Edward

appreciati[ng]

art

for Leaving Certificate

áine ní chártaigh
aidan o'sullivan

Gill & Macmillan

real
funny
crosses
at.
mighty
moyne
school

reask pillar
fahamora slab
carandonagh cross
a henny
moone
muiredach
scriptures

Subject matter = what story is the artist trying to tell: is it religous, historical, modern can I describe whats happening in artwork the subject matter is what the artist has choosen to paint, Draw or sculpt.

; composition is the dilebrit arrangment of object forms, shapes in a painting or sculpter.
is the Format of this artwork portrait or landscape is it an abstract composition is it a realistic composition, is there a background middlegroun, foreground

D1344749

Gill & Macmillan Ltd
Hume Avenue
Park West
Dublin 12
with associated companies throughout the world
www.gillmacmillan.ie

978 07171 4871 4
Design and print origination by Design Image, Dublin
Illustrations by Keith Barrett

The paper used in this book is made from the wood pulp of managed forests. For every tree felled, at least one tree is planted, thereby renewing natural resources.

Contents

Part II. The early Renaissance

Part III. The high Renaissance

Part IV. The early Renaissance in northern Europe

Part V. French painting in the 19th Century

CHAPTER 1

LOOKING AT ART

The visual arts

The visual arts are important because we live today in a world of colourful images. They surround us at every turn of our lives, from billboards on the street to advertising images in magazines and in shop windows and on packaging and food labels. Moving images entertain us at the cinema, and when we turn on our televisions or computers we are inviting images into our homes with people talking to us through these pictures. These images have an enormous impact on our lives, and the more we understand their visual and verbal messages, the greater control we have over our lives.

A message in the image

The importance of art in society has been constant throughout history and artists have always created images for various cultural and aesthetic purposes. For example, in medieval Europe few people were literate, so artists used imagery to communicate the Christian message to the ordinary people and the soaring architecture of the great cathedrals pierced the sky in a symbolic effort to reach heaven.

Nowadays we often view great works of art from the past in museums and galleries – often outside of the settings they were originally created for. Galleries are of course excellent places, good at conserving and displaying individual works in a way that makes historical sense. The pictures hang in frames around the walls of rooms organised according to the geographical area the artworks came from and when they were created. Reading the label next to the work gives the name of the work, identifies the artist and tells us when it was painted – but none of this tells us anything about the story of the work.

Learning to 'read'

Knowing how to 'read' a work of art can completely change the experience of looking at it. Whether we see it at school, in books, on television, in galleries, in public places or in museums, it is important to do more than glance and make quick judgements. But learning to look takes time and acquiring the skills and vocabulary to make observations, build understanding and respond effectively to art does not just happen. The meaning and significance of artworks – whether contemporary or historical – and indeed the enjoyment of them can remain hidden unless we dig in and do some searching.

Looking at pictures

In his book *Ways of Seeing*, John Berger points out that seeing comes before words and that a child looks and recognises before they can speak. Published in the early 1970s in conjunction with a BBC TV series, *Ways of Seeing* changed the way people look at images by concentrating on *how* we look at paintings. Its influence was enormous and it opened up a kind of cultural study that is now commonplace.

Recently, Louis le Brocquy, one of Ireland's most successful contemporary artists, said, 'Art is neither an instrument nor a convenience, but a secret logic of the imagination. It is another way of seeing, the whole sense and value of which lies in its autonomy, its distance from actuality, its otherness.'

Enjoy your visit

Because there are many ways of looking at pictures, a trip to an art gallery can be a rewarding experience. It especially helps to have some knowledge of history, because even if the artist did not intend it, what was happening at the time is reflected in the artwork.

However, with so many works of art to look at, created in so many different styles and in so many different historical periods, it is easy to fall into a daze and become only half aware of what is on the walls. Perhaps the best solution is to choose just one work in the room and take the time to enjoy that. It may mean fitting far less into the time of the visit, but it will be time well spent.

Ways of seeing

Sketching is an excellent way to learn to understand a work in a gallery, but taking the time to look carefully also works. Artists frequently placed emphasis on different parts of their work, especially if the work was created before the invention of film or television. Before film or TV, art was often a means of entertainment, and it was understood that viewers would be able to linger over works of art and uncover their details slowly.

A question worth asking

While sketching or while just looking at a painting (fig 1.1), is it a good idea to try analysing it. Looking at a painting can be quite a different experience if we ask some simple questions like:

- What is this painting about?
- Which part of the work catches the eye first?
- Why is that?
- Which way is the eye then directed?
- What is the structure or **composition** of the work?
- Does it fit into a shape like a triangle?

The artist is like an author writing a story that is told visually.
- Is there a **narrative** or a message in this work?
- Do you think the artist intended you to 'read' the whole story at once or does a certain feature keep pulling your attention back?

FIG 1.1 THE AMBASSADORS, Hans Holbein, National Gallery London

- Perhaps the artist intended this and you are meant to spend more time exploring it?
- Do you think that some details are symbols for something?
- Does the artist spell everything out for you or do they allow you to fill in the details yourself?

Colour is one of the key ingredients of visual art, so the next question could be:
- How does the artist's choice and arrangement of colour convey the importance of one element of the work over another?

Line is another basic element that can work with or against colour in a work of art.
- Can you see strong lines in the work?
- Do you think the artist preferred to work more with line than colour?

Examine *The Ambassadors*

To find out more about this intriguing painting look at the National Gallery London's website. The National Gallery in London houses one of the finest collections of western European paintings in the world. On its website it features 30 'must-see' paintings, including some of the Gallery's best-loved works. Take some time to look at these paintings in detail.

www.nationalgallery.org.uk/paintings/

In the past the surface of a painting was also important.
- What kind of surface does the painting have?
- How do you think the artist achieved this?
- Has the artist used thin glazes of colour or thicker paint?

Realist or abstract?

Many people find abstract art confusing or boring. But remember that abstract simply means *simplified* so it's worth taking the time to look at the work more closely.

The language to describe engaging with art in this way can be confusing, but it really is quite simple.

What do all the terms mean?

Painting and sculpture can be divided into three categories: figurative, representational and abstract.
- **Figurative art** – The term 'figurative art' is often taken to mean it represents a human figure or even an animal figure, but this is not necessarily so. It does, however, derive from real object sources.
- **Representational art** – Art that is based on real, objective sources. This can also be called 'realist' or 'objective' art. In other words, it represents something.
- **Abstract art** – Art that depicts real objects that have been changed, simplified or distorted in some way.

These categories can often overlap. For example, if figurative art is based on real object sources, it may also be representational.

Abstract art

Non-representational abstract works are just like magnified portions of interesting compositional elements.

These interesting areas appeal to the eye and are also found in representational pieces. However, the real or the narrative in a work often blocks that out.

Realist representational pieces appeal to the mind, but without essential abstract elements in the composition, the mind quickly filters the meaning of the painting into simplified categories and the eye is left unsatisfied.

Looking at an abstract painting (fig 1.2)
First establish:
- Is this painting representational or non-representational?
- Is it objective or non-objective?

Fig 1.2 IRELAND III, Patrick Graham, Dublin City Gallery, The Hugh Lane

- Is it figurative or non-figurative?
- What do you think it is about?
- Is there a narrative or a message in the work?
- Does it contain symbols?

Regarding colour:
- Does the colour used convey emotion, time of day and distance or some other special feature?
- What kind of paint has been used?
- Can you see brushstrokes in the work?
- Do these brushstrokes convey movement?

Now look again and ask:
- Where is the focal point?
- Why is your eye led there?
- Is your mind looking for objects and ideas while your eye is attracted to areas of high contrast?
- Are you allowing the eye (which is part of your brain) to do its work and lead your mind through the artwork?

Remember to enjoy

Visual art is not necessarily as immediately satisfying as some of the fast-moving media imagery around us today, but given time it can provide a rewarding experience.

Art can be appreciated in many different ways, and as well as appreciating a painting's visual impact – its aesthetic qualities – it is rewarding to do some research and explore the painting's style or technique, its subject matter or hidden meanings and even its deeper cultural significance.

Galleries and museums

The National Gallery of Ireland in Dublin

The National Gallery of Ireland in Dublin has numerous works of art on display. The main emphasis is on Irish art, but its collection also features examples from every major school of European painting. (See online chapter 'Painting in Ireland: late 19th century and early 20th century' at www.gillmacmillan.ie for more details.)

To see something like 10,000 paintings would take considerable time and trying to see even a fraction of this amount is impossible. Selecting some key works is therefore a good idea for a short visit, which will hopefully be the first of many.

Find out some information on the work by reading about it beforehand or asking one of the attendants at the gallery. Very often they will be delighted to talk about the work and help you to understand it.

How to look

There are many ways to look at art, but a good way is to break up your approach into three stages.
1. Look at the formal qualities like the basic shapes, composition, colour, tone, line, etc.
2. Find out the meaning or if it has a narrative or story. Are there symbols or specific images associated with this work?
3. Study the social context or background of the work.

Where to find the paintings

The paintings are divided into schools of painting. At first this may seem confusing, but after a while the different forms and genres in western European painting and the contexts in which they developed over the centuries become clear.

The Italian school

The Taking of Christ by Caravaggio (fig 1.3)

The National Gallery of Ireland's greatest treasure of recent years is the wonderful work by the Italian 16th-century master Caravaggio. The large painting (now on long-term loan to the National Gallery) was discovered quite by chance in a Jesuit rectory in Ireland in 1992. The

Fig 1.3 THE TAKING OF CHRIST, Caravaggio, National Gallery of Ireland, Dublin

4

existence of this painting was known about and many copies of it had been made but the original was long thought to be lost. The painting had been hanging in the dining room of a Jesuit house since the early 1930s and before that it was in Scotland. It was sold to a British art collector in Italy in the 18th century as a work by Gerard van Honthorst, also known as Gerard of the Night, one of Caravaggio's Dutch followers.

A masterpiece revealed
When the National Gallery was asked to clean the painting, it was immediately recognised for what it was by Sergio Benedetti, an Italian art restorer. As Benedetti carefully removed layers of dirt and discoloured varnish, he revealed the supreme technical quality of the painting. He then identified it as Caravaggio's lost painting.

Caravaggio
Michelangelo Merisi, called Caravaggio after his hometown, was a controversial artist. During his lifetime he was known to be violent and difficult and his paintings were the subject of intense criticism.

Using real-life models, Caravaggio changed the face of religious painting by depicting saints and even Jesus and Mary as ordinary people. Artists had always used life models, but adapted and changed them (as was the tradition) to make the figures look more 'holy' and idealised. In contrast Caravaggio's paintings featured figures who were dirty and ragged and his pictures conveyed a real-life setting like that found on the street.

Dramatic paintings
Caravaggio's paintings were highly dramatic. The figures are shown from an extremely close viewpoint, almost like the close-ups you can see in movies today. By using a single source of lighting, he achieved intense *chiaroscuro* (an Italian word meaning *light-dark*) or tonal contrasts that emphasised the Christian narrative in sudden flash-lit scenes emerging from darkness. Again, the lighting in Caravaggio's paintings has been compared to cinematographic lighting.

Caravaggio's artistic revolution spread through Europe quickly during his lifetime, but it just as quickly went out of favour. Caravaggio was forgotten and only regained his place in the history of art in the 19th century. He is now regarded as a pivotal figure in Western art.

In *The Taking of Christ*, Caravaggio chose a horizontal format similar to one he used in several other compositions. Even though the figures are seen in half their length only, they are depicted powerfully and dramatically.

The theme
The Taking of Christ depicts the arrest of Jesus in the Garden of Gethsemane by soldiers after Judas has identified his master by kissing him: 'The one I shall kiss is the man; seize him and lead him away safely' (Mark 14:44). Caravaggio focuses on the moment that Judas betrays him with a treacherous kiss. Christ accepts his fate with humility, his hands clasped in a gesture of faith, while the soldiers move in to capture him.

A drama
Christ, the leading actor in the drama, is pushed sideways by his assailants and by Judas. The juxtaposition (putting together) of their two heads, which are framed by an arc of dark red cloth behind them, creates a strange and poignant focal point within the composition. The contrast of these faces could not be starker. We can almost feel the tension as Judas, driven by greed, leans forward to kiss his master, changing a gentle and loving greeting to an aggressive act of treachery. Jesus remains calm, his distress shown only in his furrowed brow and downturned eyes. Stretching across this passive figure, Judas has roughly grabbed his sleeve, but the soldier's cold, shining metal armour with the hand at his neck highlights the vulnerability of Christ, whose hands are so prominently placed at the bottom of the picture and are clasped in a gesture of faith.

Christ as the central figure
If you take the scene as a whole, you see how it's designed to single Jesus out. All the other figures (the soldiers, the arresting officer, the lurching Judas, the young man running off [as described in the lines of the Bible] and leaving his red cloak that has been seized by the bearded soldier) are moving from right to left. The enormous punching force of the composition goes in that direction, but Jesus alone faces the other way – a figure of passive resistance to the great push.

Chiaroscuro
Caravaggio's extremes of light and dark give the work intensity and vibrancy. The figures are portrayed in contemporary costume and the use of light and colour add to the drama and richness of the painting's visual impact.

Behind the group on the top right is a man carrying a lantern. Not wearing any armour but dressed in a blue and red cloak, he is thought to have the features of Caravaggio himself. His lantern, however, has no role in lighting the scene because the true light source that creates the strong *chiaroscuro* is placed high on the left, beyond the view of the spectator.

Look at the painting
Ask yourself:
- What is the painting about?
- How does the artist convey the chaos and commotion of that moment?
- Which figure is central to the composition?
- How does the use of light and shade contribute to the drama of the event?

The Dutch school

The Dutch school is one of the strongest schools represented in the Gallery, with paintings from the 17th and 18th centuries. The 17th century was a time of great wealth in Holland and a strong middle-class demand for art is reflected in the paintings of the time. It is generally regarded as the 'Golden Age' of Dutch painting. Artists tended to specialise and genre painting was very popular. The term 'genre' is used to define scenes of everyday life that featured a wide range of activities, such as peasants at work, the aristocracy at leisure, community events taking place out of doors or simple domestic settings.

Johannes Vermeer

Johannes Vermeer was one of the foremost painters of the time and his genre paintings stand out for their intimacy, simplicity and style. He worked slowly and meticulously and produced only a small number of works in his lifetime.

His compositions often include objects or still life, which may hint at the prosperity and status of the people he depicts. His paintings have a distinctive style and are particularly characterised by soft textures.

Lady Writing a Letter with Her Maid by Johannes Vermeer (fig 1.4)
The scene is set in the corner of a room with light coming from a tall window on the left wall. A long, dark green curtain at the left is withdrawn, as if inviting entry, and a woman wearing a pale green dress, a white cap and sleeves and pearl earrings sits at a table covered with an oriental carpet writing a letter. Behind her stands a maid in a blue apron calmly looking out the window. She crosses her arms and waits for the woman, who is deeply

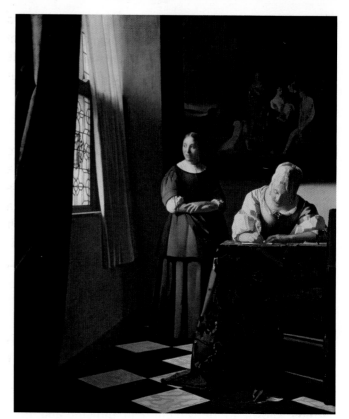

FIG 1.4 LADY WRITING A LETTER WITH HER MAID, Johannes Vermeer, National Gallery of Ireland, Dublin

engrossed in her letter writing. The elegant interior also features a black-and-white marble floor with a skirt of tiles, and a large painting depicting the Old Testament story of the finding of Moses in an ebony frame on the back wall.

A translucent lace curtain hangs down from the leaded glass window. The pattern and diffusion of light are carefully distributed by closing the lower exterior shutter on the right.

A scene of calmness
The placid scene with its muted colours suggests no activity or hint of interruption. Powerful verticals and horizontals in the composition, particularly the heavy black frame of the background painting, establish a confining backdrop that contributes to the restrained mood.

Figures in the composition
The difference between the two figures is a key aspect of the composition. The maid is the central figure and is anchored by the thick ebony frame of the picture, but standing straight and column-like, her statuesque figure leads the eye to the floor. Her calm stillness is in marked difference to her mistress, who is deeply engrossed in

her intense activity of writing and leans sharply forward on her left forearm. Strong light outlines the writing arm against the shadowed wall behind, and the angular folds on the white sleeve contrasts sharply with the regular folds of the maid's costume.

Lines of perspective

The figures function as separate individuals but are joined by the lines of perspective. These cross from the upper and lower window frames across the folded arms and lighted forehead of the maid, extending to a vanishing point in the left eye of the mistress. The result is that although the viewer's eye is drawn to the maid, it quickly passes to the woman at the table who is, in fact, the real focal point of the painting.

Painting texture

The woman and her fine clothing are painted in precise, meticulous strokes, but the maid is painted in broadly handled brushwork.

Colour

Vermeer used the exorbitantly expensive pigment lapis lazuli, or natural ultramarine, in the most lavish way throughout his paintings. This was quite unusual among his contemporaries and he used it not only where blue is the obvious colour. In *Lady Writing a Letter with Her Maid* it was used not only on the maid's apron, but also in a mixture of yellow to make green for the chair and as an undercolour to add depth to fabrics. This creates rich shadows in the white linen sleeves. It can also be seen filtering through the warm light of the painting's strongly lit interior, which reflects its multiple colours onto the wall and the floor tiles.

Leonardo's influence

In his working method, Vermeer was most probably inspired by Leonardo's observation that the surface of every object absorbs some of the colour of the objects nearby. This means that no object is ever seen entirely in its natural colour.

Stillness and serenity

By avoiding any kind of narrative or anecdote in *Lady Writing a Letter with Her Maid*, Vermeer made it a more universal image unrelated to any specific situation. All irrelevant objects have been eliminated from the composition and with a subtle manipulation of light, colour and perspective he created an atmosphere of timeless stillness and serenity.

A low viewpoint

As with all his paintings, Vermeer has divided it perfectly. For example, the edge of the table is the same distance from the bottom of the picture as the end of the picture frame is from the top. The artist has chosen a low viewpoint, scarcely higher than the top of the table, which adds to the figures' monumentality and enhances the height of the space.

Clues to the meaning

All the important elements of the painting can be seen at a glance, yet a small still life on the floor before us offers a clue to its meaning. Here a crumpled letter, a stick of sealing wax and a bright red seal could be either a letter that the lady has received or a discarded draft of the letter she is writing.

A small object might be a book. Small letter-writing manuals were very fashionable at the time and letter writers often consulted them. But in this case even a 'perfect' love letter containing all the 'right words' may not have satisfied the lady. Perhaps she preferred to use her own words to convey her sentiments.

A mystery

The red wax seal, rediscovered only recently when the painting was cleaned in 1974, indicates the crumpled letter was received, and as letters were prized in the 17th century, it must have been thrown aside in anger.

The empty chair at the table also suggests that perhaps someone was recently sitting there, since chairs of this type were typically placed against the wall when not in use.

The questions

A number of questions about the letter remain. For example, did the woman open the letter shortly before sitting down? Or was it opened by whoever was sitting in the now-empty chair across from her – presumably a man? Why was it dropped? How did the stick of wax get there? Despite much speculation over the years, no definite answers to these and other questions have emerged. The objects are small but significant signs of disturbance in the otherwise calm appearance of the lovely letter writer and create an air of mystery in the hushed interior.

Look at the painting

- Is the scene calm or lively?
- Why do we look at the figures first?
- Which of the figures is the focal point?

- Is there a clear narrative?
- How has the artist used brushwork?
- What colours did Vermeer use?
- How has the artist used colour?
- What makes the painting so calm?
- From what viewpoint is the composition seen?
- What clues do we see to solve the mystery?

Irish art

Louis le Brocquy

The National Gallery of Ireland has a very fine collection of Irish art. Among the 20th-century works is an early painting by Louis le Brocquy called *A Family* (fig 1.5).

Le Brocquy's *Family* paintings (c. 1951–54) marked a change in his palette from the comparatively colourful work he had been producing up to that time. His paintings now featured greys, black and white in what was to become known in time as his Grey Period. He continued to depict the human figure, but his images became much starker.

A Family, which hangs in the National Gallery, is considered a decisive painting in the history of 20th-century Irish art. Not only was it a turning point for the artist himself, but it also led the way for modernism as an everyday style in Irish art. *A Family* (1951) was awarded a major prize at the 1956 Venice Biennale, a major art exhibition, and it hung in the 1958 exhibition *50 Ans d'Art Moderne (Fifty Years of Modern Art)* at the Brussels World Fair, alongside paintings by Cézanne and Matisse. The painting is also an exception in that le Brocquy is the only living artist to have a work on show as part of the permanent collection in the National Gallery.

8

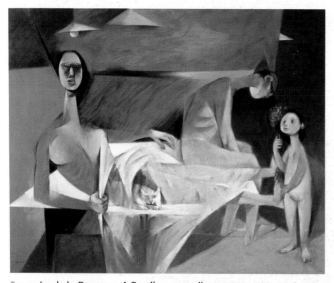

Fig 1.5 Louis le Brocquy, *A Family*, 1951, oil on canvas, 147 × 185 cm, collection National Gallery of Ireland, Dublin © the artist

At the time of painting *A Family*, le Brocquy, by his own admission, was fascinated by the horizontal monumentality of traditional Odalisque painting (the image of the reclining woman depicted voluptuously) by one master after another throughout the history of European art.

A post-war image

Le Brocquy offers a view of the human condition as he saw it in the 1950s. This suggests a family stripped back to a Stone Age state under the harsh conditions of modern experience. This was the post-Second World War period when the huge numbers of refugees and social upheaval caused by the war were very real concerns in Europe, and of course there was also the threat to humanity due to the invention of the atomic bomb.

The composition of the painting is similar to Manet's *Olympia* (see Chapter 40, fig 40.6), but the female figure has a different significance. A man, sitting alone, takes the place of the black servant in Manet's work and the bouquet of flowers are little more than a few sprigs held by a child. Instead of a black cat, a white one emerges from under the sheets.

Look at the painting

- Is this an abstract or a realist painting?
- Is it figurative or non-figurative?
- What is the subject of the painting?
- What is the mood?
- Does the colour scheme have an effect on the mood?
- Where is the focal point of the composition?
- What artists and artworks influenced the work?
- What is the painting's style?

The Yeats Museum

Jack Yeats is considered the greatest Irish artist of the first half of the 20th century. His paintings are displayed in a special room in the National Gallery. It is well worth spending time in this room examining the paintings that show the progress of his work over his long life.

The youngest of six children (four of whom survived), Jack and his brother and sisters spent a good part of his childhood in Sligo with his grandparents. As with his older brother, William (the poet W.B. Yeats), the time Jack spent in Sligo in his youth dominated his work.

The paintings in the Gallery range from early work, such as *The Liffey Swim*, which depicted the drama and excitement of a swimming race (fig 1.6), to *Grief*, a mysterious and disturbing image of war and misery he

painted late in life (fig 1.7). By this time his wife had died and he had seen two world wars and witnessed considerable turmoil in Ireland during the Rising and subsequent War of Independence, as well the Civil War.

His early works are quite realistically depicted, but his style changed considerably as time passed. The later, more abstract works are painted with thick oily paint and, as a result, the subjects of the paintings can be quite difficult to make out (fig 1.8).

Yeats had always been fascinated by horses; they reminded him of his youth and the freedom of his childhood in Sligo. They appear repeatedly in his work. In fact, as his painting style evolved he became particularly good at conveying motion.

The Irish Museum of Modern Art

The Royal Hospital Kilmainham in Dublin is the beautiful setting of Ireland's leading national institution for the collection and presentation of modern and contemporary art, the Irish Museum of Modern Art (IMMA). The building was restored by the government in 1984 and IMMA opened in May 1991. Since then, the museum has built up a collection of over 4,500 works acquired through purchases, donations and long-term loans as well as by commissioning new works. The museum has regular exhibitions that present a wide variety of art, sometimes taken from its own collection and sometimes on loan from other institutions or private sources.

The building

The 17th-century building that houses IMMA (fig 1.9) was founded in 1684 as a hospital or home for retired soldiers and was used for this purpose for over 250 years. With its formal façade and large, elegant courtyard, it is similar in style to Les Invalides in Paris.

The permanent and temporary exhibitions are displayed in a series of interlocking rooms on the long corridors that flank the sides of the courtyard.

Exhibitions

The museum's permanent collection of over 1,650 works is shown in a series of temporary exhibitions. These sometimes feature the work of individual artists or may be group exhibitions. The work is frequently that of leading, well-established international artists, but new work by younger-generation artists is often shown as well. The range and styles also vary greatly, from painting and sculpture to installation, photography, video and performance.

Dublin Contemporary 2011

A major event for art is to take place in Dublin in the Autumn of 2011. Dublin Contemporary 2011 can be seen as a successor to 'Rosc', which was a series of exhibitions of contemporary art held every four years, in Dublin from 1967, until 1988. In its early stages Rosc filled a huge gap in Ireland and gave the public a chance to see many international contemporary artists, but after the Irish Museum of Modern Art opened in 1991, and more international exhibitions throughout the country, that gap was less obvious.

Dublin galleries

The Dublin Contemporary 2011 exhibition is to feature some of the best-known contemporary Irish and international artists from all over the world in a variety of venues throughout the city. This includes many private galleries as well as The Irish Museum of Modern Art (Imma), Dublin City Gallery The Hugh Lane, the Royal Hibernian Academy (RHA) and even at the James Joyce Tower in Sandycove.

Conversations about art

When the event was announced in July 2010 the Artistic director of Dublin Contemporary 2011, Rachael Thomas said that the principal focus of the exhibition was the

many Irish world-class contemporary artists that she described at the time as 'Ireland's best kept secret'. She said they were not so well known as their literary or musical counterparts and 'the whole point was to start a conversation about contemporary art and bring art into the public eye that the public can enjoy and relate to.'

Kassel and Venice

Dublin Contemporary 2011 is based on the Documenta festival, which began in Kassel, Germany, in 1955 and takes place every five years. One of the most important exhibitions of modern and contemporary art in the world, Documenta has placed the town of Kassel on the map as an international artistic centre.

Similarly, the success of the Venice Biennale, a major contemporary art exhibition that has taken place every other year in Venice, Italy, since 1895, shows there is a real demand for contemporary art. Dublin Contemporary 2011 has the potential to be a world-class event showcasing not just the visual arts, but the city itself.

Ireland's opportunity

It is hoped that this major opportunity for Irish contemporary artists will in time reap benefits for them internationally.

Dublin City Gallery The Hugh Lane

Dublin City Gallery The Hugh Lane (or simply called 'the Hugh Lane') houses one of Ireland's foremost collections of modern and contemporary art. The Hugh Lane holds almost 2,000 artworks, ranging from Impressionist masterpieces by Manet, Monet, Renoir and Degas to works by leading national and international contemporary artists.

Today the Hugh Lane runs a programme of dynamic temporary exhibitions, which are often linked to works from its permanent collection, and it promotes new ways of expressing art (like multimedia). It also frequently holds historical and retrospective exhibitions featuring Irish art.

More recently, the importance of the Hugh Lane's cultural position in contemporary Ireland gained wide recognition when it acquired all the contents of the artist Francis Bacon's studio from London and reconstructed it as a permanent exhibit in the Gallery. Francis Bacon, who was born in Ireland but worked all his life in England, often produced quite controversial works. The studio offers an invaluable insight into the artist's life, inspirations and unusual techniques and working methods.

The Gallery also recently received a gift of paintings from contemporary artist Sean Scully, who was born in Dublin. This group of seven superb abstract paintings form the Hugh Lane's second permanent installation and are housed in a dedicated gallery in the new wing. They serve as a mainstay for the collection of non-figurative painting in the Gallery. Go to www.hughlane.ie for more information.

The first public gallery of modern art

There is an interesting story behind the origins of the Dublin City Gallery The Hugh Lane.

The Municipal Gallery of Modern Art was founded by art collector Hugh Lane in Harcourt Street in Dublin in 1908 and was the first known public gallery of modern art in the world. Later it was renamed the Dublin City Gallery The Hugh Lane and relocated to Charlemont House on Parnell Square. Today it is often called 'the Hugh Lane' after its founder.

Sir Hugh Lane

One of the foremost collectors of Impressionist paintings in England and Ireland, Sir Hugh Lane unfortunately did not live to see his gallery permanently located in Dublin. He died in 1915 when the luxury ocean liner *Lusitania* sank during the early years of the First World War, having been torpedoed by a German U-boat off the west coast of Cork. His death marked the beginning of a long dispute between Dublin and London over possession of his valuable collection of pictures.

A successful art dealer

Born in Co. Cork but raised in Cornwall in England, Hugh Lane became a successful London art dealer. His aunt was Lady Gregory of Coole Park in Co. Galway, who is well known for her role in founding the Abbey Theatre as well as for her friendship with some of Ireland's finest artists and writers, including W.B. Yeats. Through her, Lane became acquainted with the social circle at the core of Irish cultural activities and he began a campaign to establish a gallery of modern art in Dublin.

Lane convinced Dublin Corporation to find a building on Harcourt Street to hold the gallery, but as a man of passionate convictions about the way things ought to look, Lane wanted a newly built gallery for the permanent display of his Impressionist paintings. Designs for several sites were proposed for the gallery –

FIG 1.11 The Ha'penny Bridge, Dublin.

including one for Stephen's Green – but the one favoured by him, Lady Gregory and others was a building designed by the London architect Edwin Lutyens (fig 1.10) that would span the River Liffey in the form of a bridge replacing the cast iron Ha'penny Bridge (fig 1.11).

Dublin's business leaders did not agree with this plan, however, and when Lane could not persuade the Corporation to proceed he became highly irritated and took his collection of French paintings out of Ireland and gave them to London's National Gallery. Lane drafted a will in 1913 in which he left his paintings to the National Gallery to 'found a collection of Modern Continental Art' there.

The codicil to Lane's will

Lane's collection of paintings were now in the National Gallery of London, but the board of the Gallery apparently did not consider all the paintings to be good enough to show and so kept some of them in storage. Insulted, Lane withdrew his gift of the paintings from the Gallery, but he never repossessed them. Soon afterwards, he was appointed to the board of the National Gallery of Ireland, and he again became more kindly disposed towards Ireland.

Lane then altered his will in a famous codicil (or addition) (fig 1.12) in which he willed the whole collection of paintings to Ireland, provided a suitable building would be found to house them within five years of his death. Unfortunately, Lane's signature on this codicil was never witnessed and so after his death the National Gallery of London refused to recognise this change to the original will, which left all the paintings to them, and kept the

FIG 1.10 Design for the Municipal Gallery, by Edwin Lutyens to span the Liffey (Dublin City Gallery The Hugh Lane)

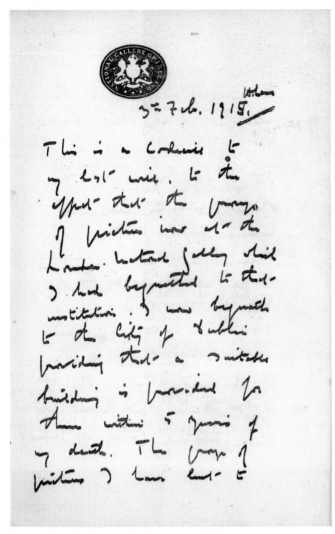

FIG 1.12 A page showing the famous codicil from Hugh Lane's will (Dublin City Gallery The Hugh Lane)

FIG 1.13 The 'empty room' at the Municipal Gallery

paintings. So began a long dispute that took on something of a nationalistic fervour and caught the imagination of many who knew nothing at all about art but saw this as a remnant of England's colonial hold on Ireland.

Getting the paintings back

In an effort to get the paintings back, the Dublin Corporation was aided by many, including the painter Sarah Purser, who founded an organisation called Friends of the National Collections in 1924, and Lady Gregory, who worked tirelessly for the cause, appealing to anyone who was sympathetic, including the Northern Irish unionist leader Edward Carson and Éamon de Valera, the Irish republican leader and founder of Fianna Fáil. In 1932, the government gave Charlemont House in Parnell Square, originally the townhouse of James Caulfeild, the 1st Earl of Charlemont and a well-known collector of art and antiques, to the city of Dublin for use

as the Municipal Gallery. The corporation then commissioned a bust of Hugh Lane and placed it in the last of the rooms of the new gallery – but the room itself remained empty, waiting for the return of the paintings (fig 1.13).

The empty room

Two students (one of whom was an IRA member) heard the message of the empty room in 1956 and set out to get the paintings back for Ireland. In a well-planned daylight robbery, they took one of the paintings from the London's Tate Gallery. The painting in question was Berthe Morisot's *Jour d'Été* (*A Summer's Day*). The incident made the headlines in all the papers (fig 1.14), but the successful return of the paintings was a much slower and less dramatic affair.

FIG 1.14 Front page of the *Irish Times* from Friday, 13 April 1956

A shared arrangement

An agreement to share the paintings was finally reached between the National Gallery of London and the Hugh Lane in 1959 and in 1961, 20 works of art were officially received by the Hugh Lane on permanent loan. The two institutions also agreed to share eight of the most important Impressionist paintings in a rotating arrangement whereby four will always hang in London and four in the Dublin City Gallery The Hugh Lane. However, all eight were made available in 2006 for a special exhibition to celebrate the opening of the Hugh Lane's new wing, making it the first time the paintings were hung together in Dublin since 1913.

The eight Hugh Lane bequest paintings include:

- Édouard Manet – *La Musique aux Tuileries* (*The Music at the Tuileries*) (fig 1.15). This was Manet's first major work depicting modern city life. A band is playing and a fashionable crowd has gathered to listen to the afternoon concert. In breaking with the conventions of composition, style and subject matter, the painting, which was first exhibited in 1863, is regarded by many as central to the development of modern art.

Another of Manet's works is *Eva Gonzalès* (fig 1.16), which Irish art audiences were already familiar with because Lane had exhibited it in 1904 in an effort to raise support for a modern art gallery. The painting is a portrait of Eva Gonzalès, an accomplished painter, pupil and friend of Manet. The artist shows her resplendent in a white dress. Later, during the controversy about finding a site for a new gallery, this painting was said to be quite shocking by some because of the portrayal of bare arms on a woman. Gonzalès died in 1883 in childbirth only a few days after Manet.

14

Fig 1.16 EVA GONZALÈS, Édouard Manet, National Gallery London

Fig 1.17 BEACH SCENE, Edgar Degas, Dublin City Gallery The Hugh Lane

- Edgar Degas – *Beach Scene* (fig 1.17). In this painting Degas shows local girls and others who are on holiday at the seaside. The locals can easily be distinguished by their uninhibited dress. They are wrapped in towels and their bare skin is still clearly visible as compared to the fully dressed girl – obviously from the city – whose hair is being brushed by her maid. With his usual wit, Degas shows the girls' swimming gear stretched out on the sand in direct imitation of her pose.

- Pierre-Auguste Renoir – *Les Parapluies* (*The Umbrellas*) (fig 1.18). This is probably the best known of the Lane bequest paintings. It features a bustling Paris street in the rain, but the composition does not focus on the centre and even cuts off figures at either edge, more like a photograph. The Impressionists, especially Degas, experimented quite a bit with this kind of unconventional arrangement, but even though the composition may look a bit haphazard, Renoir has carefully considered the pattern of angles and shapes made by the umbrellas.

The other paintings are Claude Monet's *Lavacourt under Snow* (fig 1.19), *La Cheminée* (*The Fireplace*) by Édouard Vuillard, *Jour d'Été* (*A Summer's Day*) by Berthe Morisot

FIG 1.18 LES PARAPLUIES, Pierre-Auguste Renoir, The National Gallery of London

FIG 1.19 LAVACOURT UNDER SNOW, Claude Monet, Dublin City Gallery The Hugh Lane

and *View from Louveciennes* (*Printemps, Vue de Louveciennes*) by Camille Pissarro.

The Lane Fund
At the time of his death, Hugh Lane had been a director of the National Gallery of Ireland since 1914. In his will he left it part of his considerable wealth. To this day, the Lane Fund contributes to the purchase of artworks for the National Gallery of Ireland.

Fɪɢ 1.20 The *Lusitania*

The *Lusitania* paintings
When Hugh Lane lost his life in the *Lusitania* disaster (fig 1.20), he was travelling with lead containers containing several valuable paintings. These included works by Monet as well as several by Old Masters such as Rembrandt, Rubens and Titian. A diver claimed to have identified these containers in 1994, and as the tubes were sealed, the canvases may have survived. The Irish government immediately placed a Heritage Protection Order on the *Lusitania* wreck and its contents, the first for a shipwreck under 100 years old, so if the paintings are ever recovered they will be exhibited at the National Gallery of Ireland.

Regional art galleries
Local, small-scale art galleries are to be found in many towns across the country. These can vary quite significantly and each has its own individual character. Some galleries are built around an established collection of works, while others feature contemporary work. There

16

are also art galleries that are integrated with other art forms, such as music and drama.

Cork

The Crawford Municipal Gallery
The Crawford Municipal Art Gallery, in the centre of Cork, is a small but important art museum. It has an impressive permanent collection, which is particularly strong in Irish art. The works in the collection are shown on a rotating basis, but one or two favourites are on constant display.

The gallery's permanent collection comprises over 2,000 works, ranging from 18th-century Irish and European painting and sculpture to contemporary works that include video installations.

At the heart of the collection is a special set of Greek and Roman sculpture that was brought to Cork in 1818 from the Vatican Museum in Rome and presented to the Cork Society of Arts. These white plaster casts of the original marble sculptures include such well-known pieces as

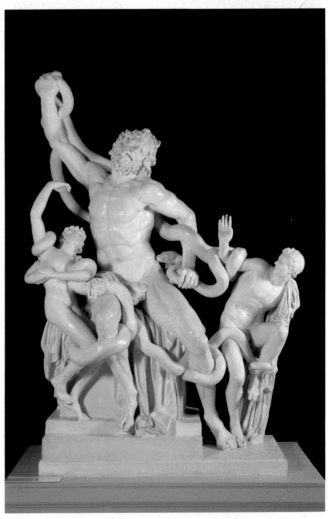

Fɪɢ 1.21 Plaster cast of THE LACOÖN AND HIS SONS, Crawford Municipal Gallery of Art, Co. Cork

Laocoön and His Sons (fig 1.21) and *Aphrodite from Melos (The 'Venus di Melos')* (fig 1.22) as well as representations of Greek athletes. They are shown in a large gallery on the ground floor with walls painted in deep red and subtle natural lighting.

Among the 19th- and 20th-century paintings are works by Irish artists Jack Butler Yeats and Louis le Brocquy. *Time Flies* (fig 1.23) by William Gerard Barry is one of the gallery's best-loved paintings. It depicts a peasant woman watching three children playing in a glade by the trees on a riverbank. The title of the picture poignantly suggests the passing of life, and this is further accentuated by the autumn colours and the shadows in the foreground that seem to mark the passing of the day.

Another of the gallery's favourites is *Men of the South* (fig 1.24) by Seán Keating, showing a group of revolutionary young men as members of a flying column sitting on a hillside, waiting for their opportunity to ambush the British military during Ireland's War of Independence in 1921.

FIG 1.23 TIME FLIES, William Gerald Barry, Crawford Municipal Gallery of Art, Co. Cork

APPRECIATION OF ART *(SECTION III OF THE LEAVING CERT EXAM)*

17

LOOKING AT ART

The Lewis Glucksman Gallery

Situated in its own award-winning building, the Lewis Glucksman Gallery (fig 1.25) is a cultural and educational institution located at the main entrance to University College Cork. The award-winning building was designed by architects O'Donnell + Tuomey, whose commitment is to work with a sense of place. They raised the timber-clad gallery space to the level of the tree tops in an interlocking suite of rooms with the intention that it would be understood as a wooden vessel, resonating with its woodland site.

Like the architecture, the gallery itself is one of the most modern venues for visual art in Ireland and is committed to the ideal of promoting research into and the creation and exploration of all the visual arts. Its aim is to showcase a range of innovative and exciting exhibitions of works not yet seen in Cork (or, indeed, in Ireland) and to initiate projects that link with the architecture and surroundings of the gallery space.

Limerick

The Hunt Museum

The Hunt Museum (fig 1.26) in the city of Limerick houses works of art assembled by the Hunt family of Limerick. The Hunts began their collection in the 1930s and 1940s and it moved with the family and then to the University of Limerick. In 1997 it moved to its present location in the restored 18th-century Customs House in Limerick city.

This extraordinarily diverse collection of antiquities and fine and decorative art includes artefacts from ancient Greece, Rome and Egypt as well as Irish archaeological

FIG 1.25 THE Lewis Glucksman Gallery, University College Cork

FIG 1.26 The Hunt Museum, Limerick city

antiquities. It also includes striking examples of silver, glass and ceramics in its 18th- and 19th-century decorative arts collection.

The Hunt Museum's Visiting Exhibition Gallery

In addition to its fabulous permanent collection, the Hunt Museum also hosts a number of temporary art shows in its Visiting Exhibition Gallery. This purpose-built space features a wide variety of exhibitions, including an annual show (held every May) of Irish art by students from the Limerick School of Art and Design.

Donegal

The Glebe House and Gallery

The Glebe House (fig 1.27), on the shores of Lake Gartan near Letterkenny in Co. Donegal, was originally a Church of Ireland rectory. From the 1950s it was the home of the English landscape and portrait painter Derek Hill. In 1980, Hill presented the house, grounds and his art collection to the state.

The house itself is of the Regency period and is decorated with period furniture and wallpapers designed by William Morris.

The Glebe Gallery is built beside the house. The converted stables are used for visiting exhibitions, while

FIG 1.27 Glebe House, Co. Donegal

the rooms of the house itself display a rich collection of paintings, sketches and numerous other items once owned by Hill, including works by Kokoschka, Yeats, Renoir and Picasso. The study has original William Morris wallpaper and there are Chinese tapestries in the morning room. The kitchen has various paintings by the Tory Island group of painters, the most remarkable of which is James Dixon's *Impression of Tory from the Sea*.

Tory Island painters

Tory Island lies off the Donegal coast and a chance meeting between Derek Hill and one of island's fishermen, James Dixon, in 1968 resulted in a school of what has been called 'primitive painters' or naïve art. Dixon, who had never painted in his life until this time, became the island's most renowned painter. Other work by this interesting group can be seen on Tory Island in the James Dixon Gallery, originally the artist's home.

Sligo

The Model Arts and Niland Gallery in Sligo is one of Ireland's leading contemporary arts centres. Built in 1862 as a model school, the present building was completely refurbished, extended and reopened to wide acclaim in 2000.

The impressive Niland art collection is housed here. This was named after Nora Niland, a local woman who was instrumental in establishing the Sligo Municipal Art Collection in the 1950s. Her awareness as county librarian of the important connection between Sligo and the Yeats family led her to organise the borrowing of five works by Jack B. Yeats to exhibit during the first Yeats Summer School in 1959.

In time, these paintings were purchased and remained in Sligo as part of the Niland Collection. These works and others by Jack B. Yeats record experiences and memories of his time living in Sligo and its environs.

The gallery holds several major exhibitions annually featuring national and international contemporary artists. Artists represented in this collection include Paul Henry, Estella Solomons and Seán Keating, among others.

Planning and mounting an exhibition

Exhibitions can take months and sometimes years to plan and develop. The designers, developers and curators who are involved usually focus on two things: the message they want to communicate and the audience it is aimed at. There are a number of different ways to get this message across using collections and environments. There are certain things you should think about when visiting an exhibition, as these are the tools that can reinforce the messages.

- **Use of space** – This is not just about elements of design, but also about the spatial experience. What is the nature, quality and design of the space used? Is it calm and contemplative or noisy and orientated towards children? How is the spatial experience enhanced by other design elements such as light, use of colour and the shape and size of spaces? How is the space used to enhance how you experience the messages or themes?

- **Lighting** – This can be really important, as not only does it create or enhance a mood but it can also affect it in negative ways. Also, textiles and paper are extremely sensitive to light damage, so conservation is a major issue when it comes to illuminating objects and displays and they can often be dimly lit for this reason.

- **Key messages** – What is the exhibition about? When visiting an exhibition it's a good idea to list the main topics and principal themes and stories or narratives.

- **Interpretive media and technology** – These can be touchpad interactive, audio and video devices, podcasts, audio guides, handling objects (objects that can be handled by visitors), text and graphic panels or live interpretation using guides or actors. How are these designed and planned to support the messages or themes?

- **Who is the audience?** Is it for experts or for people with little knowledge of the subject? Is it for students, adults, children or a range of visitors? Have the items in the exhibit been explained properly or are visitors left wondering what the exhibition is about?

- **What type of experience is provided?** Are you being allowed to form your own opinions and thoughts or are you being given a particular viewpoint? What objects and themes get priority or prominence? Has anything or anyone's viewpoint been left out?

- **Supporting, marketing and promotional materials** – These can be leaflets, advertisements, e-communications and/or catalogues. These materials are important tools for helping the organisers of the exhibition to get the messages and themes across and for reaching target audiences. Examine the graphics and images used in support materials.

- **Directions** – Note the orientation, directions and signposts used in the exhibition. Are they effective? Do they fit in with the scheme?

- **Placement** – Take some time to look at how objects are placed, such as on open display or in display cases. Also, objects in different contexts mean different things. For example, an antique clock in a science museum will take on a different meaning to one on a mantelpiece in an historic house.

A concept-led exhibition

Sometimes an exhibition is based on an idea or a concept and sometimes on a collection or objects. For example, an exhibition in an historic house like Fota House, in Co. Cork, might be a suitable venue for a concept-led exhibition.

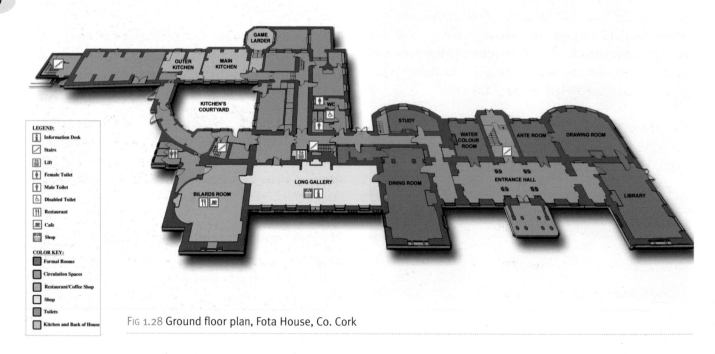

FIG 1.28 Ground floor plan, Fota House, Co. Cork

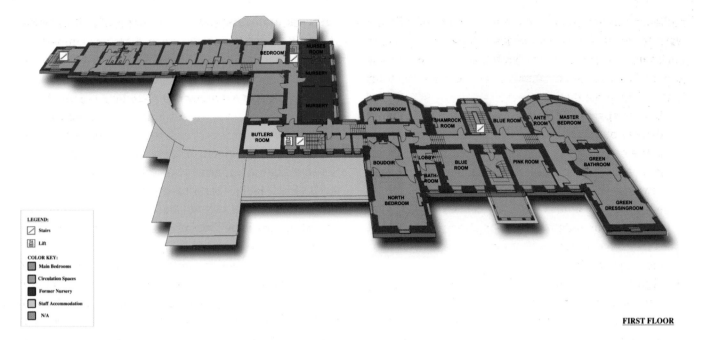

LEGEND:
- Stairs
- Lift

COLOR KEY:
- Main Bedrooms
- Circulation Spaces
- Former Nursery
- Staff Accommodation
- N/A

FIG 1.29 First Floor plan, Fota House, Co. Cork

Fota House

Originally a modest hunting lodge belonging to the Smith-Barry family, Fota House was converted in the 1820s into an elegant residence. An historic building like Fota House can be a difficult place in which to display objects because, as an old building, its interior has a fixed route that follows the layout of the house (fig 1.28, fig 1.29). This route cannot easily be changed as it would be costly, and as many historic houses are protected structures, obtaining permission to change them can be difficult.

These plans of two floors of Fota House show the circulation routes through the family area and how these relate to the house's original function as an impressive home used to display the wealth and status of the owners. Compare the size of the rooms in the main part of the house (on the left of the plan) to those in the service wing (on the right of the plan).

Use of space at Fota

Designers and planners of an exhibition at Fota cannot easily move walls or partitions, so an exhibition design

Planning an exhibition

Where would you plan an exhibition at Fota House? Have a look at the house on the Fota House, Arboretum & Gardens website.

www.fotahouse.com

has to fit around the existing circulation route – which is already a fully formed display area. Other elements to consider are the size of passageways (fig 1.30) and rooms (fig 1.31) with regard to access: some may be small, hard to get to or are bottlenecks. A lift was

FIG 1.30 Entrance hall, Fota House, Co. Cork

FIG 1.31 Dining room, Fota House, Co. Cork

recently installed in Fota House to make the building more accessible to all visitors, particularly those using wheelchairs.

Conservation both of the house and the objects in it can also be an issue. One or two people walking on delicate carpets are fine, but one or two thousand can lead to damage. Conservation concerns also affect the lighting that is used, as many historic houses are decorated with delicate textiles or watercolour paintings on paper. Many of the windows at Fota have protective film on the glass to prevent harmful UVB rays from fading or damaging the paintings and furniture.

Authentic atmosphere

The advantages of having an exhibition in a historic house is that as a former home it is full of atmosphere and it can give an authentic feel to a display, letting visitors experience it in a much more tangible way.

A family home

Another special element relating to the context of Fota House is that, as a former home to a wealthy family, it has a service wing. This wing is where the servants lived and worked and it has not been changed since it was built in the 1820s by the Smith-Barry family.

When you walk through the rooms you can get a real sense of how life was lived by different members of society in the 19th century. This is helped by the fact that the objects and furniture are in their original settings and are also on open display rather than in display cases.

Conclusion

Looking and talking about art will lead you to develop a deeper understanding and will make it a more enjoyable experience. It is also important, however, that you do not feel forced or under pressure to respond to art. It can take a while for someone to respond to art. In the same way a new song can linger in your mind, it may be some time before the response to a work of art reveals itself. The important point is to continue to visit art galleries, both large and small, whenever possible and to remain open to the experience they offer.

Questions

1. Describe some of the ways to look at a painting.
2. What does the term 'figurative' mean in painting?
3. What does the term 'abstract' mean in painting?
4. What is meant by the 'aesthetic' qualities of a work of art?
5. Describe some of the ways to ensure that a visit to an art museum or gallery is an interesting and rewarding experience.
6. How are the paintings in the National Gallery of Ireland in Dublin grouped and displayed?
7. Who was Hugh Lane?
8. Which important paintings from the Hugh Lane bequest can be seen in Dublin's Municipal Gallery?
9. How is the work of the artist Sean Scully displayed?
10. Who was Francis Bacon and where can his studio be seen?
11. Describe some of the important points that must be considered before planning an exhibition.

Essay

1. Name an important art gallery in Ireland that you have visited recently and discuss in detail two or more paintings that impressed you. Compare these works to any you are familiar with from your studies, or may have seen in a visit to another smaller or regional gallery.

2. Discuss a visit to an exhibition of contemporary art in the Irish Museum of Modern Art in Dublin or another similar museum. Comment on the venue itself and describe some works in detail and your own reaction to them. What did you learn from your experience?

3. Describe the importance of the Hugh Lane collection to Ireland and discuss two of the paintings in the collection in detail.

4. Give a brief account of the controversy regarding the establishment of the Municipal Gallery of Modern Art in Dublin.

Colour picture studies

1. Examine *Supper at Emmaus* by Caravaggio (fig 1.32) from the National Gallery in London and compare this to *The Taking of Christ* at the National Gallery of Ireland (fig 1.3). Describe the composition of the figures and how the artist conveys the emotion of the scene with gestures, expressions and colour. Comment also on the lighting and research the close connection between these two paintings and other Caravaggio paintings as part of your answer.

FIG 1.32 SUPPER AT EMMAUS, Caravaggio, The National Gallery London

2. Examine *Les Glaneuses* (*The Gleaners*) by Jules Breton (fig 1.33) in the National Gallery of Ireland and describe the scene as portrayed by the artist. Compare it to the depiction of the same scene by Jean-François Millet (see Chapter 38, fig 38.1).

FIG 1.33 LES GLANEUSES, Jules Breton, The National Gallery of Ireland, Dublin

3. Jack B. Yeats is Ireland's foremost painter of the 19th and early 20th century. Examine *The Liffey Swim* (fig 1.6), an early work by the artist, and *Grief* (fig 1.7), a late work, both of which are displayed in the new Yeats Museum room in the National Gallery of Ireland. Discuss the composition, colours and changes in style as well as the artist's use of paint. Discuss also what you already know about the artist and how you would prepare for a visit to this exhibition. What in particular do you think you would learn by examining the paintings at close hand?

4. Examine *Les Parapluies* (*The Umbrellas*) by Pierre-Auguste Renoir (fig 1.18) and describe the scene. Comment on the composition of the figures and pattern of angles and shapes made by the umbrellas. Also discuss the change of style used by the artist in this work.

5. Examine *Eva Gonzalès* by Édouard Manet (fig 1.16) and describe the scene depicted in the painting. Comment on the composition – the use of colour, the way the artist conveys the character of the sitter and the manner in which he depicts the fine fabric of her dress.

6. Examine *Montserrat* (fig 1.34) by Irish artist Sean Scully. Describe the composition, colour and the artist's use of shape. What 'message' do you think the artist is trying to convey? Do you think these abstract shapes relate in any way to our surroundings or other tangible forms?

Fig 1.34 MONTSERRAT, Sean Scully, Dublin City Gallery The Hugh Lane

CHAPTER 2

PUBLIC ART IN IRELAND

Public art – two examples

The Great Wall of Kinsale

Kinsale in Co. Cork is one of the most picturesque, popular and fashionable tourist destinations in the south-west coast of Ireland. Famous for its historical importance, its sailing and numerous gourmet restaurants, the town nestles between the hills and the shoreline in a maze of narrow streets that have changed little over hundreds of years.

A sculpture for the town

In 1988 the Arts Council for the Urban District Council of Kinsale commissioned a sculpture for the entrance to a small public park opposite the main harbour quayside. For this, they chose Eilís O'Connell, a highly successful artist who had begun to build up a career, it was to be her second commission.

O'Connell had studied in Cork and, influenced by one of her teachers, John Burke, had become one of a group of young artists working as abstract steel sculptors.

The 1988 sculpture *The Great Wall of Kinsale* (fig 2.1) marks the entrance to a park that became a fairground during the Summer months. As the site was a popular seating area, O'Connell incorporated the function of public seating into the design. The brief specified that a maintenance free material be used. The use of COR-TEN steel was agreed on by the county architect and engineer and planning permission was granted. It was a long narrow site, so to balance it, a gateway was formed by

two huge slabs of COR-TEN steel. Adjoining it were two meandering low lying curved walls with slats of teak wood to accommodate seating. Two smaller tent like structures were designed as shelters over a section of the seating. COR-TEN is a type of steel that rusts to a rich chestnut brown and then rusts no more. However, no sooner was the sculpture installed than complaints about it began.

The public

The surface was taking far longer than expected to develop evenly, due to its proximity to the sea and the fact that it was a dry summer, rust needs rain to develop its full colour. The artist took advice from the Head of Conservation at the Tate Gallery who advised her to simply give it time. The reaction of some of the local population to the sculpture was one of hatred. Many people had no idea what it was supposed to represent and simply could not understand why this large, abstract, challenging piece of rusty metal had been placed in such a lovely location. Letters were written to the newspapers, it was discussed on radio programmes and many made special journeys to Kinsale especially to see this work for themselves. Complaints were made to the town council that not only was the work an eyesore, but it also posed a danger to children, who had been riding their BMX bikes up the two lower curved shelter sections. The artist liked the teenagers reaction and she particularily liked the rubber tyre marks on the rust and regarded it as a form of drawing. The demands for its removal were so strong that changes devised by the architect were insisted upon. Copyright law in Ireland has changed since the creation of the sculpture in 1988, so such changes to an artwork today would be illegal.

FIG 2.1 THE GREAT WALL OF KINSALE, Co. Cork

The artist

This upset the artist and to her great disappointment the sculpture was painted and the county architect later added a wall parallel to the work with a number of decorative ponds. Eilís O' Connell felt that these embellishments altered the sculpture's original integrity and completely changed how she wished the artwork to be seen. The fact that nobody was really happy in the end highlights the challenges associated with such public commissions.

Including the local population

The difficulties experienced in Kinsale make an interesting contrast when compared with a more recent sculptural project in Dublin, which was especially designed to include the local population.

Hybrid Love Seat

At the St James' Hospital Luas stop in Dublin a fence has become a seat and railings are topped with magical gargoyles in an intriguing work of public art. This came about when the newly developed light rail network, or Luas, in Dublin held a competition in conjunction with St James's Hospital to commission an artist to build a boundary feature along a borderline between the Mary Aikenhead Flats and the Luas stop. The project was funded under the Per Cent for Art scheme and the competition was administered by the Irish Museum of Modern Art. Louise Walsh was the successful artist with her proposal for *Hybrid Love Seat* (fig 2.2).

Rather than build a barrier that would isolate the nearby flats from the stop, Walsh designed a curved railing piece that creates a series of seats on both sides. Although the

FIG 2.3 Gargoyles from HYBRID LOVE SEAT

final result was a division of the space, it was less of a barrier in that it offered equal usage on both sides. The semi-circular seats in the undulating railed wall picked up on the idea of a back-to-back, two-seated sofa, or 'loveseat'.

Part of Walsh's proposal was to make this a participatory project and enable the local community to experience real ownership of the art. Local teenagers working with the artist made modelled figures in clay that were later cast in bronze. Students from the Sculpture Department in the nearby National College of Art and Design (NCAD) volunteered as mentors on the project.

The finished gargoyles (fig 2.3, fig 2.4) were mounted on the railings and are an important – as well as charming – part of the overall work. The finished project was unveiled in February 2008, but these small, imaginative creatures on their lofty perches will keep passers-by smiling for a long time to come.

FIG 2.2 HYBRID LOVE SEAT, Louise Walsh, St James Luas Stop, Dublin

FIG 2.4 Gargoyles from HYBRID LOVE SEAT

Consultation and debate

This project shows the importance of participation as well as consultation and co-operation with local communities. It is also important that information as to the name of the work, the artist and the concept behind the work should be readily available so that members of the public can fully appreciate and identify with public works of art.

Public art today

Public art online

Information about public art projects can often be found on the websites of the artists involved, but this means that one has to know where to look.

Happily, a new website has been established by the Arts Council. www.publicart.ie has helped greatly in providing a forum to showcase temporary works that would otherwise have been appreciated only in books or film and has a directory of artworks with photo galleries, videos and links for some publicly funded art. It features a wide range of extremely interesting projects

Temporary projects/unusual places

Here are three examples of recent temporary projects that happened in unusual of places.

- **Hotel Ballymun** (fig 2.5) is an example of a publicly funded artwork that was recorded in book form. The project – conceived by artist Seamus Nolan and curated by Aisling Prior – transformed the 15th floor of Clarke Tower, one of the last remaining tower blocks in Ballymun, into a short-stay hotel for a few days before its demolition. Nolan worked with local residents and furniture designers Sticks and Jonathan Legge to customise and remodel the furniture left behind in the flats to create unique pieces of furniture for the hotel. A diverse programme of cultural and social events took place throughout the day and evening time, including talks, live art and music performances.

FIG 2.5 HOTEL BALLYMUN, Seamus Nolan, Dublin

FIG 2.6 DECONSTRUCTING THE MAZE, Dara Mc Grath, Co. Down

- **Deconstructing 'The Maze'** (fig 2.6), by photographic artist Dara McGrath, is a survey of the demolition of The Maze/Long Kesh Prison near Belfast. The prison with its infamous 'H Blocks' came to be associated with the worst aspects of the conflict in Northern Ireland during the 'Troubles'. It was closed in 2000 and a decision was made in 2006 to demolish the buildings completely to make way for the construction of a new national stadium on the 360-acre site. Dara photographed the demolition process over an extensive period, exploring what happens when a space comes to the end of its life. This work was published in book form as well as being exhibited in several venues in the country. It also featured in 'The Lives of Spaces', Ireland's participation in the 11th International Architecture Exhibition in 2008.

- **Medusae,** which means 'jellyfish' in Latin, is the work of well-known Irish artist Dorothy Cross and her scientist brother, Professor Tom Cross. Having secured funding from the Sci-Art fund for three years, they focused their investigations on the aesthetic, anthropological and scientific aspects of jellyfish. *Medusae* explores the notions of mystery and the relationships between art and science, the known and the unknown, the imagined and the real. This 30-minute video-based work weaves between demonstrations of the swimming techniques of the jellyfish in a documentary-style narrative and aspects of the life story of Irish amateur naturalist Maude Delap – real and imagined – who lived and worked on Valentia Island, Co. Kerry.

Problems facing public art

Information

Hopefully in time Publicart.ie will also provide information on roadside sculpture. This would greatly help the ordinary member of the public to identify and learn more about those pieces of art seen in passing on streets and roadsides. Perhaps it might also address those sculptures that the art world may not call 'art' yet which are beloved of locals and tourists alike, such as *Molly Malone* (fig 2.38) and *Phil Lynott* in Dublin and *Joe Dolan* in Mullingar.

At present, finding out about certain sculptures and who made them is a bit hit and miss. The main way to do this is through the websites of the local authorities. It seems that of the money that is spent on commissioning the work, very little of it seems to be allocated towards creating information for the public.

Local authorities

Some city councils and county councils produce excellent books, calendars and education leaflets for schools on their artworks. Their websites are equally informative and sometimes contain excellent pictures and background information on the artists. Other city and county councils provide almost nothing.

This is unfortunate as there are many wonderful projects located around the country that are almost unknown except to those living nearby. One suggestion is to take 1 per cent of the total funds allocated for art and use it to let the public know more about what their money is being spent on.

Vandalism

Another problem faced by public art is deliberate vandalism. Naturally, if an artwork has been damaged or defaced, area residents will not be pleased and may object to the artwork's presence in the locale. The fear that a proposed artwork might easily be damaged or defaced is sometimes the source of resistance by local residents to having a work of art placed in their area. Artwork can also be considered a nuisance if it acts as a gathering spot for youths engaged in anti-social behaviour.

The Per Cent for Art scheme

Most publicly funded art in Ireland has been funded by a scheme known as the Per Cent for Art scheme. Funding for art was introduced in 1978 by the Office of Public Works. The government later extended this when they established the Artistic Embellishment scheme. This now also applied to local authorities who could commission 'artistic features' as part of capital development schemes funded through the central government. At that time, funding was limited to 1 per cent of the capital cost of the scheme, up to a limit of €12,700. The Artistic Embellishment scheme quickly became known as the Per Cent for Art scheme.

Changes were made to the scheme in 1997. It was now called the Department of the Environment Per Cent for Art Scheme and was extended to all construction projects.

Recognising the important contribution made by public art, it placed a levy on building construction and stipulated that the budgets for all capital construction projects should include a sum to pay for an Irish visual art project. The scheme has been a huge success in adding to the quality of our immediate environment, but it is also a valuable support for artists and certainly creates an increased public awareness of art.

Site specific

The term 'site specific' applied to a work of art means it is created to exist in a certain place. Typically, the artist takes the location into account while planning and creating the artwork. They usually include the architectural, historical, social and/or environmental aspects and try to discover the hidden meaning of the site and find ways to enhance it.

The term 'site specific' can also apply to dance or theatrical performances.

Roadside art

Irish roads have been greatly enlivened by hundreds of figures and statues in the recent past. As the national routes are upgraded, artworks have appeared because a fraction of the road-building budget has been devoted to the placement of art at landmark junctures along them. Generally these figures and statues are permanent, prominent and site specific.

Many of the roadside sculptures that have captured the travelling public's imagination are greatly admired and widely spoken about, even by those not normally travelling on the routes. It also makes driving interesting for visitors if they are suddenly confronted with a huge white horse wearing a unicorn helmet and rearing up on its hind legs, looking out over the soft, heather-clad mountains on top of a rocky embankment.

Fig 2.7 AN CAPALL MÓR, Tighe O'Donoghue, N22 Tralee, Co. Kerry

Fig 2.9 THE SCULPTURE ROAD TO KILLARNEY, Tighe and Eoghan O'Donoghue, Co. Kerry

An Capall Mór

An Capall Mór (fig 2.7) gained immediate popularity when it was placed on the new N22 near Tralee, Co. Kerry. Made by Tighe O Donoghue, it is 4.2 m high and made from cast stone or ferro-cement over a steel infrastructure. The sculpture represents a war horse typical of those used by the Celtic chiefs during their battles. The broken chains around its front legs signify freedom.

Local people fondly call it *The Unicorn* (fig 2.8) and it has become a landmark for everyone travelling the road. Families have been known to drive along the route just to give their children the enjoyment of seeing *The Unicorn*.

The artist and his son, Eoghan, are also famous for *The Sculpture Road to Killarney* (fig 2.9), a work consisting of sculpted stones that have been placed along each side of the new part of the road to Cork. Most of these stones were excavated during the building of the road and vary between 1 to 3 tons in weight.

Equestrian statues

Horses were once an important aspect of public art in Irish towns and cities. An equestrian statue of King

Fig 2.8 AN CAPALL MÓR – detail

Fig 2.10 WILLIAM OF ORANGE ON HORSEBACK, Equestrian statue, Dame Street, Dublin

FIG 2.11 LORD GOUGH MEMORIAL, Phoenix Park, Dublin

George II once stood in the centre of St Stephen's Green in Dublin, but it has long since disappeared. William of Orange on horseback (fig 2.10) in Dublin's College Green was, by all accounts, 'the butt of countless insults. At one time decked with flowers and streamers, at others daubed with filth, or smeared with tar.' The statue suffered its final insult when it was blown up in 1929.

A symbol of oppression

The memorial to Lord Gough, 'the conqueror of the Punjaub', that once stood in Dublin's Phoenix Park met the same fate as the statue of William of Orange in 1957. Both of these statues were created by John Henry Foley, best known for the monument to Daniel O'Connell in Dublin. It was said of the Gough Memorial (fig 2.11) in 1905 that 'a finer statue than this is not presented anywhere else in the world. It sets the seal on Foley's genius as a sculptor.' However, like the William of Orange statue, it was seen as a symbol of colonial power and this completely obscured its artistic merit.

FIG 2.12 THE GAELIC CHIEFTAIN, Maurice Harron, near Boyle, Co. Roscommon

The Gaelic Chieftain

Happily, there seems to be no such hostility to one of Ireland's new public equestrian statues, *The Gaelic Chieftain* (fig 2.12). A 5 m tall horseback Chieftain in Roscommon is, according to a recent radio programme, Ireland's most popular roadside sculpture.

This imposing work is made of metal pieces and stands 2 miles north of the town of Boyle on the site of the Battle of the Curleius. The battle took place in 1599 between an English force and a rebel Irish force led by 'Red' Hugh O'Donnell. The English were ambushed and routed while marching through a pass in the Curlew Mountains and they suffered heavy casualties.

Those driving past the site today probably have little knowledge or interest in the event, but the sculpture does provide a picnic area and an opportunity to rest and take in the magnificent views over Lough Key.

'Slow release'

The artist who made *The Gaelic Chieftain* is Maurice Harron, whose sculptures have been written about in many newspaper and magazine articles as well as featured in advertisements and TV documentaries. His image of two men reaching out to shake hands in Derry (fig 2.13) has become an icon of the peace process, but his name is still virtually unknown.

FIG 2.13 HANDS ACROSS THE DIVIDE, Maurice Harron, Derry

Harron says, 'I'm not in the least bit "hard cheesed" about it. Where public art is concerned, the name doesn't matter. Once you put something like that up, you forget it. It becomes part of public property and the public imagination.' He is content to let his work do the talking for him. 'I'm not trying to be clever with people,' he says. 'I'm trying to put up a universal symbol that's very clear. You have to respect people. It is presumptuous to put up an artwork in a public zone. Thousands of people drive past my work every day, and the last thing on their minds is art.' The impact of his work is 'slow release', he says.

A landmark for Offaly

Maurice Harron is also responsible for four 7.5 m steel figurines, *Saints and Scholars* (fig 2.14), on the N52 Tullamore bypass, just off the Dublin to Galway motorway. Each holds a symbol of the world of learning and sanctity, representing the monastic settlements of Durrow and Clonmacnoise. One holds a book, one holds a chalice, one a staff and one throws aloft a flock of birds or souls. The semi-abstract patterns on the figures (fig 2.15) were

Fig 2.15 SAINTS AND SCHOLARS, detail

Fig 2.14 SAINTS AND SCHOLARS, Maurice Harron, N52 Tullamore bypass, Offaly

inspired by ancient illustrated manuscripts like the Book of Durrow, but the work is modern and so stainless steel was the material chosen. This reacts well with the rays of the sun at different times during the day.

Construction took place in Derry in a large building equipped with overhead lifting equipment and made full use of the most up-to-date industrial welding and laser-cutting techniques. When he was asked where the inspiration for his sculpture came from, Harron said, 'The location of the site was very dramatic; it had four hills and also proximity to the ancient place of learning – Clonmacnoise. I wished to honour that place.' He hoped people would like it and that the sculpture would become a landmark as well as an emblem of the locality, creating an awareness of its great heritage.

Considerations of roadside works of art

In producing such roadside works of art, there are many considerations the artist must take into account. The work must be large enough to attract attention from a distance, yet it must not distract a motorist driving at 120 kph. It also has to be robust enough to survive weather, graffiti, vandalism and even play. (It has become commonplace to 'dress' these works at the time of local sporting events or even just for fun.) Unlike art in a gallery, the public doesn't make an active choice to see it, so it must be generally inoffensive – or at least as inoffensive as possible.

Selection of the work

To add to these difficulties, as public money is being spent, the work is usually selected by committee. The result can end up being a compromise and as a result may not be taken to heart by the public, as happened with such dramatic results in the case of the two warhorses. Sculpture does, however, create interest and provides familiar or fun moments for passers-by while also marking a definite spot on an otherwise boring stretch of highway.

Art as a landmark

Many consider the large ball on the Naas dual carriageway to be a sign that they have left Dublin behind and that the real journey south or west has begun.

Not all will know that the great sphere covered in road markings is called *Perpetual Motion* (fig 2.16) or that an artist named Rachel Joynt collaborated with another artist, Remco de Fouw, to produce it in 1995.

FIG 2.17 MOTHERSHIP, Rachel Joynt, Dun Laoghaire, Dublin

FIG 2.16 PERPETUAL MOTION, Remco de Fouw and Rachel Joynt, Naas, Co. Kildare

FIG 2.18 FREEFLOW, Rachel Joynt, Custom House Quay, Dublin

Rachel Joynt is an Irish sculptor who has created some prominent Irish public art. Her commissions include *People's Island*, in which brass footprints and bird feet criss-cross a well-traversed pedestrian island near Dublin's O'Connell Bridge, and *Mothership* (fig 2.17), a cast bronze and steel sea urchin positioned on the seafront in Dun Laoghaire, Co. Dublin.

In 2006 she was commissioned by the Dublin Docklands Development Authority to insert *Freeflow* (fig 2.18), an installation of 900 small, internally lit glass cobbles in watery shades of green and blue along the north quays for 1 km, stretching from Custom House Quay to the North Wall. Joynt herself says, 'For me, a successful public artwork needs to have a sense of place, a freshness, some intrigue and playfulness, a bit like a frozen moment from a daydream.'

County councils

County councils around the country have embraced the possibilities of the Per Cent for Art scheme with enthusiasm.

Wexford

In 10 years, for example, Wexford County Council alone has undertaken 34 commissions, shifting in emphasis from permanent outdoor sculpture to time-based

installations and other explorative art forms. Artist Mick Fortune, for example, was commissioned to make a digital video of Rosslare Harbour and the lives of local people.

The Last Oak Tree

The council is also anxious to involve the local community in art. Among the most recent projects is a landmark sculpture for the N30 (New Ross to Enniscorthy). *The Last Oak Tree* (fig 2.19) is a stainless steel traditional oak tree that measures 6 m high and 5 m at its widest point. Members of the community and school children were involved in producing designs for the leaves of the tree.

Laois

Laois County Council has commissioned some major public art projects. Artists Robert McColgan and Irene Benner created a stainless steel ring over the Portlaoise bypass – *Gateway* (fig 2.20) – symbolising a gateway to the Midlands.

FIG 2.19 THE LAST OAK TREE, Denis O Connor, N30 New Ross to Enniscorthy, Co. Wexford

FIG 2.20 GATEWAY, Robert McColgan and Irene Benner, Portlaoise bypass

FIG 2.21 BRONZE
BULL, Don Cronin,
Macroom, Co. Cork

Cork

The projects of Cork County Council, which is in charge of one of the largest counties, stretch from Macroom's *Bronze Bull* (fig 2.21) by Don Cronin to *Milk Churns* (fig 2.22) on the Mallow Road by Eileen McDonagh and Bantry, where two large figures in bronze encircle a bronze mast in a sculpture called *Spirit of Love* (fig 2.23) by Patrick Campbell. As with the excellent websites of the Wexford and Donegal county councils, all the commissions are well presented on the Cork County Council website, which provides pictures and information. Other county council websites could perhaps follow the example of these county councils because this makes it easy to browse through and note the location of a public artwork for viewing during future travels in these counties. All the websites could benefit from regular updating, however.

FIG 2.24 TOMÁS Ó CRIOMHTHAIN, Michael Quane, Blasket Island Heritage Centre, Co. Kerry

FIG 2.22 MILK CHURNS, Eileen McDonagh, Mallow Road, Co. Cork

34

Limestone horses

Michael Quane is a well-known Cork sculptor who has exhibited extensively both nationally and internationally. He works with stone, usually limestone, which he carves with hundreds of thousands of chisel marks and scrapes. A particularly fine example of his work is the statue of Tomás O'Criomhtain (fig 2.24) at the Blasket Island Heritage Centre at Dun Caoin, Co. Kerry.

Quane's themes are usually centred around relationships between horses and people. Writhing animals are often carved as voluptuous beasts, sometimes locked in combat, with contorted limbs and bulging muscles. Perhaps this fascination with the power of animals and the vulnerability of that power can be traced to the artist's childhood when he saw a donkey drown in a bog hole while staying with his grandmother in Co. Offaly.

The artist has an imaginative empathy with animals, but he frequently depicts them in vulnerable positions. 'You think of a horse as something enormously strong and powerful, running on all fours. But what has he to stick out to save himself if he falls?' he asks.

FIG 2.23 SPIRIT OF LOVE, Patrick Campbell, Bantry, Co. Cork

FIG 2.25 HORSES AND RIDERS, Michael Quane, Mallow, Co. Cork

Some of his finest and most popular large-scale public works are *Horses and Riders* (fig 2.25) and *Fallen Horse and Rider* (fig 2.26).

A huge 25 ton block was carved down over nine months into an 11 ton work, depicting intertwined horses and riders. Commissioned in 1995, it is sited at a roundabout on the N20 in Mallow, Co. Cork. This group, circling in a tight knot, conveys – as the artist explains – 'a sense of the connectedness of individuals through their culture, history, evolution, dependency and need amid their own personal isolation and indivisibility'.

By all accounts, when the sculpture was first installed, passing car drivers frequently circled the junction just to take it all in its sagging and straining glory.

The Great Irish Deer

The Great Irish Deer (fig 2.27) by Kevin Holland is also on the N20 Mallow Road in Cork and has enjoyed great popularity since it was installed in 1994. This huge work is made with bronze panels over a stainless steel bar framework and its 3.5 m antler span has made it a real eye-catcher.

It refers to the natural history of the countryside and was placed at a most dramatic vantage point, standing on the edge of the bluff overlooking the road.

Cork County Council, however, needs to do some work on the site again because since the installation of *The Great Irish Deer*, gorse bushes have grown up around it and this imposing work is all but covered.

FIG 2.27 THE GREAT IRISH DEER, Kevin Holland, Mallow Road, Co. Cork

Public art in the city
Dublin

Statues and monuments have long been a prominent feature of Dublin's cityscape. Indeed, there is a unique history of witty nicknames associated with them. Controversy about their subjects and designs can also arise easily and some formerly prominent monuments have been removed or destroyed due to popular displeasure.

FIG 2.26 FALLEN HORSE AND RIDER, Michael Quane, Midleton, Co. Cork

Fig 2.28 NELSON'S PILLAR, Dublin

Fig 2.29 SPIRE OF DUBLIN – A MONUMENT OF LIGHT, Ian Richie Architects, Dublin

The Pillar

One of the most spectacular events associated with Dublin's monuments was the destruction of Nelson's Pillar (fig 2.28), which stood near the GPO and served as a landmark in the city centre for generations of Dublin people. It was blown up by a small group of Republicans in 1966. The space remained empty until January 2003. A new monument was eventually erected after a competition for a suitable edifice to take its place. The new structure, which is officially named the Spire of Dublin – A Monument of Light (fig 2.29), is not without its critics, but has become part of the Dublin cityscape. In true Dublin fashion, the tall, needle-like structure was immediately given several nicknames, of which 'The Spike' is the only one fit for inclusion in a school book!

A Monument of Light

The spire was designed by Ian Richie Architects, whose design aim was an 'elegant and dynamic simplicity bridging art and technology'. The tall, tapering, elongated cone has a diameter of 3 m at the base that narrows to just 15 cm at the top. It is constructed from eight hollow tubes of stainless steel that underwent a process known as 'shot peening' to better reflect the light. Its reflective properties also cause the metal to change colour. During the day it maintains its look of steel, but at dusk the monument appears to merge into the sky. The base is lit and the top 12 m is illuminated to provide a beacon in the night sky across the city.

O'Connell Street

The main street of Ireland's capital city has several monuments to Irish patriots.

Daniel O'Connell (fig 2.30) stands at the entrance to the street named after him on a monument designed and sculpted by John Henry Foley. Widely considered the sculptor's finest work, the foundation stone was laid in 1864 and the finished work was unveiled to enormous crowds in 1882.

The tallest statue on O'Connell Street is the Parnell Monument (fig 2.31) by Irish-American sculptor Augustus Saint-Gaudens. This striking obelisk of solid Galway granite was erected in 1911 and paid for through public subscription.

FIG 2.30 DANIEL O'CONNELL, John Henry Foley, Dublin

Oisín Kelly created the expressive bronze memorial to James Larkin (fig 2.32) in 1980. A committed and tireless trade union activist, 'Big Jim' Larkin led 20,000 workers in the great Dublin Lock-out described so well in James Plunkett's book *Strumpet City*. He is shown in the full power of his oratory, with arms outstretched, atop a granite plinth.

FIG 2.31 PARNELL MONUMENT, Augustus Saint-Gaudens, Dublin

FIG 2.32 JAMES LARKIN, Oisin Kelly, O'Connell Street, Dublin

FIG 2.33 ANNA LIVIA, Eamonn O'Doherty, Dublin

Eamonn O'Doherty

Eamonn O'Doherty's fountain *Anna Livia* (fig 2.33) features a woman as a personified River Liffey, sitting on a slope with bubbling water running down past her. The fountain is based on Anna Livia Plurabelle, a character in James Joyce's *Finnegan's Wake*, and it was placed on the central section of O'Connell Street in 1988. It immediately caused a storm of protests and quickly became known as 'the Floozie in the Jacuzzi', a nickname used by the artist himself.

A well-respected sculptor, O'Doherty had already created the quincentennial sculpture *Galway Hookers* (fig 2.34) in Eyre Square, Galway, and went on to become one of Ireland's best-known living Irish artists. His other large-scale public works include *Fauscailt* (1998) (fig 2.35) in Co. Wexford, which was a work of art commemorating the Irish Rebellion of 1798, so the local community was strongly involved. He had to incorporate a pre-established theme and local community interests. Five larger-than-life bronze figures hold long pikes and it is referred to locally and throughout the county as 'The Pikemen'.

FIG 2.35 FAUSCAILT, Eamonn O'Doherty, Co. Wexford

O'Doherty also produced *Crann an Óir* (fig 2.36) in Dublin's Central Bank Plaza. The plaza is much used in the evenings by party goers and skateboarders, but the materials used in this sculpture are hardwearing and it has required very little maintenance since its installation in 1991.

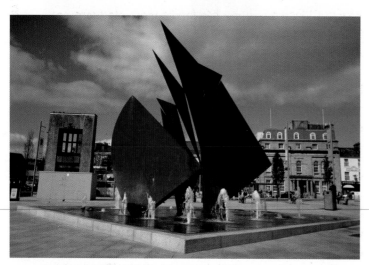

FIG 2.34 GALWAY HOOKERS, Eamonn O'Doherty, Eyre Square, Galway

FIG 2.36 CRANN AN ÓIR, Eamonn O'Doherty, Central Bank, Dublin

Anna Livia controversy

On O'Connell Street, *Anna Livia* continued to attract hostile publicity. People said the work wasn't up to the artist's usual standard and it became a target for litter and graffiti. Washing up liquid was frequently dumped into the fountain at weekends and eventually, in 2002, it was relocated to the Memorial Gardens facing Collins Barracks.

The Meeting Place

Much more acceptable to the public is a bronze statue of two women near the Ha'penny Bridge. *The Meeting Place* (fig 2.37) by Jackie McKenna has enough space on the bench for anyone who chooses to sit with the women, who are engaged in conversation with their shopping bags at their feet. They are famously known as 'The Hags with the Bags'.

FIG 2.38 MOLLY MALONE, Jean Rynhart, Dublin

FIG 2.37 THE MEETING PLACE, Jackie McKenna, Dublin

Molly Malone

Molly Malone (fig 2.38) by Jean Rynhart, located at one end of Grafton Street, is one of the most popular photo spots for visitors to the city. Nicknamed 'the Tart with the

Cart', it was erected to celebrate Dublin's millennium in 1988. Although very popular, its artistic merit is highly questionable.

Oscar Wilde by Danny Osborne is located on the corner of Merrion Square, opposite Wilde's childhood home. Composed of different-coloured stone, the writer is presented indolently reclining on a large granite boulder. He, too, has acquired some irreverent nicknames.

Rowan Gillespie – working in bronze

Rowan Gillespie is one of Ireland's most eloquent contemporary artists. He has produced numerous sculptures in Dublin as well as other parts of the country and abroad. He works in bronze, but unlike other artists he does his own casting and has built a one-man workshop and foundry where he carries out this complicated process entirely alone.

He lives in Dublin and has produced a significant body of work in the city, including the semi-abstract *The Kiss* (fig 2.39, fig 2.40) and *The Blackrock Dolmen* (fig 2.41), with three figures holding a great rock, which they overcome with a united strength. Some amusing works are *Aspiration* (fig 2.42), a figure climbing up the wall of the Dublin Treasury Building, and *Birdy* (fig 2.43), a

FIG 2.39 THE KISS, Rowan Gillespie, Dublin

FIG 2.41 THE BLACKROCK DOLMEN, Rowan Gillespie, Dublin

FIG 2.40 THE KISS – detail

FIG 2.42 ASPIRATION, Rowan Gillespie, Treasury Building, Dublin

FIG 2.43 *BIRDY*, Rowan Gillespie, Dublin

FIG 2.45 THE SINGER, Rowan Gillespie, Limerick

figure perched on the windowsill of 3 Crescent Hall, Mount Street, Dublin.

Gillespie's works outside of Dublin are found in Cashel, where his *Cashel Dancers* (fig 2.44) leap out with such exuberance that one can almost hear the music, as well as in Sligo (*W.B. Yeats*) and in Limerick city (*The Singer*) (fig 2.45).

FIG 2.44 DANCERS, Rowan Gillespie, Cashel, Co. Tipperary

Famine

Gillespie's most famous work is undoubtedly *Famine* (fig 2.46) at Custom House Quay in Dublin. It was commissioned by Norma Smurfit and presented to the city of Dublin in 1997. A commemorative work, it is dedicated to the Irish people who were forced to emigrate during the Great Famine in Ireland in the 19th century.

An image of human misery

This most moving work draws attention to world poverty today as much as it does to the Irish Famine of the 1840s. The figures are life-sized, but they seem taller due to their emaciated appearance. Nearly all of Gillespie's sculptures tell a story, but it seems as if each of these haunting skeletal figures could relate a unique tale of suffering and loss. One cannot walk past this work without being affected by the figures' predicament.

Making their way slowly and with halting steps towards emigration ships, they are hollow-eyed and clasp pitifully small bundles to their chests (fig 2.47, fig 2.48). One man carries a limp child over his shoulders and a woman at

FIG 2.46 FAMINE, Rowan Gillespie, Custom House Quay, Dublin

the rear stumbles forward, her hands hanging lifelessly at her side.

The figures stand together, yet in their misery each one looks withdrawn and utterly alone. As they pass, a mangy dog (fig 2.48) is watching them, which adds to the poignancy of the scene.

FIG 2.47 FAMINE – detail

FIG 2.48 FAMINE – detail

In June 2007, a second (and equally emotional) series of famine sculptures by Rowan Gillespie was unveiled by President Mary McAleese on the quayside in Toronto's Ireland Park to remember the arrival of these most miserable of refugees in Canada (fig 2.49).

Proclamation

A recent work by Gillespie entitled *Proclamation* (fig 2.50) is a more conceptual and abstract piece. Situated across the road from Kilmainham Gaol, it was created in memory of both the Proclamation of the Irish Republic and of his grandfather, a High Court judge and member of the Irish Volunteers. Fourteen figures stand in a megalithic circle, at the centre of which is a plaque containing a copy of the Proclamation engraved in bronze. Each figure has at its base a small plaque, engraved with their name and the British military tribunal's verdict and sentence of death. The figures are perforated with bullet holes.

Fig 2.49 MIGRANTS, Rowan Gillespie, Ireland Park, Toronto, Canada

Fig 2.50 PROCLAMATION, Rowan Gillespie, Dublin

Reflective light

The figures are without limbs and are united and blindfolded, as they would have been for execution, but they are far from lifeless (fig 2.51). The bronze has been polished and has a smooth, reflective finish with the light 'bouncing off one another', suggesting the spirit of the martyrs whose ideas passed from one to another. Gillespie sees *Proclamation* as a monument to those who gave their lives to change the course of Irish history and release the dreams of the Irish people.

Edward Delaney

In October 2009, three weeks after the death of the artist, a bronze sculpture entitled *King & Queen* sold at auction at Adam's, a fine-art auction house in Dublin, for €190,000, a world record price for a piece of Irish sculpture. Edward Delaney, born in Claremorris, Co. Mayo, in 1930, had over the course of his life become one of the leading figures in Irish sculpture of the second half of the 20th century.

Dublin sculptures

Much in demand as an artist during the 1960s and early 1970s, Delaney's public commissions for the Irish government included a statue of Wolfe Tone (fig 2.52) and a memorial sculpture to the Great Famine (fig 2.53) to be situated in St Stephen's Green in Dublin, and a statue of Thomas Davis to be located on College Green, opposite Trinity College Dublin.

Fig 2.51 PROCLAMATION – detail

FIG 2.52 WOLFE TONE, Edward Delaney, Dublin

These were made using the lost-wax (*cire perdue*) method of bronze casting and are examples of his unique style of modern expressionism, developed during the 1950s and 1960s. These minimalist and – at times – skeletal figures are said to have been influenced by the

FIG 2.53 MEMORIAL SCULPTURE TO THE GREAT FAMINE, Edward Delaney, Dublin

Holocaust and the Great Famine as well as by the work of Alberto Giacometti (1901–66).

Edward Delaney attended the National College of Art and Design in Dublin and then, with the support of the Arts Council, he studied bronze casting in Germany.

Post-war Germany

As part of a 2004 retrospective exhibition of Delaney's bronzes, Peter Murray wrote in the *Irish Arts Review* that:

> the poverty of Germany made a profound impression on the artist, providing stark images which would reappear in his later work in Ireland. His achievement lay in his ability to unite the instinctive, unpretentious approach of his rural background, where memories of the Great Famine were still alive in the memories of people, with the stricken anxiety evident in post-war culture in Germany.

Delaney's style of sculpture ranged from strongly representational to almost pure abstract until the end of the 1970s and had a particular empathy with the subject and a concern for texture. This expressionist abstraction imbued them with a naturalism and an egalitarianism that reflected a new confidence in the nation.

The artist lived in Carraroe, Co. Galway, in the last years of his life, and a large body of his work can be seen at the Open Air Sculpture Park in Carraroe.

Oisín Kelly

Oisín Kelly is one of Ireland's most famous sculptors. He worked both in a realistic and abstract style concerned mainly with ideas native to Ireland and its culture. His work shows an affection and understanding of his subject, which is especially noticeable in his sculptures of birds, animals and, of course, human beings. Subtle humour is sometimes found in Kelly's work, and his religious works are respectful but in an unsentimental manner.

The Children of Lir

Kelly's largest public work is the bronze *Children of Lir* (fig 2.54), which he made for the Garden of Remembrance in Parnell Square, Dublin, in 1970. He chose the subject to symbolise the fundamental change in Ireland brought about by the Rising in Dublin in 1916 and the subsequent War of Independence. Perhaps a more abstract form would have suited the notion of children turning into swans, which is, after all, a very abstract subject, but Kelly decided against this

FIG 2.54 CHILDREN OF LIR, Oisín Kelly, Dublin

FIG 2.55 TWO WORKING MEN, Oisín Kelly, Co. Cork

approach, fearing the public might find it too difficult to accept. The complex sculpture group was cast in bronze in Italy in 1970.

Dublin characters

Kelly's *Two Working Men* (fig 2.55, fig 2.56) are bronze figures of typical Dublin characters. They are treated in a realistic but simplified manner and unlike the *Children of Lir*, this really suits the couple. The work was intended to stand outside of Dublin's Liberty Hall, which at the time was Ireland's tallest building and the headquarters of the SIPTU trade union. SIPTU officials, however, said it would pose a traffic hazard and refused permission for the sculpture to be installed there.

It was subsequently transferred to Cork in 1969 and it was placed outside the County Hall. Here, it was an immediate hit with the public, who recognised

FIG 2.56 TWO WORKING MEN – detail

Fig 2.57 Share Building on Grattan Street, Co. Cork

Fig 2.58 Share Building on Grattan Street – Stained glass windows, James Scanlon

something of Cork's dry sense of humour in the two, who appeared not at all impressed by the height of Cork's new glass and concrete 'skyscraper', which had surpassed Liberty Hall as the tallest building in Ireland. In 2007, Desmond Rea O'Kelly, architect of Liberty Hall, reflected on the lost opportunity. He said, 'One of the other things I regret very much is that Oisín Kelly's great sculpture of the young man and the older man admiring their work was never put up outside Liberty Hall.'

Cork

Cork City Council was the first local authority to explore the full potential of the early Per Cent for Art scheme. In 1986, the newly appointed city architect, Neil Hegarty, was managing the refurbishment and renewal of a range of housing schemes in Cork. He had an interest in the urban renewal aspects of the schemes and saw the potential for some imaginative art projects. Commissions were placed within the housing schemes and artists were encouraged to consult with residents.

One of the most interesting proposals was for the Share Building on Grattan Street, part of a housing scheme for older people. Artist James Scanlon made a series of 11 abstract stained glass windows for the building. It was the first non-sculptural work of art funded by the Per Cent for Art scheme (fig 2.57, fig 2.58).

Cork City Council continues to contribute to a variety of artistic projects using the Per Cent for Art scheme. Many are temporary projects, like the one in 2002 called *Daylighting the City* that included large photographs on public billboards and walls of public buildings. Several permanent site-specific sculptures have also been erected in the city under the Per Cent for Art scheme.

Fitzgerald Park in Cork

A site of some 18 acres of landscaped gardens, Fitzgerald Park in Cork is the magnificent setting for an impressive collection of sculpture that began in the early 20th century and comes right to the present day.

International Exhibitions

In 1901, at a meeting of Cork Corporation the Lord Mayor, Edward Fitzgerald, put forward the idea of holding of an International Exhibition in Cork.

The Exhibition Committee purchased a house and lands beside the Mardyke Walk called The Shrubberies and leased adjoining lands to the exhibition, which took place in May 1902. The attractions included industrial and machinery halls, a Grand Concert Hall and amusements, such as the Great Water Chute on the river.

The exhibition was a success and it was held again the next year. This time the highlight was the visit of King Edward VII and Queen Alexandra.

Presentation of the grounds to the people of Cork

Temporary buildings were erected to house the exhibition, of which all were dismantled after the event but one. The house and its grounds were presented to the citizens of Cork as a recreational area, which was called Fitzgerald Park.

FIG 2.59 The Presidents and Lord Mayors Pavilion, The Tea House, Fitzgerald Park, Cork

Features of the great Exhibition of 1903 that remain in Fitzgerald Park to this day include the President and Lord Mayor's Pavilion still known as the Tea House (fig 2.59) and the Fr Matthew Fountain.

Sculptures

- **Adam and Eve by Edward Delaney** – These strange abstract figures with small heads and textured bodies represent a man and woman.

- **Boy with a Boat by Joseph Higgins** – Joseph Higgins attended night classes at the Crawford School of Art. His talents as a sculptor were quickly recognised and he soon received several awards. His style of clay modelling may have been inspired by the work of Rodin, but as Higgins never travelled outside Ireland, he must have learned of Rodin's work through art journals and books. He worked as a teacher, but continued to paint and to sculpt, often using his children and family as models. *Boy with a Boat* (fig 2.60), a bronze cast, was modelled on his nephew. He contracted tuberculosis and died in 1925, aged only 39. He had never received a commission and none of his works were cast during his lifetime.

- **Dreamline by Seamus Murphy** – One of the giants of Cork art and an important figure in the history of Irish art in the 20th century history is Seamus Murphy, a traditional sculptor. He worked mainly in limestone and produced a range of works from religious statues, portrait heads, commemorative plaques, public monuments, gravestones and crosses. Among these is *Dreamline* (fig 2.61).

FIG 2.60 BOY WITH A BOAT, Joseph Higgins, Fitzerald Park, Co. Cork

FIG 2.61 DREAMLINE, Seamus Murphy, Fitzerald Park, Co. Cork

- ***Little Dancer* by Oisín Kelly** – *Little Dancer*, in bronze, is one of Kelly's famous series based on the theme of movement. The movement and rhythm of Irish dancing, with arms held at the sides and all concentration on the elaborate footwork, is conveyed in the simplicity of the form. The little dancer's legs are thin and stick-like, but this adds to a feeling of airiness about the girl, who, with hair blowing in the wind, looks as if she might dance off into the woodland behind her at any moment.

Sculpture in Context

The idea of exhibiting sculpture in areas outside of the normal gallery space began in Ireland in 1985 when a group of sculptors in Dublin got together to work at providing a space for their fellow sculptors. The venture has been extremely successful over the years.

Sculpture in Context was staged at Dublin venues such as Fernhill Gardens, the Conrad Hotel, Kilmainham Gaol, the Irish Management Institute, Dublin Castle, Farmleigh

Fig 2.63 Sculpture – Botanic gardens, Dublin

House and the National Botanic Gardens in Glasnevin. It was highly acclaimed. Each year, a different panel of selectors is invited to adjudicate this open exhibition, leading to an exciting mix of mediums and styles (fig 2.62, fig 2.63).

Since 2002, the exhibition has been held every year in the National Botanic Gardens in September. These grounds provide a stunning haven of peace and tranquillity for the finest sculpture by leading Irish and international artists. More than a hundred sculptures in a large range of materials are displayed throughout the gardens and ponds, the Great Palm House and the Curvilinear Range. Smaller works are shown in the gallery above the visitors' centre.

Fig 2.62 Sculpture – Botanic gardens, Dublin

Sculpture trails and parks

One of the most exiting and interesting developments in public art has been the placing of sculpture in sensitively developed public parklands. These sculptures are created to enhance and compliment such environments and are to be found in places like the woodlands of Co. Wicklow, the rugged coastline of north Co. Mayo and the bogs of the Midlands.

The woodlands of Co. Wicklow

Sculpture in Woodland is situated in the beautiful surroundings of the Devil's Glen Wood, Ashford, Co. Wicklow. It features a unique collection of contemporary sculpture by Irish and international artists.

The woodlands

The Devil's Glen Wood is owned by Coillte and is fully accessible to the public, with car parking, picnic facilities and a variety of forest walks. It consists of both native woodlands and introduced species, but in recent years broadleaf planting in the glen has increased so that today almost 13 per cent of the glen is planted with broadleaves.

An awareness of wood

The Sculpture in Woodland project was formed in 1994 to help establish a wood culture in Ireland by creating a greater awareness of wood as an artistic and functional medium. Sculpture is ideally suited to a woodland environment. It allows artists to turn landscape into art by working with what is growing in their surroundings, safe in the knowledge that what they take will be replaced, given the renewable nature of wood. Wood is also recyclable, so sculptors can rework and return it to its natural environment long after it has made the journey from forest to sawmill or workshop.

Wood is also a versatile resource that gives quite a range of finishes, but it requires a different creative approach to other materials such as steel, bronze, stone and plastic. Wood properties vary from species to species, from tree to tree and even within a tree, so no two pieces of wood are ever the same, even when cut from the same tree.

Woodland art

Making public art, especially in a woodland, requires partnership between artists and others, including engineers, foresters, wood scientists, architects, wood workers, landscape designers and especially the woodland owners, Coillte. All the partners in this venture

Fig 2.64 THE SEVEN SHRINES, Kat O'Brien, The Devil's Glen, Co. Wicklow

have a sensitivity towards the unique Devil's Glen landscape, which has been shaped by both nature and human activity.

The area was chosen as the location for Sculpture in Woodland because of its rich historic, artistic and natural heritage. The glen was cut out gradually by meltwater during the glacial period and the River Vartry enters at the waterfall.

Permanent works

Artists commissioned on an annual basis have responded imaginatively to this challenge by using wood in the round, sawn and laminated. To date, 13 sculptures by Irish and international artists (from countries such as Japan, Latvia, Portugal, Canada and France) have been permanently sited in the Devil's Glen.

The sculptures

The collection includes work by:

- **Kat O'Brien** (Canada) – *The Seven Shrines* (fig 2.64). Made in 1996 with a variety of timbers, this work commemorates the seven generations of women born since the beginning of the Great Famine. The shrines invoke the intimacy of the forest to redirect the power of those legends towards reconsideration of the lives of seven generations of people who have no fame on the battlefield.

- **Jacques Bosser** (France) – *Chago* (fig 2.65). In his own words: 'In the African forest, drums are beating,

FIG 2.65 CHAGO, Jacques Bosser, The Devil's Glen, Co. Wicklow

FIG 2.66 ANTAEUS, Michael Warren, The Devil's Glen, Co. Wicklow

the air fills with smoke, flames rise in the sky. Chago, god of fire, appears, leaving in his wake large blackened and burned-out tree trunks. To appease the gods, the locals insert pieces of metal in their wooden objects of worship and make a wish.'

- **Michael Warren** (Ireland) – *Antaeus* (fig 2.66). This work was made from poplar and larch in 1998. Warren says, '*Antaeus* takes its name from the ancient Greek giant who drew his strength from the earth and was invincible as long as some part of his body remained in contact with the earth. The piece is sited immediately adjacent to the forest entrance and comprises three vertical elements which straddle the road and create an inverted arch-like form.'

- **Michael Bulfin** (Ireland) – *Time Alone is Changeless*, made from Douglas fir with stone in 1999. Bulfin

says, 'The rocks weather to soil. Soils provide anchorage and nutrients to plants. Trees are the largest and longest-lived plants in the valley. They celebrate with their life the nutrients, which come from the soil. All things change with time. Time alone is changeless.' Bulfin is interested in public art and, in particular, site-specific and land art. With his scientific background and knowledge, he brings a special approach to these areas of sculpture.

- **Eileen MacDonagh** (Ireland) – *Into the Dark*. This sculpture was made from laurel in 2000. MacDonagh says, 'The idea for this sculpture came from an image I saw many years ago in a wood in Japan. There were hundreds of short logs stacked against each other in rows, winding in and out between the trees, making wonderful patterns. The image remained with me and I adapted it to create this 10 m long intervention over the pathway along the river. Laurel was the ideal choice of wood for this work, not only for its organic growth patterns, but also because it had to be cleared out of areas where it has taken over in the forest.' MacDonagh was born in Sligo and has worked as a sculptor since the early 1980s.

The rugged coastline of north Co. Mayo

Tír Sáile, Co. Mayo

One the largest public arts project ever undertaken in Ireland was in north Mayo. This area has one of the greatest concentrations of Stone Age tombs in Europe as well as intact Neolithic farms, which were found in the recent past preserved beneath the thick blanket of bog that covers the region. To mark this ancient landscape in a contemporary way, Tír Sáile, the North Mayo Sculpture Trail, was created. It is a trail of permanent sculpture from the Moy Estuary to the Mullet Peninsula.

Céide Fields

The general idea for the Sculpture Trail came about after the discovery of the Neolithic site at Céide Fields, which contains the oldest known field systems in the world and dates back more than 5,000 years. It was developed by a consortium of community groups, government agencies and other interested parties that included the Mayo County Council, Moy Valley Resources, the Sculptor's Society of Ireland and Údarás na Gaeltachta (a regional state agency responsible for economic, social and cultural development in Gaeltacht regions).

Coastal art trail

The sculptures were put in place during 1993, the year of the Mayo 5,000, a year-long cultural celebration inspired by the dating of Céide Fields – the surviving human imprint in earth and stone on the Mayo landscape – back to over 50 centuries. Fourteen site-specific sculptures were placed around the coast and an exhibition site for guest sculptors and temporary exhibitions was created as a gateway to the trail at the old Culleens National School near Ballina.

Meitheal Mhaigheo

In keeping with the nature of the sculptures and the area of north Mayo, the tasks involved in creating the trail took the form of a *meitheal* (a traditional Irish method of bringing workers together to complete a task). The attitude of the *meitheal* pervaded all aspects of the Sculpture Symposium, the community involvement, the donation of sites (both public and private) and the hosting of the artists. The interest and involvement of various local communities made for a spirit of unity in identity and added greatly to an appreciation of their ever-developing cultural heritage.

The sculptures

The primary aim of Tír Sáile was to celebrate the past, relish the present and embrace the future. This has certainly been achieved through this imaginative artistic endeavour.

One fundamental requirement was the use of natural materials, but north Mayo's unique strip of rugged coastline allowed for the exploration of a variety of different sites and possibilities. The sites themselves varied from a disused quarry, small fields and sand dunes to stony ground and agricultural land.

The Sculpture Trail begins in Ballina and follows the coastal route through Killala, Ballycastle, Belderrig, Belmullet and down to Blacksod.

- *Dun Caochain Head* (fig 2.67) at Cathru Thaidhg (Carrowteige) by Walter Michael (Scotland) is best seen from the nearby coast road. This 100 m long sculpture is made of earth and local stone and is based on the local legend associated with a one-eyed giant. When it is viewed from the site entrance, this long face shrinks to present its correct proportions.
- *Tearmon na Gaoithe* (fig 2.68) at Palmerstown Bridge by Alan Counihan (Dublin) is a sculpture born of its immediate environment. The stone, quarried and thrown up by the waves, has been laid so as to form a shelter, a sanctuary, a place near the pulse of the tide, the breath of the winds. It belongs only here.

FIG 2.67 DUN CAOCHAIN HEAD, Walter Michael, Cathru Thaidhg or Carrowteige, Tír Sáile, Co. Mayo

FIG 2.68 TEARMON NA GAOITHE, Alan Counihan, Tír Sáile, Co. Mayo

- *Battling Forces* at Downpatrick Head by Fritse Rind (Denmark) is the setting for a 30 m long sculpture. It is a place where strong elements – sea, storm, land – give continuous battle to man and to each other. The work gives form to a frozen moment in an ongoing struggle between two different forces of nature.
- *Slí na nOg* at Lacken Cross was created as a joint student project involving a group of students from Lacken Cross Secondary School and Dun Laoghaire College of Art & Design. Niall O'Neill, sculptor and lecturer at Dun Laoghaire, assisted the students.
- *Stratified Sheep* (fig 2.69) at Ballinboy Visitor Farm by Niall O'Neill is constructed and carved from sandstone and granite slabs. They reflect the structure of the land and express the rural culture of the area, which has formed over thousands of years.

52

FIG 2.69 STRATIFIED SHEEP, Niall O'Neill, Tír Sáile, Co. Mayo

Enhancement

The sculpture blends perfectly with the scenic beauty and, along with the Céide Fields Interpretive Centre, contributes significantly to the wealth of the cultural heritage of the area. Given its position on one of the most western edges of Ireland's coast, this project deserves attention. The production of an excellent booklet and website on it is a positive step towards sharing this wonderful artistic development with the wider public. Let's hope that it will encourage many to make a special visit to the area.

The bogs of the Midlands

Lough Boora Parklands

Hidden at the centre of Ireland is a beautiful new landscape which, until recently, has been a well-kept secret. Lough Boora Parklands is a creative combination of nature and the human hand. New habitats are emerging on the cutaway bogs of Co. Offaly lands. Having been cloaked with great raised bogs for 10,000 years, the lands are now at the dawn of a new era. Bogs are the source of peat, which has been harvested by Bord na Móna for energy since the 1940s. Now the raised bogs are being allowed to re-establish themselves so that they can continue to provide unique and welcoming habitats for a wide range of flora and fauna.

In a pilot project covering what will be 80,000 hectares of cutaway boglands spanning 11 counties and three provinces in the Midlands of Ireland, 2,000 hectares of unique mosaic-style habitats have been developed to support a wide range of outdoor activities sensitive to the environment.

These magnificent wetlands and the wildlife wilderness also host some of the most innovative land and environmental sculptures in Ireland. Artists inspired by the rich natural and industrial legacy of the boglands have created a series of large-scale sculptures that are now part of the Parklands permanent collection.

Industrial materials existing in the bog, such as abandoned locomotives, rail lines, timber and stone, have been developed into magnificent sculptures. Over time and with the effects of nature over the seasons, some of the sculptures have changed colour and developed plant growth that blends them into the landscape.

FIG 2.70 RUAILLE BUAILLE, Patrick Dougherty, Lough Boora Parklands, Co. Offaly

FIG 2.71 SYSTEM 30, Julian Wild, Lough Boora Parklands

Sculptures

Ruaille Buaille

Sculptor Patrick Dougherty created the spectacular site-specific sculpture *Ruaille Buaille* (fig 2.70) during a three-week residency period at Sculpture in the Parklands. It was inspired by the local environment and was made from natural materials harvested from the area. The residency was made possible when Bord na Móna received an Allianz Business to Arts Award for its ongoing partnership with Sculpture in the Parklands and the Offaly County Council Arts Office and collaboration with the Crafts Council of Ireland. The artist said, 'I intend to build a walk-through work which embodies momentum and the forces of nature. The sculpture will rise above the grove of alder trees and will include hallways and swirling chambers. This will be one of my largest works to date.' The sculpture involved the help of six full-time local artists as well as community volunteers and the use of over 10 tons of willow.

System 30

Julian Wild's sculpture is part of a series of work called *Systems*, which began in 2003 and involves sculptures, installations, drawings and public art projects.

For *System 30* (fig 2.71) he collected pieces of metal scrap from the Bord na Móna workshops in Lough Boora over two years. He sees the process as a kind of archaeology in which each old cog and piece of metal tells part of the story of the site's rich industrial heritage. By welding together scrap pieces of peat wagons and cutting machinery, he constructed an 18 m long sculpture in a canal. The concept is that of a disk that appears to bounce over the surface of the canal, like a skimming

stone. This imaginative and playful piece looks like a serpentine form swimming across the surface of the canal.

Happiness

This artwork by Marianne Jørgensen (fig 2.72) was created by cutting the word 'happiness' into the surface of the top soil consisting of black peat. It is cut very deep into the turf by hand in the old-fashioned way and according to old methods in order to produce the most precise imprint of the text. The written word expresses a longing for happiness. Its fragility is emphasised by the fact that it is subject to constant change, caused by weather, wind and oblivion.

FIG 2.72 HAPPINESS, Marianne Jørgensen, Lough Boora Parklands

Ennis Sculpture Initiative

Ennis Sculpture Initiative is an award-winning model of partnership between the private and public sector and has complimented the many changes enveloping the dynamic town of Ennis. It has also received much local support and assistance. The Ennis Sculpture Initiative has installed numerous sculptures along the riverside in Ennis as well as creating street furniture in the town centre. The sculpture trail takes many forms depicting cultural, historical and sporting events as well as more abstract pieces.

A Fishy Tale

Carmel Doherty designed a limestone fish (fig 2.73) leaping out of water. She said, 'I wanted a smooth finish to show the effect of water on stone.'

Memory and Meaning

Barry Wrafter and Colin Grehan celebrate the Clare hurlers' triumph in the All-Ireland Final of 1995 (fig 2.74) after 80 years in the doldrums. Made of Irish limestone, the sculpture consists of three stones larger than life size. Two of the stones have heads carved into the apex, reflecting the old and new. The centre stone depicts two hurlers rising for the ball, which is the essence of the game.

Conclusion

Public art is all around us and takes many different forms. Art forms are often linked together and although sometimes the themes or concepts may not be immediately obvious, it is well worth finding out more about work that has be specially created for us, the public.

FIG 2.73 A FISHY TALE, Carmel Doherty, Ennis Sculpture trail, Co. Clare

FIG 2.74 ALL IRELAND FINAL OF 1995, Barry Wrafter and Colin Grehan, Ennis Sculpture trail

Questions

1. What are the problems faced by artists in designing a public sculpture?
2. Who is public sculpture for? The artist? The public? Or those educated enough to appreciate it?
3. What is the Per Cent for Art scheme?
4. What is meant by the term 'site specific'?
5. Name some examples of sculpture in Ireland that have been destroyed.
6. Why, in your opinion, did these works of art create such hostility?
7. What considerations must an artist take into account when designing roadside sculpture?

Essay

1. Discuss the reaction to public sculpture evident from the controversy in relation to Eilís O'Connell's sculpture in Kinsale, and make a comparison to the approach taken by the competition-led scheme to place a sculpture at the St James's Hospital Luas stop in Dublin. Suggest a suitable sculpture for a public area near you, and describe the measures you would take to make sure it was acceptable to the community nearby. Make sketches of your idea.
2. Do you think that roadside sculptures area a good idea? Discuss one or two that you pass on a regular basis and give your reaction to it.
3. Visit the website of Publicart.ie (www.publicart.ie), follow the links to the site's Public Art Directory and view all the public art catalogued there. Select a temporary work of art that appeals to you and discuss it. Suggest an idea of your own for a similar temporary work at a venue of your choice. Describe in detail how you would go about creating the work and the medium to be used. Mention any other art forms that might be linked with it, the reasons for your decisions and where you might get funding. Make sketches, where appropriate.
4. Sculptures have now become common in boglands, woodlands and other natural landscapes. Discuss this development and the suitability of materials chosen for such projects. Discuss one or two exhibits from a development you have visited or are familiar with from your studies. Suggest an area near you that might benefit from such a scheme and design a work you consider suitable. Make sketches of your ideas.
5. Imagine you have been asked to act as a guide on a walking tour of the sculptures of Dublin, or of another town or city with which you are familiar. Give an account of the works you would choose and draw your group's attention to the controversial as well as the positive aspects of these works.

Colour picture studies

1. *An Capall Mór* by Tighe O'Donohue in Co. Kerry (fig 2.7 and fig 2.8) and *Two Working Men* by Oisín Kelly (fig 2.55 and fig 2.56) are popular public works of art. Examine these works and discuss the reasons why you think the driving public and the people of Cork city have taken these works and others like them so much to their heart.

2. *Saints and Scholars* by Maurice Harron (fig 2.14) has been described as a landmark for Co. Offaly. Discuss the impact of this work on the viewer and describe the style of the work, the materials used and the concepts that inspired the artist. Compare and contrast this with another work by the same artist. How do you think these works may appeal to those with no previous interest or appreciation of works of art?

3. Examine *Famine* (fig 2.46) and *Proclamation* (fig 2.50) by Rowan Gillespie in Dublin and discuss the emotional impact of these works on the viewer. In comparing them, draw attention to the differences in the style and the conceptual ideas that form the basis for such works. In your answer, include a general account of the artist and his works and mention work undertaken by him outside of Ireland.

CHAPTER 3

PRODUCT DESIGN

Introduction

The term 'design' covers a wide range of activities undertaken by professionals working in architecture, engineering, product and industrial design, graphics, fashion, crafts and a number of other areas where people are designers of systems and processes. In many of these areas the design work undertaken may not be closely related to art. For our purposes, we will focus on the work of **product designers**, which in itself in a very large discipline.

A little history

People have been thinking about the shapes and functions of the things that they make since the earliest times. The first pots, baskets, tools and weapons were made to fit a purpose – and so we can say that they were 'designed'. This type of project – where the designer and maker are one person – still occurs today in the areas of craft and 'one-off designs', which are produced directly for clients (fig 3.1).

The work of the designer as separate from the maker came about when products were made on a larger scale. In the 14th century, the people who designed tapestries were paid more than the workers who made them. The people who designed for industry during the Industrial Revolution were better paid than the workers on the factory floor. **Josiah Wedgwood**, who produced ceramics on an industrial scale, had the artist John Flaxman design decorative pieces (fig 3.2) for his wealthier and more discerning customers. This is one of the earliest accounts of an artist/designer working in conjunction with industry. In 1754 the cabinet maker **Thomas**

Chippendale published a book of his designs, titled *The Gentleman and Cabinet-Maker's Director*. The purpose of the book of engravings was to show the customer the type of furniture and the style of decoration that Chippendale could make for them (fig 3.3). This was a forerunner of catalogue selling, which grew in importance in the 20th century. Ingvar Kamprad, the founder of the design company IKEA, brought out his first catalogue in 1951. Since then, IKEA (and its catalogue business) has spread throughout Europe and

FIG 3.1 Modern craft pottery

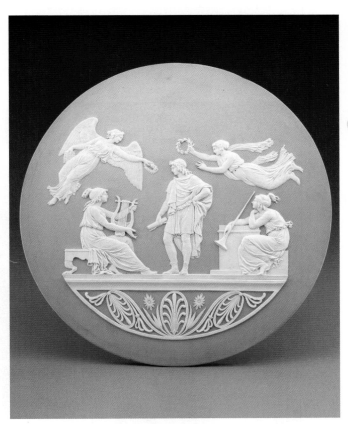

FIG 3.2 Wedgwood plate designed by John Flaxman

the USA. Today it is one of the largest sellers of household and interior design products worldwide. Online selling is the most recent adaptation of the catalogue sales business.

FIG 3.3 Chippendale Design for a Gentleman's Toilet Table

The Crystal Palace Exhibition (a 'Great Exhibition of the Works of Industry of All Nations') was held in Hyde Park in London in 1851. Its purpose was to demonstrate what could be achieved by the manufacturing industry of the time (fig 3.4). Most of the items on display were highly decorated and produced in lavish materials.

The art critic Thomas Ruskin and designer **William Morris**, of the **Arts and Crafts Movement**, were very critical of the work on show in the Crystal Palace. They felt that most of the designs at the exhibition were not true to their processes of manufacture and that the over-decorated products broke the basic rules of design, as they understood them. These were:

- *Truth to materials* – They felt that the shape of an object should be influenced by the materials from which it was made. For example, a wooden chair was different by its nature from an iron chair, so it should look quite different.
- *Fitness for purpose* – By this Morris and Ruskin meant that an object should do the job that it was designed for, without bending or breaking or causing an injury to the user. This may seem very obvious, but it is surprising how many early factory products were not fit for purpose.
- *Form follows function* – The shape of a product should be influenced by the job that it does, and any decoration should be part of its function and not merely an add-on.

FIG 3.4 Illustrated plate taken from Dickinsons 'Comprehensive Pictures of The Great Exhibition' (1854). Note the range of elaborately decorated goods on display.

The reforms that Ruskin and Morris wanted to see in what they considered to be bad taste in design led in turn to the 20th-century modernist design movement (fig 3.5).

Henry Ford is credited with building the first moving assembly line to build his automobiles in 1914 (fig 3.6). He produced the Model T automobile, which was relatively inexpensive and easy to repair and maintain. Soon, however, General Motors was outselling him because it provided their customers with a range of designs. The various models – Cadillac, Pontiac, Buick, Chevrolet and others – all used the same basic chassis, but each was different in the range of colours and style that it offered. Each General Motors model was aimed at a different segment of the car-buying public. Ford soon found that the public liked to be given a choice, even when they were being offered good value (fig 3.7).

The Deutscher Werkbund was formed in Germany in 1907. It brought together manufacturers, retailers, politicians, architects and designers to create products that could compete with British and American designs. The principles of its members were similar to those of the Arts and Crafts Movement – they felt that form should follow function and decoration and ornament should be eliminated. Richard Riemerschmid, a designer with the group, produced small-scale, machine-made furniture (fig 3.8). Peter Behrens, another group member, linked up with the AEG manufacturing company and produced product designs, advertising and factory buildings which were all integrated, in a very early version of the kind of 'company identity' that became a feature of large businesses in the 20th century (fig 3.9).

The Bauhaus school of design in Weimar, Germany, opened in 1919. It was founded to unify the arts and design under principles similar to the Arts and Crafts Movement. It moved in 1925 to Dessau, into revolutionary modern buildings designed by Walter Gropius and students of the college. The school concentrated on design for industry, producing prototypes in their workshops that could be mass produced. The workshops also made furniture and fittings for the new buildings. Marcel Breuer's tubular steel furniture was a modern sensation of the time (fig 3.10).

FIG 3.10 Bauhaus-classic WASSILY SESSEL by Marcel Breuer, 1925

FIG 3.11 BIBENDUM CHAIR and E-1027 (top) by Eileen Gray. E-1027 is designed to reach over a bed or chair.

The International style evolved during the 1920s and 1930s, based on the principles of the Dutch De Stijl movement, Russian Constructivism and the German Bauhaus. It was an abstract style based on elementary structures. It included architecture and the applied arts.

Eileen Gray (1878–1976) was born in Ireland, near Enniscorthy, Co. Wexford. She lived and worked most of her life in Paris, designing furniture and interiors. Her Bibendum Chair, which is made of tubular steel and leather, and a table made of tubular steel and glass, E-1027, became icons of the International style. Grey was also known for her lacquer work, particularly her screens, and also for her architectural designs. Though Gray was underappreciated for most of her life, there was a revival of interest in her work when some of it sold for very high prices at auction in Paris. In 1972, Zeev Aram, a London-based furniture company, put some of her designs back into production. There is a permanent exhibition of her work in the Decorative Arts & History branch of the National Museum of Ireland at Collins Barracks in Dublin (fig 3.11).

Henry Dreyfus (1904–72) was the founder of a New York City design company that still operates today. He was one of the leading American designers in the 1930s and 1940s and worked on an enormous range of projects, from streamlining railway trains to telephones and steam irons. In the 1960s, he published *The Measure of Man*, a reference book on ergonomics that became very influential (fig 3.12). **Ergonomics** is the science of designing the job, equipment and workplace to fit the worker. Ergonomics has two goals: health and productivity. Ergonomically designed offices and workplaces should reduce stress for workers as they move through the workplace and as they interact with furniture and machinery in it.

The Volkswagen Beetle was in production – with only a few small modifications ever made – from 1938 until 2003. It was the world's most popular car. Asked by Hitler to design a *Volkswagon* (literally, a 'people's car'), the Ferdinand Porsche Company came up with the design. The Beetle was mechanically simple and reliable,

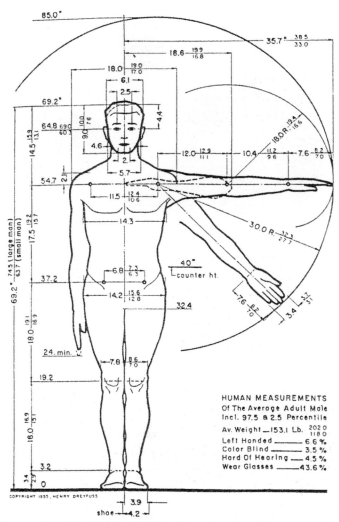

FIG 3.12 THE MEASURE OF MAN by Henry Dreyfus

FIG 3.13 1953 Volkswagen Beetle

FIG 3.14 Porsche 911

compared to its contemporaries. It had a rear-mounted, air-cooled, flat four-cylinder engine, which was unusual for its time. It had rear-wheel drive. It also had a novel suspension system (fig 3.13). After World War II, the Beetle gained in popularity. From 1950, crates of partly assembled Beetles were imported into Ireland and assembled in a factory on Shelbourne Road in Dublin, where there is still a VW dealership today. Porsche based his first sports cars on Volkswagen parts and the Porsche 911, which has a water-cooled rear/mid engine, is still competitive in the 21st century (fig 3.14). A fashion for retrospective design in the late 1990s produced a new Beetle, which is related to the original only in terms of styling. The new car has a water-cooled, front-mounted engine and front-wheel drive (fig 3.15).

The fashion for redesigning economy cars from the 1950s and 1960s has produced a number of models around the world. Fiat has redesigned its 500, which was in

FIG 3.15 1998 Volkswagen Beetle

FIG 3.16 Original Austin Mini

FIG 3.17 2010 Mini Cooper

production from before the Second World War until 1975, and the Austin/Morris Mini, which was such a design and fashion icon in the 1960s that it has been redesigned for the 21st century (fig 3.16, fig 3.17).

Change of materials

From the 1960s on, a wide range of plastics could be produced in bright colours. Plastics can be moulded into a great variety of shapes, which allows the designer to play with colours and contour in a way that would not have been possible previously. Mass-produced and cheap plastic objects need to be almost disposable in order to justify their low price. Plastic food storage containers and inexpensive kitchen and picnicware became popular in the late 20th century. In the 21st century, new technology provides the designer with previously unimaginable options in the choice of materials and structures (fig 3.18).

The constant search for new and better materials has led to a revolution in sports and leisurewear, particularly footwear. Clever marketing and promotion of company identity have led to people wearing tracksuits and training shoes with no intention of taking any exercise.

Miniaturisation

Integrated circuit boards were invented in 1958. The Japanese were quick to respond to the opportunities this electronic component created and moved to produce a number of inexpensive electronic devices that took the world by storm. Sony produced miniature TVs and radios and in the late 1970s created a new concept in listening to music with the Sony Walkman (fig 3.19). The Walkman was a miniature cassette tape player that allowed users to listen to their music on headphones while they were out walking or jogging. It was the forerunner of all the personal listening devices that are used today.

FIG 3.18 Plastics allow designers flexibility in colour and shape

FIG 3.19 Sony Walkman, 1970s model

FIG 3.20 Modern electronic gadgets

FIG 3.21 Interior of the Royalton Hotel, New York. Design by Philippe Starck.

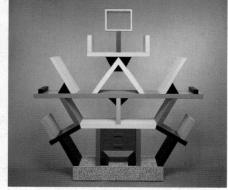

FIG 3.22 Designed by Ettore Sottsass (Italian, 1917–2007). 'Carlton' Room Divider/Bookcase, designed in 1981. Plastic on wood laminate carcass; 196.2 × 190 × 40 cm. The Cleveland Museum of Art. The May Spedding Milliken Memorial Collection, Gift of William Mathewson Milliken

Further miniaturisation has been possible since the invention of the microchip. New materials and computer-aided design have also played their part in the design of ever smaller electronic gadgets (fig 3.20).

Post-modern design

Following the oil crisis of the 1970s and the recession of the 1980s, designers had to re-examine their role and motives. There was a greater interest in the home and people increasingly saw their choices in furniture and decoration as a statement of their taste and their social status. There was a focus on 'good' and 'bad' design, which was played out in TV programmes and magazine articles. Design shops such as IKEA and Habitat encouraged homeowners to see themselves as designers in their own right. The 'less is more' concept became popular in the home of the late-20th-century educated middle classes, while less-educated people preferred accumulation (fig 3.21).

The Italian design company Memphis, whose chief designer was **Ettore Sottsass**, produced a range of furniture and household items for Milan's furniture fair in 1981 which created a sensation, challenging ideas of good taste and functionality (fig 3.22). Its multicoloured and dramatically patterned designs were much more about expression than function. Sottsass also did some work for the Alessi design company in Italy and he produced an elegant stainless steel oil and vinegar set which is sold with his name on it. Alessi commissioned famous architects and designers from around the world to design tea and coffee sets and kettles, which they then put on display in galleries and museums, as if to say, 'These are works of art, not just functional items.' The designs were often humorous, poking fun at function or referring to the past. The French designer **Philippe Starck** designed one kettle, which he called *Hot Bertea*, and a lemon juicer, which he called *Juicy Salif* (fig 3.23). He said, 'My juicer is not meant to squeeze lemons; it is meant to start conversations.' A great self-publicist, Starck brings the role of designer closer to that of fine artist.

FIG 3.23 HOT BERTEA kettle and JUICY SALIF juicer by Philippe Starck

FIG 3.24 Versace designed dinner service

a brightly coloured, see-through case, the iMac was made of plastic, it was portable, it was quiet and it was easy to use. Clearly, the designer had thought about its appearance as well as the technology inside it. Ive went on to design the iPod and the iPhone, which offer cutting-edge technology with easy human access (fig 3.26).

FIG 3.26 Apple iPhone

Designer as a marketing tool

Designers' names can be used as a marketing tool to add value to quite ordinary objects. Names like Giorgio Armani or Gianni Versace, when applied to ordinary jeans and T-shirts, turn them into high-fashion 'designer' wear. These and other designers lend their names to household goods and furnishings to enhance their value and marketability (fig 3.24).

New technology

The Apple Corporation has been extremely successful in making the connection between technology and lifestyle. Its commitment to making computers and other electronic equipment user friendly and its practice of including design right from the start when developing a new product have led to its great success. **Jonathan Ive** designed the iMac for Apple in 1999 (fig 3.25). Housed in

The new technology that went into **James Dyson**'s cyclone vacuum cleaner has been copied by his competitors, but his use of strong colours and continuous innovation set his designs apart. The DC25 Dyson Ball vacuum cleaner puts a further twist on vacuum design by doing away with fixed wheels (fig 3.27).

FIG 3.27 Dyson Ball DC25

Collect all five.

The new iMac. Now in five flavours. Think different.

FIG 3.25 Ad for the Apple iMac, 1999

Computer technology and design

Some people feel that computer software challenges the need for the designer. Today, graphics programs are commonly used to do the work of a graphic designer. In addition, computer-aided design (CAD) programs have transformed the work of architects and product designers, who can create and explore their designs in three dimensions and even produce prototypes through computer technology (fig 3.28).

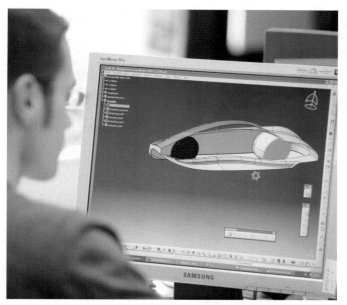

FIG 3.28 Product designer working with a CAD program

Modern designers should take into account the vulnerability of the planet and global trends towards overconsumption. Sustainable materials should be used. Products should be made to last and be easily disassembled for recycling.

The mass media has a strong influence on taste. TV programmes on interiors, food and fashion all influence the consumer. Fashion and taste in design are constantly changing. The 'anything goes' expressive style of the post-modern period will probably be overtaken by new ideas and criteria for design. Ultimately, there is no formula for 'good design' – all that can be said is that the basic ideals that date back to William Morris and the Arts and Crafts Movement are still valid today.

The design process

The design process is a series of steps used by designers to help organise their work. Whether they are designing a building or a bicycle or even a computer game, this process helps the work to progress in an orderly fashion.

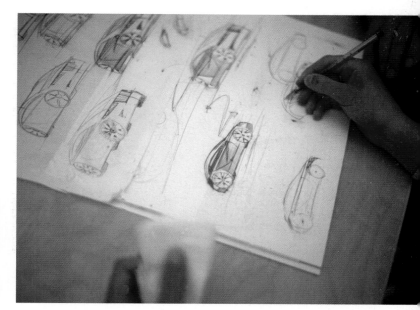

FIG 3.29 Product design sketches

Below is just one version of a range of processes used by different companies and individuals to help them with their design work.

Pre-production

Most of the work of the designer takes place before a product is manufactured.

A **design brief** should state the goals of the project. For example, one might be asked to design an electric car for city use by young people or an armchair with easy access for an older person. A detailed plan of the project will be written out, including all the limitations in terms of cost, materials, manufacturing and use. The possibilities in design and innovation that must be considered would also be noted. All these requirements should be discussed with the client.

Research into similar products and systems and related areas of design is carried out. Simple sketches and notes should be made to create a variety of possible designs (fig 3.29).

Presentation/choosing a solution comes next. Fully worked up drawings and/or models are made showing the preferred design solution and giving all the relevant dimensions, materials and colours and highlighting any special features. These drawings and models are shown to the client for their approval. At this stage, a full set of technical drawings is produced in consultation with engineers and technicians (fig 3.30). A manufacturer works from the technical information, selecting machines, materials and processes to carry out the project.

FIG 3.30 Product design presentation for the Airvod media player by Cian and Matt O'Sullivan.

During production

Development and testing of the product should take place in order to improve the manufacturing process and to enhance safety and the appearance of the finished item. With modern computer technology, a good deal of testing can take place in virtual environments. This saves time and avoids having to make expensive changes to machinery and processes during production (fig 3.31).

FIG 3.31 Production line testing

Post-production

Implementation, or putting the product into use, is the ultimate object of the process. Evaluation and post-production testing help to discover if the process and the product were a success. Constructive criticism and suggestions for further improvement can be made at this stage.

Redesign can happen at any stage of the process to make improvements and corrections.

Examining a designed object

The criteria guiding good design that William Morris laid down in the 1850s still hold good today. The usefulness of following 'truth to materials', 'fitness for purpose' and 'form follows function' have generally held true for designers in the intervening years. These ideals are restated in simpler form below, along with some examples that should help to clarify how they can be used when examining products.

FIG 3.32 Oxo Good Grips kitchen tools

- *A product should suit the requirements of those for whom it was designed.* This is where ergonomics comes into play. If you are examining something small, like kitchen utensils, then how they fit in the hand is important (fig 3.32). (They should be comfortable to use and do their job properly.) Larger items (such as pieces of furniture) should be shaped to their purpose. A dining chair or an office chair will have different requirements to an armchair. The body position of the user has to be considered. For larger items like, say, a motorcar, there should be a comfortable and adjustable driving position and all switches and controls should be visible and easily accessible. The area of the market it is being

FIG 3.33 Bosch electric lawnmower

FIG 3.34 Modern electric kettle

designed for is also important. The specifications for a family saloon will be quite different from a sports car.

- *A product should function properly and efficiently.* A product needs to be mechanically sound and safe. If we take the example of an electric lawnmower, it should obviously cut grass, but it should also be safe to use. On/off switches should be at the operator's fingertips. If it operates on a long flex, there should be an automatic cut-off in case the mower cuts its own cable, or preferably, it should have a rechargeable motor so that a cable is not necessary and does not present a hazard. Any product with switches and motors needs careful examination and assessment (fig 3.33).

- *A product should be made of suitable materials.* With modern developments in materials, a lot of equipment has become safer and easier to handle. If we take the example of the domestic electric kettle, modern heat-resistant plastics have made them much safer to use (fig 3.34).

- *A product should look well and be pleasing in shape, colour and texture.* This is where styling and colour choice come into play. What looks good can be very different in different times and places. If we look at the shapes of the Volkswagens we saw earlier, we can see how taste changes over a generation. While there is a general similarity between the original model and its modern incarnation, the details are quite different. Culture and fashion partly dictate what is acceptable, but well-designed objects should be ageless (fig 3.35).

FIG 3.35 Anglepoise lamp by the Terry Spring Company, manufactered since 1932

This outline just skims over some of the more obvious points. A full analysis of any design would need to be planned out and examined using the four points above as a guide. The names of designers and famous design houses should be included in your analysis where they are relevant and you should have a little background for these.

Questions

1. What were the design principles of the Arts and Crafts Movement?
2. Describe a product designed in the Bauhaus.
3. Describe a piece of furniture designed by Eileen Gray.
4. Name a publication by Henry Dreyfus. What did it describe?
5. What do you think of retrospective car design?
6. What did manufacture in plastic bring to design?
7. How has miniaturisation helped design?
8. What is ergonomics?
9. What is meant by post-modern design? Give two examples.
10. Describe the interaction between new technology and design through two examples.
11. What is the design process?

Essays

1. Describe the characteristics of a well-designed modern laptop computer, noting the style, function and materials it is made of.
2. Examine one of the objects from the list below, noting the suitability of design, the form, the function, the materials it is made from and the style.
   A mountain bike, an electric car, a hairdryer, a personal music player, an electric kettle, an armchair or an electric screwdriver.
   Note the work of a designer you admire to support your points.

Colour picture study

1. Compare the photographs of the 1950s Beetle (fig 3.13) and the 1998 model (fig 3.15) and note the differences in design that have been brought about by changes in materials and technology.
2. Look at the photograph of the DC25 Dyson Ball vacuum cleaner (fig 3.27) and offer some opinions on the advantages or otherwise of the ball over conventional wheels. What design features have made Dyson vacuum cleaners successful in the market?

CHAPTER 4

FILM STUDIES

Film, which some believe to be the most powerful art medium, is a relatively new art form. The combination of sound and vision makes it the most complete artistic experience available. It is also the most accessible, being available cheaply in public cinemas or at home on television or on DVD, or downloaded from the internet.

When looking at film we try to become aware of how the elements of sound, colour, lighting, camerawork, special effects, direction and editing affect our enjoyment of the film and how the art director uses make-up, costumes, sets and props to support the storyline and atmosphere of the film.

The technology of film

Once workable cameras and projectors had been produced in the 1890s, refinements and improvements arrived in quick succession. Soon cameras were better engineered and larger, so that bigger reels of film could be accommodated. The first films of Auguste and Louis Lumière (French pioneers of film making) were often less than a minute long. In the following years, films stretched out to 10 or 15 minutes, which was the length of one reel of film. Up to the 1920s these 'one reelers' were often shown between variety acts in vaudeville theatres. Dedicated film theatres gradually opened in Europe and around the world. In America, they were called nickelodeons.

The camera

Early cameras and projectors were simply cranked by hand (fig 4.1). The operator controlled the speed of film by winding the handle faster or slower. Filming at high speeds created a slow-motion effect when the action was played back at normal speed on screen, and slow filming speeds created the high-speed chases often associated with early film. Clockwork motors were then devised to run at a constant 16 frames per second, which produced a smoother movement. Corresponding refinements in shutters and the invention of the Latham loop, which controlled film feed into the camera or projector, made cameras more reliable and more capable of taking longer films. This basic arrangement continued in use until the end of the silent movie era. With the addition of sound to the mix ('the talkies'), films began to be shot at faster speeds (24 frames per second, which is still the standard speed for filming and projection). The soundtrack was recorded on the film at the same time.

Fig 4.1 A Lumière Camera could also be used do develop the film and operate as a projector.

Fig 4.2 Cameras of this type are used in modern film making

This basic set-up – with the addition of electric motors and light-fast film cassettes, which can be changed in daylight – remain the norm for film cameras today. Digital cameras are becoming more common as the technology improves, however (fig 4.2).

The lens

Most early cameras had a 35 mm lens, which gives a slightly wider view than the normal focal length of the human eye, which is about 50 mm. A single fixed lens was all that was available on early cameras. By the early 1900s, some cameras had interchangeable lenses, from wide angle to telephoto. The range of lenses allowed a greater range of shots and allowed filming in confined spaces or at a longer distance. Bell and Howell made the first zoom lenses available to cinematographers in 1932, which permitted a whole range of effects that were not possible before. Some cameras were fitted with a number of lenses, which could be rotated in front of the aperture to speed up lens changes. These cameras were useful for filming news events and documentaries where the action could not be stopped to change the lens. Modern lenses are very sophisticated and are capable of moving from wide angle to zoom while remaining in focus.

Film stock

From the time the Edison Company first produced the Kinetoscope, an early device for viewing film, it was necessary that a standard size of film be established. The company settled on 35 mm film, which became the industry norm. Biograph, the first US company devoted entirely to film production and exhibition, produced movies on 68 mm film from 1895 into the early 1900s, but even though it was renowned for the quality of its productions, Biograph could not compete with the mass production of 35 mm films. Over the years a number of innovators made films in different formats for multiple cameras and projectors to create panoramic effects (the most recent being IMAX), but the 35 mm format has retained its popularity through the introduction of sound, colour, wide screen and 3D.

Soundtrack

Strictly speaking, the strip on the side of the film, which records sounds, is referred to as the 'soundtrack', but the term has come to mean all the sounds that accompany a film, including voices, sound effects and particularly music. In movie making, sound is normally recorded separately on precision audio equipment. The beginning of a take is marked by the **clapperboard**, which is used to record scene numbers and other essential information that the film editor might need (fig 4.3). The noise made by the shutting clapperboard allows the sound and picture to be synchronised. The film stock manufacturer prints a series of unique identification numbers along the edge of the film, which can be recorded in conjunction with the audio time code during editing.

Editing

The editing process is used to connect a number of shots together in sequence. The editor's role is a creative one, working with images, story, music, rhythm and pace. The editor can even shape the performance of the actors. There are endless possibilities open to the editor. The editor can take small pieces of sound and images and arrange them into a coherent whole. Originally, film was physically cut and rejoined using an editing machine, which also allowed the editor to view a positive copy of the original film, which could be experimented with without damaging the negative (fig 4.4).

Editing starts as soon as filming starts. The editor and the director look at the scenes shot each day and discuss how the film should fit together. When filming is complete the **editor's cut** is made, which is the first draft of the film. The director and editor then go through the film in great detail, looking for plot holes, missing shots

FIG 4.3 Clapperboards being used on the set of GREEN ZONE, 2009

FIG 4.4 A film editor's desk can be used to mix sound and vision, segments from different spools of film can be recorded and played in any order the editor wants

FIG 4.5 Computer-generated special effect in AVATAR, 2009

FIG 4.6 Special effect using a model in GODZILLA, 1998

or sections that might have to be filmed again. They then make the **director's cut**, which is shown to the producers and other interested parties before the **final cut** is made.

Special effects

Special effects (sometimes abbreviated as SFX or SPFX) are used to create scenes that could not be made by live-action filming or by normal means. A scene with crashing aeroplanes or burning buildings might be too expensive or dangerous to make in the real world, so it could be done with models or computer graphics. There are broadly two kinds of special effects:

- Optical, visual or photographic effects, which are created in the camera as filming tricks or with computer-generated images (CGI) (fig 4.5)
- Mechanical or physical effects, which are filmed live and can involve mechanical props and scenery, models or pyrotechnics (fig 4.6)

Projection

Early projectors were sometimes cameras fitted with a lamp and reflector to project the images. As cinemas became larger and more light was needed to show the images over greater distances, special projectors were made. Though early films were shot at 16 frames per second or thereabouts, they were normally projected at faster speeds to avoid the lamp burning the highly flammable film. Early projectors were hand cranked, so the operator could control the pace of projection, varying it to suit the events on screen.

When sound was introduced, films needed to run faster to give clear, synchronised sound and images. Running 24 frames per second was selected as the optimal speed

since it was the slowest speed that could be used which gave good results. (Faster speeds would use more film and therefore be more expensive.) Over the years, different formats of film and multiple projections were used to create panoramic images. Most modern cinemas use digital projectors (fig 4.7).

FIG 4.7 A modern film projector

Video/digital film

Video was originally developed for television as a method of recording, processing, storing and transmitting images electronically. The first video was recorded on magnetic tape, but now it is digitally processed using DVD, QuickTime or the MPEG-4 systems. The quality of the video depends on the capturing method and the storage used. Quality video cameras used commercially can produce cinema-quality images, whereas images captured on lesser devices (such as a mobile phone) are of more limited quality (fig 4.8).

Fig 4.8 Shooting a TV programme with a video camera

The language of film

Many visual storytelling techniques were developed during the silent era. Intertitles were simply short sentences projected on screen between scenes to help the viewers understand what was going on, but they could not be relied on to explain fully what was happening on screen. The first films were filmed using a stationary camera and the actors performed as if they were on a stage. Film makers quickly discovered that they could tell stories and convey ideas more clearly with a range of angles and images (fig 4.9).

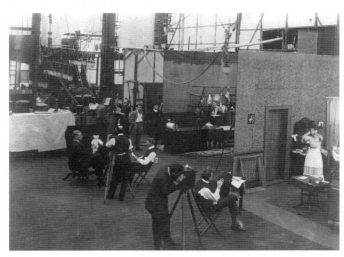
Fig 4.9 Filming with a stationary camera, ca. 1924

Mise-en-scène

A French theatrical phrase which could be translated as 'putting into the scene' or 'setting in scene', *mise-en-scène* has come to mean everything that goes into the scene to be filmed, including the sets, props, actors, costumes and lighting. It even includes the location and movement of the actors, which is called blocking. *Mise-en-scène* is a broad term, which draws together all the physical parts which designers and directors use to create the scene. It can be used to create mood and atmosphere in a film. For example, a film director can help portray aspects of the film's characters by showing a scruffy, untidy apartment or a neat and orderly office, which give clues about the kind of person we are about to meet (fig 4.10).

Fig 4.10 Mise-en-scène for PANDORUM, 2009

The framed image

Many of the same rules and aesthetic concerns that are used in composing a painting are also used in framing a shot for a film. The director and cinematographer plan where the focal points will be and how the camera or actors will move through the scene. A storyboard can be used to plan the composition of the shots (fig 4.11).

Fig 4.11 framed image from INCEPTION, 2010

FIG 4.12 The George Méliès film CINDERELLA combines camera tricks and painted scenery

FIG 4.13 A scene from GRANDMA'S READING GLASSES by George Albert Smith, 1900. When the child looks through the magnifying lens there is a cut to a close up of what he is looking at.

The film shot

A French cinematographer and magician, Georges Méliès, accidentally discovered the effectiveness of camera shots when his camera temporarily broke down in the middle of filming a street scene. When he reviewed the results of the stop and restart, he noticed that people and carriages disappeared or seem to change shape because of the break in continuity. He realised what might be done by filming short scenes of 10 seconds or so and joining them together. He produced the first fantasy films, combining live action with painted sets. These were the first edited films made, starting in about 1898 (fig 4.12).

Once the notion of shots and editing spread, directors were quick to innovate. The **close-up** was first seen in about 1901 when G.A. Smith used it in his movies *Grandma's Reading Glasses* and *The Little Doctor*. A child sees everything close up when he looks through Grandma's glasses and a close-up of a cat getting a spoon of milk was used in *The Little Doctor* (fig 4.13). Close-up can be used to observe facial expression and emotion and show details of a story. It soon became one of most frequently used techniques of the cinematographer.

The **long shot** was often used to set the scene or show the audience a wider context for the events in the story. **Medium shot** is the term used to describe scenes where the actors are seen from the waist up or where the middle distance is in focus. The **zoom** became possible with the arrival of the zoom lens in the 1930s during the early years of sound. It is useful for focusing in on the detail of a scene or for drawing back to create context.

Before the zoom lens, the whole camera would have to be wheeled forward or drawn back, with the focus puller constantly adjusting the lens, to get the same effect.

Editing

The editor uses a variety of techniques to connect scenes together or to note a change of time or place. The **cut** is the basic way of connecting two clips of film together. In the Hollywood tradition, cuts are generally hidden to create a smooth transition. In more experimental European films, the **jump cut** is used, where changes in time and space occur abruptly and without explanation.

Fade in/fade out, an editing technique where one shot is gradually blurred out to light or dark and the next take gradually sharpened, is a useful effect for noting a change of time or place or thinking. A **dissolve** is where the end of one scene is superimposed over the beginning of another to create a gradual transition. The **wipe** is an effect where one shot appears to wipe another from the screen. A whole range of special wipes are used, including iris wipes, flip wipes, star wipes and many others.

Camera angle

The angle of view recorded by the camera can have a dramatic effect on a scene. Filming from a **low angle** can make the characters and scene look dominant and threatening as if the viewer was small or low down by comparison (fig 4.14). Conversely, a **high angle** shot can make the viewer feel like they are in a controlling position and may like to help or be sympathetic towards the characters. The **flat, or eye-level**, view is often used

FIG 4.14 Low angle shot, from 28 DAYS LATER, 2002

for filming interaction between characters on screen. Conversations or confrontations are often filmed in this way so the viewer can feel that they are in on the action. A **bird's eye view** is filmed from directly above the scene. In an **oblique angle shot** the camera is tilted to the side so that a sloping horizon is created on screen.

Camera position/point of view, camera movement

The director can help the audience to understand the situation by literally showing the events from the character's point of view. Action and reaction can be observed by changing the camera position. Camera position can often determine the level of involvement that the audience feels with the action in the screen. The **pan** is where the camera is moved horizontally from a fixed position. It is used to follow movement or to show a wider context in a scene. The **tilt** is where the camera is pointed up or down from a fixed position. The **tracking shot** (or **dolly shot**) is most often used to follow action. The camera is wheeled along on a little truck, often on rails, so that it can be kept steady and on the same plane while it is moving.

The **Steadicam** is a counterbalanced camera strapped onto the camera operator. It remains relatively steady while it is carried through the scene. It can be very useful in confined spaces where a camera crew would not fit. It can be used to follow complicated action that could not

be filmed otherwise. A camera **boom** is a mechanical device used to film shots where the camera has to move up or down in space while being held at a constant angle.

Focus

The effectiveness of the **focus pull** was noticed from the early days of cinema in another of A.G. Smith's films, *Let Me Dream Again* (1900), in which a man is seen kissing a beautiful woman. The picture gradually goes out of focus and when the image comes back into focus, he is kissing his less attractive wife. This focus pull became the standard way of introducing a dream sequence. A long lens with a large aperture creates a shallow depth of field where only a narrow band is in focus at any time. This can be used in close-ups, as the actor's face is sharply focused while the background is fuzzy. In large productions, a focus puller makes sure that the focus is accurate in every shot. The **zoom** is also a function of focus, where the camera operator can change the focal length of the lens from close up to wide angle without losing focus (fig 4.15).

FIG 4.15 Only the actors are in sharp focus in this scene from THE LOVELY BONES, 2009

Colour

Though some early films were colour tinted by hand and colour film was available from the late 1930s, colour movies were not common until after the Second World War. The popularity of television in the 1960s led studio management to introduce colour in most films in order to compete.

Colour can be important for mood and atmosphere in a film. Reds have associations with violence and danger, blues with cold and sadness. The whole range of colours can help to create atmospheres of mood, time and place.

FIG 4.16 Scene from THE WIZARD OF OZ, 1939, an early colour film

Directors can colour enhance a scene or a whole film to create a particular atmosphere (fig 4.16).

Lighting

Lighting has been a basic component of filming from the beginning. When Edison built his first films studio, the Black Maria, in 1893, he used artificial lighting to film in the darkened room. Early European films were shot in natural light, but as filming techniques improved, lighting became an integral part of the film-making process. Lighting can help set the atmosphere and create an emotional response. The quality and colour of light, its direction and intensity form an essential part of any scene (fig 4.17).

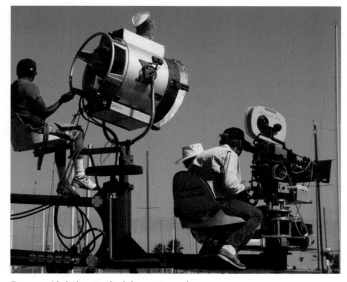

FIG 4.17 Lighting technicians at work

Sound

Sound can be a very evocative part of the film. A scene in a darkened room where we hear sirens and traffic noises can locate us in a city. Bird calls or the sound of running water or the sound of a breeze in the trees place us in the countryside. An actor's accent or tone of voice can give a sense of place or atmosphere. Music played as accompaniment to a scene can heighten our senses, such as screeching violins in a horror movie or the rhythmic sounds when the shark approaches in the film *Jaws*. Sometimes the soundtrack music from films has become as famous as (or even more famous than) the film for which it was written. **Sound effects** are usually added at the editing stage, when they are synchronised with the soundtrack and the images. The sound of slamming doors, footsteps, the sounds of nature, explosions – whatever is required – are not normally left to chance at the time of shooting but are separately recorded and added to the finished product later on.

Genre

Genre is a word which comes from literary and musical criticism to describe categories of artistic composition. In film, it has come to describe work which is similar in form, style or subject matter. Genres go in and out of fashion, but here's a list of ones that have been very popular over the years: action, adventure, comedy, crime, documentary, drama, epic (historical drama), family, fantasy, horror, musical, mystery, romance, science fiction, sport, suspense, thriller, war, western. When you are discussing film, it can be useful to categorise a film into one genre or another so that you can make comparisons with similar productions.

Professions and crafts

The scale of a production usually dictates the number of staff and the levels of specialty that will be involved. It is possible for an individual to make a complete film on their own, in which case they are the producer, director, cinematographer and editor – the whole show. At the other extreme are productions that involve hundreds of people, from studio bosses through the layers of production and technical experts, actors and extras – the complete range of staff.

Some of the people involved in film making are well known to the public. Actors and directors are often household names. Others involved in key roles in the film-making process may never come to the public's attention, though they would be well known and respected within the industry. The film-making process took on an industrial character in America from the early years of cinema.

Film production

The production team has the final responsibility for all aspects of a film. On big movies there would be executive producers, producers, production assistants and a whole range of financial and technical people responsible to them, all trying to turn the ideas in the story into a profitable cinema entertainment. The **producer** brings together the screenwriter, director, cast, financiers and a production team in a creative environment. Producers are ultimately responsible for the success or failure of a film. At the **development stage** of a film the producer may be responsible for the original idea. He or she may have had the impulse to make the film, in the first place or might own the rights to the story. The producer may employ a screenwriter and a story-editing team, if necessary. The production team will also have to raise finances. In **pre-production**, the producer brings together the key people, including the director, the cinematographer and the leading cast. In some productions, all these people will be involved in the effort to get financial backing for the film. In big organisations, like Paramount or MGM, there is a

dedicated team to look after finances so the creative people can get on with their own work without this added concern. Members of the production team take part in choosing locations, commissioning sets and music and organising production and shooting schedules and budgets. The producer has the final say over all these elements of the production. During the **production period** (when the filming is taking place), the producer may delegate day-to-day operations to producers and associate producers, who keep track of shooting schedules and budgets and the management of all aspects of the filming. The producer liaises with the director and the other creative people, approves of script changes and cost reports and is the primary contact with all the production partners, investors and distributors.

Post-production and marketing are also the responsibility of the production team. The editor, composer, special effects team and marketing people all answer to the producer. All the necessary business and creative skills for the production of a large-budget film may not be available in one person, so roles may be delegated to executive producers, co-producers, line producers and assistant producers (fig 4.18).

Direction

The **director** is ultimately responsible for the creative vision and style of a film. Directors can be the initiators of a film project, working in a combination of roles, such as producer/director, writer/director or any number of roles. In smaller films, the director can control the whole production process as well as writing script, arranging finance, casting, filming, editing and looking for outlets to show the film. Whatever the size of the endeavour, the director is normally involved from an early stage, writing or commissioning the script or taking charge of the draft screenplay. The director takes charge of casting and will normally pick leading actors, even in a large production where there is a separate casting director. The crew is also the director's responsibility and the choice of locations and settings for the film must also be approved by him or her. The director is the link between the production, creative and technical teams and provides the creative vision to turn the script into the images and sounds that the audience sees on screen. The direction of actors during rehearsals and filming is an important part of the work. The technical aspects of cameras, sound, lighting, design and special effects are also key in a successful film and the director needs to motivate these teams to produce the best results (fig 4.19).

Fig 4.18 A poster for the film THE CRAZIES, 2010

FIG 4.19 Director Clint Eastwood at work on the set of GRAN TORINO, 2008

When filming is over, the director works with the editor to produce the final cut of the film for approval by the production company and financiers. The director may also be involved in the promotion and marketing of the film and has responsibility for the artistic and commercial success or failure of the film.

Art department

The art department is responsible for the visual world or setting of the film. The **production designer** provides the initial visual identity for the film in consultation with the director. **Concept artists** may be employed to provide illustrations for big-budget science fiction, fantasy and historical films or films where complicated special effects may need to be visualised first. These illustrations can be used to help sell the idea for a film to production companies or to financiers. In the film series *Lord of the Rings*, concept artists played a key role in providing the images for characters, settings, colour and atmosphere. The production designer uses this type of input to help realise the director's vision for the film and to decide on sets and locations. The drawings may be used to decide what will be built or adapted and what special effects need to be commissioned. The production designer and director will also decide if there will be recurring visual themes or if elements need to be designed to help the emotional feel of the film. Sometimes **researchers** are used to check historical information or to look for images and references from works of art or from other films. The

production designer may produce sketches detailing the mood, atmosphere, lighting, composition, colour and texture of every scene. A **storyboard artist** can be used to produce a series of comic book-style illustrations, which the director uses to show the heads of departments what is needed in a scene. Whole films may be storyboarded where there is a lot of action or CGI, complicated chases, fights or battle scenes. The storyboard is designed from the camera's viewpoint, framing the shots as they would be seen on the cinema screen (fig 4.20).

FIG 4.20 Alexander Witt working on a storyboard for RESIDENT EVIL

The **art director** works as a project manager for the production designer and may be in charge of the creative vision for sets and locations, providing solutions for visual problems that may turn up during filming. The art director begins work long before filming starts, overseeing the production of sets, which are drawn up from a prop list taken from the script. **Draughtsmen** draw up plans for sets and locations, which are then given to construction teams. The art director makes sure that all the settings are ready for filming and the sets are 'struck' (dismantled) and locations cleared when filming is over. The **set decorator** provides all the furnishing details on sets, including the action props (which are used by the actors or are mentioned in the script and are involved in the action of a scene) and the dressing props (which are used for background atmosphere and to create the impression that the scene is a real location). Dressing props can include pictures on the walls, items left casually on tables and chairs, the contents of a fridge or a drawer – all the details of life that need to be included in a realistic scene. **Costume design** can be a separate department in productions, designing and making or hiring costumes for the actors and the extras. Costumes

Fig 4.21 Adjusting costumes for PIRATES OF THE CARIBBEAN: AT WORLD'S END

can be an important element in the overall look of the film. The designers make costume plots for all the actors and scenes to avoid clashes and to highlight the emotional journey of the characters through the film. Colour palettes, sketches and fabric samples are checked with the production designer and the director (fig 4.21). **Hair and make-up** people look after the design, application, continuity and care of hair and make-up during the production. The 'look' that is created may be contemporary or historical, or special prosthetics may be needed to change a face. Noses and chins can be enlarged and scars and injuries can be added. Style can be a very important element in a film and helps to match the time, place and mood of costumes and sets (fig 4.22).

Fig 4.22 Film make-up being applied, from THE OTHER BOLEYN GIRL, 2008

Camera department

Camerawork can tell more about what is going on in a scene than dialogue or music. The **director of photography** (or **cinematographer**) helps to give a unique look to the film. He or she consults with the director and production designer to decide on the kind of cameras and lighting that are needed in the production. The cinematographer is involved in pre-production. Working from the screenplay, he or she carries out research and preparation, considering style and technical aspects, planning camera positions on sets and locations and identifying the lights and equipment that will be needed for each shot. Camera cranes, Steadicams, cameras on wires and filming from the air all have to be considered, planned and costed.

The cinematographer and director go through each scene to work out blocking (where the actors will be in a scene and what movements the cameras or actors will make during the scene). During rehearsals, the actors walk through the scenes and the cinematographer works out camera moves and lighting. Each scene is marked up for focus and framing (fig 4.23).

Fig 4.23 Cinematographer at work with a steady cam, from GLORIOUS 39, 2009

Teamwork is very important during filming. The cinematographer may operate the camera on smaller productions, TV programmes, advertising and promotional work. The **camera operator** carries out the camerawork that was planned and may have creative input in reacting to what is happening in the scene or spotting an image that has not been planned. The camera operator also keeps the actors informed about what can and cannot be seen on screen. The **grip** builds, maintains and operates all the equipment and supports for the camera. This includes tripods and dollies, tracks, jibs, cranes, static rigs, etc. The grip also works for the cameraman during filming, moving dollies and operating jibs and rigs. In large productions there might be several camera crews operating together or at different locations. The **Steadicam** is a counterbalanced unit that allows smooth movement with a hand-held camera. It is a specialised piece of equipment and weighs up to 40 kilos, requiring a strong and agile operator. It is used for shots that require complicated camera movements.

Editing and post-production

The raw material shot by the camera crew and recorded by the sound crew is edited together to form a completed film. Filming frequently takes place out of sequence. The editor and director study the rushes each day and editing begins while the filming is still in progress. An overview of how all the scenes fit together may not be available until all filming is complete. The **editor** works closely with the director. Assembling shots into scenes, they check technical standards, continuity of lighting and colour and the performance of the actors. An editor needs to be creative, noting opportunities and moments of spontaneity from the actors that might improve the story. An editor's cut is made to see if the storyline fits together, which is examined minutely along with the director to spot flaws in the storyline or images and to plan any filming that might be necessary to fill gaps. A director's cut is then made, which is a more complete version of the film and which would be shown to the production company and financiers before the final cut is made. The editing team mixes the sound, music and images, adding any special effects that are needed.

Special effects, as we have already seen, can be mechanical/physical or visual. Computer-generated images (CGI), especially 3D computer graphics, are now frequently used instead of building miniatures or hiring extras for big crowd scenes. CGI can produce images not feasible otherwise. Blue or green screen can be used for human action that needs to be superimposed on an imaginary background or in a physically impossible location. Mat paintings, animation, miniatures, models and many other tricks are available to the special effects department.

The **music department** can be central to film production, and in the case of a musical, it can be used as part of the storyline when an actor sings or performs on screen. The film score can be a critical element of a film, creating atmosphere and defining characters, locations, period and ethnicity. A **composer** is usually commissioned to write an appropriate musical score that will enhance the director's vision of the film. The music should guide the audience through the story, creating an atmosphere, raising and relaxing tension and creating pace for the

Fɪɢ 4.24 Scene from the film ONCE, 2006, which won an Oscar for Best Original Song in 2007 with the theme song 'Falling Slowly'.

film. The composer assembles a team of orchestrators, copyists and programmers and supervises the whole musical process from early in pre-production, through shooting and assembly, to the final mix. The composer holds spotting sessions with the director to note particular locations for music in the film. The composer picks a style for the film and decides on the theme and the purpose of the music in the film. He or she works with the editor to match sound and images, making sure that there is a smooth transition between scenes (fig 4.24).

Case study

As there are many aspects to making a film, it is impossible to examine all of them or to look at every shot in it. A better approach might be to break the film down into key scenes and sequences. The categories that are used at the Academy Awards might be a useful way to look at the various elements involved. Producers (best picture), writers, directors, actors, cinematographers, make-up artists, art directors, costume designers, editors, score composers and more receive awards each year at the award ceremony.

Production poses the question of context – what social or historical conditions surrounded the making of the film? What were the conditions of production? Was it a Hollywood blockbuster, a small-budget or experimental film? What was the target audience? Was it a commercial or artistic venture? These are some of the questions you

FIG 4.25 PARANORMAL ACTIVITY (2007) was a small budget production

might ask yourself about the production of a film you wish to study (fig 4.25).

Writing is the starting place for most films. The **script** is not just the dialogue or storyline; it includes stage directions, descriptions of settings, camera movements and the overall mood of the film. When looking at the way the story is told in a film, the plot can be noted. For example, it might be a linear plot, that is, the events described in the film happen in a natural sequence, one event following another in normal time, or it might have flashbacks, cross-cuts or repetitions – all to help tell the story.

Direction is always important. The director oversees all aspects of the film and determines how the screenplay will be interpreted on the screen. It is worth noting whether film has been made by a 'big name' auteur director who might bring a certain style or theme to the work. When you are writing about a film, you need to know the director's name and a little bit about their background.

Actors can be an important element too. Some films are made as 'star' vehicles expressly designed to take advantage of the talents or marketability of a popular actor. Other films are made with comparatively unknown or even amateur actors. The style of acting can also affect the film. Whether the performances are natural, melodramatic or deadpan influence the reaction of the audience. You should know something about the main actors in any film you study and consider what they bring to the style of the film.

Cinematography is the term used to cover all the techniques of motion picture **photography**. Important technical aspects of photography include framing, camera movements, film speed (slow or fast motion), film stock (black and white or colour, coarse or fine grain, digital),

exposure, camera angles, lenses (deep focus, wide angle, zoom), shot selection (wide, medium, long shot, close-up) and lighting (natural or artificial, high or low key). In the classical Hollywood tradition, cinematography is designed to be unobtrusive in order to help the storyline. Modern film makers often push the boundaries of this convention. It might be worth getting some background on the cinematographer in a film you look at, noting other work they have done and what they bring to the project.

The **art department** can be the largest contributor to the visual qualities of a film. If you look at the roles of the art specialists that were discussed in the 'Professions and crafts' section above, you can get some idea of the range of contributions made by artists in films. You can use these headings when examining the visual content in a film.

Editing determines the pace and rhythm of the film by putting shots together and assembling sequences and scenes into the unfolding narrative. In the Hollywood tradition, **continuity editing**, which tries to make cuts invisible, is used to make a seamless visual and narrative storyline. Alternatives to this style are increasingly common. They include montage theory, invented by the Russian director Sergei Eisenstein, which proposes that two shots placed side by side can imply ideas beyond the two images in the viewer's mind. Surreal images and jump cuts have also been incorporated into mainstream cinema from experimental films. When watching a film, you might try to work out why the various editing techniques have been chosen.

Sound, which includes spoken dialogue, sound effects, music and all aural aspects of a film, is most frequently added artificially in post-production. Sound is generally added artificially because of the control it gives the sound engineers. (Natural sound is more unpredictable.) Actors and directors sometimes rely on the post-dubbing process to improve vocal performances, smooth over flaws and hide gaps in the narrative. **Diagetic sound** is the sound which is heard by the characters and which is part of the narrative, on screen and off screen. **Non-diagetic sound** includes all the sound effects, voiceovers and musical scores that are produced after filming and matched to the visual track during postproduction. It can be interesting to play a scene from a film with the sound turned off just to appreciate what it brings to the film.

Remember, good film analysis avoids emphasising the obvious aspects of a film, such as retelling the whole plot, reproducing parts of the dialogue or simply listing visual techniques. You should look for the meaning behind the surface, taking examples from the film to support points you make. Draw sketches of key scenes and effects to show your understanding of the film-making process. In the end, we all take our own meaning from the moving images that we see, but when making an argument or carrying out an analysis, it is always important to back up your ideas with evidence from the film.

Questions

1. Write a short description of early movie cameras and lenses.
2. What are special effects? Describe some computer-generated images you have seen.
3. Give two or three examples of different camera shots.
4. Describe some of the techniques an editor can use to connect scenes together.
5. How can camera angle or position affect a scene?
6. Describe the use of colour in a film or music video you have seen.
7. How can sound affect a scene?
8. What is meant by the term 'genre'?
9. What does a film producer do?
10. Name a director you admire and say what he or she brings to a film.
11. What roles can artists have in a film?
12. Describe some of the work a cameraman does.

Essays

1. Write an account of a film you have seen under these headings: Camerawork, Colour and lighting, Special effects and Costume/make-up.
2. Describe a film by a director you admire and say how he or she uses the visual elements, camerawork, colour and lighting to enhance the story. What part does sound or music play in the production?

Colour picture study

1. Describe the *mise-en-scène* in fig 4.10.

ART IN IRELAND
(SECTION I OF THE LEAVING CERT EXAM)

PART I. PRE-CHRISTIAN IRELAND

CHAPTER 5

THE STONE, BRONZE AND IRON AGES

The visual arts

Most art in pre-Christian Ireland was abstract. It reflected the technical, social and intellectual developments of the time. The pace of change in art and technology was slow at first; it took 5,000 years from the arrival of the first Stone Age people for metal technology to be developed in Ireland with the introduction of copper and bronze. It took another 1,500 years for iron technology to arrive and 500 more years for the major social and intellectual changes that came with Christianity.

One can see the increasing pace of change as each major cultural innovation was built on the knowledge and experience of previous generations.

The Stone Age (7000 BC to 2000 BC)

Human settlement began in Ireland around 7000 BC, during the Mesolithic or Middle Stone Age. The earliest people were hunter-gatherers; they probably crossed by boat from Britain at a spot where the Irish Sea was narrow enough to enable them to see the coast of Ireland in the distance. The forests and rivers of Ireland would have made rich hunting grounds for these nomadic people, who would have moved with the seasons to where food was most plentiful.

During the Neolithic or New Stone Age (3700 to 2000 BC), farming and animal-rearing people settled in Ireland, clearing forests to plant crops and fencing off areas of land to control domestic animals. There is evidence of permanent communities all over Ireland and contacts with Britain and Europe. These were the people who built the Megalithic structures we can still see today.

Stone Age structures (architecture)

The works of art and construction that survive from the Stone Age are generally associated with ritual sites and places of importance to these first Irish people. Little evidence of their everyday lives or language survives, but we can find remains of the tombs they built to revere their dead. These early farmers brought seeds for crops and domestic animals to Ireland and had developed skills beyond the simple hunting and gathering society that first lived here. They had enough spare time to think out, plan and build large structures, which can still dominate their local landscape. This Megalithic people (from the Greek words *mega*, meaning 'large', and *lithos*, meaning 'stone') used large stones to build their tombs.

Stone Age technology

Wood and stone were the only materials available for building and making tools and weapons during the Stone Age. Some hard stones could be broken and shaped to produce sharp edges that could be used as knives, scrapers, chisels, axes, spearheads and arrowheads. Experiments with Stone Age tools have shown that they were surprisingly effective in spite of their crude appearance (fig 5.1). An arrowhead embedded in part of a human pelvis was found during excavations at Poulnabrone in Co. Clare, demonstrating the power of a Stone Age bow and the sharpness of a stone arrowhead. Axes for felling trees and chopping wood were made by tying carefully shaped and polished stone axe heads onto wooden handles. Wood was used to make tools for digging and ploughing and some vessels were made of wood. Clay was dug and built into a variety of simple pots, which were probably fired on an open fire. Domestic buildings were generally round in plan and probably made with stone, wood and mud with thatched roofs. Stones for large structures would have been moved by dragging and levering and possibly using logs as rollers to ease the progress of the largest stones. Beasts of burden and the wheel were not yet available.

FIG 5.2 Poulnabrone portal dolmen, Burren, Co. Clare

Portal dolmens

Portal dolmens were the simplest of the megalithic structures. They are presumed to have been tombs because human remains from cremations and burials have been found within them, along with some Stone Age artefacts. They are constructed of between two and seven stone legs supporting one or two large capstones. The stones at the back of the tombs are generally lower than those at the front, suggesting to some archaeologists that the capstones may have been dragged up an earthen ramp to rest on the uprights. There are dramatic examples at Poulnabrone in the Burren in Co. Clare (fig 5.2) and at Kilcooley in Co. Donegal. There are 170 or so portal dolmens in Ireland.

Court cairns

As the name suggests, court cairns were a combination of a burial chamber inside a mound (or cairn) of stones, with an open court in front of it. The covered chamber was sometimes divided by jambs and sills, creating doorways between spaces. Outside, a semicircular area created a formal entrance or ceremonial area. There were a number of variations to this basic layout (fig 5.3).

Dolmens and court cairns have no added decoration, though they were formally constructed to a preconceived design, which does put them in the realm of art.

Passage mounds (graves)

There are over 200 known passage mounds in Ireland. (There is a growing preference for the term 'passage mound', rather than 'passage grave', as the understanding of their function grows.) They come in a variety of layouts and sizes and many have decorated stones as part of their construction. There is a

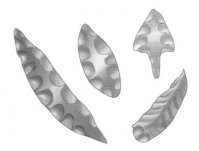

Blades, scrapers, arrows and lance heads were made from flint, shaped by flaking or knapping the stone to create a sharp edge.

Polished axe heads were used to chop down trees. They might also have been used as weapons.

FIG 5.1 Stone Age tools and weapons

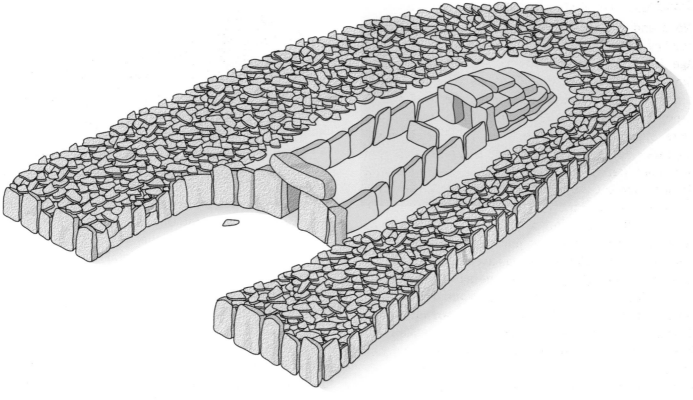

FIG 5.3 Court cairn reconstruction

concentration of these structures in Co. Meath, particularly at Brú na Bóinne, an area 4 km long and 3 km wide and enclosed by a bend in the River Boyne. There are close to 40 mounds in this area, including three large mounds at Knowth, Dowth and Newgrange with smaller satellite tombs surrounding them.

Knowth

The oldest and largest of these mounds is at Knowth, which dates back to 4000 BC. The mound has two passages – one facing east and one facing west. It is surrounded by a kerb of 127 large stones, most of which

are decorated. The mound covers an area of 1.5 acres and is the largest man-made structure in Western Europe dating from the Stone Age (fig 5.4).

The western passage is 34 m long and is of the undifferentiated type (that is, there is no clearly separate chamber at the end of the passage) (fig 5.5). A basin stone with the remains of cremation burials and some

FIG 5.4 Knowth – looking towards the entrance to the eastern passage.

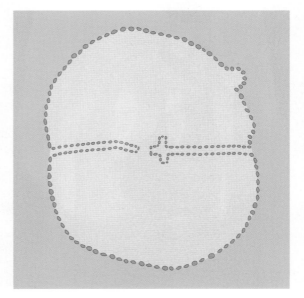

FIG 5.5 Plan of Knowth

FIG 5.6 Knowth basin stone

grave goods was found in this passage. The grave goods included stone balls and pendants, coloured beads, shell necklaces and stone tools, such as arrowheads, knives, chisels and scrapers. A number of the orthostats (upright stones) in the passage are decorated.

The eastern passage is more elaborate. It is 40 m long and has a cruciform chamber with a corbelled vault 7 m tall at the centre. A beautifully decorated basin stone

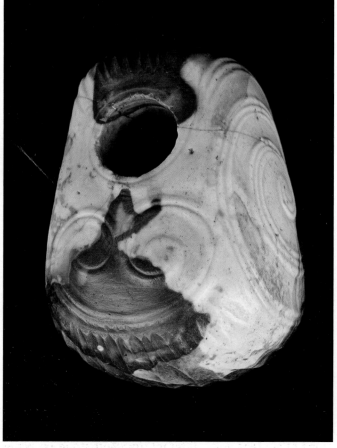

FIG 5.7 Knowth mace head

(fig 5.6) was found in the recess at the northern side of the chamber and a mace-head carved from a piece of flint from the Orkney Islands off the coast of Scotland was also found (fig 5.7). It is a remarkably well made and finely finished piece for such an early date. Many of the kerbstones that surround the base of the mound are elaborately decorated with patterns which have been interpreted as relating to the phases of the moon and movements of the planets.

Dowth

Dowth has not been thoroughly excavated yet, but it has two passages facing west. One is a short passage with a circular chamber, while the other has a longer passage with a cruciform chamber, while containing a large basin stone. There are many decorated stones in this mound as well. We will know more about it once a complete survey has been done.

Newgrange

The most famous of the Boyne Valley mounds is noted for the roof box over its entrance, which allows the sun to shine down the 18.7 m long passage into the furthest recesses of the chamber each year on the 21st of December (the midwinter solstice, the shortest day of the year) (fig 5.8). The passage is formed by upright stones with lintels on top, some of which are decorated. Between the first and second roof slabs of the passage, over the entrance, is a rectangular opening built in stone, which forms the roof box. The upper lintel stone of this opening is carved with triangles, which create a pattern of raised X shapes separated by vertical lines. The chamber at the end of the passage is roughly 6 m in diameter and 6 m tall. It has three recesses, which create a cruciform plan like the east passage at Knowth.

FIG 5.8 Newgrange

FIG 5.9 Newgrange entrance stone and light box

Newgrange was built around 3200 BC. It was excavated from 1967 to 1975, when it was reconstructed into the shape that we see today. The wall of white quartz stones and grey, water-worn granite stones stands on the row of kerbstones at the front of the structure. The quartz came from Co. Wicklow and the granite beach stones came from Dundalk Bay in Co. Louth. They were arranged in this way on the instructions of the Professor Michael J. O'Kelly, the chief archaeologist, who imagined, based on his research, that the mound had been built like that when it was first constructed. Ninety-seven kerbstones surround the base of the mound. Many have decorations, ranging from simple lines and spirals to fully decorated stones, such as the curvilinear patterned entrance stone and kerbstone 52 on the opposite side of the mound (fig 5.9). There is a further circle of monoliths at a distance of about 15 m out from the kerbstones. Only 12 undecorated stones remain standing, out of the original 32. This ring of standing stones may not be contemporary with the mound.

Construction

The building of these large structures was an heroic task for people of the Stone Age. Their technology was limited to what they could carry, pull or lever into place, they had no beasts of burden and the wheel was not yet invented. They had to move large stones up to 5 tons in weight across the countryside, which may have still been forested. It has been estimated that it might have taken up to 80 men three weeks to pull one large stone the 15 km from the quarry at Tullyallen up to Knowth. At this pace, it may have taken 50 years to build one mound.

Construction probably began with the layout of the passages, as their orientation to the sun or moonlight was an essential part of the purpose of the structure. The line of the kerb would need to be laid out early on, as it was the retaining structure for the stones, sod and earth that made up the body of the mound.

Corbelling

The corbelled roof over the chamber might have been constructed as the level of the mound built up, allowing access to gradually higher levels. These corbelled chambers are the oldest roofed structures still standing in Western Europe. The vaults were built on the standing stones of the chamber in gradually decreasing circles of large flat stones, sloping slightly outwards. At Newgrange, grooves were cut in the top surface of the stones to help shed any water that might have percolated down into the mound. This outward lean of the stones would also help to distribute the weight away from the centre, minimising the risk of a collapse of the completed dome or vault (fig 5.10).

Decoration

The range of designs used by Stone Age artists is quite limited. They consist of circles, dots in circles, spirals, serpentiforms, arcs, radials (star shapes), zigzags, chevrons, lozenges (diamond shapes), parallel lines and offsets or comb devices. All the shapes are drawn freehand and are abstract, but they may have held some meaning for the people who made them (fig 5.11).

At Knowth, we find the greatest number of decorated stones, making up about half of all the Stone Age art in Ireland. Many of the 127 stones in the kerb are elaborately patterned. Kerbstone 15, which looks like a sundial, can be interpreted as a lunar calendar recording the phases of the moon (fig 5.12). Kerbstone 78, which is also supposed to refer to the phases of the moon, has a range of designs quite different from Kerbstone 15. Wavy lines and circles dominate the pattern, which flows over

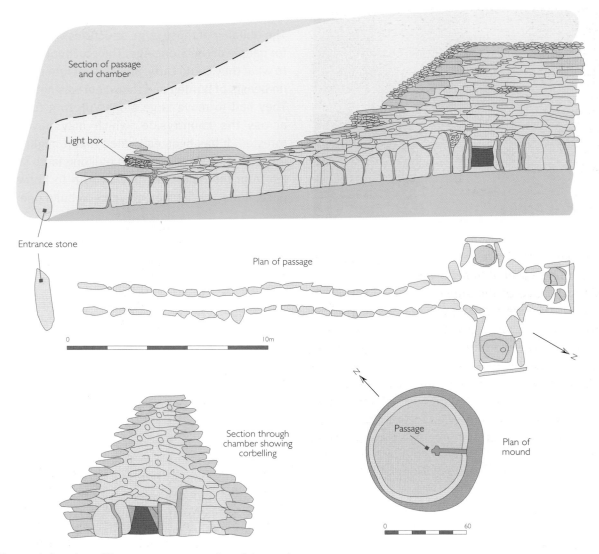

Section of passage
and chamber

Light box

Entrance stone

Plan of passage

0   10m

Section through
chamber showing
corbelling

Passage

Plan of
mound

0   60

FIG 5.10 Plan and elevation of Newgrange, construction of the tomb

FIG 5.11 Drawings of the range of Stone Age designs.

FIG 5.12 Knowth kerbstone 78

the whole surface of the stone. At Newgrange, the entrance stone is covered in a curvilinear pattern which emphasises the size of the stone. A groove at the top centre lines up with the entrance and the roof box, left of the groove is a triple spiral and beyond this a series of lozenges covers the end of the stone. On the right of the centre, two double spirals sit on top of a wave pattern that connects back to the triple spiral. Lozenges, curves and zigzags cover the right-hand end of the stone. Kerbstone 52 on the opposite side of the mound has an even more varied range of patterns covering most of its surface (fig 5.13).

Techniques

Most of the stones of Knowth and Newgrange have been dressed, that is, a hammer-driven stone chisel or point was used to remove rough areas and to take away a thin layer of stone and improve its colour. The lines and patterns on the stones are made by **chip carving**, cutting into the stone with a sharp flint or other hard stone tool or by picking or pecking with a stone chisel or point driven by a hammer. On the surface of the stones, marks may have been smoothed out by hammering or rubbing with coarse textured stone (fig 5.14).

FIG 5.13 Newgrange kerbstone 52

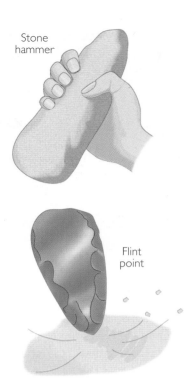
Stone hammer

Flint point

FIG 5.14 Chip carving

Interpretation

Passage mounds seem to be much more than graves for revered ancestors. The sheer scale of commitment from the Stone Age people who spent generations constructing them must have made them the most important endeavour in the lives of the community. They were the largest structures in the country for thousands of years and were the source of legends. The earliest records describe Brú na Bóinne as the home of the Tuatha Dé Danann, the ancient Irish gods who descended from the skies to inhabit Ireland. In later generations, the mounds were thought to be the burial places of ancient kings. The number of cremated remains inside the passage mounds is relatively small in relation to the size of the community and the length of time for which the mounds were used, however. This might mean that only very special members of the community were buried there or that they were ritual or sacrificial burials.

There is a growing body of support for the theory that designs on the stones relate to movements of the sun, moon and the planets, which would be a way of keeping track of the seasons and important community events. Kerbstones at Knowth in particular can be interpreted as recording lunar events and patterns (fig 5.15). The passages at Knowth received the light of the rising and setting sun at the equinoxes in March and October, which

FIG 5.15 Decorated kerbstone 15, Knowth

The Bronze Age (2000 BC to 500 BC)

The changes that marked the arrival of a new culture in Ireland began in the north and east of the country. Burials of cremated human remains under the cover of a new type of pottery, often in a stone-lined cist grave, mark the arrival of the Beaker People, called after their distinctive pottery. During the Early Bronze Age (2000 to 1500 BC), Stone Age culture survived for some time in the south and west of the country, while Bronze Age society and technology were developing in the north, east and Midlands.

The clear differences between Bronze Age and Stone Age art suggest that the people who developed metal technology in Ireland were of a different culture to the Stone Age people. The Beaker People originated in mainland Europe and probably came in search of copper and gold deposits. There is certainly evidence of Irish gold and copper being traded into Europe and Britain, which suggests links with the wider European community.

The nature of the **decoration on Bronze Age objects** is fundamentally different from Stone Age design; it is the result of combining basic geometric shapes with the most up-to-date technology of the time (fig 5.16). Metal was cast, hammered, twisted and cut to shape to create the range of forms preferred by the Bronze Age artists (fig 5.17). Forms and designs were created by mechanical means using a compass and straight edge rather than the freehand designs found in Stone Age art.

are important seasons for planting and harvesting in a farming community. At Newgrange, the light of sunrise on the solstice (21 December), the shortest day of the year, may have celebrated the death of the old year and the birth of the new. Other passage mounds also received the light of the sun or the moon at significant seasons and are the focus of ongoing research.

Rituals and ceremonies might have been held in procession around the mounds, stopping at significant stones relevant to the season. There are areas outside the east and west entrances at Knowth that are paved with quartz and granite stones like those on the front of the mound at Newgrange. These areas may have been the focus of ceremonies or they might have marked forbidden areas. Whatever their function, these stones had to be transported by boat or raft from far away (80 km for the quartz from Wicklow and 50 km for the smooth granite stones from Dundalk Bay).

Conclusion

The ancient mounds of Brú na Bóinne have a long history and their construction speaks of an intelligent and inventive people, deeply motivated over generations to construct the largest structures of their time. Newgrange represents the pinnacle of wood and stone technology and freehand abstract design.

Their art was the result of carefully planned and often repeated images, which took time and effort to construct and must have had deep significance for the artists. It seems likely that the images are more than random doodles, but we know so little about the lives and language of these early people that we can only guess at the meaning.

FIG 5.16 Late Bronze Age object

FIG 5.17 Bronze Age pottery

Bronze Age structures (architecture)

The design of tombs changed during the Bronze Age, which again suggests a new type of culture in Irish society. In the greater part of the country, the dead were laid to rest in pits or cists. These usually took the form of a small stone-lined box about a metre in length which contained an upturned pot with cremated remains underneath. In the west of Ireland, wedge tombs, which were related to the court cairns built in the Stone Age, were still being constructed. None of these burial sites had the drama of the Stone Age monuments.

Ceremonial sites made of circular earthen banks or standing stones and hilltop forts (once thought to have been from the Iron Age) are now regarded as Bronze Age structures that continued in use into the Iron Age (fig 5.18). Stone carving seems to have been little practised except for a few examples of rock art found in counties Cork, Kerry and Donegal. Designs were very simple, mainly little hollow 'cup marks' surrounded by circles, sometimes with radiating lines (fig 5.19). Little remains of Bronze Age human settlement. Houses and fences seem to have been made of wood, which would have rotted away over the centuries, though evidence of a widespread population has survived through burial sites and finds of Bronze Age objects (fig 5.20).

Metalwork

Mining for gold and copper was carried out at a number of locations in Ireland during the Bronze Age. Evidence of Bronze Age metalworking has been found at Mount Gabriel in Co. Cork, the Vale of Avoca in Co. Wicklow and in the Mourne Mountains. It was low-technology mining. Gold was probably found in nuggets or by panning alluvial deposits in rivers. Copper was mined by roasting ore-bearing rock with fire and cracking it by throwing cold water on it. The broken stone would then be dug out and the bits with the highest concentration of copper oxides would be selected and smelted over a charcoal fire. The resulting molten copper was poured into stone moulds and was cast into the shapes of axes, knives, sickles or whatever shape was required (fig 5.21). As technology improved, more sophisticated moulds were made and tin (imported from Britain) was mixed with the copper to make the alloy bronze. Bronze is harder than copper and can hold a sharp edge for longer.

FIG 5.18 Stone circle, Drombeg, Co. Cork

Designs made by incision: cutting into the surface

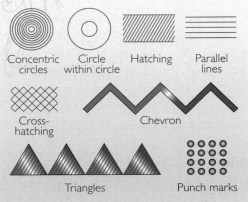

Concentric circles

Circle within circle

Hatching

Parallel lines

Cross-hatching

Chevron

Triangles

Punch marks

Designs made by the repoussé technique: designs raised on the surface

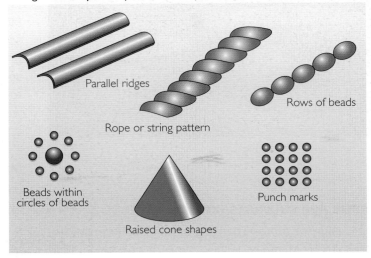

Parallel ridges

Rope or string pattern

Rows of beads

Beads within circles of beads

Raised cone shapes

Punch marks

Some combinations of designs

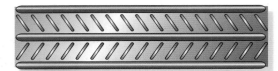

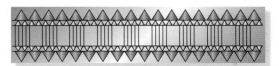

Some combinations of designs

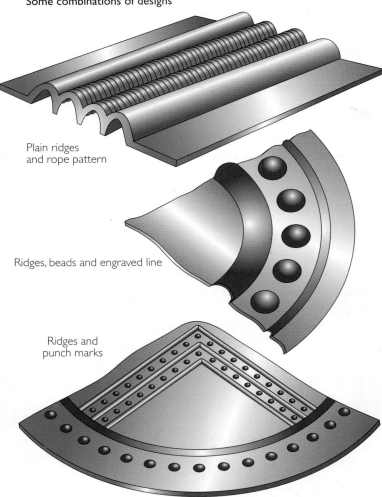

Plain ridges and rope pattern

Ridges, beads and engraved line

Ridges and punch marks

92

FIG 5.19 Bronze Age designs

FIG 5.20 Rock art, Derrynablaha, Co. Cork

FIG 5.22 Sun discs from Tedavent, Co. Monaghan

Decorative gold objects

Early Bronze Age objects were made from a single piece of gold, as the technology for joining pieces together with gold solder was not yet developed in Ireland. Craftsmen hammered gold into thin flat sheets and cut it to shape. Decoration was added simply incising (cutting) lines and patterns into the surface or by raising designs from the surface using the repoussé technique (hammering from the reverse side). Early Bronze Age gold objects were decorated with simple geometric patterns. Circles, triangles, dots and straight lines were combined in various ways to make up the design repertoire of the first goldsmiths in Ireland.

The **sun disc**, from the early Bronze Age (c. 2000 BC), is circular in shape and about 11 cm in diameter. It is cut from a thin sheet of beaten gold. The surface is patterned with ridges, chevrons and dots created by the repoussé technique. Two holes near the centre suggest that the discs might have been sewn onto a garment or belt. The discs, which are from Tedavent in Co. Monaghan, have bands of dots, ridges and chevrons around the perimeter, with a cross shape in the centre. Triangles are

formed at the centre and the ends of the arms. Triangles also appear between the arms of the cross shape against the surrounding circles. (This design, from 2,000 years before Christ, is simply a result of the geometric pattern and has no Christian religious symbolism.) These discs from Tedavent show some of the earliest examples of repoussé work (fig 5.22). To apply a repoussé design, gold sheet would have been laid face down on a firm surface – in more recent times, a leather sandbag or a bowl of mastic would have been used by goldsmiths. A pattern could then be created on the surface using tracers (chisel-like tools with a variety of shapes cut into the tip which were pressed or hammered into the surface) to produce a design. With the work completed, the sheet of gold was turned face up to reveal the design projecting from the surface. The work required careful craftsmanship, as a careless stroke could tear the thin gold sheet and the work would have to be started all over again (fig 5.23).

The **lunula** is the most commonly found gold artefact from the early Bronze Age and are dated to after 1800 BC. A lunula was a neck collar probably worn as a status or magical item. It was made of gold hammered into a thin sheet and cut into a crescent moon shape (hence the name), often with a plain surface but frequently decorated with incised lines (fig 5.24). A lunula from Ross in Co. Westmeath has a pattern of lines, triangles and chevrons incised into its surface. The pattern is concentrated in the narrow ends of the crescent. Four patterned areas on each side have parallel lines with chevrons inside separated by hatched lines. There are rows of hatched triangles on each side of the parallel lines. The main body of the lunula is plain and is surrounded by two rows of lines edged in triangles.

FIG 5.21 Bronze axe in stone mould

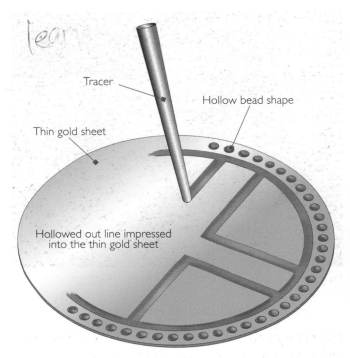

FIG 5.23 Repoussé technique

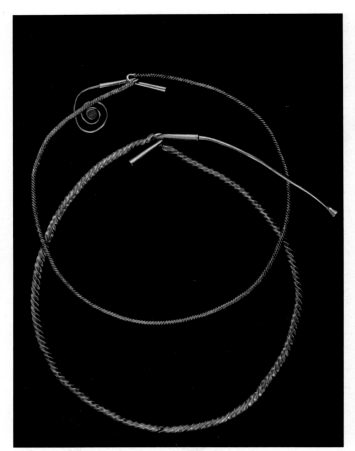

FIG 5.25 Long torcs with elaborate catches, probably to be worn around the waist.

A completely new form of ornament largely replaced sheet gold work from about 1400 BC (the Bishopsland phase). These new objects, called **torcs**, were made by twisting gold into a variety of decorative forms. The **ribbon torc** was made from a flat strip of gold twisted into an even spiral (fig 5.25, fig 5.26). Twisting round, square or triangular-sectioned rods of gold into a spiral shape made a **bar torc**. A variation of the bar torc was made by hammering flanges out from the angles of square or triangular-sectioned bars before twisting (fig 5.27). By varying the size of the flanges, the length of the bar and the degree of twist that was applied, craftsmen could make a great variety of these **flanged**

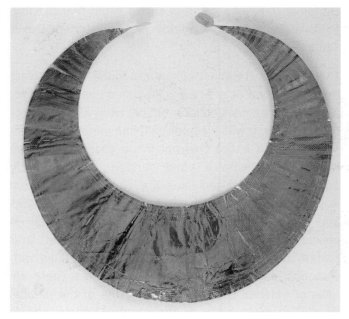

FIG 5.24 A lunula and a close up of the incised design

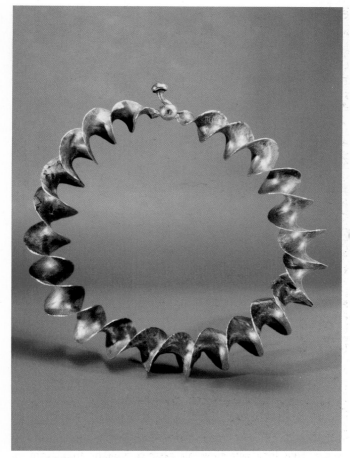

FIG 5.26 Ribbon torc from Belfast

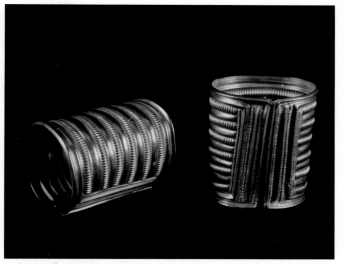

FIG 5.28 Derrynaboy armbands

torcs. Catches and terminals also ranged in style from simple to elaborate. Hammering the ends of the torc into the required shape created catches. All torcs are made of one piece of gold and were made to fit the neck, waist and arms or to be worn as earrings.

The repoussé technique continued in use at this time. A pair of armbands from Derrinaboy, Co. Offaly, is boldly patterned in alternate smooth and rope patterned rows (fig 5.28).

The Golden Age

After 800 BC (the Dowris phase), there was a huge upsurge in metalwork production in Ireland. New types of bronze tools and weapons and gold ornaments have turned up in buried hoards found in numbers all over the

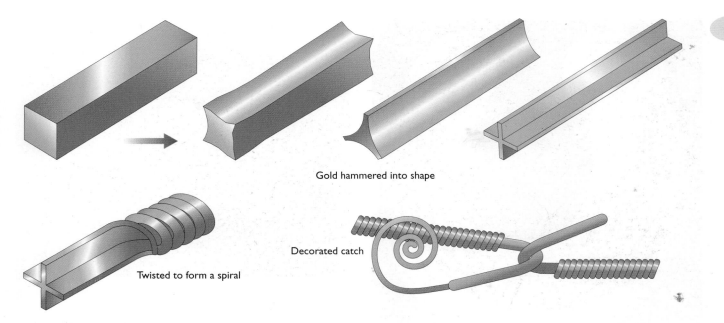

Gold hammered into shape

Twisted to form a spiral

Decorated catch

FIG 5.27 Method of making flanged torcs

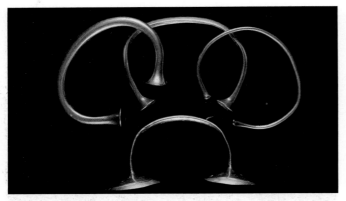

FIG 5.29 Selection of fibulae

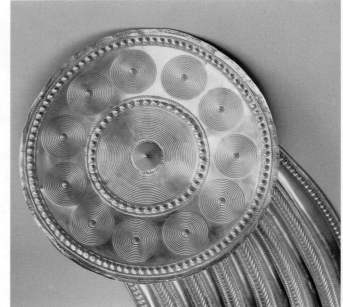

FIG 5.30 Clones Fibula

country, but particularly in the counties surrounding the lower Shannon River. This was Ireland's first 'golden age'. A greater quantity of gold objects has been found in Ireland from this time than from any of our European neighbours.

The **fibula** may have been a type of dress fastener adapted from northern European models, although some of the larger ones would have been too heavy to be practical and were probably only for ceremonial use. A fibula is made up of a gold bow or handle with a cup-shaped or flat disc at each end. The basic form would have been cast and the cups or discs at the end of the bow could be hammered out into the required shape. Fibulae come in a variety of forms and are both decorated and undecorated (fig 5.29). A beautiful example comes from Clones in Co. Monaghan. It is made

from a kilo of solid gold and it has large, open-cup ends, which are decorated with rows of small, concentric circles with a little hollow in the centre of each. There are three grooves cut into the outer edge of each cup. The area where the bow joins the cup is decorated with incised triangles and bands of lines. There are also triangles on top of the bow (fig 5.30).

The **gorget** is a semicircular collar with a gold disc at each end. It would have been worn at the neck and would have been a high-status item. Gorgets are perhaps the most beautifully made objects from the Bronze Age. There are several examples of gorgets in the National Museum of Ireland, the most perfect of which is the Gleninsheen Gorget (fig 5.31), which was found in a rock crevice near the tomb of the same name in the Burren in Co. Clare. The crescent-shaped body of the collar has

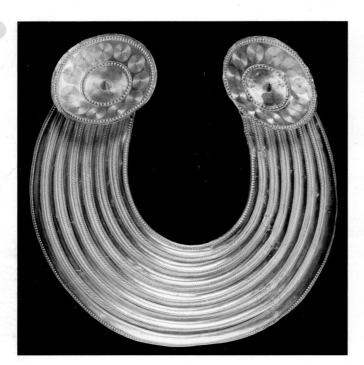

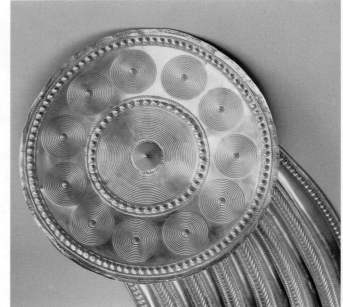

FIG 5.31 Gleninsheen Gorget

rows of repoussé decoration, which are alternately plain and rope patterned. The discs at each end are patterned in rows of beads and concentric circles, with a smooth cone at the centre. Similar designs appear on sunflower pins and little gold boxes of the same period. The alternately smooth and textured patterns on the surface of the collar catch the light beautifully, creating an impression of movement and dancing light. Gorgets were constructed from a number of parts. The outer and inner edges of the collar were finished with a strip of gold wrapped around it to create a smooth finish. The discs were made from two layers, with the edges of the larger back disc wrapped over the edge of the upper disc, again creating a more finished edge. The discs were connected to the collar by stitching with gold wire or, in some cases, by a hinge-like arrangement.

Lock rings seem to be a uniquely Irish invention. They may have been used as hair ornaments. Structurally, they are the most advanced work of the Bronze Age goldsmiths in Ireland. A pair of lock rings from Gorteenreagh in Co. Clare was made from fine gold wires soldered together into a double cone shape with a narrow opening down one side. A plait of hair could be slipped through this opening into a tube at the centre, which could then be turned out of line to hold the hair in place (fig 5.32).

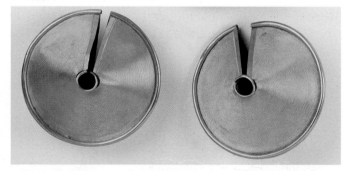

FIG 5.32 Gorteenareagh Lock rings

Craftsmanship

The art of the metalworker reached a very high standard of craftsmanship in the late Bronze Age, both in gold and bronze work. Clay moulds made of a number of parts were now used to cast more complicated objects. Bronze was beaten into sheets and joined with rivets to create large cauldrons and other vessels. Sophistication in design and workmanship is a hallmark of late Bronze Age metalwork (fig 5.33).

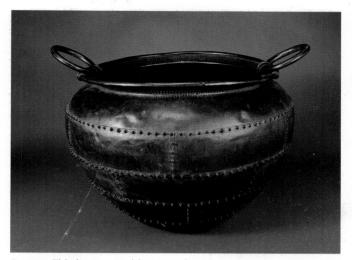

FIG 5.33 This bronze cauldron was found at Castlederg, Co. Tyrone. It is 56cm in diamter. It is from the Down's phase of the late Bronze Age.

Conclusion

The abstract art of the Bronze Age was linked to the art of a large part of Western Europe. We are lucky to have exceptional examples of Bronze Age design in Ireland. The gold and bronze objects of the Dowris phase of the Bronze Age demonstrate the most advanced technology of the time combined with sophisticated designs and a high level of craftsmanship, showing what could be achieved with simple geometric patterns.

The Iron Age: The Celts in Ireland (500 BC to 400 AD)

The Celts

The Celts were a group of tribes that populated much of Europe in the 700 years before the birth of Christ and for a few centuries after. They were known to the Greeks and the Romans as the Keltoi. They were renowned as warriors (fig 5.34), horsemen and craft workers, skilled in the production of a wide range of goods and weapons in gold, bronze and iron.

Strabo, a Roman historian writing in the 1st century AD, describes the Celts thus:

> To the frankness and high spiritedness of their temperament must be added traits of childish boastfulness and love of decoration. They wear ornaments of gold, torcs on their necks and bracelets on their arms and wrists, while people of high rank wear garments besprinkled with gold. It is this vanity that makes them so unbearable in victory and so completely downcast in defeat.

The Celts, unfortunately, kept no written records, so the only written evidence we have of Celtic culture and society are second-hand accounts kept by their enemies.

FIG 5.34 THE DYING GAUL OF PERGAMUM. This Celtic warrior is naked for battle except for a torc around his neck. His weapons and trumpet are around him on the ground.

The Celts spoke an Indo-European language, which evolved as they gradually migrated into Europe during the Stone and Bronze Ages. By the Iron Age the Celts consisted of a large group of tribes with similar languages and culture and inhabiting most of Europe from the Black Sea to the west coast of Europe and Britain.

The Celts in Ireland

When the Celts arrived in Ireland and how they got here is still open to debate. In the early 20th century it was assumed that the Celts invaded Ireland, but this is not so certain anymore. Significant sites like hill forts and places of burial seem to have been in continuous use from the Bronze Age into the Iron Age, so a Celtic cultural influence may have arrived ahead of any Celtic people by trading, migration and assimilation, with large numbers of Celtic people only arriving in Ireland as the Romans invaded Gaul (France) and Britain. By the 1st century BC, Ireland had a Celtic culture of some depth and substance.

Irish myths and legends from the oral tradition are an important source of evidence about the Celts. They were first written down by Christian monks hundreds of years after the events they were supposed to describe, but they probably give a flavour, seen through later Christian eyes, of what Celtic Ireland might have been like. The picture that comes through the myths and legends is one of a tribal society based on family ties where wealth took the form of cattle ownership. Princes and heroes led cattle raids and wars of honour, combining physical prowess, cleverness and magic to win the day. Places described in the sagas, such as Eamhain Macha (Navan

Fort), in Co. Armagh, do exist and based on archaeological excavation were significant Iron Age sites.

There may have been an extended period when Celts and earlier native people lived quite separately. Most early La Tène culture artefacts were found in the northern part of the country. Late Bronze Age hill forts and burial sites seem to have continued in use in the southern part of the country. Certainly, by the time Christianity arrived in Ireland, the country had one Celtic language and a uniform social and political system, but how it evolved is not certain.

The development of Celtic art

The development of the art of the Celts into the style we know in Ireland began during the centuries when the Celtic peoples were growing in power and influence in central Europe. The Hallstatt style (called after a town in Austria where a great quantity of artefacts that define the style were first found) was the earliest development. Most of the work is in bronze and gold and is finely crafted and in an abstract style (fig 5.35). These Hallstatt Celts developed iron technology, which improved farming and military equipment and allowed them to expand their influence east and west. Some hints of this art and technology reached Ireland in the 6th century BC, but it did not seem to take root.

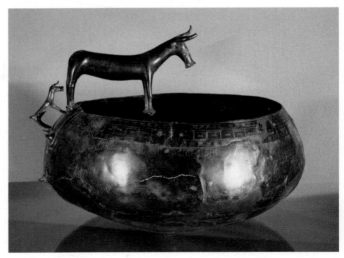

FIG 5.35 Hallstatt art

The La Tène style

By the 5th century BC a new style of Celtic art had developed. It combined influences from classical Greek and Roman art, the Etruscans, the Scythians and Oriental art with the Celtic style. This style is called La Tène after a site on the shores of Lake Neuchâtel in Switzerland where the diagnostic examples were found (fig 5.36).

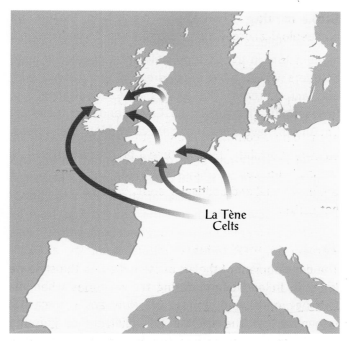
FIG 5.36 Areas of Celtic influences in Europe

FIG 5.37 Celtic designs

Leafy palmate forms

Vines

Tendrils and scrolls

Lotus flower   Spirals

Lyre   Pelta

Trumpet

FIG 5.38 Ballyshannon sword hilt

This new style combined leafy palmate forms with vines, tendrils, lotus flowers, spirals, S-scrolls, lyre and trumpet shapes into a sinuous, abstract style which the Celts used to decorate ornaments and weapons (fig 5.37). The migrations and invasions of the Celtic peoples throughout Europe in the 5th and 4th centuries BC helped to spread the style. By the 3rd century BC, La Tène art was evident in Ireland, initially in the form of imports. Gold collars found in Co. Roscommon, scabbard plates found in north-east Ulster and a sword hilt in the shape of a human figure found in the sea at Ballyshannon were all probably imported from Europe (fig 5.38, fig 5.39). These finds of weapons and valuables in rivers, lakes

FIG 5.39 Scabbard plate design

and at the seashore speak of rituals and offerings among the Celtic people associated with water. (The legend of King Arthur, for example, contains a story of a sword being thrown into a lake following the death of a warrior, returning the power associated with it to the other world.)

Insular La Tène

The style of art used by the first native craftsmen in Ireland is called Insular La Tène. It is a modified version of the European style. It consists of S-scrolls, leaf and vine forms, trumpet ends and spirals. Some of its characteristics are peculiar to the islands off the west coast of Europe, which gives the style the name 'insular'. The patterns on the Turoe Stone, in Co. Galway, and the Broighter Collar, discovered near Lough Foyle in Co. Derry, are in this style.

Iron Age structures (architecture)

Much of our knowledge of Stone and Bronze Age structures is based on the tombs and burial sites of the time. Little is known of the burial rites of the Iron Age people in Ireland, but habitation sites and ring forts in earth and stone are relatively common throughout the country. Some forts were built for defence, some were ritual sites and smaller ones were just homesteads. The circular enclosure (with houses and animal pens inside) continued in use in Ireland after the Norman invasion, at a time when the rest of Europe had long since developed towns and cities (fig 5.40).

Stone carving

The first objects we can confidently claim to be of Irish manufacture in the La Tène style are a number of large boulders which have been dressed and carved with abstract patterns. The stones at Castlestrange, Co. Roscommon, Killycluggin, Co. Cavan, and Derry Keighan, Co. Antrim, have a linear pattern carved into the surface.

The **Turoe Stone** has been dated to about 50 BC. This 4 ton boulder, which is 1.68 m tall, is of pink feldsparred Galway granite. It is a glacial erratic which was carried 40 km by moving ice during the last Ice Age, from its source in Connemara to the Loughrea area, where it was worked on, thousands of years later, by a Celtic stonemason (fig 5.41). The pattern on the Turoe Stone (fig 5.42) takes the form of abstract leaf and vine shapes, trumpet ends and spirals all flowing in a casual symmetry. It was sculpted in low relief; the background was cut away to a depth of about 3 cm. The design is in four segments. Two semicircular areas of design take up most of the stone's surface and between these are two smaller triangular segments of pattern, which connect over the top of the stone. A triskele (a motif of three curved limbs which spring from the same point and turn in the same direction) appears in one of the triangular segments. The flowing pattern takes up the domed top of the stone. Some of the spaces between the raised pattern can also be read as part of the design, showing

FIG 5.40 Dún Aengus on Inis Mór in the Aran Islands was in use from the late Bronze Age into the Iron Age.

FIG 5.41 Turoe Stone

FIG 5.42 Turoe Stone schematic drawing

FIG 5.43 Tricephalic head from Corleck

the Celtic love of the play between positive and negative spaces. A brick or step pattern forms a band below the decorated dome and separates it from the plain base.

The purpose of these decorated stones is not known; they may have been boundary markers or ceremonial objects. Some stone figure carvings may also be from the Iron Age, but it is difficult to date them accurately. The tricephalic head (*tricephalos*, with three faces) from Corleck, Co. Cavan (fig 5.43), is generally accepted as Celtic, as is the Tandragee Idol from Co. Armagh (fig 5.44), but some other figures and heads once assigned to the Iron Age are now thought to be of later date.

Metalwork

The arrival of iron technology in Ireland improved and simplified the production of tools and weapons (fig 5.45). Iron was readily available in the environment in the form of clay ironstone nodules, bog iron and other less easily worked sources. It was not melted and cast, but heated until the impurities were burned off or melted away and then it was hammer forged and shaped. Smiths were often itinerant, setting up wherever they were needed and moving on when the work ran out. There is evidence of small-scale smelting all over the country. Iron would

FIG 5.44 Tandragee Idol

FIG 5.45 Iron objects

Not many gold finds can be dated to the Iron Age, but the quality of some pieces makes up for the lack of quantity. The Broighter Hoard (fig 5.47) was turned up by a ploughman near Lough Foyle in Co. Derry. It includes some of the finest examples of the goldsmith's art. The collection consists of a model boat and a bowl made of thin sheet gold, two chains, two twisted bracelets and a gold collar.

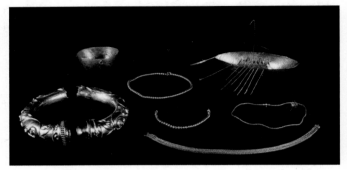

FIG 5.47 Broighter Hoard

also have been recycled. The smith would have had similar tools and skills as any village blacksmith would have had up to the middle of the 20th century. Metalworkers were highly valued members of society and were equal in status with physicians.

Much of the decorative work from the Iron Age was made of bronze, such as horse trappings, tools and utensils, brooches, armbands and rings, all beautifully crafted (fig 5.46). The lost wax method of casting in bronze allowed for complicated pieces, such as horse bits, to be made. Sheet bronze was also turned and hammered to produce vessels and decorative pieces.

The collar is the most accomplished piece. It is of Irish manufacture in the Insular La Tène style. The tubes that are the main element of the piece are made from sheet gold onto which the foliage pattern was chased. (Chasing is a technique by which a design is brought into relief by pressing back the surrounding area by hammering. In some ways, chasing is a reverse of the repoussé technique.) The design would have been applied while the gold was still a flat sheet. The patterned gold sheets were then rolled into tubes, which were soldered shut and then filled with hot mastic (a wax-like substance) so that the tubes could be curved without being torn or crushed. The pattern is symmetrical and is based on interconnecting S-scrolls. It combines a variety of plant-based forms, culminating in spiral bosses, which were made separately and pinned on (fig 5.48). The background area between the pattern elements has been incised with compass arcs to create a contrast with the smooth surface of the raised design.

The buffer terminals are riveted onto the ends of the tubes and a row of beading has been raised along the edge to disguise the rivet heads. A raised pattern of

FIG 5.46 Early Iron Age objects

FIG 5.48 Broighter collar schematic drawing

lentoids and hollowed bosses with a little gold bead soldered in the centre meets the tubes. One of the terminals has rows of beading. A T-shaped bar is used as the lock, which holds the two terminals together, and another terminal, which is now missing, would have joined the other ends of the tubes together.

The gold chains and twisted bracelets from the Broighter Hoard are probably imports of Roman origin. The gold boat is a model of an ocean-going craft, probably a hide-covered boat driven by oars and a square sail, and it is an interesting indication of how Celtic people travelled around the coast of Europe.

The Ultimate La Tène style

Later in the Iron Age there was a change in the style of design and the patterns became lighter and more symmetrical. The vegetal designs of the Insular style gave way to the more geometric forms of the Ultimate La Tène, which continued into the Christian era. The objects below are in this style.

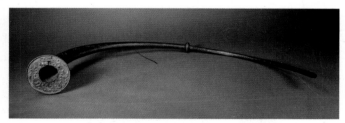

FIG 5.49 Loughnashade Trumpet

- The Loughnashade Trumpet (fig 5.49), found in Co. Antrim and dating from the 1st century AD, is made of two tubes of sheet bronze joined by a knob in the middle and having a decorative plate on the open end. The tubes are expertly made; the edges are rolled together and riveted onto an internal strip of bronze. The plate at the open end has a four-part pattern raised by the repoussé technique. It is based on the Roman *pelta* motif and is almost perfectly symmetrical. The design is lighter and more linear than earlier work, with broader areas in relief at the ends of the curves (fig 5.50).
- The Petrie Crown is an object of unknown origin from the collection of the 19th-century antiquarian George Petrie (fig 5.51). It consists of an open-work band with a cone and two discs fixed to it. The top and bottom edges of the band are perforated, which would have allowed it to be sewn to fabric or leather or fixed to wood or metal. It is not known how long the band was intended to be or how many horns or

FIG 5.50 Pattern on plate at the open end of the trumpet

discs were originally fixed to it, so is difficult to imagine its original function. The raised outlines of the design were created by cutting back the surrounding metal. The openings in the band create the impression of a series of connected semicircles which are decorated with spirals ending in crested bird heads. The concave discs, which are mounted on this band, have a slightly off-centre boss, one of which still has a red enamelled bead in its hollow middle. Enamelled beads were probably fixed in the eye sockets of some of the bird heads. The deceptively simple designs on the discs combine

FIG 5.51 Petrie Crown

palmate, lotus bud and triskele motifs created by slim trumpet curves (fig 5.52). The artist made use of both positive and negative shapes to create the design, a tendency which becomes even more common in the Christian period. The bird heads found on the band, discs and horn are among the earliest zoomorphs (animal forms) found in Irish art.

- The Cork Horns (fig 5.53), probably some kind of ceremonial headgear, are nearest in design to the *Petrie Crown*, though not as elaborately decorated.

FIG 5.53 **Cork Horns**

Conclusion

The Celtic period is as mysterious and enigmatic as some of the designs created by the artists of the time. There is little archaeological evidence of how the people lived. There are almost no house remains, and hilltop forts once thought to belong to the Iron Age are now dated back to the late Bronze Age, although they continued in use during the Iron Age. Elaborate burials of warriors with chariots, weapons and valuables found in Britain and on the Continent are not found in Ireland. Pottery hardly features in Irish sites, though it is relatively common in the rest of Europe. Containers may have been made of wood, leather or metal, which would have suited nomadic people, pottery being more easily broken in

learn   *this*

Background bronze openwork strap

Concave discs

Bronze cone-shaped attachment

Bird head decorations, early zoomorphs

Long triskeles made of trumpet ends

FIG 5.52 **Petrie Crown patterns**

104

transit. Many of the Iron Age objects decorated with La Tène designs are not easy to interpret; we can only say that by the time records were beginning to be written in the 5th and 6th centuries AD, people speaking a Celtic language and having a largely Celtic culture populated Ireland.

The work left to us from this time displays the elements of design and pattern that formed the basis for the decorative art that followed in the Christian Celtic period. Plant forms (vegetal decoration), animal forms (zoomorphs), simplified human figures and geometric patterns were brought together to create a style of art that was flexible, harmonious, imaginative, ambiguous and, above all, beautiful.

Questions

1. What is a dolmen?
2. Describe the construction of a passage mound in words and sketches.
3. Describe three objects made of sheet gold from the Bronze Age.
4. Write an illustrated account of the techniques used in torc making.
5. Describe some characteristics of the La Tène style.
6. Make a sketch of the decoration on the Turoe Stone and describe the techniques used in its creation.
7. Describe two objects made in the Ultimate La Tène style.

Essay

1. Compare and contrast the design of the Stone and Bronze Ages, using two examples from each. Demonstrate why the technology and social needs of each society created such different forms of design.
2. Write an account of the Broighter Collar. In words and sketches, describe its decoration and the techniques used in its construction.

Colour picture study

1. Look at the picture of the entrance at Newgrange. Describe the construction of the roof box and the decoration of the entrance stone (fig 5.9).
2. Examine the picture of the Gleninsheen Gorget and describe its construction and decoration and the techniques used to achieve them (fig 5.31).
3. Look at the illustration of the Petrie Crown. Describe its structure and decoration with particular reference to positive and negative shapes within the design (fig 5.52).

CHAPTER 6

THE ARRIVAL OF CHRISTIANITY IN IRELAND (5TH AND 6TH CENTURIES)

Early medieval Ireland had a society based on kinship. The *tuath* (or 'tribe') was the basic social unit, which expanded into small kingdoms through alliances or tribute. It was a society without towns or coinage. Trade was by barter, exchanging goods or services of equal value. There is evidence of the importation of wine, oils and other luxury goods from areas within the old Roman Empire and from farther afield.

Stock rearing and farming were the main activities, which supported craft workers, musicians, poets, lawyers, priests and nobles. It was an illiterate society, with the exception of the crude ogham script, dependent on an oral tradition to maintain its laws and folklore.

The Roman Empire was in decline in Britain by the 3rd century AD, and the final legions departed in 406 AD. Irish raiders were able to set up colonies in northern and southern Wales on the edge of the empire and they took over large areas of west Scotland in Argyll. This contact with the outside world had effects on lifestyle and art in Ireland.

The arrival of Christianity in Ireland

The Christian message seems to have arrived in Ireland in a number of ways. Traders and raiders in and out of Ireland would have met Christians on mainland Europe and in Britain; this influence may have penetrated back into Ireland. Anchorite monks and hermits looking for places of isolation along the coast of Europe settled on the islands off the Irish coast. The heroic self-denial and endurance of these hermits would have appealed to an Irish society brought up on tales of the valour and strength of the old Celtic heroes and gods.

Palladius and St Patrick

In 431 AD Pope Julius I sent Bishop Palladius 'to the believers in Christ in Ireland'. The bishop brought books and religious objects in the Roman style with him, and craftsmen to make more. Following this initiative from Rome, St Patrick and others succeeded in converting the country to Christianity without the creation of martyrs and after little conflict with the pagan priesthood. In later centuries, the role of Palladius was played down in favour of the cult of St Patrick, which was promoted by the archdiocese of Armagh (which claimed a special tie with St Patrick) to reinforce its position as the senior *paruchia* (united group of monasteries and dioceses) in Ireland.

Church organisation

Initially, the Christians of Ireland were organised under the European model, with the bishop controlling a diocese of parishes in a geographical area, but this did not suit the non-urban make-up of Irish Celtic society. A system of monastic federations evolved in Ireland, based on kinship or allegiance to the founding saint of one of the great monasteries. Columba (Columcille) founded Derry and Iona, along with other monasteries; Patrick – Armagh (the prime monastery of Ireland); Brigid – Kildare; Brendan – Clonfert; Comgall – Bangor; Medoc – Ferns; and Enda – Aran. The abbot of the leading house of each of these federations was called the Comarba (successor to the founder) and was generally a kinsman of the founder. In some cases, sons succeeded fathers. Some of these Comarba would have been laymen or in minor orders.

This monastic system coexisted with a similar political system where the local king and abbot would often be of the same family, keeping religious and political power in the same *tuath*.

Monasticism in Ireland

The monastic way of life originated in the deserts of the eastern Mediterranean and arrived in Ireland via the Gallican Church in France. Irish monks seem to have maintained contacts with churches of the eastern tradition throughout the 5th and 6th centuries. It may have been safer to sail to the eastern Mediterranean than to try to cross Britain and Europe, which were in a politically unstable condition following the fall of the Roman Empire.

The founders of monasteries were revered as saints and their burial places and institutions holding their relics became centres of pilgrimage over the years. Some saints were associated with many sites and holy wells, particularly Patrick and Brigid, while others had a more local following.

During the 6th century, Irish monastic sites became great centres of learning and strict spiritual practice. Students came from Britain and Europe, where the Church was in some disarray and scholarship was at a low ebb. In the following centuries, Irish monks travelled throughout Britain and Europe, spreading the word of Christ and founding new monasteries. Columba used Iona as an outpost for the conversion of Scotland, which became a political colony of Ireland at the same time. *Scot* had been the Roman word for 'Irish man' up to this time.

Constructing the early monasteries

The layout of the early monasteries

Early monasteries were laid out following the local building style: an enclosing bank or wall surrounded an area with the church or oratory at the centre of the bigger sites and towards the south-east in smaller enclosures. The cemetery was located near the church and the monastic buildings. The area around the perimeter of the enclosure would have been for domestic dwellings and craftwork (fig 6.1).

FIG 6.1 Monastery of St. Molaise on Inishmurray Island, off the Donegal coast

Most of the early monasteries were made of wood (fig 6.2) or were of post-and-wattle construction (fig 6.3), but they were built over or used as burial grounds in the following years, so little can be discovered about them. In the west of Ireland and on some coastal islands, monasteries were built in stone and the remains of these are better preserved.

Cogitosus describes the monastery of Kildare in his 7th-century *Life of St Brigid*, saying it was 'a vast and Metropolitan City ... with suburbs which Brigid had

FIG 6.2 A wooden church

FIG 6.3 A wattle and daub church

marked out' and an 'ornate cashel', a 'spacious site' and a 'Cathedral Church' of 'awesome height' which was divided internally into three parts by wooden screens. The remains of St Brigid and Bishop Conleth, the co-founders of this rare community of both nuns and brothers, were placed at either side of the altar that was 'adorned with a profusion of gold, silver, gems and precious stones'.

The style of early buildings

We have some idea of how these early buildings may have looked from written accounts in the Annals and from images created in other crafts, such as the painting of the temple on the 'Temptation of Christ' page in the Book of Kells (fig 6.4) and a number of house-shaped shrines. The cap of Muiredach's Cross at Clonmacnoise is also house shaped (fig 6.5). The little 12th-century stone church on St Macdara's Island in Co. Galway copies the detail of the wooden construction of an earlier church down to carvings in the shape of shingles on the roof (fig 6.6). The sheer plainness of these early churches reflects the austerity and self-denial of the early Christian monks in Ireland.

FIG 6.5 Muiredach's Cross cap

FIG 6.4 BOOK OF KELLS, temptation of Christ, folio 200v

108

Churches had a simple, rectangular plan and varied from being almost square to being, more commonly, twice the length of the width. They had a small window in the east gable and the western doorway would have allowed little natural light to penetrate. Some later churches had additional small windows towards the eastern end of the sidewalls. Wooden churches had steeply pitched roofs covered in thatch or wooden shingles; this design tradition was followed when churches were built in stone. There has been much debate about the age of the simplest stone churches in Ireland. There is little mention

FIG 6.6 Church on St McDaraghs Island, Co. Galway

FIG 6.7 Monastery on Skellig Michael

of stone buildings in the texts before the 9th century. Carbon dating has produced a timescale of 640 to 790 AD for some of the corbelled buildings on the Dingle peninsula, which puts them close to the beginning of the development of stone churches in Ireland.

Skellig Michael

The well-preserved monastic settlement on Skellig Michael off the Kerry coast consists of a group of corbelled buildings and stone enclosures (fig 6.7). Corbelling was an ancient method of construction dating back to the Stone Age. It was used at Newgrange. Corbelling allows the builders to create a dome or arch of stone by laying each progressive course of stone a little further inside the one below, creating an inward curve which continues until the walls meet at the top. There are both dome-shaped and rectangular corbelled buildings on Skellig Michael. Some are as large as 9 m in diameter and 4.5 m tall. The settlement on the Skelligs would not have been a typical monastery, clinging as it does to the crags of an island 180 m above the Atlantic, but it does give us an idea of the scale and complexity of early monasteries (fig 6.8).

FIG 6.8 Oratories on Skellig Michael

Gallarus Oratory

Gallarus Oratory on the Dingle peninsula is the best-preserved and most complete of the group of corbelled rectangular oratories on the mainland. The sidewalls form one continuous surface from ground to ridge and are supported by inward-leaning gables. The doorway has inclined jambs (the opening is narrower at the top than at the bottom) and a plain lintel. The tiny east window has a round top cut from two stones, not a true arch (fig 6.9). The dry stone construction uses carefully selected stones, larger at the corners and at the base, smaller and lighter towards the top and centre, where a cave-in was more likely to happen. The stones were laid down sloping out from the centre of the wall and trimmed to an even surface on the outside to shed the rain and wind.

FIG 6.9 Gallarus oratory, south and west sides, Dingle peninsula, Co. Kerry. The thickness of the wall can be seen through the doorway

Stone carving

As we have seen in relation to the construction of monasteries, stone was not the material of choice during the 5th and 6th centuries. The development of carved stone monuments evolved over several hundred years. Because of gaps in the progression of design and technique, it is difficult to work out the reasons for the form and variety of the monuments that remain.

The carved pillar

Ogham stones

The earliest form of vertical stone monument from the Christian period is the ogham stones. Dating from the 4th and 5th centuries AD, they are found mainly along the southern end of the country, from Co. Wexford to

FIG 6.10 Ogham stone at Traigh an Fhiona on the Dingle peninsula. The inscription is translated as CUNAMAQQI CORBBI MAQQS

Co. Kerry. A few examples are found in Britain in areas which once supported Irish colonies, but they are mainly of Irish origin (fig 6.10).

Ogham was a form of Latin script simplified down to marks across a line or around the corner edge of a stone. Its origins may be in the marks made on counting sticks which were used to keep tally in trade with the Roman colonies.

Most ogham stones are plain, untrimmed pillars set up to commemorate an important person from the community. The name of the deceased person and the father's name is usually all that appears on the stones. Ogham writing is also found on stones with Latin inscriptions and cross designs.

Cross-inscribed pillars

Upright pillars and slabs with crosses inscribed into their surfaces are found at some of the earliest monastic sites. The decoration is usually a simple linear pattern carved into the surface of untrimmed stones. It can include Latin and Irish inscriptions with Greek, Latin or Maltese crosses, sometimes inside a circle. The Chi-Rho monogram (a symbol for Christ), swastikas, simple knots, fretwork, spirals and curves can also appear as part of the design repertoire. Most of these elements, except the Christian symbols, were in the La Tène style already in use during the Iron Age in Ireland (fig 6.11).

110

FIG 6.11 Cross inscribed pillar from Kilshannaig graveyard, Co. Kerry

Cross inscribed pillar from Mount Brandon, Co. Kerry

Engraved slab from Inishkea, north Co. Mayo

Cross-inscribed pillars are often found close to early churches and tradition suggests that some of them mark the grave of the founding saint, which would have become a focus for pilgrimage in the following centuries. The majority of this type of monument is found in the western part of the country from Co. Kerry to Co. Donegal.

Reask Pillar

The cross-inscribed pillar in the walled monastic enclosure at Reask (fig 6.12) on the Dingle peninsula in Co. Kerry dates back to the 7th century. It has a Maltese cross excavated in low relief, surrounded by a circle. A pattern of spirals extends down from the circle, ending in a pelta shape. The letters DNE are inscribed on the left of the shaft; they probably stand for the Latin word *domine*, meaning 'lord', and may refer to the 'Lord our God' or possibly the 'Lord Abbott'. All the design elements on this pillar relate to late La Tène design, and the delicate line contrasts with the crude surface of the stone on which it was carved.

Pillars and slabs are difficult to date because they are so simply decorated and many have no inscription, which could help put them in a context. Cross slabs could date to any time from the 5th to the 10th centuries AD, and

FIG 6.12 Reask Pillar, on the Dingle peninsula, Co. Kerry

they are not necessarily the forerunners of the Celtic high cross, but a separate type of monument. Whatever future research may find, it is interesting to look at these simple monuments here before we come to the more elaborate high crosses.

Manuscripts (book painting)

The importance of books in an Irish monastery

The books of the Bible were central to the practice of Christianity. A monk in an early Christian monastery needed a copy of the Bible and other texts for the daily readings and singing that were the centre of his life. Before the invention of printing in the 15th century, all books had to be copied by hand. This included not only Bibles, but books of prayers and services, texts on Latin grammar and all kinds of scholarly works that were needed for the education of members of the clergy and nobility.

Latin was the language of educated people throughout Europe; clerics and educated nobles could join in Church services and communicate with each other anywhere on the Continent. All Church ceremonies were conducted in Latin. Education began with Latin so that students could read the texts and further their knowledge.

Books were very precious, not simply because of the time and effort that went into their making, but as sources of knowledge and, often, as the word of God. Carelessly copied texts would be regarded as an insult to God, whose words were being transcribed. Monks offered their work as a prayer, so they tried to make it as perfect and beautiful as they could.

Making books

Not only had books to be written by hand, but every part had to be produced from raw materials. There was no source of ready-made pages, inks or pens. The scribe had to make everything from what was available locally or what could be imported. Pages had to be made and assembled into book form.

Vellum

In Ireland, vellum was the preferred material from which to make pages. Vellum is calf skin. To prepare it, it was placed in a bath of water and lime, or excrement, for some days to loosen the hairs on the skin. Timing was an important element because if the skin was left too long in the bath, it would become prone to bacterial attack. (The Book of Kells has suffered a little from this problem,

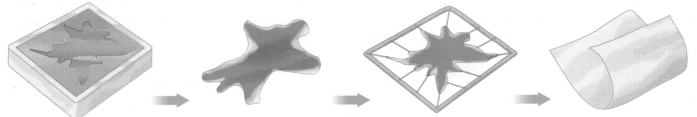

| Calf skin soaked to loosen hair and impurities | Impurities scraped off calf skin | Stretched flat on frame | Cut into bifolium (double page size) |

FIG 6.13 Making vellum

for example.) After the bath, the skin was cleaned and scraped free of hair and impurities with a blade. Next it was rubbed smooth with a pumice stone. The hide was then stretched flat and dried before it was cut into pages. The vellum could be sewn into rolls or made into a codex (groups of pages sewn together into book form). The codex became the more popular form, as it was easier to refer to and to store (fig 6.13). (Pages were also made from goat or sheep skin, which is known as parchment.)

Inks and pigments

Black and dark inks were made in a variety of ways. Carbon inks were made from burnt wood or animal fat and remained black, but they were prone to flaking off the page. Iron gall ink was made by mixing iron sulphate with crushed oak galls and gum to bind them together. This mixture was carried in a solution of water, wine or vinegar. Disadvantages of iron gall ink were that the iron etched into the vellum and the gall sometimes faded to shades of brown.

The earliest books that have survived used very little colour, just a little red or yellow dotting around the capital letters at the beginning of new sections.

The Cathach

One of the earliest surviving Irish manuscripts is The Cathach, or the Psalter of St Columba. It is the oldest extant Irish manuscript of the Psalter (a copy of the Book of Psalms) and the earliest example of Irish writing. Traditionally, this book is from the hand of St Columba (Colm Cille, the 'Dove of the Church'), who lived from 521 to 597. He was the founder of the Columban order of monks who continued the tradition of manuscript writing and missionary work begun by their first abbot. Unfortunately, only 58 damaged pages of the work survive (fig 6.14).

The name *Cathach*, an Irish word meaning 'battler', was given to the book by the O'Donnells, clansmen of Columba, who carried it with them into battle, invoking the protection of the saint. This is reputed to be the book which Columba transcribed in haste without the permission of his master, Finnian, bringing about a court case which ruled 'to every cow its calf, to every book its copy'. Columba's clansmen disputed the court case and fought the battle of Cuil Dremhne for ownership of the book. The story goes that Columba was so horrified by the death and destruction of the battle that he banished himself on permanent pilgrimage and exile from home. This *peregrinatio* involved a life of prayer and self-denial while spreading the word of God to the heathen. His travels took him first to Iona, an island off the coast of Scotland, where he founded a monastery, which was to

FIG 6.14 Folio 21a of THE CATHACH

become the chief house of the Columban *paruchia* (family of monasteries) for the next 200 years. The missionary work then continued through Scotland to Northumbria in northern England.

The tradition of care and love of manuscript writing which Columba fostered in his followers can be seen in the quote from his biographer, Adamnan:

> I beseech all those who may wish to copy these books, nay more, I adjure them through Christ, the judge of all the ages, that, after carefully copying, they compare them with the exemplar from which they have been written, and emend them with the utmost care.

This care can be seen in The Cathach, which is written in a clear majuscule script with enlarged capitals introducing each Psalm. The lettering is in a peculiarly Irish style, different from the Roman models, examples of which the first missionaries must have brought with them. In a few generations Irish Christians had not only learned to read and write in Latin, but had created a style of lettering and decoration of their own, quite different from the Roman books they had first encountered.

Majuscule is a style of rounded capital letter written between two ruled lines with very few ascenders or descenders above or below these lines. The decoration employed by the scribes seems to follow from the La

Tène style, as it incorporates trumpet ends, spirals and a few animal and plant forms, along with the Christian cross and fish symbols.

The writing was carried out with reed or quill pens, in dark ink with some dotting in red and yellow surrounding the capital letters. Folio 6a of The Cathach (fig 6.15) shows the *diminuendo* effect where the initial letter takes up four lines and the following letters gradually reduce in size until they are back to the general text size. This is a characteristic feature of Irish script, not seen in Roman models. The opening letter Q of Psalm 91, which begins 'Qui habitat. . .' (fig 6.16), shows a range of the designs used in this manuscript. A little spring spiral, an animal head and a cross are all added to the tail of the Q and a row of pen flourishes decorates the inside. The *diminuendo* effect can clearly be seen over these opening words. The letter M, which opens the psalm on Folio 21a, is decorated with spirals and trumpet ends. The simple decoration employed in The Cathach is echoed in contemporary stone and metalwork. A small repertoire of designs and patterns forms the basis for the amazingly elaborate work produced by the following generations of craftsmen.

FIG 6.15 **Folio 6a of THE CATHACH**

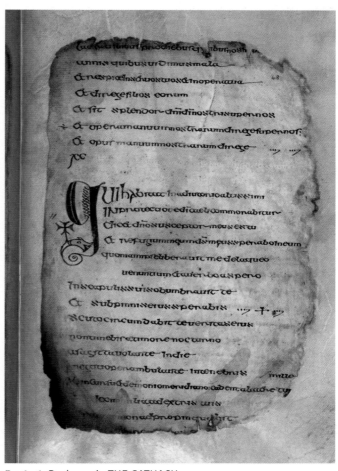

FIG 6.16 **Psalm 91 in THE CATHACH**

FIG 6.17 Simple penannular brooches

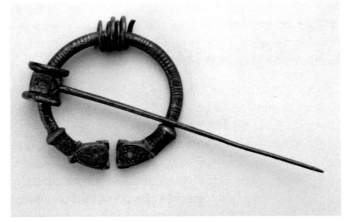

FIG 6.18 Ballinderry Penannular Brooch

Metalwork

Roman designs found their way into Ireland through contacts with Britain and Gaul. At this time a new range of objects appeared in Ireland, among them hand pins, penannular brooches, latchets and hanging bowls.

Of these, penannular (broken circle) brooches might best show the kind of development that took place. The earliest brooches were simple wire dress fasteners, with the ends beside the opening in the ring bent back to retain the pin, which was connected to it by a loop. Later brooches were cast in bronze or silver (fig 6.17). As time passed, the decorated areas beside the opening of the ring and the loop connecting the pin to the ring were enlarged to incorporate more elaborate designs.

The Ballinderry Brooch

This brooch, which was found at a crannog near Ballinderry, Co. Westmeath, is a beautiful example of the style (fig 6.18). There is millefiori glass decoration on the ends of the ring and on the pin head and there is a range of textures and patterns on the cast bronze brooch that form a zoomorph on each end of the ring. Later brooches became even more elaborate and new techniques emerged through trade with Europe. Gold-wire filigree is found in a few small pieces dating back to the 6th century. A small bird-shaped button was found in Lagore Crannog, where millefiori glass was also discovered in an enameller's workshop.

The new designs, which first appeared on Celtic high crosses and in illuminated books, also made their way into metalwork. The Ardakillin Brooch, for example, has ribbon interlace as part of its design, and the relief patterns at each end seem to have something in common with a capital M from The Cathach.

Conclusion

The Christian mission to Ireland brought with it new ideas and influences from abroad which were incorporated into all the crafts. Further opportunities were created by the introduction of decorated books and the demand for beautiful metalwork and stone carving in the new and rapidly expanding monasteries. During the 5th and 6th centuries, technical skills and the repertoire of designs gradually increased to the point where all the elements needed for the explosion of creativity that happened in the 7th and 8th centuries were gathered together in the workshops of the larger monasteries.

Questions

1. Describe the layout of an early monastery and identify the function of its buildings.
2. List the different kinds of construction methods that might have been used to build an early monastery.
3. How did Christianity come to Ireland and how was it adapted to Irish society?
4. Describe two pieces of metalwork from the 5th and 6th centuries, noting any Continental influence.

Essay

1. Write an account of how books were made in an early monastery. Use words and sketches to describe the decoration of one early manuscript.

Colour picture study

1. Look at the examples of the early carved pillars and explain their function and decoration in words and sketches (fig 6.12).

CHAPTER 7

THE GOLDEN AGE (7TH AND 8TH CENTURIES)

Political and social background

In the 7th and 8th centuries, Europe became more stable through the establishment of strong kingdoms in the areas that are now France and Germany. Much of Europe was converted to Christianity and the influence of the papacy had become stronger. Clergy from France converted southern Britain.

In Ireland, there was also a strengthening of political and monastic dynasties. The Uí Néill, kings of Tara, controlled the Midlands and a good part of Northern Ireland. They made an alliance with the Dál Riata, who were kings of Antrim and Argyll, which extended their influence into Scotland. The Uí Néill were in conflict with the Eóganachta dynasty of Munster for 400 years.

There was a growth in the importance of monasteries in Ireland. They had become centres of learning and places of refuge for pilgrims, the sick, widows and orphans. Kells, Armagh, Glendalough, Clonmacnoise and other large monasteries grew in size and population and took on a new economic importance in the community. The simple austerity of the early monasteries was replaced by wealth and power, which resulted in conflicts between monasteries. In 790 AD, a war was fought between the monks of Clonmacnoise and the monks of Durrow.

The missionary work which began on Iona in the previous century spread to Britain and Europe. St Aidan, a follower of St Columba, was invited by King Oswald of Northumbria to build a monastery on the island of Lindisfarne, off the east coast of England. He had great success in converting the people of Northumbria to Christianity. St Columbanus, another Columban monk, set up monasteries in France, Switzerland and Bobbio, in northern Italy.

When the Irish monks came in contact with European clergy, differences in their practices created difficulties. The Irish Church, which had been out of direct contact with Rome, had retained some ancient practices, particularly a way of calculating the date of Easter, which was not acceptable to the papacy. The Synod of Whitby in 664 AD settled these differences, but they were slow to make the required changes in Ireland.

Influences on design

Over a number of centuries, influences from outside Ireland mixed with native Irish design and evolved into a style that was used in all the crafts during the 7th and 8th centuries. These include:

- Spirals and pelta shapes, which had their origins in Celtic design and which had already been in use for 800 years at this time.
- Interlace, which is Coptic in origin and which probably came to Ireland via the Mediterranean countries and Rome in particular, which was strongly influenced by the Middle East in early medieval times.
- Animal ornament, which was of Germanic origin and would have been introduced through Anglo-Saxon influences in Northumbria, which had close Irish connections.

Iconography

Iconography refers to the identification, description and interpretation of images. Though it is difficult to be certain about the meanings or significance that the artists of the early Middle Ages intended to include into their work, we are able to understand and interpret a certain amount today. (As we move forward, the meanings will be given with the work as it is examined. This may result in some repetition but, it is hoped, less confusion on the part of the reader.)

Structures (architecture)

Very little architecture survives that can be dated with any certainty to the 7th and 8th centuries. A few stone churches that would originally have had wooden roofs may date from this time. These churches have antae, projections of the side walls beyond the surface of the

FIG 7.1 Church with antae, Scattery Island, Co. Clare. Later alterations to the roofline can be seen.

gables, which may be an imitation in stone of corner posts from wooden buildings (fig 7.1).

At this time monasteries seem to have been laid out in the same way as they were in the previous century, with a surrounding bank of earth or stone enclosing small stone or wooden buildings. This kind of enclosure could easily be expanded by adding more small buildings and moving the bank farther out to enclose a wider area (fig 7.2).

Stone carving

Cross-decorated slabs, simple crosses and grave slabs became more common in the monasteries of the 7th and 8th centuries.

The Fahan Mura Slab

At Fahan Mura in Co. Donegal, on the site of the monastery founded by St Columba for his disciple Mura, stands a stone 2.10 m tall dating to the end of the 7th

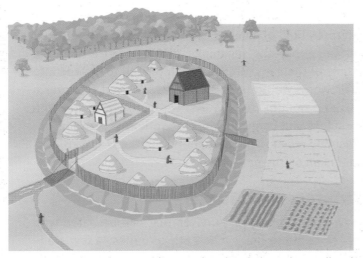

FIG 7.2 Monastic enclosure with a wooden church, boundary wall and huts made of wattle and daub with thatched roofs.

FIG 7.3 Fahan Mura Slab, west face

century AD (fig 7.3). This decorated slab marks a further development in the art of stone carving in Ireland. Fully trimmed and dressed, the design of the stone is related to Pictish slabs found in Scotland. A pattern of ribbon interlace is formed into a cross shape on both faces. On the west face, simple human figures stand at the left and right of the cross shaft. Each of these figures has an undeciphered inscription on their tunic. There are little stubs projecting from the side of the slab, which some commentators regard as the beginnings of the arms that appear on later crosses. This is a far more sophisticated piece of stone craftsmanship than we have seen before, and the accuracy of the design and the refinement of the low-relief carving mark an important development in the evolution of Irish stone carving.

The Carndonagh Cross

The cross at Carndonagh in Co. Donegal (fig 7.4) has been regarded in the past as the transitional piece between stone slabs and pillars and the fully formed Celtic high cross. Scholars now contend that this cross is more likely to be contemporary with the early wheel-head crosses,

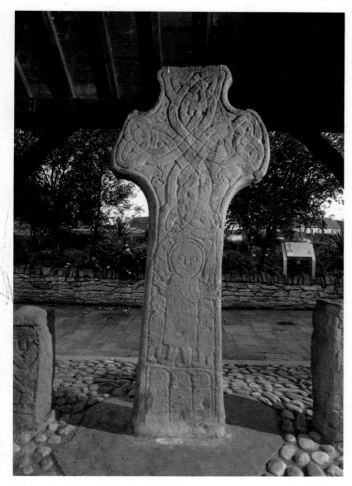

FIG 7.4 Carndonagh Cross, east face

monastic connections between Donegal and Scotland. The design in ribbon interlace on both faces of the cross has echoes in the designs found on Pictish cross slabs in Scotland. The unevenly shaped cross stands 2.53 m tall and the ribbon interlace on the east face forms a cross on the upper part of the stone, with a little group of birds forming a triskele pattern in the crook of each arm. On the shaft there is a crucifixion scene. Other groups of figures are not clearly identified. There are small pillars beside the cross, carved with figures representing David playing the harp, Jonah and the whale and ecclesiastics with bell and crosier, all of which are themes that occur on other crosses. The figures and patterns are simple and linear with a few areas of low relief. Detail could have been added by painting, creating an effect like the figure pages in the Book of Durrow.

Decorated grave slabs

Stone markers, laid flat on the ground, were the traditional style of gravestone from the 7th to the 10th centuries AD at the important monastic sites. The monastery at Clonmacnoise in Co. Offaly preserves a particularly good collection in a variety of sizes and patterns. Small slabs with a Greek cross inside a square seem to be the earliest type. A simple inscription, giving only a name, is all that accompanies the linear cross design. Larger, more elaborately carved slabs asking a prayer for the departed are probably from the 9th and 10th centuries, the period of the Viking invasions (fig 7.5). These slabs were enhanced by accurately

but in a different style tradition. Like the slab at Fahan Mura, the Carndonagh Cross design may relate to the

FIG 7.5 Two grave slabs. On the left is a decorated cross in a square frame, Durrow, Co. Offaly. The inscription reads 'OR DO CATHALAN'. On the right is a decorated cross with ring and terminals, Durrow, Co. Offaly. The inscription reads 'OR DO AIGIDIU'

carved crosses with fret and spiral patterns decorating the centre and terminals. The designs executed on the grave slabs often resemble patterns in metalwork and book illumination and are elegant linear designs accurately executed on the flat surface of the stone.

Manuscripts (book painting)

The Insular style

New Irish establishments founded in Britain and Europe would originally have been stocked with books made in Ireland, and Irish monks probably trained the scribes in these monasteries. Influences from British and Continental traditions in art also found their way back into Ireland with migrating monks. Books in the style called Insular survived in many European monasteries. Scholars today can't be certain about where every book was actually written, but there is a strong element of the Irish Celtic tradition in them all.

Not many books survive from the 7th century. There are some from the monastery of St Columbanus at Bobbio in northern Italy. We are very lucky to have an outstanding example in this country – the Book of Durrow.

The Book of Durrow

The Book of Durrow is the earliest example of a fully decorated manuscript in the Insular style. It is a copy of the Four Gospels with some preliminary texts. It contains 248 folios (leaves) of vellum, most of which have writing or decoration on both sides. There are 12 fully decorated pages and many more with decorated capitals. The script is in the Irish majuscule style, written in long lines across the page. Books of a similar type written in Lindisfarne and other Northumbrian monasteries with Irish connections were generally written in two columns. Smaller pocket gospels were also written in columns.

The text is a copy of the Latin Vulgate version of the New Testament, which St Jerome compiled for Pope Damasus in the late 4th century AD, in an effort to create a correct and standard translation of the books of the Bible.

The origins of the book

There has been much discussion in the past as to the origin of the Book of Durrow. Its associations with the Columban monastery at Durrow can be verified as early as 877 AD as well as in 916 AD, when it was enshrined in a metal case (which is now lost). The book seems to be older than these dates, so it was probably written in the late 7th or early 8th century. The interlace pattern relates to designs on the Fahan Mura Slab and the Carndonagh Cross, which were near the Columban monastery of Derry. The animals on the carpet page at the beginning of the Gospel of John relate to Saxon or Germanic designs that might suggest a Columban monastery in Northumbria, where Saxon influence was strong. It may have been given as a gift from the chief Columban monastery of Iona or it might have been produced at the scriptorium of Durrow itself.

The book we see today is in remarkably good condition considering the ups and downs of its 1,300 years of existence. It was knocked about during its enshrining in a metal *cumdach* in 916 and its value as a miraculous object led its custodians in the 17th century to dip it in water they used to cure sick cattle. There is some staining and loss of colour due to this treatment. It has been in the care of Trinity College Library in Dublin since the late 17th century and was completely restored and rebound in 1954.

Making the book

The Book of Durrow was written on vellum pages. (The process for making vellum is described above.) To assemble the pages into a codex, the vellum would have been cut into bifoliae (a bifolium is a strip of vellum that is doubled over to create two pages), which were collected into groups called gatherings. These gatherings were then sewn together to form the codex or book.

Writing tools

Pens were made from the tail feathers of the goose or swan or from cut reeds. Brushes could be made from a variety of hairs tied into a goose quill ferrule. The hair of the marten could have been used for the finest brushes. A straight edge, a compass and dividers would have been needed for ruling out the pages and laying out designs.

The colours

Colours for the Book of Durrow were made in a variety of ways. The orange-red was made from red lead, which is white lead that is heated, pulverised, washed, put back in an oven and stirred for two to three days until it reaches the correct intensity of colour. The resulting pigment was quite toxic. A yellow colour could be made from ox gall, but it often discoloured to brown. A purer, brighter yellow was made from orpiment (from the Latin *auripigmentum*, which means, 'gold pigment'), a yellow arsenic sulphate which had to be imported from parts of Europe or Asia and is both toxic and foul smelling. Chemically, it reacts with lead or copper-based colours. Green was most commonly made from verdigris, which is copper acetate, created by the action of ascetic acid and heat on copper. Sheets of copper smeared with honey and ground salt were placed in a hollowed-out section of oak which was filled with vinegar or hot urine, capped with wood and buried in dung for four weeks. Pigment could be scraped from the copper plates at intervals after this time. (Verdigris can be unstable, however, and it has eaten through the vellum in parts of the Book of Durrow.)

Scheme of decoration

The Book of Durrow is a richly decorated codex designed for use on the altar and for display on special occasions. The book opens with some decorated pages. The first is a carpet page with a design in the shape of a double-armed cross (fig 7.6). In the Coptic tradition of the eastern Mediterranean, double-armed metal crosses were used to house a fragment of the true cross, and the design may invoke the protection that such a relic would bring. The cross design includes eight squares, which may refer to the eighth day of Christ's Passion, The Resurrection. These symbols would announce the core message of the Bible – the death and resurrection of Christ for the sake of his faithful followers and mankind in general.

The Four Evangelists

The second decorated page (Folio 2r) consists of a cross surrounded by the symbols of the Four Evangelists. These are framed in a pattern of squares in red, yellow and green that is quite faded and damaged (fig 7.7). The origins of the images of the Four Evangelists is based on text in the Old Testament (Ezekiel 1:5–14) and in the New Testament (Revelations 4:6–8). The creatures of these visions became associated with the Four Evangelists through the writing of St Irenaus in the 2nd century, who compared them to the four regions of the cosmos and the four winds, which together symbolised the spread of

FIG 7.6 BOOK OF DURROW, folio 1v

FIG 7.7 BOOK OF DURROW, folio 2r

the gospels. St Gregory, writing in the 4th century, identified the visionary figures as four stages of Christ's life: he was born as a man, put to death as a sacrificial calf, resurrected with the power of a lion and ascended into heaven like an eagle. St Jerome identified the man with Matthew, the lion with Mark, the ox with Luke and the eagle with John. In the Book of Durrow, the symbols are assigned by an older arrangement where the lion is John and an eagle is Mark. On the Four Evangelists page, the artist has arranged the figures so that if you read them clockwise you get the older order and anti-clockwise you get the more correct version according to St Jerome.

Carpet page

The third page (Folio 3v) is also decorated. It is a carpet page, so called because of the resemblance of these abstract patterned pages to the design on Turkish carpets. The design is based on circles decorated with trumpet and spiral patterns set in a border of six-ribbon interlace with four knots in each roundel (fig 7.8). The pattern of trumpets and spirals resembles contemporary metalwork. There are 42 spirals on this page, which may be a reminder of the 42 generations of the ancestors of Christ mentioned in the Gospel of Matthew.

Canon tables

The pages following the decorated ones discussed above contain the canon tables and additional writings that are included to help the reader with context for the books of the New Testament. The canon tables divide the gospels into sections, which are laid out in a grid so the reader can locate a passage or incident from one gospel in the others.

The Four Gospels

Beginning on Folio 21v are the books of the Four Gospels. Each begins with an evangelist symbol page, followed by a carpet page. (The one exception is in the case of the Gospel of Matthew, which is missing the carpet page. It was probably misplaced sometime over the centuries. Indeed, the book was quite jumbled up before it was restored in 1954.) The first page of each gospel has a decorated capital letter and the opening lines are usually larger than the general text and are surrounded by red dotting.

The 'man symbol'

The 'man symbol' at the beginning of the Gospel of Matthew is shaped like a contemporary Irish bell; there is no sign of arms or details of clothing (fig 7.9). The check pattern looks like millefiori glass decoration created in

Fig 7.8 BOOK OF DURROW, folio 3v

Fig 7.9 BOOK OF DURROW, folio 21v, the man symbol

7th- and 8th-century metalwork and the overall shape of the figure is like those on the Carndonagh Cross and the Cross of Moone. There is an area of plain vellum around the figure, which is surrounded by a border of ribbon interlace in shades of yellow and green. The area between the ribbons has been darkened for dramatic effect and a triangle of plain vellum breaks each dark, triangular space into three parts, probably a reference to the Holy Trinity which is picked up again on Folio 23, the Chi-Rho page, where the name of Christ is mentioned for the first time in the gospel.

The Chi-Rho

The Greek letters *X*, *P* and *I* are the first three letters of the Greek word meaning 'Christ'. They are combined into a monogram for Christ called the Chi-Rho (after the first two letters, *chi* and *rho*). Here, the Chi-Rho monogram is beautifully decorated with fine spring spirals and trumpets and surrounded inside and out by a field of red dotting, except for the space between the *X* and *P*, which has little triangles of dots. The centre of the A has a trinquetra knot, a symbol of the Trinity (fig 7.10). The little cross at the top of the X is similar to the one on the tail of the Q at the beginning of Psalm 91 in The Cathach. The enlarged letter-size at the beginning of each passage is a development of the *diminuendo* effect we saw in The Cathach. The most elaborately decorated letters are the opening lines at the beginning of each gospel.

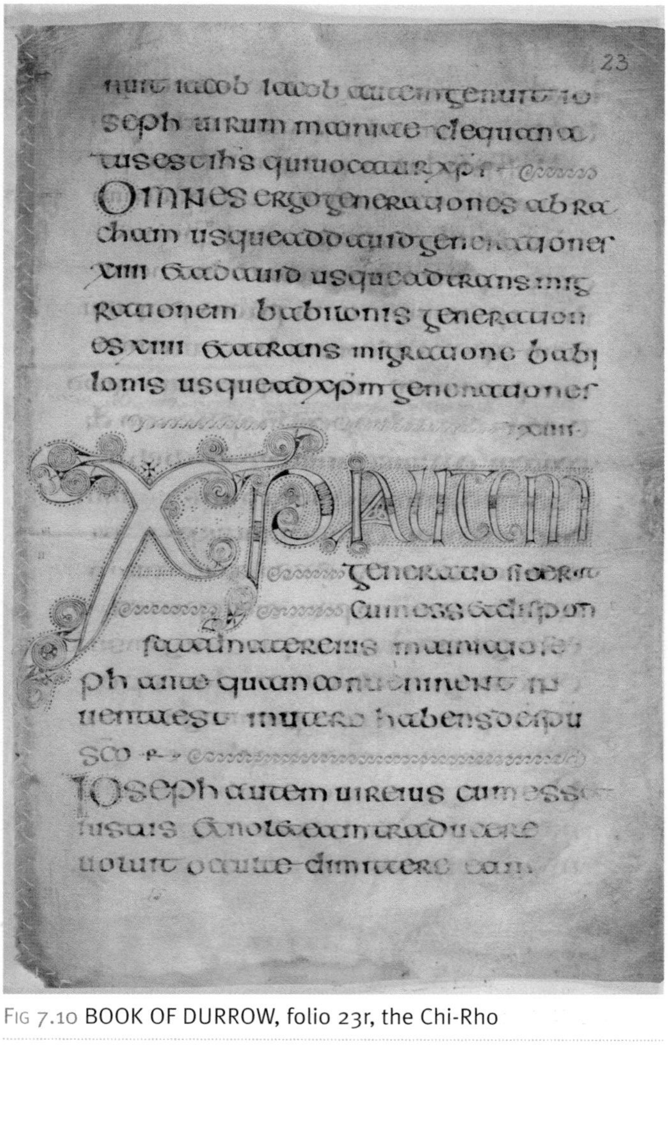

Initial letter pages

The Initium page (Folio 86r) at the beginning of the Gospel of Mark is the best preserved of the initial pages (fig 7.11). The letter *I* takes up three-quarters of the height of the page with a sharp diminuendo to the *N*, *I* and *T*. The first three lines are surrounded with red dotting. The spirals and trumpet scrolls that decorate the ends of the *I* and *N* become zoomorphs on closer inspection.

Interlace and number symbolism

In some cultures, interlace patterns are considered to be a protection from evil. Intricate patterns, particularly those with animal heads, were thought to be capable of confusing and intimidating evil spirits. This may be a reason for the inclusion of such patterns at the beginning of the manuscript and at the start of each gospel.

Fig 7.10 BOOK OF DURROW, folio 23r, the Chi-Rho

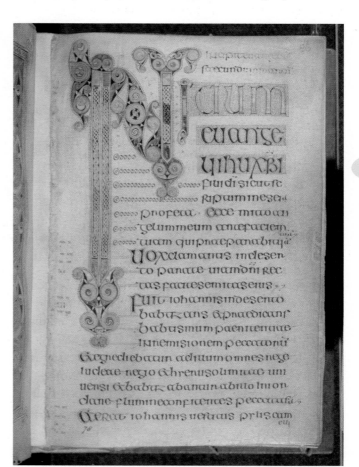

Fig 7.11 BOOK OF DURROW, folio 86r, the Initium page

FIG 7.12 BOOK OF DURROW, folio 192v, animal interlace page

Number symbolism is a common theme in early medieval Christian art. It was designed to aid the contemplation of the reader and to help divine new layers of meaning in the texts. A four-part design could imply a range of associations, including the Four Gospels, the Four Evangelists, the four cardinal virtues, the four rivers of Paradise, the four rings which carried the Arc of the Covenant, the four qualities of Christ and other biblical meanings, depending on the context of the design.

The page of interlaced animals on Folio 192v at the beginning of the Gospel of John is one of the highlights of the Book of Durrow; it is full of number symbolism (fig 7.12). The circle in the middle of the page has a cross at its centre, which is surrounded by a three-part interlace pattern in red, yellow and green. (Notice the repeating patterns of green triangles.) Three discs with a black-and-white step pattern, making crosses, punctuate the rim of the circle. These discs look like glass studs with wire grilles, of the type found on the Ardagh Chalice and the Derrynaflan Paten. The emphasis on three-part patterns within the circle is a reference to

the Trinity; the panels of three biting dogs to left and right might also have this underlying meaning. The panels of elongated animals in the top and bottom sections are alike, but they are not mirror images of each other. (It can be interesting to unravel an animal interlace and see how the leg, tail or jaw can be extended to loop around other limbs or back on itself to fit the artist's pattern.) The inner rows of eight animals refer to the eighth day of the passion of Christ, the Resurrection. The top and bottom patterns have 10 animals in each panel, a reference to St Augustine's perfect number, 10, which symbolised unity. There are 42 animals on the page, which may be a reference to the 42 generations of the ancestors of Christ.

A number of 8th-century gospel books survive. There are three in Great Britain: a gospel book fragment (in the Durham Cathedral Library), the Lindisfarne Gospel and the Lichfield Gospel. Gospel books in Echternach, in Luxembourg, Maihingen in Germany and the Cathedral Library of St Gall, in Switzerland, are all written in the Irish style of script. They all have portraits of the evangelists, carpet pages, decorated initials, animal interlace and a wide range of colours. These books give us a wider picture of the style and quality of Irish manuscripts (fig 7.13).

FIG 7.13 The Lindisfarne Gospels Cross carpet page

It is notable that at this time an increasing number of books were being written in Irish, such as commentaries, legal documents and books of a more secular nature. They are among the earliest European books written in a non-classical language.

Metalwork

The metalwork produced in Ireland in the 7th and 8th centuries is of a very high quality. It is easily the most elegant and technically refined work created in any part of Europe during the early Middle Ages. Before we look at the objects themselves, let's take a look at some of the techniques metalworkers used at the time.

Techniques

Enamelling

A variety of techniques were used in enamelling.
- Cloisonné: Areas of design were surrounded with silver, gold or bronze wire and filled with enamel.
- Champlevé: An old Celtic technique, in which areas of a surface were carved away or beaten hollow and the spaces created were filled with enamel.
- Millefiori: Rods of coloured glass were heated and drawn together in a molten state and stretched into long, thin rods from which fine sections could be cut off and applied to enamel surfaces. The sections can look like flowers, hence the name, *millefiori*, meaning 'a thousand flowers'.

Studs

Studs were cast in clay moulds. Some had wire grilles fitted into the mould and were then filled with coloured glass enamel. Other studs were cast with hollow spaces, which then could be filled with a second colour.

Filigree

Filigree consisted of fine gold wires that were twisted together into a fine rope. Sometimes wires of different sizes were twisted together to create a more glittering effect. The filigree was bent into shape and soldered to a gold foil background that could then be fixed in its place (fig 7.14).

Chip carving

Chip carving was a technique of carving metal in high relief, creating sharp outlines and deep shadows.

FIG 7.14 Detail of Ardagh Chalice showing a variety of manufacturing techniques, such as filigree, enamel and engraving.

Casting

A variety of methods and techniques were used in casting. Clay and bone moulds were used to create both plain and decorated objects. The lost wax technique was used for more complicated objects. Chip carving was sometimes imitated in cast designs.

Engraving

Engraving involved cutting a design into a metal surface with a sharp point. Sometimes two metals were laid one on top of the other so that the colour below would be revealed when the upper metal was engraved.

Die stamping

Die stamping involved stamping a thin sheet of metal, usually gold or silver, with a design that had been carved into a block of wood or cast into metal.

Turning

In turning, a sheet of metal was pressed onto a former, rotating on a lathe, and gradually shaped into a bowl or cone shape as required. The lathe was also used to polish beaten metalwork.

Amber

Amber, which is fossilised resin, was cut to shape and used like enamel studs as a contrast to areas of filigree or chip carving. The amber could be heated and lightly moulded into shape (fig 7.15).

FIG 7.15 Detail of the Tara Brooch showing a variety of manufacturing techniques. The cast frame is a variety of filigree and enamelled areas.

Trichinopoly

Trichinopoly is a type of wire mesh made in copper, silver or gold. It is formed into chain on the Tara Brooch and is used to cover and the rim on the Derrynaflan Paten.

Gilding

There were two methods of gilding bronze or silver. Metalworkers could attach gold leaf mechanically, but this was not often done. The other method is fire-gilding. To do this, gold was dissolved in mercury and applied to the surface of the object. The object was then heated so that the mercury would evaporate, leaving a thin layer of gold on the object.

Objects

At the beginning of this chapter we noted three sources for the origins of Christian Celtic design. In the following metalwork objects, you will see how these basic elements were elaborated and distorted to create designs of the most extraordinary quality. There is nothing second-hand or copied in these designs – the elements were used with flair and originality to create a unique and subtly balanced art.

Penannular brooches

Penannular brooches continued to develop, with larger decorated areas covering up to half of the ring. This type of brooch is called pseudo-penannular because they look like penannular brooches, but the circle has been closed. Large numbers of penannular and pseudo-penannular brooches, ranging in size from 7 cm to 13 cm in diameter, are known from the 7th and 8th centuries. Of these, the Tara Brooch is the finest.

The Tara Brooch

The Tara Brooch was found near the mouth of the River Boyne, beside the sea, at Bettystown, Co. Meath, in 1850. Though some sections are damaged, enough remains to give a clear impression of the quality of craftsmanship and design that went into its manufacture (fig 7.16).

The body of the brooch, which is 8.7 cm in diameter, was cast in silver, creating a raised framework. The front face of the brooch is divided into panels of filigree, separated by amber and enamel studs. Most of the filigree is very

FIG 7.16 TARA BROOCH, front view

fine and is wrought into spiral and interlace patterns. In the panel that remains at the centre left of the brooch there is an amazing dog design. His body, which is made up of a range of different-textured filigree strands, turns back on itself in a pattern which tightly fits the triangular space. The dog, which is upside down when viewed from the front, would have been right way up for the wearer looking down at it. There is another animal like him on the head of the pin.

The reverse side of the brooch has sections cast in high relief, with zoomorphs and spiral patterns. Every part of the brooch that has not been decorated separately has been gilded. There are two flat, silvered copper plates with fine spiral patterns engraved into them, which are like the spiral patterns used in the Book of Durrow. These designs are in the triangular spaces at each side of the centre of the brooch. Glass and amber studs were also used on the back (fig 7.17).

Fantastic animals seem to be the theme of the Tara Brooch. They appear in the filigree sections, in cast areas on the back, at several places on the perimeter, on the pin and on the chain connection. The trichinopoly chain is attached to the rim by an intriguing series of animal heads with interlocked jaws. This link also contains two tiny human faces made of moulded blue glass.

At the time, there were laws controlling the size and quality of brooches that could be worn by people from different levels of society. Brooches may have been part

of clerical garb. They are shown on some of the figures carved on high crosses. One could read the pattern at the centre of the front of the Tara Brooch as a cross, so the animal patterns could have a Christian meaning.

Communion vessels

The large chalice and paten that survive from 8th-century Ireland (the Ardagh Chalice and the Derrynaflan Paten) are in a style not common in Europe. The closest comparable pieces are of an earlier date and from Syria. This does not necessarily mean that there were direct connections between Ireland and Syria, but it does point to differences in religious practice between Ireland and the rest of Europe. The large size of the vessels points to ceremonial use. The chalice was probably a *calyx ministerialis*, which would have been used to distribute wine to the congregation and was probably brought to the altar in an offertory procession.

The large paten would also have been used for distribution to the congregation and in procession. There are instructions in the Stowe Missal (a mass book of the early Irish Church) for the ceremonial breaking of bread, laying it out in the form of a wheeled cross on the paten, with different sections assigned to different parts of the congregation.

The Ardagh Chalice

The Ardagh Chalice was found in 1868, along with a small bronze chalice and three large brooches, in a hoard at Ardagh, Co. Limerick, by a boy digging potatoes. It is made up of a silver bowl connected to a conical foot by a gilt bronze collar. It is 17.8 cm high and 19.5 cm in diameter (fig 7.18).

FIG 7.17 TARA BROOCH, back view

FIG 7.18 ARDAGH CHALICE, front view

FIG 7.19 ARDAGH CHALICE, underside of foot

Many of the techniques that were used in making the Tara Brooch were also used in making the Ardagh Chalice. The decoration of the chalice is a masterpiece of subtlety and refinement, with an almost perfect balance between areas of sumptuous decoration and the plain silver of the bowl and foot (fig 7.19). A band of decoration just below the rim is made up of panels of gold filigree punctuated with 12 glass studs; the filigree is a mixture of animal and abstract panels. The names of the apostles are lightly engraved in a field of dots just below this band and are probably symbolised in the 12 studs.

The handles and the plaques, which attached them to the bowl, are decorated with gold filigree, red and blue enamel and glass studs inlaid with silver wire. Two medallions in the shape of a Greek cross in a circle are placed centrally on each side of the bowl of the chalice; they are also decorated with filigree and glass studs. The collar joining the bowl to the base is cast, in imitation of high-relief chip carving, in spiral and interlace patterns. A rim around the upper surface of the conical foot is decorated with filigree panels punctuated by squares of blue glass.

Underneath at the centre of the foot is a large glass crystal (which hides the bolt connecting the foot to the bowl). This is surrounded by three bands of decoration: the inner, an animal interlace, is in gold filigree; the middle has a chip-carved spiral decoration punctuated by small glass studs with gold granulations; and the outer has an abstract interlace pattern in the chip-carved style.

The Derrynaflan Paten

This paten is the only one of its kind to come to light so far. It was found in 1980 at the monastery of Derrynaflan in Co. Tipperary. It was buried under a bronze cauldron with a chalice and other objects (which will be discussed later). The paten is 35 cm in diameter and made of over 300 components. The beaten silver dish has a gilt bronze rim, which is decorated with gold filigree panels and enamel studs (fig 7.20).

FIG 7.20 *Derrynaflan Paten*, overall view from above

The design of the filigree panels relates closely to those on the Ardagh Chalice, as do the enamel studs. The quality of the decorative elements is very high. Animal, human and abstract designs are used in the filigree (fig 7.21). There are 24 glass studs around the upper rim of the paten; the number is probably a reference to the 24 elders of the Apocalypse who were seated around the throne of God. These studs are in two groups – 12 larger and 12 smaller. Perhaps this is an allusion to the apostles? The 12 smaller studs are set in little cups containing fine filigree; these studs hide the rivets that join the components of the paten together. All the studs are more patterned and colourful than any we have seen before. A ring of trichinopoly wire, in copper and silver, frames the decorated upper rim and conceals the joint between it and the side panels. The die-stamped gold panels on the side of the rim are decorated with interlace and scroll patterns. The panels on the foot are similar, but not as finely made.

FIG 7.21 Filigree panel with human figures and elaborate enamel studs.

FIG 7.22 The Emly Shrine

The discovery of this paten shows that work of the quality of the Ardagh Chalice and the Tara Brooch was not a rarity in Ireland in the 8th century. It adds to our understanding of the richness and quality of the craftwork of the period.

Shrines

When pilgrims arrived at a monastery, they wanted to see evidence of the saints associated with that place. A practice grew up of enclosing relics or objects associated with a saint in a decorated case that could be put on display in a prominent place in the monastery.

House shrines (a small house- or tomb-shaped shrine) were used to contain the bones or relics of a saint. The shrines had a leather neck strap so that they could be carried in processions or from place to place. Three of these Irish house shrines have been found in Italy, where they were brought in ancient times, possibly to collect relics of Italian saints or to carry Irish relics to Rome in order to have them blessed. Relic boxes and parts of them have also been found in Norway, where they were brought back with other treasure and broken up for reuse by raiding Vikings.

Book shrines were made to contain books associated with an important saint. While these shrines preserved the book from human interference, they often served to damage the pages of the book, which could be knocked into the sides of a box when it was moved. (This type of damage can be seen on The Cathach and the Book of Durrow.)

The Athlone Crucifixion Plaque is a gilt bronze decoration that was probably once attached to a wooden book box.

Holes around the perimeter would have allowed it to be pinned to the wood. The figures in the crucifixion scene are similar to ones we have seen on the Carndonagh Cross and in the Book of Durrow. An angel sits on each of Christ's shoulders and the sponge and spear bearers are at his sides. The figures are decorated with spirals based on triskeles and bands of interlace.

Shrines were also made in more unusual shapes. The Moylough Belt Shrine contains the remains of a leather belt, and other shrines were made to contain an arm, crosiers and other holy relics.

The Emly Shrine is house or tomb shaped. It is a portable reliquary made of yew wood and decorated with silver, gold, enamels and gilt bronze. The whole surface is covered in a step pattern of silver inlay, which creates a pattern of silver crosses against the dark wood. The circular medallions fixed to the box have a simple pattern in green and yellow champlevé enamel. The decoration at the top of the shrine takes the form of a ridgepole, such as you might find on a wooden house or a church. It has an animal head at each end, again in green and yellow enamel (fig 7.22).

The Tully Lough Cross is an Irish altar cross of the 8th or 9th century (fig 7.23). It is almost 2 m tall. The metal parts on the surface of the cross are nailed onto an oak core and the edges are finished in tubular binding strips. The ends of these strips are decorated with cast animal heads. The front of the cross is more decorative than the back and is divided into areas of interlace and figure panels interspersed with cast bosses and areas of plain

FIG 7.23 The Tully Lough Cross

metal. Originally, the decorated areas were gilt and the flat areas were tinned, which would have created a much more glittering effect than the exposed bronze plates and castings that we see today. The two openwork figure panels are almost identical and show a kilted figure with an open-mouthed animal on each side, which may represent Christ between two beasts or Daniel in the lion's den. The central pyramid-shaped boss originally had amber studs in the settings at the centre and corners. All the bosses have chip-carved designs using a range of La Tène motifs. Large crosses like this were probably carried in procession on important festivals.

Conclusion

The 7th and 8th centuries were a high point in Irish art and learning. Ireland was the repository of scholarship for Europe, which was just coming out of the Dark Ages. It is extraordinary that the finest craftsmanship and scholarship of the age should have come from a society without towns and cities. Work of extraordinary technical skill and subtle design characterises the period.

Questions

1. Describe the development in design and technique from pillar stones to the first cross-shaped pillars.
2. Write a short account of the range of colours and the writing and painting techniques available in an 8th-century monastery.
3. Describe the layout, design, colour and symbolism used in a page from the Book of Durrow.
4. List some of the techniques available to an 8th-century metalworker.

Essay

1. It is believed that elaborate Church ceremonies were part of monastic life in the 8th century. Describe two metalwork objects that you believe were made for ceremonial use and note their structure and decoration.
2. Write an account of the human figure as it appears in 7th- and 8th-century art, giving examples from book painting, stone carving and metalwork.

Colour picture study

1. Examine the photographs of the Tara Brooch and note the range of designs and techniques used in its construction (fig 7.15, fig 7.16, fig 7.17). What do you believe the function of a brooch like this was?
2. Choose a page from the Book of Durrow and describe its layout, colour and decoration. Do you know of any meanings that lie behind the images or patterns (fig 7.6–12)?

CHAPTER 8

Viking raids on Irish monasteries began in the year 795 AD when several islands off the north and west coast were plundered. The island of Iona, where the chief monastery of the Columban order was located, was raided in that year, and again in 802 and 804, when 68 people were killed. By 807 the Columbans had moved their headquarters to Kells, in Co. Meath, which was away from the coast and out of immediate danger of Viking attack. In the first 40 years of the 9th century, most Viking raids in Ireland took place on the northern coast, but in 842 the Vikings overwintered in a defended ship harbour in Dublin and established a settlement there. In the following years, they established settlements at Arklow, Wicklow, Wexford, Waterford, Cork and Limerick. They were – to an extent – absorbed into the Irish tribal system, though periods of warfare and raiding were common until the end of the century.

The Vikings caused a good deal of destruction by raiding monasteries, which were centres of population and wealth in Ireland. Many pieces of Irish art have been found in graves in Norway, such as parts of book covers and reliquaries which were cut up to make jewellery. The Vikings also took slaves in their raids and traded them for silver in the Middle East. The Vikings traded and raided all over western Europe, from Russia to the Mediterranean, gathering great wealth, some of which came back to Ireland.

There was also a positive side to the Vikings. They established the first towns in Ireland. They introduced coinage and paid tribute to the local Irish kings, often in the form of silver, which, as a result, became more readily available to Irish craftsmen. Precious metals were not easy to obtain up to this time in Ireland and were only used in tiny quantities to gild bronze. Pure precious metals had been used in only the most important pieces before this time.

Structures (architecture)

The monasteries

In spite of the Viking raids, Irish monasteries grew as centres of learning and pilgrimage. Expansion and

Fig 8.1 An aerial view of the monastery at Clonmacnoise. The round tower and the remains of the cathedral can be seen on the left. The monastery covered a much wider area in the 10th century.

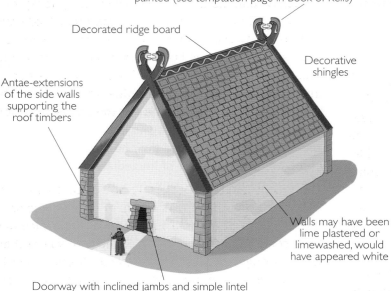

Zoomorphic heads on roof timbers. May have been painted (see temptation page in Book of Kells)

Decorated ridge board

Decorative shingles

Antae-extensions of the side walls supporting the roof timbers

Walls may have been lime plastered or limewashed, would have appeared white

Doorway with inclined jambs and simple lintel

FIG 8.2 A conjectural reconstruction of the cathedral at Clonmacnoise

reorganisation became necessary. A cross-slab or a tomb shrine often marked the grave of the founding saint. Sometimes an oratory (house of prayer) was placed over the tomb of the founder, as at Clonmacnoise and Glendalough. Crosses were erected near the entrance of the monastery and by the 10th century, most churches were built in stone, with a round tower towards the west side, with its doorway facing the church. The outline of some of these early monastic sites can still be seen in the banks and mounds that remain or in the street and property patterns that overlay them. In Armagh, the Church of Ireland cathedral and cemetery lie at the centre of the old monastery. The circular pattern of streets in the older parts of the town follows the expansion of the monastery over the years.

In the 9th and 10th centuries, the building of stone churches became more common. At **Clonmacnoise**, Co. Offaly, there are a number of examples (fig 8.1). Temple Ciaran, which is only 3.8 by 2.8 m internally, may have been an oratory to house the remains of the saint. The cathedral, which originally measured 18.8 by 10.7 m, was the largest stone church in Ireland until Norman times. It was built between 908 and 909 AD. Most of these simple rectangular churches have *antae*, which are projections of the sidewalls beyond the gables, considered by some art historians to be a copy of corner posts from wooden buildings (fig 8.2). The roofs of these early stone churches were steeply pitched in the style of the wooden buildings, which they copied, though many gables were trimmed in later years during medieval reconstructions.

A few 10th-century churches have a chancel at the east end, separated by a round-headed arch from the nave. These churches have a mixture of ancient and more up-to-date features; the *antae* are gone, replaced by corbels to carry the roof timbers. Trinity and Refert Churches at Glendalough, Co. Wicklow (fig 8.3), have small, flat-headed doorways and small windows with arches cut from a single stone, which harkens back to the earliest churches.

Irish buildings were designed in a conservative style and were very small in size compared to contemporary European churches; this was probably a result of the different, non-urban social structure and the style of monasticism practised here. Ultimately, adherence to the

FIG 8.3 Reefert Church at Glendalough. Note the arch separating the nave and chancel.

ancient rules of the founding saints created problems when the Irish Church came in close contact with the revitalised monastic orders of Europe.

Round towers

From early in the 10th century AD, round towers became part of the range of buildings found in Irish monasteries. An entry in the *Annals of the Four Masters* for the year 960 AD is the first written reference to a round tower: 'The Belfry at Slane was burned by the foreigners' [the Dublin Vikings] ... full of relics and distinguished persons, together with Caeineachair, lector at Slane, and the crosier of the patron saint, and a bell, the best of bells.' Obviously, the belfry was built before this date, which gives us an approximate starting point (fig 8.4).

The Irish word for a round tower is *cloicteach*, literally 'bell house', which describes its primary function of calling the monks to prayer from their various duties around the monastery and surrounding fields. From the entry in the *Annals* above, we can see that towers were also used as a treasury to keep the relics and valuables of the monastery safe and as a place of sanctuary in times of trouble – but that sanctuary was not always respected.

FIG 8.4 The round tower at Killmacduagh, Co. Galway. Note the very high doorway on this tower.

Round towers would have been outstanding buildings in a society that normally built small-scale, low-profile buildings. They would have been important landmarks and status symbols, pointing out places of pilgrimage and learning and distinguishing monastic sites from secular settlements. Remains of over 60 towers exist in Ireland today, and there is evidence of far greater numbers having been built during the 250 years before the Norman invasions.

Origins

The origins of round towers is not clear. There is no evidence of wooden predecessors or simpler versions – they seem to begin as a fully formed idea which may have come from Britain or the Rhineland, where there were strong contacts with Ireland through pilgrim monks. Towers in these regions would have been attached to the west front of churches, which were larger than Irish buildings. There was a tradition of freestanding bell towers in Italy, but they were more often square in plan. The Irish towers were generally built at the west end of the main church in the monastery, with the door of the tower facing the west door of the church, which is, in effect, a looser arrangement of the Rhineland style. There are some later Irish churches with towers attached, as at Clonmacnoise and Glendalough, though these do not seem to have been a common type.

Construction

Round towers are a uniquely Irish construction. They were frequently around 100 feet tall. (The number 100 was considered to be a perfect number in medieval times.) In proportion, towers were often twice the height of the circumference of the base. This not only leads to an elegant shape, but also a stable structure. Construction followed the ancient tradition of building on a circular plan. (Churches, built on a rectangular plan, were the exception.) Towers generally had quite shallow foundations, less than 1 m deep, and were constructed of large stones built in layers gradually stepping inwards to the diameter of the base of the tower. The cylinder of the tower was built of an outer and inner skin of carefully selected or cut stone. The space between was filled with rough stone and lime mortar. It was this infill of stone and mortar, which turned to concrete when it set, that gave the towers their structural strength. When construction reached about 1 m in height, wooden scaffold was built and connected to the tower by put lock holes, which would have received wooden beams to support the scaffold. Put lock holes can be found on the exterior of many towers, showing where the scaffold was connected to the rising walls.

Doors and windows

Doors and windows in round towers vary significantly in shape, size and design, from openings with plain lintels to decorated Romanesque arches on the later towers. A few towers had a door at ground level, though generally they were located well above the ground, which would have given added security. Most doorways have inclined jambs (like contemporary churches do). Windows were small and splayed inwards (openings were larger on the inside of the wall). Some windows had simple lintels while others had a triangular or round-headed top. The windows of the bell floor, at the top of the tower, were

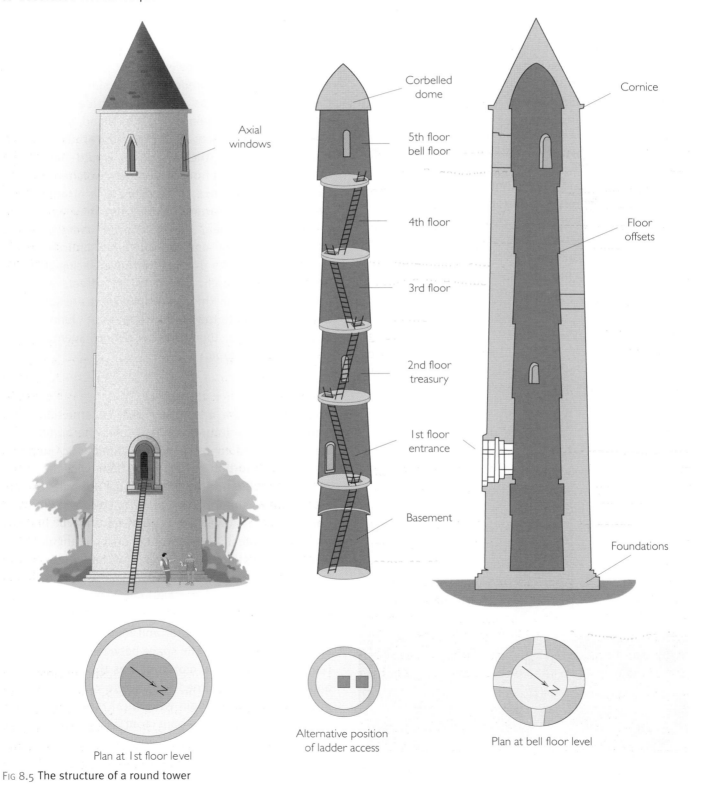

132

Fig 8.5 The structure of a round tower

Antrim
Simple lintelled doorway

Monasterboice
False arch

Kells
True arch

Timahoe
Romanesque

Fig 8.6 Round tower doorways.

generally larger and faced north, south, east and west. Towers had between five and seven floors, some of which had no windows (fig 8.5). The wooden floors were supported on offsets in the walls or on corbels protruding from the inside of the walls. The cap was a cone, set on a cornice; internally, it was a shallow corbelled dome, the whole construction being solid masonry. When the structure was completed, the masons would have dressed the surface to a smooth finish using hammers or axes to create an even exterior and continuous slope from top to bottom. Towers were constructed in a variety of finishes, from rough unwrought stones to carefully cut blocks, depending on what stone was available locally, the skills of the craftsmen and the funds provided.

Stone carving

The Celtic high cross

There are many theories about the origins of the Irish high cross and the various local styles of decoration that are used in different parts of the country. The earliest written mention of a high cross is in the *Annals of the Four Masters* for the year 951 AD, but crosses are clearly older than this. There are written accounts of crosses made of wood and stone from Northumbria in Britain, an area that had strong Irish connections, dating back to 750 AD. The Tully Lough Cross (now on display in the National Museum of Ireland in Dublin) is a rare survivor of these wood and metal crosses, which may have been part of the inspiration for the shape and design of high crosses.

Numbers

Remains of over 200 high crosses exist in Ireland, but this may represent only a part of the number that once existed. Several crosses are found at some sites, though the same Bible scenes are not often repeated at the same monastery. Not all crosses have figure scenes or decoration; there may be as many as 16 large, plain crosses and over 40 with geometric ornament or an inscription, but no figure scenes. The majority of the crosses were erected in the 9th and 10th centuries when the Columban Order, which was based in Iona and Kells, created an impetus for cross construction.

The ringed cross (jewelled cross)

The reason for the shape of the Irish high cross seems to originate in the large jewelled cross which was erected on Golgotha in Jerusalem by the Emperor Constantine to celebrate the finding of the 'True Cross' by his mother, St Helena, in the 4th century AD. Images in early mosaics, manuscripts, sculptures and wall hangings show the cross on a stepped base, which represents Golgotha, with a wreath or circle surrounding the crossing of the shaft and the arms. This ring represents Christ's victory over death and at the same time represents eternity, or the universe. (Multiple layers of meaning attach to many parts and scenes on Irish high crosses. This was a common element in medieval art and writing.) The cap on the top of crosses is thought to represent the church that Constantine built over the Holy Sepulchre; it can be seen as a symbol of resurrection and eternity (fig 8.7).

The function of the high cross

The high cross standing in a monastic enclosure in Ireland represented the True Cross, the symbol of resurrection, which was the centre of Christian belief. Viewers were also reminded of the relics and holy places that a pilgrim might see on a visit to Jerusalem, the holiest place in the Christian tradition. Respect for the

House-shaped cap represents the chapel Constantine built over the holy sepulchre

The ring represents the wreath of victory (Christ's victory over death). The circle also represents eternity and the universe.

Shaft

Base

The whole image represents the cross erected in Jerusalem to celebrate the finding of the True Cross

FIG 8.7 The parts of a high cross

psalmist like David, the son of Jesse, a distinguished sage like Solomon, the son of David, the lawgiver to hundreds like Moses. . . .

These and other Old Testament figures frequently appear on crosses and may have been a reference to the character of some local saints. Local saints do not appear in the scenes carved on the crosses, but we do know through written accounts that devotion to their memory was strong in the early Christian church in Ireland.

The crosses

The Ahenny Crosses

The Ahenny group of crosses are situated in a river valley north of Carrick-on-Suir, Co. Tipperary, on the border with Kilkenny. They are located at Kilkieran, Killamery, Kilree and Ahenny itself. They seem to be a manifestation of the jewelled cross (see above) in Ireland. The shaft and arms are covered with curves, knotting, fretwork and spirals, which have close relationships with contemporary metalwork. A raised border of what looks like woven wire translated into stone surrounds the cross and ring, like

FIG 8.8 The east face of the North Cross at Ahenny, Co. Tipperary

134

symbolism of the high cross gave them an importance as markers of the boundaries of sanctuary in the monastery. They were also a focus for prayer and repentance; most of the crosses with Bible scenes were designed to be read from the bottom up, starting from the eye level of a penitent kneeling in prayer. Scenes on Muiredach's High Cross at Monasterboice echo the penitential litanies that the monks would have chanted.

The high cross had many functions in an Irish monastery. The symbolism and imagery would have drawn pilgrims in a country that had little large-scale art. Crosses may also have symbolised local saints in the way that St Brendan is characterised in the opening lines of the account of his life:

This Brendan was the head of the belief and devotion of the great part of the world like faithful Abraham, a pre-eminently prophetic

FIG 8.9 The west side of the base of the North Cross at Ahenny

the border on the Derrynaflan Paten, which hides the edges of the metal plates. Stone bosses appear in high relief at the centre of the cross, and where the ring passes through the arms and shaft, they look like the studs which are used in metalwork construction to hide the rivets which join metal plates together.

The North Cross at Ahenny stands 3.13 m tall on its stepped base (fig 8.8). The cross itself is completely encrusted in abstract pattern, including one panel of human interlace on the west face of the shaft. The base, on the other hand, is decorated with human and animal figure scenes, which, Peter Harbison suggests in his great survey of Irish high crosses, can be read as lessons in the power and gifts of God and the victory of good over evil. On the west face of the base is a group of seven figures with crosiers, representing Christ's mission to the apostles (fig 8.9). On the east face, a man sits under a palm tree facing a group of animals – Adam being given dominion over the animals. On the north side, David charges into battle on a chariot, while on the south side, David carries Goliath's head in a procession with Goliath's headless body tied to a horse. The style of carving is simple and non-classical, more in the Celtic tradition of symbolism in preference to realism. The low-relief panels on the base of the North Cross are worn and difficult to see clearly, except in good light.

The panels on the base of the South Cross (3.9 m tall) are even more difficult to make out; each face on the base is divided into two panels, with animal and human figure scenes (fig 8.10). One of the scenes on the eastern side may represent Daniel in the lion's den, but the meaning of the other panels is difficult to work out. This group of

crosses was once thought to belong to the 8th century, but now they are placed in the early 9th century, along with the majority of high crosses.

FIG 8.10 The east face of the South Cross at Ahenny

The granite crosses

Most of the Irish high crosses are carved in sandstone, but in the area around Kildare there are a number of crosses carved in granite. This hard granular stone presents a problem for the sculptor. Fine line and small detail are not possible and a smooth finish is hard to achieve. Despite these difficulties, interesting, even beautiful crosses were created in a style of design that relates back to the Celtic traditions rather than the more classical style, which we will see on the scripture crosses.

The Castledermot Crosses

The monastery at Castledermot was founded after 812 AD for the Columban order, which was undergoing reform by the Cele De (literally, 'servants of God') movement. The movement was trying to bring piety and order back into the Irish monasteries, which had become very irregular in their practices during the 8th century, even to the extent that wars were fought by rival monastic alliances.

The crosses at Castledermot reflected the piety of the Cele De. Both crosses have scenes from the lives of St Paul and St Anthony, who were the founders of ascetic monasticism and were seen as an example of piety and self-denial for monks to follow. Other scenes show examples from the Old and New Testaments of how God provides for his faithful followers and saves them from damnation. The cross to the north of the church has a representation of Adam and Eve on the west face of the head (fig 8.11), on the opposite side to the Crucifixion.

Fig 8.11 The North Cross at Castledermot, Co. Kildare. Viewed from the south east, The Crucifixion can be seen at the centre of the crossing

This placement of the scenes may illustrate that Christ's sacrifice on the cross was needed in order to redeem the original sin of our first parents.

The figure panels on these crosses are tightly composed to fit within the frames that surround each scene. The figures are relatively flat, defined by cutting away the background areas. Detail is kept to a minimum, since it would have been difficult to achieve on this hard stone.

The Cross of Moone

The monastery at Moone was probably another Columban house, contemporary with Castledermot. The cross on the site is unique in style and layout. Over 7 m tall, it is the second tallest cross in Ireland, its height being emphasised by the narrow shaft and small wheel-head. Most of the upper part of the cross, the shaft, arms and head, is carved with patterns. A figure of Christ in majesty appears on the crossing on the east side and animals appear in panels on the west side of the shaft. The tall base, which is almost square in plan, has figure scenes on every side, set in panels (fig 8.12).

The theme of the Cross of Moone seems to be the help that God gives his faithful followers. This is illustrated in scenes from the Old and New Testaments. A medieval monk looking at the scenes on this cross would have deciphered layers of meaning in all the scenes. Events recorded in the Old Testament were often understood as a prefiguration (an early indication) of events in the life of Christ and his followers. Beginning on the east side, the scenes on the base of the cross can be read – unusually – from top to bottom. In the first scene, Adam and Eve stand under a stylised tree with the serpent (Satan) coiling around the trunk. This represents man's original fall from grace. Below this is the sacrifice of Isaac from the Book of Genesis in the Old Testament. The scene shows Isaac bent over the sacrificial altar. Abraham leans forward from an interesting-looking chair to strike the fatal blow, and the ram, which takes Isaac's place as the sacrifice, is squeezed into the top left-hand corner. The scene of the father about to sacrifice his son is regarded as a prefiguration of the Crucifixion. At the bottom of this side is the scene of Daniel in the lion pit, with seven lions, rather than the more common Daniel in the lion's den, with four lions. The pit scene comes from an apocryphal part of the Book of Daniel in the Old Testament and can be read as God saving his faithful follower and as another prefiguration for the sacrifice of the Crucifixion. It could also be understood as a symbol of redemption (fig 8.13).

Moving onto the south side, the three children (Hebrews) and the fiery furnace, from the Book of Daniel, are seen protected by an angel. The flight into Egypt and the

FIG 8.12 The west face of the Cross Moone, Co. Kildare. Animal Panels on the shaft, and The Crucifixion and apostles on the base

FIG 8.13 The east side of the base of the Cross of Moone. Adam and Eve in the top panel, the sacrifice of Isaac and Daniel in the lion pit below

miracle of the loaves and fishes from the New Testament complete the scenes on this side (fig 8.14).

On the west side is the Crucifixion scene arranged in its most frequently used form in Ireland, the sponge and spear bearers beneath the arms of the Christ figure. The 12 apostles fill the remainder of the base; simple

FIG 8.14 The south side of the base of the Cross of Moone. The flight into Egypt is represented in the middle panel.

rectangular bodies with large heads and prominent noses form three rows, without individual details. The north side of the base of the Cross of Moone seems to be dedicated to St Paul and St Anthony, who appear in two scenes above a seven-headed monster (probably a figure from the Apocalypse).

Painted crosses?

The style of the figure panels is similar to those at Castledermot, but there is more space surrounding the figures, which gives them greater clarity. The armless figures of Daniel and the apostles, and the bodiless Christ child in the flight into Egypt scene, suggests that details and decorative elements may have been painted onto the carvings, creating images like those in the Book of Durrow. The lions in the Daniel in the lion pit scene look like they might be related to the lion symbol of St Mark in the Book of Durrow.

Scripture crosses

Although the crosses we have just looked at have scenes from scripture, like the ones below, they are very different in style and detail. The crosses found in the Midlands from Clonmacnoise to Monasterboice have similarities in style, technique and subject matter, though each should be considered separately as a unique work of art and symbolism.

Origins of the designs

The iconography of the scripture crosses is not simple to work out. The images and subjects relate to designs found on Roman sarcophagi (box tombs) from about the

4th century AD. These tombs were often reused for later burials, so an Irish pilgrim or cleric on Church business in Rome who went to see the relics of saints or famous churchmen would have seen many of these sarcophagi (fig 8.15).

The images that appear in early Byzantine art also share themes and styles with scenes found on Irish crosses. This similarity may be due to common influences from Rome and an emphasis on the same messages throughout the early Christian world.

Images may also have come second-hand through Britain or the Carolingian Empire, which had contacts with Ireland (fig 8.16). There are accounts of written descriptions of the relics and sites of Rome being circulated, so drawings may conceivably have been available as well.

However it evolved, a style based on classical art was in use in Ireland in the 9th and 10th centuries. While the subjects and layout were often based on Roman designs,

FIG 8.15 The Twelve Apostles sarcophagus from the basilica of Sant'Apollinare in Classe – Ravenna, Italy

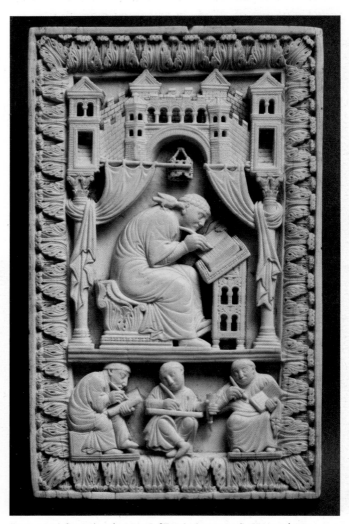

FIG 8.16 An ivory book cover of Pope Gregory the Great (590 - 604) being inspired by the holy spirit

the details were based on local observations; hairstyles and clothing were in the Irish style, not the classical togas seen on the sarcophagi.

The crosses at Kells

There is an important group of crosses at Kells, Co. Meath, which was the senior monastery in the Colombian tradition in the years that followed the Viking raids on Iona in the early 9th century. Kells would have been a centre of power and influence in the Irish Church, active in the spread of new ideas and art forms. Four crosses carved in sandstone survive at the site: the Cross of Patrick and Columba (3.30 m), the Market Cross (3.35 m), the Broken Cross (shaft is 3.44 m tall) and an unfinished cross.

The Cross of Patrick and Columba

This cross may have been erected to commemorate the founding of the monastery at Kells in about 804 AD. The inscription '*Patricii et Columbae crux*', unusually written in Latin, may indicate an agreement between the *paruchia* (group of allied churches and monasteries) of

FIG 8.17 The east face of the Cross of Patrick and Columba at Kells, Co. Meath

St Patrick, based at Armagh, and the *paruchia* of St Columba, then centred on Iona. This cross is unusual among Irish crosses as it is not divided into panels. Figure scenes and areas of decoration meet without borders. The figures in the Bible scenes are more vigorous and animated than on other crosses, and some areas of the cross have different subjects side by side. A section on the east face (fig 8.17) depicts Adam and Eve covering their nakedness with Cain killing Abel side by side. In another area, the children in the furnace are shown, with devils forking firewood on top of them, just under the feet of Daniel in the lion's den.

On the left-hand arm of the cross there is a carving of the sacrifice of Isaac and on the right a raven brings bread to St Paul and St Anthony (a prefiguration of the Eucharist). The top of the cross has a figure scene, the meaning of which is disputed. Françoise Henry reads it as the miracle of the loaves and fishes and Peter Harbison interprets the scene as David playing his harp for Saul, to banish evil.

The west face of the shaft has a Crucifixion scene above an area of human interlace. At the centre of the cross is a Christ in glory or Last Judgement scene. The sides of the cross have areas of pattern and some figures, which are difficult to interpret. The base has horses and riders and chariots on the west face and a man hunting animals on the east. If this cross can be interpreted as the earliest one at Kells, its unusual style could be attributed to influences from Iona and the Scottish style of carving.

The Broken Cross and the Market Cross

These crosses seem to have been moved from their original orientation. The panels include some scenes not found on other crosses, deeply carved into designs, which fit closely into their panels.

Together with the unfinished cross, which we will look at later, these crosses at Kells may have been the models on which the designs of the scripture crosses in the rest of the country were based.

The Cross of the Scriptures at Clonmacnoise

One of the most beautiful and complete of the high crosses, this stands 3.90 m tall in the interpretive centre specially built to protect the crosses at Clonmacnoise. Modern copies now stand in the original locations. The theme of this cross is the Passion, death and resurrection of Christ. The Old Testament scenes on the lower panels of the east face of the shaft can be interpreted as a prefiguration of the resurrection, which

FIG 8.18 The west face of the Cross of the Scriptures at Clonmacnoise located in front of the westdoor of the Cathedral

FIG 8.19 The east face of Muiredach's Cross at Monasterboice, Co. Louth

is illustrated in two panels on the base and lower shaft of the west side, which would have been the focus of a person kneeling in prayer before the cross.

The sculpted panels are carved in high relief, with some of the figures almost projecting free from the surface. The designs are neatly composed and carried out in greater detail than we have seen on previous crosses (fig 8.18). The ring at the head of the cross passes over the shaft and arms, which is different from other crosses, where the ring is set back from the surface of the shaft and arms.

The crosses at Monasterboice, Co. Louth

Mainistir Buite is on the site of the monastery founded by the 5th-century monk, Buite. He prophesied the importance of St Columba. Tradition says that Columba was born on the day in 521 AD on which Buite died. This made Monasterboice an important place of pilgrimage, connected to Kells, which may explain similarities in the style between the crosses at Kells and Monasterboice.

Muiredach's Cross

Another local tradition stated that Muiredach's Cross was sent from Rome. This may relate to the themes and messages that are on the cross and even to the origins of the designs which some scholars say are based on images from early Christian tombs in Rome. The cross stands 5.20 m tall and is one solid piece of stone, except for the cap and base. Artistically and technically, it is the finest high cross in Ireland.

The east face

The Old Testament scenes on the east face are crowded into panels of multiple subjects or large groups (fig 8.19). The lowest panel shows Adam and Eve and Cain killing Abel. The scene above this depicts David killing Goliath, while Moses strikes the rock in the next scene, providing water for the large group of Israelites included in the panel. The uppermost scene on this side of the shaft shows the Adoration of the Magi in which four kings, representing people from the four corners of the Earth, come to adore the infant Christ in the arms of his seated mother.

Across the arms of the cross is a Last Judgement scene (fig 8.20) with Christ at the centre, holding a staff and sceptre; an eagle is above his head. The staff, sceptre and eagle were all ancient symbols of power from Egypt and Rome, which became incorporated into Christian

FIG 8.20 The Last Judgement scene on the east face of Muiredach's Cross

FIG 8.21 The lower panels on the west face of the shaft of Muiredach's Cross. Note the Irish style hair and clothing on the figures.

symbolism. At Christ's right hand is David playing his harp, an angel writes the judgements in a book and the good souls face Christ. On Christ's left hand is a flute player and behind him is the Devil with his trident, driving the souls who turned their backs on Christ into Hell. Below Christ's feet is a small panel in which St Michael the Archangel weighs souls and the Devil tries to upset the balance. This scene is common in Romanesque art, which developed in Europe in the following centuries.

The west face

On the bottom of the west face of the shaft is an inscription written in Old Irish, which reads: 'OR DO MUIREDACH LAS NDERNAD————RO', meaning 'A prayer for Muiredach, who had (the cross) erected'. This inscription, which gives the cross its name, appears in a small panel behind two cats. The inscription does not help to clarify a date for the cross, as there were several abbots called Muiredach and the cross cannot be associated with any one in particular. Above the inscription is a mocking of Christ scene, in which soldiers, who look like Vikings, have dressed Christ in an elaborate cloak fixed with a penannular brooch, like the Tara Brooch, to mock him as king of the Jews (fig 8.21).

The next panel is interpreted by Peter Harbison as the raised Christ, hovering above the world with St Peter and St Paul, while Christ gives the keys to the kingdom of Heaven to St Peter and the book of the New Testament to St Paul in the uppermost panel on this side of the shaft.

The Crucifixion is at the centre of the west face of the cross. It shows Stepathon offering the sponge to Christ and Longinus piercing his left side with a lance. An angel hovers above each shoulder, and patterns and bosses surround the scene. At the end of the arms there are figure scenes, which may represent the denial of St Peter on the left-hand side and the resurrection on the right. The scene above the ring is the Ascension of Christ (fig 8.22).

The narrow sides and base

The north and south sides of the cross are decorated with interlace patterns on the shaft and figure scenes on the ends of the arms and at the top of the cross. The base is divided into panels, which contain figure and animal scenes on the upper row and interlaced patterns along

FIG 8.22 The west face of Muiredach's Cross at Monasterboice

FIG 8.23 The hand of God on the underside of the arm on the north face of Muiredach's Cross

the bottom. On the underside of the arms of the cross (the parts that have been least weathered), there is a pair of animals on the south side and the hand of God on the north. Heads with entwining snakes are carved on the underside of the ring (fig 8.23).

The message of the cross

Because of the layers of meaning associated with each scene, a number of messages can be taken from this cross. Christ the King can be seen in the mocking scene, the Crucifixion and the Last Judgment; in fact, the whole west face could be interpreted in this way. The importance of the Eucharist can be noted in a number of scenes and the Passion, death and resurrection of Christ were also emphasised (fig 8.24).

Carving

The quality of the carving on Muiredach's Cross is unsurpassed on any other Irish cross. There is a crispness of detail and depth of modelling rarely found

elsewhere. Features of hairstyles, clothes and weapons can be seen on the larger figures, which are carved almost in the round. The style of the figure carving and the design of the scenes predates Romanesque versions by more than 100 years. Could it be that Irish pilgrim monks brought their sculptural designs to Europe as they had done with their book designs?

FIG 8.24 The mocking of Christ scene on the end of the arm, on the north side of Muiredach's Cross

FIG 8.25 The west face of the Tall Cross at Monasterboice

The Tall Cross

Near the round tower at Monasterboice stands the Tall Cross (fig 8.25), which, at over 7 m, is the tallest cross in Ireland. Because of its great height, the Tall Cross has the largest number of figure scenes found on any cross. Scenes appear on all faces, illustrating the life of David and God's help for his faithful followers on the east face, and scenes from the life of Christ on the west. The figure style is more animated but less detailed and deeply carved than Muiredach's Cross.

The crosses in the North

In counties Fermanagh, Monaghan, Armagh, Tyrone and Down, there is a group of crosses that are related in style and choice of subject. These crosses are now in poor condition, but the scenes can still be deciphered on many of them. The subjects are strictly separated into Old Testament scenes on the east face and New Testament scenes on the west face. Many of the crosses have the same arrangement of subjects.

FIG 8.26 The west face of the Tall Cross at Arboe, Co. Tyrone

Armagh, with its associations with St Patrick, was the most important monastic centre in Ireland and was probably at the heart of the development of high crosses in the surrounding counties, but only fragments remain of the crosses that once stood on the site.

The cross at Arboe in Co. Tyrone is 5.70 m tall (fig 8.26). It is the third-tallest cross in Ireland and is almost complete. The themes on the cross are the common ones: God's help for his faithful followers, baptism, Eucharist and a large number of scenes from the life of Christ. It is difficult to judge the original quality of the carving as the cross is now very worn, but the arrangement and design of the panels bears a resemblance to the Tall Cross at Monasterboice.

The construction of the high crosses

We can get some idea of how crosses were made from the unfinished cross at Kells, Co. Meath. The basic blocks from which the cross was to be built would have been roughed out at the quarry, the mortises and tenons which were to connect the parts together would have been cut to fit each other, and all the parts were then transported to the site where the cross was to be erected.

At the site, the stonemason would have marked out the areas for decoration and checked the shape of the stone for accuracy with a square and compass. The measurements of mouldings and panels seem to correspond with inches and feet, used in the imperial system, which was based on the Roman measuring system.

Blocking out

Different depths of carving were allowed for during the blocking out process. This can be seen on the unfinished cross at Kells (fig 8.27), where panels are left projecting above the surrounding area to accommodate higher relief. All the surfaces were first trimmed flat so that drawings could be transferred onto them, providing guidelines for the carver. When the preliminary work was complete, the parts would have been assembled in their final position before the panels were cut into, so that

Blocks roughed out at the quarry.
Mortices and tenons cut to make joints.

Panels blocked out on site. Different thicknesses allowed for different depths of carving.

Cross erected on site.
Carvers begin carving designs.

FIG 8.28 The construction of a high cross

edges and joints could be carefully matched, giving continuity to the design (fig 8.28).

Tools

The sculptors would have used iron chisels similar to the tools used by modern sculptors, but this is only an assumption since tools from this time have not been found as yet. Crosses of the 9th and 10th centuries have

FIG 8.27 The unfinished cross at Kells

144

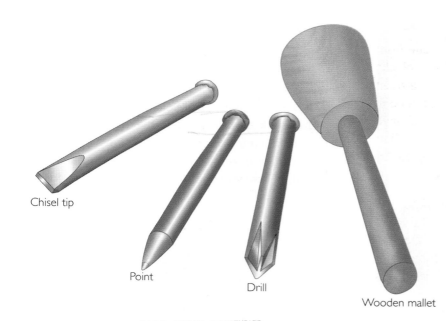

Chisel tip

Point

Drill

Wooden mallet

Moyne College
BALLINA, CO. MAYO.

a greater depth of carving, which may be accounted for by improved iron technology brought by the Vikings. Drill marks can still be seen on Muiredach's Cross in the areas under the arms and ring that have been least weathered. The drill would have been used to bore down to the deepest areas of the design, followed by a chisel, which would have formed the details of the design (fig 8.29).

We know from later history that medieval masons had pattern books of abstract designs and figure scenes that they could choose from when they were carving decorations on churches. Irish masons may have had similar records to help them. In any case, there are close relationships between some of the designs and patterns found on Irish high crosses, which indicates that designers were at least aware of the work on other crosses.

Manuscripts

We have seen earlier the simplicity of the buildings in an Irish monastery and how few comforts were available for the monks. The beautifully decorated and elaborately laid out books of the 9th and 10th centuries seem to be in contrast with this simple life, but they are also an expression of the attempt by Irish monks to lead a spiritual and intellectual life free from worldliness. Beautiful bibles had a value beyond the everyday; they were an expression of the commitment of the community to spiritual ideals.

Colours

The range of colours in the Book of Kells includes the yellow, red and green that we have seen in the Book of Durrow, but some more exotic and expensive pigments were also used. Blues were obtained from indigo (a plant imported from the Orient), woad (a northern European plant) and lapis lazuli (which is ultramarine blue – *ultramarine* means 'from across the sea' – a mineral from northern Afghanistan). Lapis lazuli was a very precious and expensive pigment usually reserved for the most important areas in a design. Kermes red was obtained by crushing the bodies and eggs of the *Kernococcus vermillio* insect, which lives on the kermes oak. Vermillion is red mercuric sulphide, which probably came from Spain. Folium comes from marsh plants grown around the Mediterranean and it produces a range of purple and plum colours. White lead was used both as a colour and a ground for over-painting; it was much used in spite of its toxicity.

Most of the organic pigments were extracted in ammonium (urine) and fixed in an insoluble mineral salt (aluminium hydroxide). Colours may have been traded in the form of small rags of dyed cloth from which the colours could be diluted out as required. Colours could be bound in egg white, yolk, natural gums or animal gelatine so they would stick to the vellum page.

Writing tools

The scribes and artists who produce manuscripts used a variety of equipment: pens, which were made from the tail feathers of the goose or swan; brushes of varying fineness (the hair of the marten was suitable for the finest-quality brushes); and knives, which were used to scrape away mistakes. To create the decorated pages, artists would have needed a ruler, a compass and

FIG 8.30 Folio 291v. The Saint John portrait from the Book of Kells.

The Book of Kells

The Book of Kells is the most elaborately decorated manuscript codex in the Insular style to have survived the ravages of time. The text is very similar to that of the Book of Durrow. The Book of Kells was created 100 years after the Book of Durrow, but the Four Gospels and related preliminary writings in it could have been copied from a common exemplar. Both books were transcribed in Columban monasteries, which may account for the closeness of the texts.

The book

The origins of the Book of Kells

Scholars now generally agree that the Book of Kells was written at Iona, the chief monastery of the Columban order, and then brought to Kells when Iona became unsafe due to Viking raids. The book could have taken decades to write, so it may have been started on Iona and continued in Kells. These monasteries were regarded as one unit under the authority of one abbot in the early part of the 9th century. The book was probably written in the years around 800 AD, but it was never fully completed – two pages are blank and a few have decorative elements begun but left unfinished.

The Book of Kells today

The Book of Kells now measures 330 by 255 mm. It was cut down for rebinding in 1830, which damaged the design of a number of pages. It was badly rebound again in 1895 before it was restored in 1953. The decoration suffered damage from wetting the pages to flatten them at each rebinding. The book still preserves some of the most amazing examples from any era of the illuminator's skill. Three hundred and forty folios remain, and it is estimated that about 30 are lost, including some fully decorated pages.

Vellum

Calf vellum was used to make the pages for the Book of Kells. Skins of newborn or inter-uterine calves were preferred to produce the finest vellum. Only one bifolium could be made from each skin of this size. Stronger vellum for the fully decorated pages was obtained from two- or three-month-old calves, producing two bifoliae from each skin, though decorated pages were often on single leaves, which could be worked on separately and later sewn into the book. It has been estimated that the hides of up to 185 calves could have been needed for the complete book; this suggests a monastery of great wealth, capable of affording these resources.

probably templates to lay out the designs and patterns. Cow horns were used as inkwells. The portrait of St John in the Book of Kells (Folio 291v) shows the scribe with a pen in his right hand and a book in his left, and an inkwell sitting just above his right foot (fig 8.30).

We can now see that the work of scribes and artists entailed much more than simply writing text or painting designs. They had to work with foul-smelling and poisonous materials and spend long hours preparing colours and pages. Even after all this work, the book still had to be bound together by sewing groups of pages along the spine and attaching them to wooden boards, which formed the covers. A layer of decorated leather was sometimes used to create a final cover. The most precious books, or books associated with the saints, were sometimes enclosed in decorated metal plates and fixed to a wooden box. These book shrines prevented use of the books and sometimes did physical damage to them, but helped to preserve them for posterity. Books for everyday use were generally carried and stored in leather satchels. These satchels could be hung up on hooks in the scriptorium or library. There are records in the Annals of books being stored in round towers.

FIG 8.31 Folio 2r from the Book of Kells is a page of canon tables. Symbols of the Four Evangelists appear in the decorative section at the top of the page.

FIG 8.32 Folio 7v. Virgin and Child surrounded by angels, from the Book of Kells.

The scheme of decoration

The first surviving page from the Book of Kells has a list of Hebrew names on the left side and the symbols of the Four Evangelists on the right. The next five pages are canon tables, which are laid out in columns and connected by arcades, with the symbols of the evangelists in an arch at the top of the page. (Folio 2r is one of these pages (fig 8.31).) The four columns of text refer to passages or incidents that are common to all four gospels. The decorated pillars between the rows of text have human and bird interlace. The pillars at the left and right of the page are decorated with flowing spirals. The symbols of the Four Evangelists in the upper arch are crossed and turned to create a balanced design within the space. In the spandrels (the triangular spaces between the curve of the arch and the corners of the frame), there are opposing pairs of peacocks, which in medieval times symbolised the everlasting nature of Christ. Already at this stage the themes and nature of the design are clear. Almost all the images referred to Jesus, his characteristics and his words. The design elements of spirals, zoomorphs, human figures and interlace are all used in various combinations.

The Virgin and Child page

The first page completely devoted to decoration is Folio 7v, a portrait of the Virgin and Child surrounded by angels (fig 8.32). This page precedes a beautifully decorated page of lettering about the birth of Christ. Mary sits in a purple cloak on a throne of gold with a step pattern creating crosses of various shapes on the side. There is a lion's head terminal on the back of the chair. The Christ child is larger than the newborn baby mentioned in the accompanying text. He tenderly holds his mother's hand and she enfolds him in her arms. The four angels at each side of the throne are usually identified as the archangels Michael, Gabriel, Raphael and Uriel, who will appear a number of times throughout the book, witnessing important events in the life of Christ. Three of the angels carry a flabella and one a flowering bough. (The flabella was a fan used in the Coptic Church to keep flies away from the chalice during the celebration of the Eucharist. It became a symbol of purity in the early Christian Church.)

The small rectangle enclosing six figures looking to the right seems to have been a convention for linking two pages together; they look across to the text on the birth of Christ on the opposite page. The three crosses in Mary's halo and three arcs filled with interlace on the inside of the frame probably refer to the Trinity. This painting is the earliest surviving image of the Virgin and Child from a Western manuscript, though there are written accounts of panel paintings and icons of this scene, now lost, which may have been models for its composition.

The next 37 pages consist of the *Breves causae* (gospel summaries) and *Argumenta* (short biographies of the evangelists), which were designed to provide the reader with background information referring to the gospels and the evangelists. The opening line of each section of these texts is decorated with interlace capitals and parts of the texts are highlighted with borders, colour and interlace.

The Four Gospels

The Gospel of Matthew, which is the first of the Four Gospels, begins on Folio 27. In the original plan, each gospel began with a page illustrating the symbols of the Four Evangelists. This was followed by a portrait of the evangelist for each gospel and a full-page decoration surrounding the opening lines of each gospel. The portrait page from the Gospel of Mark is missing, and the Gospel of Luke is missing the pages that would have contained the images of the Four Evangelists and the portrait of St Luke.

The Four Evangelists page from the Gospel of Matthew

Folio 27v (fig 8.33), the Four Evangelists page from the beginning of the Gospel of Matthew, is richly coloured and patterned in the style of enamelled jewellery. Translucent layers of colour are built up to create rich blues and purples, balanced with the bright orpiment yellow. The central cross form is emphasised by the arcs on the outside of the frame. There is human, animal, bird and snake interlace in the border. Panels of spirals and black-and-white maze and interlace patterns, in very fine lines, are used to separate the coloured sections. The man symbol for St Matthew seems to be skipping lightly forward in his gorgeous robes and wings, holding a processional cross. St Mark's lion symbol is shown in a leaping pose; he has a curling tongue and mane and fabulously decorated wings. The ox or calf symbol of St Luke has four wings, the flight feathers entwining with his legs on one side and with the second wing on the

Fig 8.33 Folio 27v. The Four Evangelists page from the Gospel of Matthew. St Matthew is symbolised by the man, Mark by the lion, Luke by the calf or ox and John by the eagle.

other. The three white circles with crosses inside them, on his haunch are a reference to the Eucharist. The eagle symbol of St John has a halo with three crosses, a device that recurs a number of times, and appears to be a reference to the Trinity. The beautiful tail of this eagle connects to the body in a sweeping S curve.

The portrait of St John

The painting of St John on Folio 291v (fig 8.30) portrays the author as a scribe, his quill pen in his right hand, a book held aloft in his left and an ink horn down by his right foot. John has an elaborate halo and the folds in his garments are arranged in a symmetrical way. The patterns in the border seem to be mirror images of their opposite number until one takes a closer look to discover differences in pattern and colour. The crosses at the top, bottom and sides of the border emphasise the head, hands and feet, which protrude beyond the frame, a reference to God the Father, who is behind everything, unseen. The crosses could be a reference to the fact that John was the only evangelist present at the Crucifixion of Christ.

FIG 8.34 Folio 188r. The opening letters of St. Luke's Gospel, 'Quoniam'.

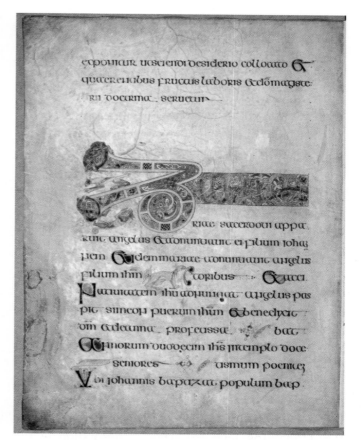

FIG 8.35 Folio 19v, from the Breves Causae illustrates the 'turn in the path'. At the end of the third line up from bottom 'doce' is finished 'bat' on the line above and is separated from the rest of that line by a decoration.

The *Quoniam* page

The opening word of the Gospel of Luke, '*Quoniam*' (fig 8.34), is given a full page to itself. The first three letters (QUO) are overlapped into one shape framed in purple, while the remaining letters (NIAM) are surrounded by little groups of figures. The group to the left and inside the A seemed to be overindulging in drink, and two at the bottom have their heads in the mouths of lions, which are formed from the ends of the letter M. This group of figures is sometimes thought to represent the Last Judgement or the punishments of Hell. Above the lettering is another group of figures forming an interlace pattern. Interlace patterns of a very high quality can be seen inside the circle at the bottom of the letter Q and in the panels that make a frame around the right and bottom sides, which end in a large dragon head that shares teeth and an outline with lion and eagle heads. This is the work of an artist with an amazing sense of design. On the Tara Brooch there is a link connecting the chain to the frame, which is designed in a similar way.

Other decorated pages

Decoration is not confined to the opening pages of the gospels only.

In the **Gospel of Matthew** the genealogy of Christ (a list of his ancestors) begins with the words '*Liber generationem*' ('The book of the generation'), which is given a full page of decoration. The two following pages, which list the generations, were planned to have decorated borders, but these were never completed. The name of Christ appears for the first time in the gospels at the end of this list. To celebrate the introduction of the name of Christ, the designers of the book introduced three pages of decoration: a portrait of Christ, a carpet page of eight circles and the Chi-Rho (symbol of Christ) page. The text of the gospel that follows is decorated throughout with enlarged capitals. Scrolls and marigolds are used as line fillers with occasional animal and human figures. Some decoration is used to mark the ends of passages or to highlight words in the texts. Decoration is also used to point out a 'turn-in-the-path' or 'head-under-wing' (that is, a place where a line of verse is finished in the space above or below the original line.) All the copyists in the Book of Kells seem to have used this space-saving device (fig 8.35). A few of the interlinear drawings seem to illustrate a piece of text. The arrest of Christ illustrated on Folio 114r is a scene often carved on high crosses of the time. On the back of this page is Folio 114v, a fully decorated page of lettering beginning with the words *Tunc dixit*. Further on in the Gospel of Matthew we come to the *Tunc crucifixerant* page, which begins the story of Christ's Crucifixion. Opposite this, on Folio 123v, a page remains blank, probably intended to carry an illustration of the Crucifixion.

The **Gospel of Mark** is much more sparsely illustrated. The four-symbol page and the initial page, which open the text of the gospel, are decorated, and only one other page of lettering from the beginning of the story of the Crucifixion – '*Erat autem hora tercia*' ('It was in the third hour') – is fully decorated.

The **Gospel of Luke** is missing the Four Evangelists and portrait pages at the beginning, but it does retain the glorious '*Quoniam*' initial page, which we have seen earlier. There are five pages from the genealogy of Christ, with decorated capitals forming a border down the left side of the page, and there are some interesting interlinear decorations. An illustration of the temptation of Jesus by Satan on Folio 200v (fig 8.38) is followed by the decorated opening letters of the story of the temptation. The final full page of decoration in the Gospel of Luke is the *Una autem* page, the opening lines of the resurrection story. The four archangels appear again on this page.

The three opening pages of the **Gospel of John** are intact: the Four Evangelists, the portrait and the decorated initial page. No other fully decorated pages survive. This is the most damaged part of the Book of Kells; four chapters are missing from the end of the Gospel of John.

Scribes and artists

A book as large as the Book of Kells and as elaborately decorated would have taken many years to produce. It could have been worked on by many hands over the years. Scribes and artists trained in the same scriptorium would have learned similar styles and techniques, so the work of individual artists is not easy to identify. More than one artist may have worked on individual pages, making it even more difficult to separate out the creations of different hands.

The scribes

Scholars have identified a number of different scribes. Françoise Henry, in her study on the Book of Kells, identified three, which she designated A, B and C. Other commentators think that different artists were involved in the work of C and so add the fourth scribe, D.

- Scribe A is regarded as the most conservative. He wrote 18 or 19 lines to the page in a clear majuscule script. The decoration is controlled and may have been added by another hand. His work appears at the beginning of the book, in the preliminaries, and at the end of the Gospel of Luke and the Gospel of John (fig 8.36).
- Scribe B has quite a different style. He used coloured inks and ended his pages in a line of minuscule script. This scribe added the rubrics (instructions and comments on the text, written in red) and other pieces throughout the text. He may have had the task of filling in gaps and finishing off incomplete sections of the book. The number of lines he wrote to the page varies.
- Scribes C and D copied most of the gospels of Matthew, Mark and Luke. Their work seems to combine both script and decoration. Their style is very close and some scholars treat all their work as by the same hand.

The quality of the lettering is very high, but it is sometimes difficult for the modern reader to make out because the conventions we use today regarding word spaces and punctuation were not yet in use in the 9th century. Some of the more elaborately decorated capitals and the opening pages can be difficult to decipher. Most of the monks reading the book would have known the texts by heart, however, so they would have known which letters to expect.

The artists

The artists may not have been separate people from the scribes, but so much time would have been needed to complete the decorated pages that it would seem logical that some monks would be dedicated to this work alone. Françoise Henry identifies three main artists from the different styles she found on the fully decorated pages. She calls them the Goldsmith, the Portraitist and the Illustrator.

The Goldsmith

Henry calls the first artist the Goldsmith because of the relationship between his work and metalwork in gold and silver. He is credited with the eight circles carpet page, the Chi-Rho page and the opening words of the gospels of Matthew, Mark and John as well as with some other smaller pieces of decoration. It is interesting to compare the Chi-Rho page in the Book of Kells (fig 8.37) with the same passage in the Book of Durrow (see Chapter 7, fig. 7.10). In both cases, the letters are decorated with spirals and

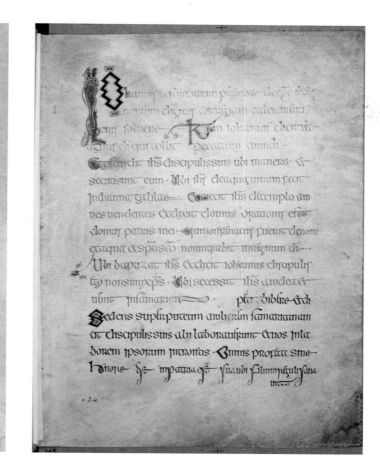

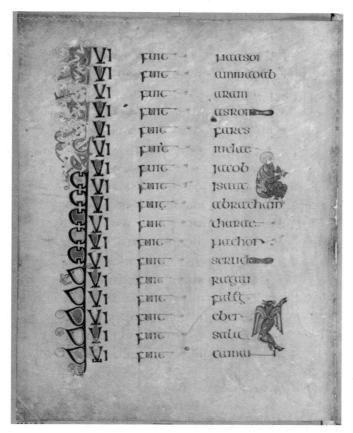

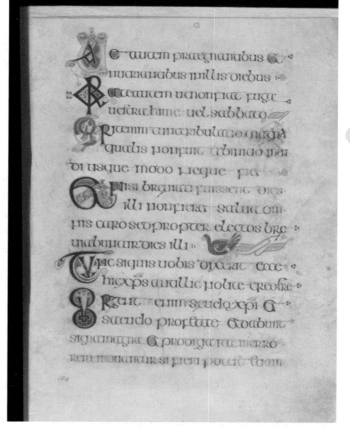

FIG 8.36 Folio 309r the work of scribe A. Folio 24r the work of scribe B.
Folio 188v the work of scribe C. Folio 104r the work of scribe D.

FIG 8.37 Folio 34r. The Chi-Rho page, it is a monogram of Christ taken from the first two letters of his name in Greek. It is used near the beginning of Matthew's Gospel where Christ's name is first mentioned.

FIG 8.38 Folio 200v. The Temptation of Christ, work by the artist known as the Illustrator.

trumpet curves, but in the Book of Kells the Goldsmith elaborates on everything – there is an almost endless variety of circles, spirals, triskeles and trumpet ends, twisting and turning together like the wheels of an old-fashioned clock mechanism. Between all these moving parts are panels and spaces filled with interlace, and men, birds, lions and snakes are interwoven in the most intricate patterns. The colour scheme is subtler than some of the other pages; delicate blues and violets make a counterpoint to smaller areas of bright red and yellow, which outlined the letters. This page is also heavy with Christian symbols: the cross in yellow and red at the foot of the letter P, the presence of angels to the left of the down stroke on the X, the God the Father figure appearing at the top of the X, the cats and mice with the Eucharist bread and the otter with the fish (another symbol of Christ) on either side of the cross at the bottom of the design. Three-part patterns occur regularly (referring to the Trinity) and four-part patterns could refer to the Four Gospels or the stages of Christ's life, or they might have other meanings.

The Portraitist

The Portraitist is the name given to the artist who painted the images of Christ, St Matthew, St John and the

symbols page for the Gospel of Matthew. We already looked at the Four Evangelists page (fig 8.33) and the portrait of St John (fig 8.30), which demonstrate a use of colour and space that is quite different from the work of the Goldsmith. There is less interest in tiny detail and areas of open vellum were left to contrast with the painted areas.

The Illustrator

The Illustrator is thought to be the artist behind the paintings of the Temptation, the arrest of Christ and the Virgin and Child (fig 8.32) paintings, which we have already seen, and the symbols of the evangelists before the Gospel of John. He may also have had a part in some other pages. The temptation of Christ page (Folio 200v) (fig 8.38) shows Christ at the apex of the temple, which can be interpreted as the Church, the body of Christ. To his right is a group of figures, which may represent his faithful followers, who he protects from the Devil. One of the group holds up a small shield (the Shield of Truth from Psalm 19:5), which the Devil quotes in the temptation story. The Devil, at Christ's left side, holds up a snare to trap the unwary. Four angels accompany Christ, as they do in the other scenes from his life. The beautifully decorated temple with the lion-head finials on the roof may give some idea of how an Irish wooden church looked in the 9th century. The figure in the doorway may represent Christ the judge. The two groups of 13 torsos at the bottom of the page could represent the apostles and the prophets, who were the foundation of the Church, or if the rectangle in the middle of the group can be seen as an empty table, they could be clergy fasting to see off the Evil One. The panels of snake interlace inside the crosses and at the bottom and sides of the border can be understood as representing the presence of evil in this scene.

One has to be careful about interpreting the symbols and images in these paintings, as they can be deliberately ambiguous. It is difficult to look at the scenes through the eyes of a 9th-century monk and see how he would have understood the images. The lives of the early monks were centred on a belief in Christ and the study of the Bible and related texts. They understood the world in a way that is difficult for observers in the 21st century to fully appreciate.

The Faddan More Psalter

The Faddan More Psalter was discovered in a bog in Co. Tipperary on 20 July 2006. It appears to be a complete book of Psalms contained in a leather satchel. Damaged when it was found and suffering the effects of spending 1,000 years in a bog, it is the most significant Irish archaeological discovery in decades and the first discovery of an Irish early medieval manuscript in 200 years. It is a large format codex of 52 or 54 folios (104 or 108 pages), written in Irish magiscule with decorated pages. The nature of the decoration will be seen once the conservation work on the book has been completed (fig 8.39).

Metalwork

Metalwork continued largely in the same style as the century before, but there were fewer colours used. Enamel was less frequently used and the fine detailed filigree work of the 8th century was transformed into looser and simpler designs. Precious materials, such as silver, gold and amber, were widely used. Craftsmen were still highly skilled and work was well constructed and carefully finished, but there appears to have been a loss of creative ingenuity. Designs and patterns were repeated more frequently.

By the 10th century a Viking influence was evident. An Irish version of the Viking Jelling style (a style of animal

FIG 8.39 The Faddan More Psalter before conservation

art) appeared alongside Irish motifs. Brooches took on new shapes and forms, probably in response to a Viking preference for larger pieces cast in solid silver.

A brooch from Roscrea, Co. Tipperary (fig 8.40), is a good example of this new style. It is cast in silver and decorated with gold filigree and amber. The design is much broader and simpler than the Tara Brooch; the pin

FIG 8.40 A pseudo pennanular brooch in silver with gold filigree decoration and amber studs

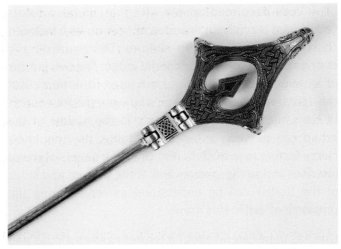

and ring are boldly outlined in a crest of semicircles filled with amber. A band of simple animal interlace inside this border surrounds panels of loose spirals in filigree. The overall effect is simpler and bolder than the Tara Brooch, but it does not have the subtlety of design and ingenious craftsmanship of the older brooch.

New brooch types were also introduced at this time: large silver kite (or almond-shaped) brooches, bossed penannular brooches and thistle brooches (fig 8.41) became more common in the 10th century. The laws that dictated the size and value of brooches that could be worn by people from different strata of society were still very much in evidence at this time.

The Derrynaflan Chalice

The Derrynaflan Chalice (fig 8.42), found in the same hoard as the Derrynaflan Paten that we looked at earlier (see Chapter 7, fig. 7.20), is the finest piece of 9th-century metalwork yet discovered. It is 19.2 cm high and 21 cm in diameter. It is made of silver and is decorated with gold filigree and amber studs. The decoration is laid out in a similar way to the Ardagh Chalice: there is a band of filigree and amber studs just below the rim, the handles have large decorated escutcheons, the collar between the bowl and the foot has bands of filigree and amber studs, which are also used on the decorative rim around the foot. Bird and animal shapes are the main elements in the filigree decoration (fig 8.43). The designs are simpler than those on the Ardagh Chalice. The artist relies for his effect on the contrast between the warm tones of the gold and amber decoration and the cooler silver colour of the bowl and foot.

FIG 8.42 *The Derrynaflan Chalice*

FIG 8.43 A Filigree animal from under the rim of the Derrynaflan Chalice.

154

The manufacture of other kinds of metal artefacts continued in the 9th and 10th centuries, including crosiers, book boxes and shrines (fig 8.44). Although none survive in very good condition, these items indicate the range of objects that were made at the time. Skills and techniques had not fallen away greatly since the 8th century, but the taste for intricate design seems to have changed in favour of bolder work. Possibly this bolder work was more suited to the taste of Vikings, who were important trading partners.

Conclusion

The period of the Viking invasions brought great changes to Ireland. A society that had lived in comparative isolation for nearly 1,000 years was violently opened up to new values and ideas. The notion of an island of saints and scholars was dealt a death blow. Irish book painting as a recognisable style almost vanished in a few generations, and though stone carving and metalwork would have a revival in the Romanesque era, the style was heavily overlaid with Viking and European influence. The unique combination of Celtic society and Christianity that proved to be so creative was at an end.

Fig 8.44 The 'Soiscel Molaise' book shrine from Dernish Island, Co. Fermanagh, early 11th century. Images of the Four Evangelists surround a central ringed cross.

Questions
1. Write a short description of a monastery of the 9th and 10th centuries.
2. Describe the function and construction of a round tower.
3. What was the symbolism of the ringed cross?
4. Sketch and describe one panel from the base of the Cross of Moone.
5. Compare and contrast a cross from the Celtic design tradition with one in a more classical style.
6. Give a short description of Muiredach's Cross at Monasterboice in words and sketches.
7. How were high crosses constructed?
8. Outline the scheme of decoration in the Book of Kells.
9. List the main artists in the Book of Kells.
10. Describe the Viking influence on 10th-century Irish metalwork.

Essay
1. The human figure frequently appears in designs of the 9th and 10th centuries. Describe the various forms and styles using examples from stone carving and book painting.
2. Write an account of the high crosses in the 9th and 10th centuries, using two examples to point out developments in design and technique.

Colour picture study
1. Choose an illustrated page from the Book of Kells. Examine the layout and colour scheme of the page and interpret the meaning of the images.
2. Using a photograph of a scripture cross as your starting point, describe the layout and decoration of the scenes and the meaning that was taken from them (fig 8.18).

CHAPTER 9

THE HIBERNO-ROMANESQUE REVIVAL (11TH AND 12TH CENTURIES)

Political and social background

The 11th and 12th centuries were a time of great religious and social change in Ireland. These changes brought new styles and forms or art, which were incorporated into the existing repertoire of Irish design. The style, which has become known as Hiberno-Romanesque, is a particularly Irish version of the Romanesque style. It mixes old Celtic elements and Scandinavian designs with some aspects of the more formal European style. In Ireland, Romanesque was more a style of decoration rather than a significant structural advance in architecture.

In spite of efforts in previous centuries to reform the Irish Church, a number of irregularities still remained and practice had not come into line with the diocesan system, which was the norm in the rest of Europe. When the Vikings converted to Christianity, they wanted to stay independent of the Irish Church organisation, so they sent their clergy to be educated in England at Worcester and Canterbury and had their bishops consecrated there. Pope Gregory VII wrote to Toirdelbach Ua Briain (Turlough O'Brien), High King of Ireland, and the archbishops, bishops and abbots of Ireland, offering assistance with reform. The synod held in Dublin in 1088 AD was attended by the king and the Anglo-Norman

Bishop Lanfranc of Canterbury. In 1101 AD Muirchertach, son of Toirdelbach Ua Briain, called a synod at Cashel and made a gift of the site to the Church, to be used as the centre of an archdiocese for the southern half of the country (fig 9.1). Armagh was made the centre of the northern archdiocese. In the following years, further synods were called to set the boundaries for dioceses and to introduce further reforms. By the mid-1100s there were archdioceses at Armagh, Cashel, Dublin and Tuam, and the boundaries of the dioceses were generally settled. It was at this time that there was an upsurge in building Romanesque churches or adding Romanesque features to existing churches, very often at diocesan centres.

Pilgrimage

Pilgrimage was at its peak in Europe in these centuries. Rome and the shrine of Santiago de Compostela (St James the Apostle) in northern Spain were the main centres of pilgrimage in Europe, but every church tried to have its own relics to encourage local pilgrimage. Much of the surviving metalwork from the 11th and 12th centuries is in the form of shrines. These were mainly metal covers made to house the remains or an article associated with a saint. Bones, bells, books, crosiers and other relics were enclosed in cases of decorated and precious metals, often paid for by the local royalty.

Patronage

Inscriptions on shrines, crosses and doorways offer praise and blessings on the kings who paid for their construction and the clergy who commissioned them.

FIG 9.1 An aerial view of Cashel with Cormac's Chapel on the left, the round tower on the right and the 13th century cathedral which was built on the top of the earlier diocesan site

The craftsmen who carried out the work were sometimes mentioned, which shows how highly esteemed craft workers were in Ireland. In Europe, the names of craft workers are rarely known. Patronage seems to have been an important aspect of kingly power at this time. The annals often record the presentation of gold or silver on the occasion of a visit by a king to a church or monastery and the purpose of the gift, to enshrine relics or to build a church, is usually noted. Kings seem to have sought power by association with these artefacts, which were important in the eyes of the people. Patronage may sometimes have had political ends; lands given to the Church along the border with a neighbouring kingdom could solve a problem over disputed territory. Cistercian monks from Europe were encouraged to come to Ireland by St Malachy of Armagh in the 1140s and they were given land by Irish kings to build and farm on. The effect of this was to introduce a new type of monasticism into Ireland as well as new types of buildings, which were completely at odds with the traditional Irish forms.

Politics

Irish society went through a complete structural change in these centuries. It evolved from a local tribal system into the feudal system, which was the norm in the rest of Europe. Under the feudal system, local kings looked on their land as a way of producing tax revenues from the peasants and of gathering men for an army when it was needed. In return, the king offered leadership and protection to his subjects. This new feudal system created the need for symbols of power and authority, and God, through the Church, was the ultimate authority. It is interesting to note that by the middle of the 12th century, many of the ring forts had been abandoned and people were living in closer community around the fort of the king or near the church.

There was a lot of manoeuvring for power among local kings. Diarmaid Mac Murchada (Dermot MacMurrough), the King of Leinster from 1132 to 1171, was a patron to many churches. He brought Augustinian priors in to reform the abbeys of his kingdom and he gave lands to Cistercian monks at the edge of his territories with the subordinate kingdom of the Ua Tuathails. He made Lorcán Ua Tuathail (St Laurence O'Toole), who was the abbot of Glendalough, into the Archbishop of Dublin, and married his half-sister to confirm the family bonds. Diarmait later abducted Derbforgaill, wife of Tighearnán Ua Ruairc (Tiernán O'Rourke), King of Breifne, and for this and other misdemeanours he was exiled in 1166. He returned in 1169 with Strongbow and his Anglo-Norman

Fig 9.2 Some surviving ruins of Mellifont Abbey. The first Cistercian house built in Ireland in 1142.

mercenary army to retake his kingdom and unwittingly change the course of Irish history.

The monasteries

The tradition of building small, simple churches continued into the 11th century. Most new church buildings had a chancel attached to the nave, with a round-headed arch connecting the two parts. Round towers with Romanesque doorways are found at a number of monasteries. The layout of the monasteries did not change until European orders were introduced

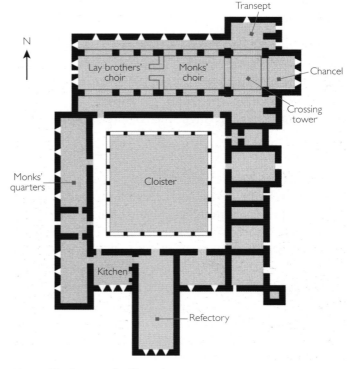

Fig 9.3 The layout of a Cistercian monastery

FIG 9.4 St. Kevin's Church at Glendalough from the east. The small chancel arch connected the nave to a chancel which has collapsed. Traces of the chancel can be seen on the ground and on the gable.

into the country in the 1140s. The Cistercian order built their first monastery at Mellifont, Co. Louth, in 1142, under the direction of Robert, a monk from Clairveaux in France. The first community of monks there were from France (fig 9.2).

The Cistercian order had a standard layout for their monasteries. The buildings were organised around a square cloister, with the church on the north side and the living and working areas around the other three sides (fig 9.3). The new monastic communities seemed to appeal to the Irish, because there were 30 Cistercian monasteries operating by the year 1200 and many of the old monasteries had gone over to Augustinian rule. The style of building in these converted Augustinian monasteries did not change much before the second half of the 12th century.

Structures (architecture)

Even though the technology existed to build round-arched doorways from the beginning of the 11th century, they did not become common for over 100 years. The traditional small door opening with inclined jambs and a large lintel must have had some important significance. St Kevin's Church at Glendalough, which has been dated to the end of the 11th century, is unusual in that a round tower is included in its roof structure. Its west door has a lintel with a relieving arch over it, which illustrates the point about lintels being a choice of style rather than technology (fig 9.4). Internally, St Kevin's is barrel vaulted, that is, it has an arched stone ceiling, and there is a triangular space above the arch and below the stone roof. This type of stone vault and roof was not common at this time in Ireland, but there are a few examples at important sites: St Columba's House at Kells, St Mochta's House at Louth and a few others. The oratory of St Sennan was built at Killaloe, Co. Clare; this was the centre of the Munster kingdom of the Ua Briains (fig 9.5). This building is similar in structure to St Kevin's, but it has no tower. It has a simple Romanesque doorway in the English style. The largest and most elaborately decorated version of this type of structure was at Cashel in Co. Tipperary.

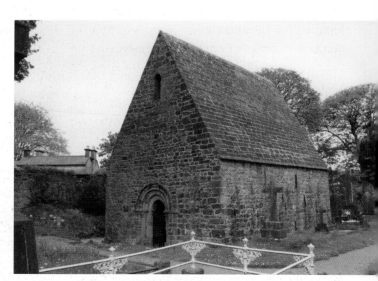

FIG 9.5 St Sennan's oratory at Killaloe, Co. Clare

The north wall is the most richly decorated. There is a door with a gable pediment over it and rosettes and heads form part of the design, along with chevrons in the English style. This wall originally faced a courtyard in front of the old church and the round tower. The courtyard was built over during the construction of the 13th-century cathedral, which is tight up against the chapel.

The south wall has three stages of arcading and a colonnade on top, like the one on the north wall. The decoration on the doorway is saw-tooth chevron, and chevron is also used to decorate the arches at ground level.

The stringcourses, which run horizontally along the building and the arcades, continue around all the elements, creating a unity of design not normally seen in Irish churches of this time.

The interior of the building, which was restored in the 1990s, reveals the remains of colourful murals and painted stonework. Some scenes have been deciphered, such as the Adoration of the Magi, the Magi before Herod and a shepherd scene (fig 9.7). The architectural features are again finely detailed, with arcades and pillars supporting the ribs of the barrel vault in the nave and the rib vaulting in the chancel. The chancel arch is decorated with human heads, and heads appear again on all sides of the vault in the chancel (fig 9.8).

The style of the decoration on Cormac's Chapel seems to owe so much to the contemporary Anglo-Norman style that it has been suggested that English craftsmen carried out the work. There are other influences present here:

FIG 9.6 Cormac's Chapel, Cashel, from the east

Cormac's Chapel

Built between 1127 and 1134 under the patronage of Cormac Mac Carthaigh, King of Munster, Cormac's Chapel was constructed on the site donated by Muirchertach Ua Briain in 1101. Cormac's Chapel is a unique building in Ireland in its architectural completeness. It is a simple nave and chancel church with two square towers, one on each side of the east end of the nave. There is a Romanesque doorway in the north and south walls with arcades (rows of arches) and stringcourses on all sides of the exterior. It is 15 m long and 5 m wide internally and the towers are 18 m tall (fig 9.6).

FIG 9.7 The tympanum over the north door has a centaur shooting a lion-monster with an arrow. Rows of chevron moulding decorate the arches.

FIG 9.8 Cormac's Chapel interior. Traces of paint can be seen on the arches and ceiling.

FIG 9.9 The west door of Clonfert Cathedral with its decorated triangular 'gable pediment'

the arcading corresponds with some French examples and the overall appearance from the east of the building is Germanic. This last element may be explained by the presence of Benedictine monks, who were brought from the Scottenkirche (Irish church) of St James at Regensberg in Bavaria, Germany, to run the church. The Scottenkirche had long-time connections with Ireland.

Romanesque decoration

The decorated north doorway at Cashel seems to have impressed some influential people, as there are eight other doorways with pediments, mainly around the Midlands. The latest and most elaborate of these is at Clonfert Cathedral in Co. Galway.

Clonfert Cathedral

Clonfert Cathedral is more typical of the Irish Romanesque style. It is a simple nave and chancel building with *antae* (projections of the sidewalls beyond the gables), much altered over the years. The decorated area surrounding the west door is 8 m tall. It consists of

a doorway with six orders of Romanesque arches, with a pediment on top (fig 9.9). The inside arch of grey limestone was added in the later Middle Ages and is not part of the rich brown sandstone of the original design, which we are studying. The pillars on each side of the doorway are decorated in matching pairs, with lightly carved patterns of geometric and vegetal designs. The capitals have animal heads and human faces, again in matching pairs on either side of the door.

The arch rings are more deeply carved and come in a variety of designs (fig 9.10). The inner row is decorated with plant forms, and the next one has animal heads holding a roll-moulding in their jaws. The third row is made of square crosses connected to a roll-moulding at the outer edge. Flat disks are carved on both faces of the next arch and are alternately pierced or decorated with spirals, serpents and flowers. The fifth row has an open-ended cable moulding surrounding bosses on both faces, enclosing a roll-moulding on the outer edge. The sixth row is made of semi-spherical bosses decorated

with interlace, and the outer ring that separates the arches from the pediment has an interlace pattern in the Scandinavian Urnes style (tight patterns of slim and stylised animals).

The pediment is surrounded at its outer edges by a double cable moulding. There is a final at the top, which has a human head on each side. The lower part of the pediment has a row of five arches with a head placed in each. Above this is a pattern of triangles, decorated with plant forms. There are 10 heads set in the hollow spaces between the decorated triangles.

The carved doorway at Clonfert Cathedral has some parallels in England and France. It may have been built at the time of the synod, which was held there in 1179.

Romanesque features

There are Romanesque features at over 100 sites around the country, ranging from simple chancel arches to elaborately carved doorways. Most of these features are added to small, plain buildings. The Nuns' Church at Clonmacnoise was completed in 1167 by the same Derbforgaill who had been abducted by Diarmaid Mac Murchada. It was a family church patronised by her father, Murchad Ua Máelsechlainn, King of Meath. The west door and reconstructed chancel arch are all that remains of the decoration. The doorway has four decorated arches resting on pillars with chevron decoration on both faces, creating a lozenge pattern down the outer edge. The second arch has animal heads with patterned faces holding a roll-moulding in their jaws. The other arches

have geometric patterns (fig 9.11). The chancel arch has some human and animal heads on the capitals and the arches are carved with geometric patterns.

FIG 9.11 Doorway & chancel arch of the Nun's Church at Clonmacnoise

Irish sculptors combined European and Viking influences with La Tène designs, which had already been in use for hundreds of years. Interlace, animal forms and geometry formed the basis for most design. Repetition of designs and patterns and balancing of composition was more common than it had been in earlier work.

Sculpture

During the Romanesque period in Europe, sculpture formed a decorative element on architecture. In Ireland, almost the opposite was true. Buildings were smaller, plainer and without many architectural qualities, but the decoration was of a very high standard. The decorative carving discussed above under the heading 'architecture' could just as easily be called sculpture. Many of the design elements – geometric and animal interlace, high-relief carving and plant forms – recur in the carving of high crosses.

High crosses

There is a gap of almost 200 years between the great period of Irish high cross carving in the 9th and 10th centuries and this final phase of development.

The Drumcliffe High Cross (fig. 9.12) is an early example of this new series of crosses. It has many of the same features that the earlier crosses had, such as a wheel head and tall base, but it is not divided into panels. The cross is carved from two blocks of pale sandstone and a bead moulding surrounds the decoration on both faces, leaving a plain border around the outline of the cross. There is a mixture of interlace designs and figure scenes, all over the cross. A lion in high relief is superimposed midway up the shaft on the east face, and a monster is in the same position on the west. More traditional scenes, such as Cain killing Abel and Adam and Eve, are also included. Interlace relates closely to contemporary metalwork and manuscript designs.

FIG 9.12 The western face of the High Cross at Drumcliffe

FIG 9.13 High Cross at Cashel

Romanesque crosses at Tuam, Roscrea and Cashel are badly weathered and damaged. They appear to have had a large, high-relief figure and areas of interlace designs (fig 9.13). The design of the cross at Cashel is similar in design to the Volto Santo, a wooden crucifix from the cathedral in Lucca, Italy, which is on the pilgrimage route to Rome. Small copies of this cross were sometimes carried by pilgrims who visited Lucca on their way to or from Rome, so it may have influenced the design of Irish crosses.

In Co. Clare, a number of crosses survive, the latest and most unusual of which is at Dysert O'Dea. This cross has no traditional wheel head, though sockets at the ends of the arms may have held some further decoration (fig 9.14). A figure of the crucified Christ wears a long robe in the style of some contemporary European sculptures. The figure of a bishop below Christ's feet has a socket at waist level, from which a separately carved arm once projected.

FIG 9.14 Dysart O'Dea High Cross, Co. Clare

Other surfaces of the cross are carved in low relief with patterns and a few figure scenes. Viking influence can be noted in the design of the interlace patterns of snakes and animals on the base, which relate closely to designs on metalwork.

Irish Romanesque sculpture

Irish Romanesque sculpture, whether on doorways and arches or carved high crosses, combined influences from England and Europe with the earlier Celtic tradition. Interlace patterns were modified through Viking influence into battles between fantastic creatures. Geometric patterns often seen on doorways and chancel arches had their origins in English carving, and high-relief figures found on crosses or on doorways relate to sculpture from France and Italy. All these influences were brought together in this final phase of truly Irish sculpture, in which Celtic roots were still clearly visible, providing the harmonising element in the style.

Manuscripts

A number of interesting books survive from the Romanesque period. Most of these books are interesting for their texts and associations rather than for their decoration, but there are a number of decorated books. The Liber Hymnorum is an 11th-century book of hymns in Irish and Latin kept at Trinity College Library in Dublin. It has decorated capitals with animal and plant forms painted in yellow, red, green and purple. These colours are now faded due to the passage of time. The text is written in Irish majuscule across the full width of the page (fig 9.15).

The Psalter of Cormac includes some Continental influence, which might have been introduced through the Cistercian monasteries. The script is more regular and some background areas within the letters are coloured. The capital letters that begin each psalm are decorated with blue, purple, yellow and green against a red background (fig 9.16). The Psalter of Cormac is one of the most completely decorated texts surviving from this period. Decorated capitals and small animals appeared throughout the text in a scheme that reminds one of the Book of Kells.

The few decorated books that survive from the Romanesque period mark the end of the true Irish manuscript. All that followed were written in Britain or Europe or were copies of European models. Only rarely in the following centuries did an Irish decorated capital make an appearance in a manuscript.

FIG 9.15 Decorated capitals from the Liber Hymnorum from Trinity College

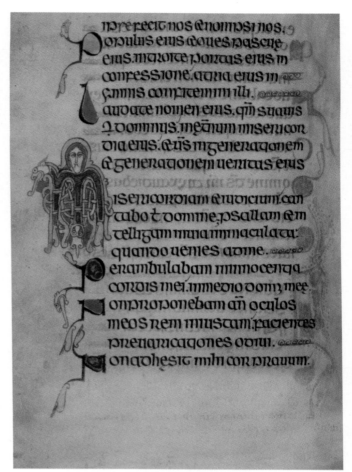

FIG 9.16 A page from the Psalter of Cormac which shows the continuity of manuscript design into the 12th century

Metalwork

Most surviving examples of 11th- and 12th-century metalwork are reliquaries, which have probably survived because of their importance to the Church as objects of veneration. Their hereditary custodians kept many of them until the 19th century. Little else survives. Brooches, which were such a feature in earlier centuries, may have gone out of fashion. Although few examples of any quality survive, we know of the existence of chalices and decorated drinking horns from the accounts in the annals.

A number of pieces from the Romanesque period were inscribed with the names of the craftsmen who made them and the bishops or patrons who commissioned them. Cudulig O'Inmainen and his sons made the Shrine of St Patrick's Bell in their workshop in Armagh (fig 9.17). It includes finely cast panels in the Urns style (a Scandinavian version of Irish animal interlace, combining snakes and ribbon-bodied animals in a thin

FIG 9.17 The Shrine of St Patrick's Bell

FIG 9.18 The handle cover from St Patrick's Bell shrine showing interlace patterns in gilt cast bronze

linear style). Most of the Shrine of St Patrick's Bell is as it was originally designed, except for a few semi-precious stones, which were added to the box in later medieval times (fig 9.18). The handle cover at the top of the box includes an openwork bronze cast of two interlaced birds.

Other bell shrines, book boxes and crosiers survive, encased in elaborate metalwork. The Lismore Crozier has a row of interlaced dogs and monsters on its crest (fig 9.19). The panels between the enamel studs once contained filigree, none of which remains. The whole crosier is covered in bronze plaques held together by three cast bronze knobs, which are decorated in plant and animal interlace. Other croziers of this type survive,

FIG 9.20 The Crozier of the Abbots of Clonmacnoise

FIG 9.19 The Lismore Crozier. The filigree has all fallen out but many of the fine enamel studs survive.

decorated in a variety of styles and techniques. All seem to have had a little box at the outer end of the crook, probably to hold the precious relic of a saint.

The Crozier of the Abbots of Clonmacnoise (fig 9.20) is an elaborate reliquary made of bronze plates enshrining a wooden staff. The crook is a simple horse's head shape, in the Irish style. About half of the original crest – dogs biting the rear of the preceding animal – remains. The sides of the crook are inlaid with silver in a pattern of ribbon-like snakes entwining with finer threads with spiral endings. The pattern was outlined in niello.

The designs on the Crozier of the Abbots of Clonmacnoise show Scandinavian influence in the style of the patterns, which relate to Ringerike and Urnes designs, though adapted into an Irish style. Some elements of the interlace patterns cut through each other rather than weaving under and over each other, as they did in earlier designs. A grotesque face with an elaborate beard and moustache tops the reliquary box at the front

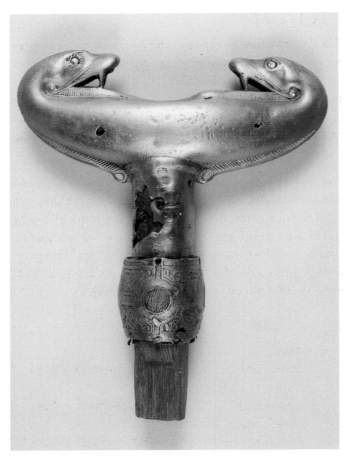

FIG 9.21 A tau crosier with animal head terminal

FIG 9.22 The Shrine of St Lachtin's Arm

of the crook; the little cast figure of a bishop was added in the 14th century.

The upper knop (ornamental knob) of the crosier has triangular insets made of copper with champlevé enamel patterns in foliate and geometric designs. There are blue enamel studs at the points of the triangles. Below the knop are two pairs of cast animals – their forelegs are entwined and they have spiral patterns on their chests and haunches, which were inlaid with silver and niello. Triquetra knots are formed by their tails, which end in an animal head. (Paired animals like these appear on the Cross of the Scriptures at Clonmacnoise and on Muiredach's Cross at Monasterboice.) The middle knop is decorated with a geometric interlace, and below this the shaft tapers down to a ring with a point below it.

Crosiers in other shapes also existed. The National Museum of Ireland houses a tau crosier with a fine top consisting of a cast of two animal heads (fig 9.21). An ivory crosier with a spiral crook found in Aghadoe, Co. Kerry, shows Jonah emerging from the whale.

The Shrine of St Lachtin's Arm is a well-preserved example of a type of relic once common all over Europe

(fig 9.22). It is 40 cm tall and is made of bronze plaques held in place on a wooden core by cast rings. The hand is a separate cast. The plaques are inlaid with silver and niello in a ribbon decoration of thread-like animals with open jaws. The hand has some panels of filigree, silver nails and the gilded silver palm is decorated with foliage and tendrils. The bands, which held the shrine together, are decorated with interlace. Some glass studs survive around the base.

The Cross of Cong was made to display a fragment of the True Cross, taken from a larger fragment, which was brought to Ireland from Rome in 1119 AD. Like the Tully Lough Cross that we discussed earlier, it is made of bronze plaques and mounted on an oak core. The cross is 76 cm tall and the surface is covered in a network of ornament (fig 9.23). The cross is outlined by a tubular, silver edging and punctuated with glass studs on the front and enamel discs on the back. Rows of mounts, which once held glass or enamel studs, divide the front of the cross into panels. The centre of the cross has a semi-conical mount holding a rock crystal. The fragment of the True Cross was displayed behind this transparent

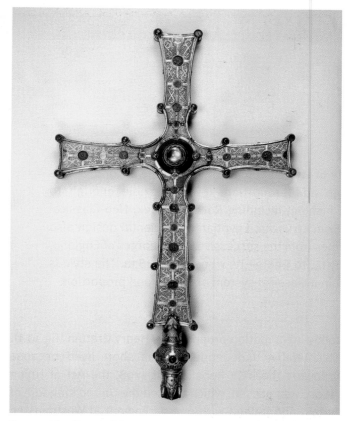

FIG 9.23 The Cross of Cong

crystal. Each panel on the front is filled with gilt bronze animal interlace, in the Urnes style. Four bronze openwork plaques that have been skilfully cast and gilt, again in the Urnes style, make up the back of the cross. A pair of animal heads with blue glass eyes forms the mounting, which joins the shaft to the cross. The animals, clamping the cross in their jaws, have scaly heads with mustachios and eyebrows of niello and silver.

Metalwork of the 11th and 12th centuries is quite different in style from the 8th-century work, which is considered to be the high point of Irish metalwork. The later work relied for its impact on bolder designs and colour effects, though pieces like the Cross of Cong are beautifully balanced and subtle in their design.

Conclusion

The changes that began with the arrival of the European monastic orders and the Norman knights created an enormous social upheaval in Ireland. The Celtic monasteries, which had been the focus of Irish society for hundreds of years, became less popular, with large numbers of monks joining the new monastic orders, the Cistercians, Augustinians and Benedictines.

The adoption of the feudal system by the Irish chieftains and the development of towns added to this change in society. For a while, the patronage of new foundations by the Irish chieftains and kings and the need for reliquaries created a blossoming in the arts, but the European orders' preference for plain buildings and simple altar vessels soon put an end to this crafts revival.

Questions
1. Write and sketch a short description of Cormac's Chapel at Cashel.
2. Describe the decoration of the doorway of the Nuns' Church at Clonmacnoise.
3. Describe the style of high crosses in the Romanesque period.
4. Describe a reliquary from the Romanesque period.

Essay
1. Influences from outside Ireland became very noticeable in the designs of the 11th and 12th centuries. In words and sketches, describe two objects from the time that illustrate this point.

Colour picture study
1. Look at the illustration of the west doorway at Clonfert Cathedral. Describe the elements and the layout of the design and give your opinion of the significance of Romanesque design in Ireland in the Middle Ages (fig 9.9, fig 9.10).

CHAPTER 10

THE GEORGIAN PERIOD

The term 'Georgian' refers to a variety of styles in architecture and the decorative arts based on classical ideals of design and proportion. It was flexible enough to accommodate changes in taste and fashion, including Rococo, Greek, Neo-Classical and Gothic Revival, with influences from Etruscan, Egyptian and Oriental design also holding sway for a time. The name comes from the successive King Georges of England, from George I, who became king in 1714, to George IV, who died in 1830. The style is characterised by good craftsmanship in a classical system of design and proportion.

Political and social background

In the 18th century, Ireland had just come out of a period of rebellions, wars and plantations, ending in the defeat of the old Irish aristocracy who had fought alongside Catholic King James II of England. The victory of William of Orange at the Battle of the Boyne in 1690 brought about the Flight of the Earls. The Penal Laws that followed denied political and civil rights to Catholics and gave political control to the Protestant Ascendancy, who ruled via a parliament in Dublin (albeit subject to approval from the English parliament in Westminster).

Through agitation and political pressure, the Irish parliament achieved legislative independence in 1782, following a motion proposed by Henry Grattan (fig 10.1). This relative independence was short lived because following the Irish Rebellion of 1798, the Act of Union (1800) was passed, which created the United Kingdom of Britain and Ireland with one parliament in Westminster, putting an end to 'Grattan's Parliament'.

The loss of the Irish parliament had a huge economic effect on Ireland, and particularly on Dublin. The parliamentary sessions had brought elected representatives and lords to the town, where they all owned or rented large houses. They entertained and socialised, creating jobs in services and supplies, development and construction. When politics moved to

FIG 10.1 THE IRISH HOUSE OF COMMONS, a painting by Francis Wheatley (1780). Shows all the commons and the spectators in the gallery above during Grattan's famous speech on the repeal of Poynings' Law. It is the only record of what the house of Commons looked like as it was destroyed in 1803 following the Act of Union.

London, the social and economic benefits went with it, leaving Dublin in a depressed state. Over time many of the fine houses were divided up into tenements to be rented out to the poor, while others were sold off as offices.

Prosperity was brought about in the 18th century by a strong export trade in wool, linen and agricultural produce, particularly salt beef, pork and butter. (The result today is that the old trading and export centres in the towns and ports of Ireland often have well-built streets of Georgian buildings and market houses.) While the wealth and patronage were largely in the hands of the Protestant minority, the artisans and tradesmen were often native Irish Catholics (fig 10.2).

The Dublin Society

Organisations were set up for the improvement of infrastructure, agriculture, industry and the arts. The Dublin Society, founded in 1731, sponsored research and awarded premiums to encourage industry and crafts. The Wide Streets Commission, set up in 1757, regulated planning and street design in Dublin, which was going through a phase of unprecedented expansion.

The Grand Tour

This was the age of the 'Grand Tour', when people of wealth and education visited the sights of Europe with particular attention given to classical and Renaissance arts and architecture. The sights of Rome and Florence and the works of art being revealed at Pompeii influenced returning tourists to attempt classical design in their own public and private buildings.

Palladianism

Andrea Palladio (1508–80) had an enormous influence on architecture through his books *I Quattro Libri dell'Architettura*, which were published in 1570 and published in English translation as *The Four Books of Architecture* between 1715 and 1720. These books contained drawings of plans and elevations of Palladio's buildings and advice on proportions, building materials, the 'correct' classical orders, porticos, columns and other useful details. Palladio offered a system of proportions 'as immutable as the harmonies of music', which governed the relationships between all the elements of his designs, both plans and elevations. His theories were based on the books by the Roman architect Vetruvius and his own measurements of classical buildings in Rome (fig 10.3).

Palladio designed country houses for wealthy Venetians in the countryside of the Vento region. They combined elegant living space for the owner with outbuildings for animals and farm work. This arrangement proved popular with Irish and English country gentlemen who built a great number of houses, both large and small, in

FIG 10.2 Georgian buildings in Birr, Co. Offaly

Ionic capital

Corinthian capital

Composite capital

Doric

Tuscan capital

FIG 10.3 The classical orders

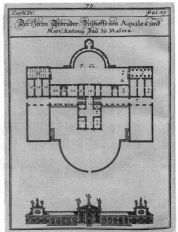

FIG 10.4 The Villa Barbaro, Maser, Italy. 1558 by Andrea Palladio (above). Plan and evelation of the Villa Barbaro from 'The Four Books of Architecture' by Andrea Palladio (on the right).

the style. The central block was often square in plan with a temple front of columns and a triangular pediment forming a portico over the formal entrance. Generally, the buildings had three floors. The basement was often of rusticated stone, containing the kitchen, services and minor rooms. The ground floor, referred to as the *piano nobile* ('noble floor'), would have been reached by a flight of steps leading to the entrance. Inside were the main reception rooms and master bedroom. This floor would have the tallest windows and most spacious rooms. The top floor had lower ceilings and contained bedrooms and rooms of less importance. The windows were often square on this level (fig 10.4).

Irish Palladianism

Palladian buildings in Ireland were often truer to Palladian ideals than English examples. This may be because some of the architects who worked in Ireland came directly from Europe and were not influenced by the English version of the style. Irish interiors were often quite flamboyant, with Rococo plasterwork in high relief.

Sir Edward Lovett Pearce

Sir Edward Lovett Pearce (1699–1733) was born in Co. Meath. After the death of his father in 1715 he went to England to study architecture with his father's cousin, the famous English Baroque architect Sir John Vanbrugh, who was working on the design of Blenheim Palace at the time. After a spell in the army, Pearce travelled to France and Italy for three years, studying architecture. He had a copy of Palladio's *Quattro Libri*, which he annotated with his own sketches and observations of the buildings he saw. He met Alessandro Galilei, the designer of Castletown House, in Florence. Pearce was

one of the most influential architects of his day and is credited with bringing the Palladian style to Ireland. Castletown House, Drumcondra House (All Hallows College), Bellamont Forest and Cashel Palace were among the large country houses that he worked on. The Parliament House (now the Bank of Ireland) in College Green, Dublin, was his greatest and most influential public building.

Castletown House, Co. Kildare (fig 10.5), is the earliest and largest of about two dozen large country houses that were built in Ireland between 1716 and 1745. It was built for William Connolly, who had risen from humble beginnings to become one of the richest and most powerful men in Ireland. He made a vast fortune from land deals and rose to political prominence as the Speaker of the Irish House of Commons.

The Italian architect Alessandro Galilei was commissioned to design the house. He came to Ireland in 1719 and spent less than a year on the job. He produced drawings of the front elevation and probably the plan for the house before departing, leaving others to carry out the work, which was begun in 1722. Sir Edward Lovett Pearce took over the project in 1724 on his return from his Grand Tour in Europe. He designed the quadrant Ionic colonnades that join Galilei's central block, which is built in pale limestone, to the two end pavilions, which are in a warm brown limestone.

Castletown is the first large country house in Ireland to be designed by a professional architect using classical proportions. The central block, which is in the style of an Italian town palazzo, is 13 bays wide. The building is four storeys tall. A set of broad steps reaches the main entrance across the area in front of the basement. The

tallest windows are on the ground floor. The first floor windows each have a pediment, alternately curved and triangular. The windows on the top floor are square. A balustrade at roof level helps to conceal the hipped roof. A matching balustrade runs along the top of the colonnades and continues along the roof level of the wings, creating a unity in the whole composition.

Inside there is a double-height entrance hall, which was designed by Pearce. He used Ionic columns around the walls and to support a balcony, which connects to the central corridor on the first floor. The columns in the hall match the colonnades outside. This balconied hall with its black-and-white stone floor tiles was frequently copied in other Irish houses. It is the only part of Castletown House that survives unchanged from William Connolly's time (fig 10.6).

Many of the features of Castletown House's interior date from the late 1750s, when Tom Connolly, grandnephew of

FIG 10.6 The entrance hall at Castletown designed by Sir Edward Lovett Pearce

William, inherited the estate. He married Lady Louisa Lennox in 1758. She was the daughter of the Duke of Richmond and a granddaughter of Charles II of England. Louisa was only 15 at the time of her marriage, but she took over the management and decoration of the house with some enthusiasm. She ordered the beautiful cantilevered stairway built in Portland stone and the plasterwork on the walls of the stairwell, which was carried out by Paulo and Filippo Lafranchini, the Swiss-Italian *stuccodores* (plaster modellers). The plasterwork consists of floral swags, cherubs and family portraits in a high-relief Rococo style. In the 1760s, Louisa with her sister and friends decorated the walls of one of the ground floor rooms with mezzotints and engravings, creating the only 'print room' still surviving in Ireland.

In the 1770s, **the Long Gallery** was completely redecorated (fig 10.7). This room, which is more than 24 by 7 m, is on the rear of the first floor. It has decorative wall paintings in the Pompeian style by Thomas Ryder. The room has eight windows overlooking the gardens; Connolly's Folly (1740) can be seen in the distance. The wall opposite the windows has two doors with a niche between them, which contains a statue of Diana the Huntress. Above the doors is a large semicircular (lunette) oil painting, a version of Guido Reni's *Aurora*. There are other oil paintings incorporated into the scheme of decoration, including portraits of Tom and Lady Louisa Connolly over the fireplaces at each end of the room. All the elements of the room design, including paintings, niches, sculptures, mirrors – even the coloured glass chandeliers specially ordered from Venice – were carefully balanced in a symmetrical arrangement of all the parts. The Connollys used this enormous room as their family living room, where they could have family meals, play games or music and entertain close friends. Several activities could go on at the same time without interfering with each other.

Bellamont Forest, Co. Cavan (fig 10.8), begun in 1730, is a smaller villa that Pearce designed for Charles Coote. Compared to Castletown House, it is a very plain structure, almost square in plan. The building is constructed of locally fired red brick, with details picked out in cut limestone. The entrance front has a portico, which consists of a pediment supported on Doric columns approached by broad steps. The windows on the ground floor are also pedimented. Pearce uses stone to outline the *piano nobile*, a stringcourse runs around the building at portico level and corner stones are used to create a kind of frame to emphasise the most important rooms of the house. The basement is of rusticated stone, with deep joints and a roughened surface. The upper floor has square windows. There are Venetian windows on the side elevations, and on the inside there is a colonnaded lobby on the top bedroom floor, which is lit from above by a lantern window. These are among the features that Pearce designed for Bellamont which were often borrowed in later houses. There is some good high-relief plasterwork in the interior.

The Parliament House (Bank of Ireland) is considered to be the most important early Palladian public building in Britain or Ireland (fig 10.9). It was the first structure designed to hold two houses of parliament. It contained chambers for the Commons and the Lords of the Irish Parliament. The House of Commons was at the centre of Pearce's design. A large octagonal space covered by a dome, it was damaged by fire in 1792 and removed when the building was converted to a bank in the early 19th century. This chamber was surrounded on three sides by

FIG 10.9 The Irish Parliament (now the Bank of Ireland), designed by Sir Edward Lovett Pearce

FIG 10.10 The House of Commons in the Irish Parliament building retains many of its original features

a corridor of top-lit domed squares, which became a feature of Pearce's work. The House of Lords, which is set off to the east side of the Commons, retains many of its original features (fig 10.10). In plan, the building is quite like a church with an apse at the eastern end. It still retains its original plasterwork and a carved oak fireplace. The decoration includes large tapestries of the Battle of the Boyne and the Siege of Derry by John Van Beaver and a Waterford crystal chandelier made of over 1,000 pieces of glass.

Pearce's design for the entrance incorporates three temple fronts. The ends facing the street combine round-headed arches with pediments overhead. The central portico supports a pediment on four Ionic columns. An Ionic colonnade connects these three elements. In plan, it is like a letter E. The central portico is set back from the ends, creating a piazza forecourt where parliamentarians could make a formal entrance, arriving in their horse-drawn carriages. The Parliament House would have been the most impressive building in Dublin in its day. It influenced the design of other public architecture in Britain and Ireland.

The building in its present form includes a Corinthian temple front entrance on the east (Westmoreland Street) side, designed by architect James Gandon in 1782 as a separate entrance for the House of Lords. Gandon also designed the curved wall with niches that connects his entrance to Pearce's colonnade. Later, a portico and screen wall was built on the west side and pilasters were added to Gandon's wall to harmonise the whole composition.

Pearce spent only seven years working in Ireland, but in that time he changed the direction of Irish architecture. He died in 1733 at the age of 34, with some of his work unfinished. Richard Cassels, who had been his assistant on a number of projects, took over the practice and became the leading architect in the country, working in the Palladian style.

Richard Cassels

Richard Cassels (1690–1751) was born in Hesse-Cassel in Germany of a Huguenot family with a background in architecture. (He later anglicised his name to Castle.) He trained originally as a military engineer, but became interested in Palladian architecture when he was working in England in 1725. Sir Gustavus Hume brought him to Enniskillen, Co. Fermanagh, in 1728 to design a house for him. Cassels was also working with Pearce on the Parliament House that same year.

Cassels's first independent project was the Printing House at Trinity College. It has a portico in the form of a freestanding Doric temple front. Cassels's later buildings use engaged columns or pilasters rather than a freestanding frontispiece. He was an innovator in his plans for country houses. He designed an oval drawing room at the rear of Ballyhaise House in Co. Cavan and he put semicircular bay windows on the side elevations of Belvedere House in Co. Westmeath. These features became popular in Ireland and England, but not until years later.

Russborough House, near Blessington, Co. Wicklow (fig 10.11), is a high point in Irish Palladian country house design. It was begun in 1741 for Joseph Leeson, the 1st Earl of Milltown, and built in local granite. The façade is over 200 m long and includes a central block, six bays wide, connected by quadrant arcades to two pavilions, each seven bays wide. Walls continue beyond the pavilions to outbuildings at each end. There is a Baroque arch topped with a cupola at the centre of each wall to add interest and relief to the composition. It is a perfect example of Palladio's idea of combining the master's house within the structures of a working farm. The buildings on the west side contained the stables. The kitchens and other out offices were on the east side. A lot of the original features have survived intact. Stone, statuary, inlaid floors, mantles and plasterwork are all original and in good condition.

The central block of Russborough is two storeys over basement. The entrance is reached by a stairway, which is the full width of the frontispiece. This consists of four

FIG 10.11 Russborough House, Co. Wicklow, designed by Richard Cassels in 1741

engaged Corinthian columns, with floral swags between the capitals. These support a triangular pediment, which is applied to the wall. There is a semicircular fanlight over the door. Stringcourses at pediment and roof level create a horizontal emphasis. Cassels used urns as roofline sculptures on the main house as well as on the arcades and the wings.

The simplicity, even severity, of the exterior of Russborough is in contrast with the lavish Baroque and Rococo interior. On the *piano nobile* there are seven interconnected reception rooms. All of them are 6 m tall and – with the exception of the dining room – have coved ceilings (curved where the ceiling meets the wall). Dado rails in carved mahogany 1.2 m high help to reduce the apparent height of the rooms. Carved mahogany is also used on the doors, stairs and banisters. The floor of the saloon is also mahogany with satinwood inlay (fig 10.12). The Lafranchini brothers, whose work we noted at Castletown, decorated several of the ceilings. In the saloon, the 'the loves of the gods' are represented by cherubs and figure groups framed by plant forms and swags. The plasterwork at Russborough is considered to be the finest in the country.

Cassels designed many of the great Georgian country houses in Ireland, including Powerscourt (Co. Wicklow), Carton (Co. Kildare) and Westport (Co. Mayo). He also designed some large townhouses in Dublin, the first to be built in cut stone in an otherwise brick streetscape. Newman House (85, St Stephen's Green), Tyrone House (Marlborough Street, now part of the Department of Education and Skills), Powerscourt Townhouse (now a shopping centre) and the largest of them, Leinster House (Kildare Street,), the building housing the Oireachtas, the national parliament of Ireland.

Leinster House, originally built for the 22-year-old James Fitzgerald, the 20th Earl of Kildare and the 1st Duke of Leinster, in 1745, is basically a Palladian country mansion relocated into the city (fig 10.13). The entrance front on Kildare Street is built in fine Ardbraccan limestone and the simpler Leinster Lawn front is built in granite. It is set back from the building line behind its own forecourt. The central block is three storeys tall and

FIG 10.12 The saloon at Russborough

11 bays wide. The entrance is emphasised by a three-bay breakfront, which runs the full height of the building. The ground floor of this section is rusticated and a plain moulding surrounds the doorway. At first-floor level, a balustrade connects four Corinthian columns, which support a triangular pediment at roof level. The windows of the first floor have curved and triangular pediments like those on the *piano nobile* at Castletown.

Inside Leinster House there is a double-height hall with a balcony like the one at Castletown. A surprising amount of the original decoration survives, considering its changes of use over the years, including some good plasterwork by the Lafranchini brothers.

The Rotunda is a public building by Cassels. Founded as a charity hospital for expectant mothers by Dr Bartholomew Mosse, it is still a maternity hospital today (fig 10.14). Assembly rooms and a pleasure garden, where games and entertainments were held, were built with the hospital in order to raise funds to support the charity. The design is like Leinster House – it is 11 bays wide with a temple front – but it does have curved arcades connecting the central block to the wings and

176

Fig 10.14 The Rotunda Hospital in Dublin designed by Richard Cassels in 1750

FIG 10.15 Trinity College, front façade

the round building, further east, which is now a theatre. There is nice plasterwork by Bartholomew Cramillion in the chapel over the main entrance.

Cassels died before work had begun on his design for the Rotunda, but he left an impressive legacy of fine houses built to the highest standards.

Trinity College

Trinity College in Dublin is considered by some to be the finest collection of 18th-century university buildings in Britain or Ireland. The west front and Parliament Square behind it are thought to be the work of the amateur architect Theodore Jacobsen. It was built in granite with Portland stone details in 1752. The façade is four storeys tall and 19 bays wide. The seven central bays and the end pavilions are projected a little forward and framed with Corinthian columns to add interest to the long façade. A temple front of four attached Corinthian columns supporting a triangular pediment at roof level makes up the frontispiece. The end pavilions have large Venetian windows with swags above them and an attic storey at roof level. The pavilions and entrance were intended to carry domes, but these were never built (fig 10.15).

FIG 10.16 The Provost's House, Trinity College, designed by John Smyth in 1759

The oldest part of the existing complex of buildings is the Library, designed by Thomas Burgh in 1712. Burgh, an Irish-born architect, was the Surveyor General of Ireland. He was also responsible for the design of Collins Barracks (Royal Barracks) and Dr Steevens' Hospital, but the Library is considered to be his finest work. Cassels designed the Doric Temple, which is the Printing House, in 1734 and the Dining Hall in the 1740s. Sir William Chambers, of whom we shall see more later, designed the Theatre and the Chapel in the 1780s.

Of all the buildings at Trinity, the Provost's House is considered to be a gem. Designed by John Smyth in 1759, it is based on a drawing by the supporter of the Palladian style, Richard Boyle, Lord Burlington, who in turn based his ideas on work by Palladio. The beautifully decorated interior retains most of its original contents since it has always been occupied as a house (fig 10.16).

Davis Ducart (Daviso de Arcort), a Sardinian architect and engineer, worked mainly in the south of Ireland in the 1760s. The Custom House (now the Hunt Museum) in Limerick is thought to be one of his earliest designs (fig 10.17). His style was a Franco-Italian version of Palladianism, which sometimes looked more modern than contemporary work. The entrance front of the Custom House faces the river. It has a rusticated ground floor with three arches at the centre supporting the frontispiece, which has fluted pilasters supporting a simple entablature. He uses a straight arcade as the connection to the end pavilions, rather than the curved versions used by other architects in Ireland. Ducart designed several buildings in Cork: the Mayoralty House, Lota House and Kilshannig House, which has beautiful

plasterwork by the Lafranchinis in their later, lighter style.

Ducart's masterpiece is considered to be Castletown Cox in Co. Kilkenny, which is seven bays wide and three storeys over basement. It is built in fine cut limestone. Straight arcades again connect the house to domed pavilions, which form the corners of two L-shaped courtyards at the rear of the house. There is a very fine interior with plasterwork by Patrick Osborne of Waterford.

Plasterwork

'Stucco' is the term used for 18th-century decorative plaster. Stuccowork reached a high point during the Renaissance, Baroque and Rococo periods. Very fine sand, crushed white Carrara marble, gypsum, alabaster dust and other, sometimes secret, ingredients were mixed with water to create the stucco, which could be cast in moulds or applied freehand. When it was dry, the surface could be polished to a smooth finish.

During the building boom of the 18th century in Ireland, decorative stucco was introduced, first in the compartmented style, which was a continuation of 17th-century design, where the ceiling was divided into decorated geometric shapes (fig 10.18). In the 1740s the Lafranchini brothers introduced a Baroque style, with the human figure in high relief surrounded by acanthus leaves, swags of flowers and putti. Their later work was more Rococo, lighter and with more movement. The human figure was less evident.

The classical scenes and decorations were probably borrowed from French and Italian engravings. It was the

FIG 10.18 The compartmented ceiling of the chapel in the Royal Hospital Kilmainham, now the Irish Museum of Modern Art, is 17th century, but this style continued into the early Georgian period.

practice in the 18th century to use engravings as a reference for all kinds of decoration. Books of patterns and designs were produced so that architects and craftsmen could copy from them.

Robert West was an Irish *stuccodore* who worked in the Rococo style of the Lafranchini brothers. He is known for his high-relief birds and human figures, combined with plant forms. Some of West's best work can be seen in the house he built for himself at 20, Dominic Street, Dublin.

From about 1780, stucco design changed to the Neo-Classical style. Readymade decorative plasterwork became available from designers such as Robert Adam of England. Michael Stapleton, master plasterer and architect, was the finest exponent of the style in Ireland. He used moulds and freehand work to produce the sophisticated designs that were used in buildings such as the Theatre at Trinity College and Belvedere House in Dominic Street in Dublin. These sometimes delicate designs often show up best against a coloured background.

The Lafranchini brothers were born in Ticino in the Italian-speaking part of Switzerland. Paulo (1695–1770) and Filippo (1702–79) were the most influential *stuccodores* (plaster modellers) to operate in Ireland. They worked in an Italian Baroque figurative and ornamental style on about 15 Irish houses. They are often associated with the buildings of Richard Cassels. At Carton House and Newman House (fig 10.19) they produced figures of classical gods and goddesses, surrounded by swirling acanthus cartouches and swags. Classical figures are used again at Riverstown House in Co. Cork, where personifications of the virtues decorate

FIG 10.19 The Lafranchini's plasterwork combining figures and floral swags can be seen in this reception room at Newman House, Dublin

FIG 10.20 A portrait surrounded by leaf designs from Castletown House

FIG 10.21 A sketch of Robert West's decorative plasterwork from 20, Dominic Street, Dublin

the walls and a copy, in plaster, of Nicolas Poussin's painting of an allegory on truth appears on the dining room ceiling and is the highlight of the stuccowork in the house. (Copies of the plasterwork at Riverstown were made for Áras an Uachtaráin, the residence of the President of Ireland, in 1948.) There are figure scenes at Kilshannig House, also in Co. Cork, made in 1766, but these are unusual, as the Lafranchinis had generally changed to a lighter, more Rococo style from the 1740s on. At Russborough House the lighter style is more evident: acanthus leaf and floral swags with occasional putti make up the rhythmic patterns, which decorate the ceilings of the saloons (fig 10.20). The walls in the stair hall at Castletown are also decorated in this lighter, lively, asymmetrical Rococo style. While Paulo went to work in England in the 1750s for a number of years, Filippo remained in Ireland into the 1770s.

Robert West (d. 1790) came from a family of *stuccodores* whose work was recorded from the early 17th century. He was also a master builder. He was producing foliate and pattern-work stucco for the Rotunda Hospital at the time

the French *stuccodore* Bartholomew Cramillion was working on the chapel and was influenced by him. He would also have seen the work of the Lafranchinis, whose skills impressed and influenced him. West's best work is high-relief birds and human heads emerging from curved plant forms. These almost freestanding birds appear at his house, 20, Dominic Street, Dublin (fig 10.21), and at 28, St Stephen's Green, surrounded by leaves, flowers, fruits and musical instruments. West or his studio also decorated some country houses, such as Dowth Hall (Co. Meath) and Dunsandle (Co. Galway).

Michael Stapleton (1740–1801) was a master builder and *stuccodore*. He was a pupil of West and was able to do creative, freehand plasterwork as well as make copies of the work of English designers, such as Adams. His stuccowork was in the Neo-Classical style. A large collection of his drawings and engravings survive in the National Library of Ireland, and they show that he designed original compositions as well as copying from published sources. Stapleton's Neo-Classical designs look like lace or embroidery. Delicate white plant forms arranged in geometric patterns against a coloured background form the basis for most compositions. Figure

FIG 10.22 Michael Stapleton's neoclassical plasterwork combined figure scenes with more formal geometric patterns of plants and musical instruments.

scenes and classical devices like urns or musical instruments are used as centres of interest in the designs (fig 10.22).

Stapleton's work appears in the Theatre in Trinity College, Lucan House, which is now the Italian embassy, and Mount Kennedy House. His masterpiece is considered to be Belvedere House in Great Denmark Street in Dublin, which he completed for the 2nd Earl of Belvedere in 1786. (The Jesuit order bought the building in 1841 to use it as a school and has run it since as Belvedere College. James Joyce is its most famous past pupil.) Stapleton was the architect and *stuccodore* on this project. He produced some of his most creative work for the stairs and the main reception rooms.

The availability of plasterwork from commercially mass-produced moulds brought an end to the handcrafted work we have just seen. Decorative mouldings could be obtained quickly and cheaply, which suited the needs of Irish developers in a market where prices were falling, following the Act of Union in 1800.

Townhouses

At the beginning of the 18th century, Dublin was still a small, walled medieval city with narrow streets and alleys. Houses were built of stone and wood. By the end of the century, it was the second city of the British Empire and had elegant streets and squares and impressive public buildings. The city developed outwards from the area around Dublin Castle (fig 10.23).

The Duke of Ormond set land aside for the Phoenix Park, which was to be a deer park surrounding a royal residence. He approved the development of houses on both sides of the River Liffey, set back from the river behind broad paved quays. Much of the early development began on the north of the Liffey; Sir Humphrey Jervis developed lands around Capel Street and Jervis Street. The Earl of Drogheda owned lands that were developed into Henry, Mary and Earl Streets. Luke Gardiner bought out many of the interests and became

FIG 10.23 A view across Grattan Bridge to the Royal Exchange, now City Hall, at the top of Parliament Street

the main developer north of the Liffey from 1714 onwards.

On the south side of Dublin, Sir Francis Aungier and the Earl of Meath were the early developers. Joshua Dawson, Viscount Molesworth, planned Dawson, Molesworth, Nassau and Kildare Streets from 1710 on. The Fitzwilliam family (Lords Mountjoy) were the main developers on the south side after 1780. Other towns in Ireland have Georgian elements as well: the redbrick terraces of Newtown Perry in Limerick, the Mall in Cork and parts of many towns contain Georgian streets or civic buildings.

The Wide Streets Commission was established to control planning and to create order and uniformity in the development of Dublin city. They had powers of compulsory purchase and to enforce regulations. The commission was made up of members of parliament and the mayor, so they had considerable political clout. They cut through old parts of the city to create Parliament Street, which connected Dublin Castle to Capel Street Bridge and the north side of the city. Later, they built another bridge further down the river connecting Sackville (now O'Connell) Street with new developments at Westmoreland and D'Olier Streets. These streets were designed in the 1790s with integrated shop fronts, a feature which did not appear in London until later.

The earlier squares, such as St Stephen's Green and Parnell Square, were developed piecemeal, a few buildings at a time. Later squares, such as Mountjoy

Square on the north side and Merrion and Fitzwilliam Squares on the south side, were laid out in advance. Some streets were intended to have centrepieces and end houses, but plain redbrick terraces were the most common solution. Most streets and squares had a continuous building line, but there are streets with houses that vary in height, width, size of windows and doors and the colour of the bricks. Some houses have basements and first floors in cut stone and a few of the larger houses were completely stone built. The North and South Circular Roads outlined the urban area, which was later redefined by the Royal and Grand Canals (fig 10.24).

The **Georgian redbrick terraced house** can vary in size from being a single bay wide, which is rare, to five or even seven bays for some of the largest houses. The basements are at natural ground level. The streets were built on brick arches. The spaces beneath the arches were used as storage areas for the houses. Circular manholes on the pavements opened into chutes where coal, which was used to heat the houses, could be poured into the stores below. The streets were cobbled and the footpaths in the better parts of Dublin had granite kerbs. An open area between the street and the house allowed light into the basement windows. This area was protected by a cast-iron railing set in a low stone plinth at street level. Railings continued up the sides of the steps to the front door. The steps formed a bridge over the area. Cast iron was also used for

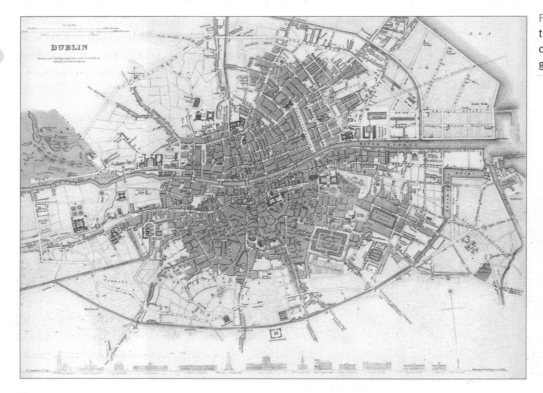

FIG 10.24 A map of Dublin from the 1840s shows how the canals created an outline for the growing city

DUBLIN

FIG 10.25 Cut away view of a Georgian terraced house

balconies and for foot scrapers and other street furniture.

The doorways provide one of the main decorative features of the Georgian street house. They come with a variety of fanlights and porticoes made up of classical elements. Some houses have a small window on each side of the door to help light the hallway inside. The sash windows vary in size, according to the importance of the rooms within. The tallest windows were on the first floor reception rooms and the smallest on the top floor bedrooms. The houses were built of red Bridgwater Brick, which came as ballast in ships trading with Bristol. The plainness of the façade is emphasised by the parapet, which partly conceals the roof. Fire-prevention regulations required the parapet to avoid rising sparks catching in the eaves and setting fire to the roof. Roofs were double-pitched; rainwater was carried through to the rear of the house and collected in down pipes. Houses had a garden at the rear with a carriage house at the far end. This could be accessed from a mews lane, which ran along behind the houses (fig 10.25).

Interiors

Most Georgian terrace houses were family residences, lived in by successful merchants and members of the professions. Some of the gentry used them as townhouses. They were most often four storeys over basement, with two reception rooms on the ground and first floors, one at the front and one at the rear, with a stairway and passage running down one side. The formal stairs normally stopped on the second floor, where the bedrooms of the master and the lady of the house were located. Smaller stairs gave access to the top floor, which was usually divided into four smaller bedrooms for children or servants (fig 10.26).

FIG 10.26 A three bay Georgian red brick house with a cast iron balcony. The roof is not visible from street level (left.) A Georgian bedroom interior (above).

Fig 10.27 One of the earliest Georgian terraces on Henrietta Street

bars, fine patterned framing on fanlights, and all carried out to the highest standards.

Henrietta Street (fig 10.27), which is just off Bolton Street on the north side of the city, was the earliest example of the Georgian terrace. Large four-storey houses, which were four or five bays wide, had big areas of plain brick between their well-proportioned windows. Door cases and pediments were in stone – London houses had wooden door cases – and the spacious interiors were based on country house designs. Sir Edward Lovett Pearce designed numbers 9 and 10. Number 9 has a Palladian compartmented ceiling in a colonnaded entrance hall, which is a scaled-down version of Castletown. Numbers 2 to 5 Henrietta Street were built by the banker Nathaniel Clements, one for his own use and the other two for speculation. Robert West's house, 20, Dominic Street, has the strongest contrast between plain exterior and decorated interior, with the flamboyant plasterwork he created in the stairway and reception rooms. The plain façade of 7, Ely Place conceals the exotic plasterwork of Michael Stapleton, representing the labours of Hercules. These are just some of the more outstanding early redbrick houses that line Dublin city's streets and squares. Later in the century, houses became more standardised and were mainly three windows wide with a wide arch enclosing the door case (fig 10.28).

The Neo-Classical style

In the late 18th century, there was a change in thinking about architectural design, which emphasised original Roman and Greek designs rather than the Renaissance interpretation of them through architects like Palladio. There was a movement away from Baroque and Rococo and a return to true classical design based on direct observation while on the Grand Tour or from books of engravings that showed Roman ruins or reconstructions of them. Giambattista Piranesi (1720–78) produced several influential books of engravings that exaggerated the size of Roman buildings. Another book of engravings, *The Antiquities of Athens* (1762), led to a Greek revival. The discoveries at Pompeii and Herculaneum helped create the Etruscan style that influenced the Adam and Empire styles.

Lord Charlemont

James Caulfeild, Lord Charlemont, spent a number of years on the Grand Tour in Europe. His cultural interests led him to spend a lot of his time in Rome, where he was friendly with artists and architects. On his return to

The basement contained the kitchen and rooms for servants to work and live in. Ceilings were relatively low and there was little or no decoration. The rooms on the ground and first floors were taller and had decorative plasterwork. The quality and quantity of the stucco depended on the wealth of the owner and the skills and talents of the builder or architect. The drawing room was normally more elaborately decorated; some of the finer houses have fully patterned ceilings surrounded with a frieze up to 30 cm deep. Dining rooms were less elaborately decorated. Rooms in the reception areas of the more ordinary houses would have had a plaster ceiling rose as a centrepiece and elaborate cornices. The ceilings of the basement and the top floors would have been quite plain. Stucco was also used for overdoors, which decorated the doorways of the main rooms. Swags, urns, heads or simple fluting were among the repertoire of designs used in these areas. Fine joinery was a feature of Georgian houses, including panelled doors and shutters, decorative door frames and balustrades, well-made sash windows with tin glazing

FIG 10.28 Some examples of the range of styles used on Georgian doors

Dublin in 1755, he wanted to bring Italian style to his Irish properties, so he employed a friend that he made in Rome to make the designs for him.

Sir William Chambers (1723–96) was the leading English architect of his day. He designed a townhouse and a garden temple for the country estate of Lord Charlemont at Donnycarney, which he renamed Marino in memory of his time in Italy. Marino House is long demolished, but the garden temple, the Casino at Marino and his townhouse, Charlemont House in Parnell Square, now the Hugh Lane Municipal Gallery, still stand (fig 10.29). Charlemont House, which was built in 1763, formed the centrepiece for the north side of Parnell (originally Rutland) Square. The house is connected to the redbrick terraces on each side by quadrant walls, which are decorated with niches. The ground floor is of rusticated stone, while the two upper floors are finished in smooth, cut stone. The entrance has a simple entablature supported on Ionic columns. It is a relatively simple exterior when compared with the early Palladian townhouses of Dublin.

The **Casino at Marino** was built during the 1760s. It is basically a garden ornament on a grand scale (fig 10.30). Chambers designed it as an architectural gem first; function was not of primary importance. The building is deceptively large; a second attic storey is almost hidden above the cornice. In plan it is a Greek cross inside a Doric colonnade. It stands on a podium, which is stepped

FIG 10.29 Charlemont House, the Sir Hugh Lane Municipal Gallery, designed by Sir William Chambers for Lord Charlemont

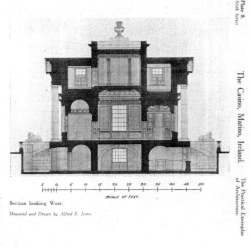

Section looking West.

Measured and Drawn by Alfred E. Jones.

FIG 10.30 The Casino at Marino designed by Sir William Chambers for Lord Charlemont (left). A section through the Marino Casino shows the amount of accomodation created within the building (right).

on the north and south side and has a balustrade on the east and west. The columns support an entablature decorated with ox skulls and concentric circles. The walls are rusticated to create a contrast with the smooth columns. A pediment creates a centrepiece on the north and south sides and the attic storey – decorated with swags and figure sculptures – forms part of the centrepiece on the east and west sides. Chambers never came to Ireland, so the English sculptor Simon Vierpyl, who had also befriended Lord Charlemont in Rome, supervised the work. Vierpyl was in charge of the stone carving and the exquisite detailing of the building, as well as having overall responsibility for the construction. All the functional parts are incorporated into the design: the urns on the roof are chimney pots and the pillars are hollow in order to channel rainwater from the roof into cisterns in the basement, where it could be used for household needs.

The glass in the windows is curved, which causes a reflection that prevents someone on the outside seeing in. This provides some privacy and disguises the fact that partitions and stairs, which form part of the ingenious interior, cross some of the window spaces. The basement has a kitchen and workrooms for the servants. The ground floor has a formal entrance hall and three reception rooms, with geometric patterned floors in exotic woods and fine plasterwork by Giovanni Battista Cipriani, another of Lord Charlemont's friends from

Rome. The highlight of the interior is the stateroom on the first floor, which is richly coloured in contrast with the pure white interiors on the ground floor. Sir William Chambers designed other buildings in Ireland, including the Chapel and Theatre at Trinity College and Lucan House in Co. Dublin, but none compare with the refinement and perfection of the Casino, built with the best materials and to the highest standards. It cost £20,000 at the time, a considerable fortune. The Casino was an influential building; aspects of its design appear in several important buildings in the following years.

When Parliament Street was opened up by the Wide Streets Commission, it needed a focus at its south end near Dublin Castle. An architectural competition was opened to design a new **Royal Exchange**, which would be the heart of trade and business in the city. Architects from Ireland and England entered the competition and designs were put on public display, which brought new ideas and influences into the city (fig 10.31).

Thomas Cooley (1749–84), an English architect, won the competition and spent the remainder of his life working in Ireland, mainly designing for the government and the Archbishop of Armagh. The design for the Royal Exchange, built between 1769 and 1779, shows a French influence. It is designed as a Neo-Classical domed temple with a giant Corinthian portico on the entrance front, which faces north down Parliament Street. The

columns and pilasters reach over two storeys to support the entablature; the walls are rusticated to create a contrast in texture. Inside the ground floor was all one open space, with a circle of columns at the centre supporting a deep entablature with a coffered dome overhead. It is a magnificent building, beautifully detailed and finished, but almost useless as a functional space.

The **Blue Coat School**, now home to the Law Society of Ireland in Blackhall Place, Dublin, was so called because of the colour of the uniform of the students at King's Hospital. Another architectural competition was called

for the design of a suitable school. This time an Irishman won the competition (fig 10.32).

Thomas Ivory (1732–86) was born in Cork and worked as a carpenter before turning to architecture. He had picked up some Neo-Classical ideas from the drawings exhibited at the time of the Royal Exchange competition and put them to good use in his design for the school. The layout follows the plan of Palladian country mansions with the main central block connected to two wings by curved walls with niches. The whole ground floor, including the quadrant walls, is rusticated, except for the frontispieces on the wings. The central block is

FIG 10.32 THE BLUE COAT SCHOOL, by James Malton, National Gallery of Ireland, Dublin

still generally Palladian, but the wings are treated differently, relying more on form than detail for their effect. Round-headed niches create hollow spaces at first-floor level, as do the large relieving arches over the central windows. Recesses with swags and oval niches also form part of the design. Balustrades at the windows and niches on the first floor support a stringcourse that runs the full length of the building, tying all the elements together.

Ivory had a major influence on Irish architecture through his role as the first master of the School of Architectural Drawing at the Royal Dublin Society. One of his pupils, James Hoban, designed the White House in Washington, DC.

James Gandon (1743–1823), an Englishman and a student of Sir William Chambers, became the leading architect of the Neo-Classical period in Ireland. He was brought over to design a new Custom House in 1781, almost a mile downriver from the old building. This was part of the eastward development of the city away from the medieval centre around Dublin Castle.

The **Custom House** was built on previously undeveloped and marshy ground, which made for complicated and expensive construction. In plan, the building is a square with long façades on the north and south sides connected to corner pavilions (fig 10.33). The east and west sides are more functional, consisting of storage areas and offices. The riverfront, which faces south, is two storeys tall. The entrance is a temple front with a pediment supported on freestanding Doric columns reaching over two storeys. An attic storey helps to emphasise the slightly projecting central block. Arcades at ground level make a bridge between the central block and the end pavilions. Columns set in recesses create a feature on the end pavilions and on each side of the entrance. A cornice runs the full length of the building, and above this, balustrades connect the roofline of the pavilions to the attic storey. Enormous sculptures of coats of arms and urns on the rooflines of the pavilions continue the vertical emphasis created by the columns below, making a contrast with the horizontal nature of the building. The riverfront can be seen reflected in the surface of the River Liffey, which also helps to increase the apparent height of the building. A tall, columned drum supports the dome, which has a figure representing commerce on the top. The darker stone of the drum is an Irish limestone, which was used during the reconstruction following the destruction of the building by fire in 1922. This change of colour makes the dome look a little heavy when compared with the paler Portland stone of the original structure. Edward Smith was responsible for much of the sculpture on the Custom House.

Gandon was commissioned to design many of the major buildings in Dublin and a number of the projects ran simultaneously, including the extension to the House of Lords, the Four Courts, Carlisle (O'Connell) Bridge and the King's Inns.

FIG 10.33 The Custom House, Dublin, designed by James Gandon in 1781

FIG 10.34 The Four Courts, Dublin, designed by James Gandon in 1786

The **Four Courts** building, built in 1786, is considered by some to be one of the finest Neo-Classical buildings in Britain or Ireland. It has a central block, which is square in plan, supporting a large pillared drum with a saucer-shaped dome. The ground floor has a large circular reception area with four courts leading diagonally off it (fig 10.34). Originally the courts were only separated from the hall by pillars; curtains were hung shortly after construction, then timber and glass screens were built and the partitions were built in masonry when the building was reconstructed following its burning in 1922, when all the interior decoration was lost. Screen walls with triumphal arches at the centres connect the main building to the wings. Large carved crests are mounted on these arches, again sculpted by Smyth.

Gandon also designed some buildings outside Dublin: Waterford Courthouse, which is now demolished, Coolbanagher Church in Co. Laois and Emo Court nearby, a fine country mansion, which was only just begun at the time of Gandon's death. Emo was one of a few houses that Gandon designed, mainly for his patrons. Abbeville, which was built for Sir John Beresford, and Emsworth are both in Co. Dublin.

Edward Smyth (1749–1812), an Irish sculptor, was responsible for much of the carving on the Custom House and other buildings designed by Gandon. The riverine heads that decorate the keystones of the arches

FIG 10.35 The river head keystone representing the Blackwater from the Custom House, Dublin. Carved by Edward Smyth.

on the riverfront show Smyth's bold style to advantage (fig 10.35). Carved in high relief and classically proportioned, they are based on Greek and Roman models. Fourteen heads represent the rivers of Ireland: the Foyle, the Erne, the Liffey, the Boyne, the Nore, the Blackwater, the Atlantic, the Ban, the Shannon, the Lee, the Lagan, the Suir, the Barrow and the Slaney. The hair or headdress of each head carries symbols in the form of plants and animals to represent each river. The keystone over the main door represents the Liffey, the only female figure in the group.

Country houses at the end of the 18th century were generally smaller than the palaces that we saw earlier; they were also less lavishly decorated. Interiors were often in the Adam style. Chambers and Ivory designed some country houses, but James Wyatt (1746–1813) was the leading figure in country house design in the later part of the century. He supplied designs for the renovation and alteration of many houses and schemes for the decoration of others. His earliest work in ireland was Mountkennedy in Co. Wicklow, which he designed in 1772, but which was not built for ten years. He designed Castlecoole Co. Fermanagh for the Earl of belmore in 1793. The house is nine bays wide and is finished simply, with no window mouldings and little decoration. Four ionic columns reach over two storeys to support the plain pediment over the entrance. Straight doric collonades make the connection to the end pavillions (fig 10.36). Wyatt was also responsible for the design and furnishing of the elegant interior. His renovation of Slane Castle in Co. Meath in 1785 demonstrates a new romantic fashion in Gothic decoration. Towers and battlements were added to a classical building in a style known as Gothick (with a K, to separate it from the more serious Neo-Gothic of the next century) (fig 10.37).

The applied arts

At the beginning of the 18th century, Irish craftwork followed the English style, but it was usually a few years behind the fashion. A number of changes occurred around 1850. Some trade restrictions between Ireland and England

FIG 10.37 The gothic façade of Slane Castle designed by James Wyatt in 1785

were lifted and the first students who had been trained in the Dublin Society schools were now beginning to offer their work for sale in Ireland. A good deal of the work by Irish craftsmen was of high quality, and there was an Irish style that was different from English and European work. There was a new middle class in Ireland – large farmers and professional people – who wanted to furnish their town and country houses in some style.

We have already seen the work of the European and Irish *stuccodores* who produced the decorative plasterwork for the larger houses and public buildings in the country. There were silversmiths, glass workers and joiners in most of the larger urban centres in Ireland providing quality products for their local markets.

Silver work

Silver work in the late Rococo style was produced in workshops in Dublin, Cork and Limerick. Repoussé,

FIG 10.36 Castlecoole House, Co. Fermanagh

190

FIG 10.38 A three-legged silver cream jug

Furniture

Trade with the West Indies brought new and exotic timbers to Britain and Ireland. Mahogany, which is a dark, fine-grained wood, was ideal for turning and carving. It produced strong, elegant furniture. Irish carvers developed a style of high-relief decoration in the form of foliage, animals and masks. They often finished the ends of the table and chair legs with big, hairy paws (fig 10.39). Today, chairs, cabinets and, particularly, side tables carved by Irish joiners are highly regarded by collectors worldwide.

Glass

Irish glassmakers got a boost in 1780 when trade restrictions were dropped and a tax was put on English glass. A period of great productivity followed, and glass factories in Dublin, Belfast, Cork and Waterford all produced thick, deeply cut glass work. A typically Irish product was a large serving dish with a turnover rim with deeply cut designs (fig 10.40).

chasing and open work were features of this style. Country scenes, flowers, birds and masks were among the designs that appeared on silver work. Dish rings, three-legged sugar bowls and helmet-shaped cream jugs were particular to the Irish market (and they are much sought after by collectors today) (fig 10.38).

FIG 10.39 A mahagony chair with carved details including paw feet

FIG 10.40 A collection of 18th century glass

Other crafts

Ceramics, bookbinding and fabric printing were also flourishing industries in Ireland, which produced work of the highest quality equal to any in Europe.

Conclusion

During the 18th century, Irish architecture and design joined the mainstream of European development. It came out of the backwater that it had been in for centuries and enjoyed a period where it was at the forefront of fashionable taste. Although many of the architects and designers came from outside Ireland, there was a short period when Dublin in particular had finer public buildings and more elegant streets than London. It's true that only a privileged few actually led the life of culture and refinement that is represented by the architecture, decoration and furnishings that we associate with the Georgian period, but this would have been the case in any country at that time.

The Dublin Society schools played an important role in creating high standards for their students in painting, sculpture, architecture and crafts. Many graduates of the schools went on to successful careers, not just in Ireland, where the pool of patrons was small, but in England and further afield.

At the close of the century, Ireland was again in political turmoil. The sense of national pride that had grown with the achievements in architecture and the arts, and the prosperity that had developed, led some to believe that Ireland would be better off separate from Britain. The French and American Revolutions created an atmosphere of rebellion, which led to the Rising in 1798. The rebellion was quickly put down and the Act of Union was signed in 1800, which made Ireland part of the United Kingdom of Great Britain and Ireland. With Dublin's parliament closed, politics and influence moved to London, leaving Ireland again at a financial disadvantage and in a political and cultural backwater.

Questions

1. What was Palladianism?
2. Make a sketch of Castletown House.
3. Describe the decoration of one room in Castletown House.
4. Write a short account of the Irish Parliament building (Bank of Ireland).
5. Describe the design and decoration of an Irish country palace.
6. Name the architect and write a short description of Leinster House.
7. Describe a Dublin redbrick terrace house.
8. What was the Neo-Classical style?
9. What is stucco work? Give two examples.
10. Write a description of the structure and decoration of the Casino at Marino.

Essays

1. James Gandon was one of the most important Georgian architects in Ireland. Describe one of his buildings, noting its Georgian characteristics in design and decoration.
2. Describe a building by the architect Richard Cassels, noting the Georgian characteristics in its design and decoration. Compare this building with a building of the same type by another architect.

Colour picture study

1. Look at the picture of Russborough House, noting the location of the building in the surrounding landscape. Describe the function of a house like this, noting the features of its design (fig 10.11, fig 10.12).
2. What can you observe in the photograph of the Four Courts that is typical of Georgian design? Name the architect and mention another building by him (fig 10.34).

PAINTING IN IRELAND:
LATE 19TH CENTURY AND EARLY 20TH CENTURY

Details on leading 19th- and 20th-century Irish artists and some of their most important works can be found online at www.gillmacmillan.ie. Just search for Appreciating Art and look under 'Additional Resources'.

This information will complement studies of works made by visiting the National Gallery of Ireland in Dublin, Dublin City Gallery The Hugh Lane and The Crawford Gallery in Cork.

See Chapter 1: Looking at Art and Chapter 2: Public Art in Ireland.

The study of contemporary Irish artists and their work is best served by visiting the Irish Museum of Modern Art and reading contemporary reviews.

Featured artists are as follows.

Nineteenth- and twentieth-century painters:
Nathaniel Hone (1831–1917)
Walter Osborne (1859–1903)
Roderic O'Conor (1860–1940)
John Lavery (1856–1941)
William Orpen (1878–1931)
Paul Henry (1876–1958)
William Leech (1881–1968)
Jack B. Yeats (1871–1957)

Stained glass – An Túr Gloine:
Sarah Purser (1848–1943)
Harry Clark (1890–1931)

Twentieth-century painters:
Patrick Collins (1910–94)
Louis le Brocquy (1916–)
Tony O'Malley (1913–2003)

EUROPEAN ART
(SECTION II OF THE LEAVING CERT EXAM)

PART I. MEDIEVAL ART AND ARCHITECTURE

CHAPTER 11

THE ROMANESQUE PERIOD

Romanesque and Gothic were the two major movements in art and architecture in medieval Europe. Together they had the kind of impact on the visual culture and the built environment in Europe not seen since the Roman Empire. These movements occurred from the 11th to the 14th centuries at a time when Europe was going though dramatic social, religious and artistic change.

What is Romanesque?

The term 'Romanesque' (fig 11.1) was first used in the mid-19th century. Until then, art and architecture of the Middle Ages had traditionally been considered heavy and crude compared to that of the Renaissance, but the negative image changed when art historians began to describe the style as 'Roman'. Once the link was made to the ancient Roman art of building, 'Romanesque' became the accepted name for all the art of the period and it is now considered as one of the great phases of Western culture.

It is difficult to give precise dates at which the Romanesque period began and ended because it varied considerably from country to country. The Romanesque style in art was widely established across Europe by the middle of the 11th century and had reached its peak in the 12th century. Several important social reasons that influenced its development were:

- **Peace had come to Europe by the 11th century**, bringing prosperity to a large part of the Continent.
- **New farming methods** led to a population increase and the gradual **growth of cities and trade**.
- **A middle class and merchant class emerged** with the rise of the cities.
- **Learning and education** increased.
- The **Roman Catholic Church** held an extremely **dominant position** as an international and very well-organised institution.

FIG 11.1 Abbaye de Ste-Foy, Conques, south-eastern France

Medieval society

Emerging from the Dark Ages

The Roman Empire began to weaken around the year 400 AD. Barbarian tribes from the north swept across Europe, overwhelming towns and cities and their inhabitants, and eventually the great world power collapsed after the city of Rome itself was invaded. Europe fell into disarray in a long period of gloom known as the Dark Ages. The luxury and riches associated with Roman civilisation disappeared and advances in science, technology, medicine and literature were all but forgotten. The Continent divided more or less along the lines we know today, but strong rival warriors ruling small kingdoms were constantly at war with each other.

The dreaded year 1000

In the years coming up to the year 1000 a widespread fear existed that this was the year of the Last Judgement, or the end of the world, as described in Christian writings. However, as the new millennium dawned it seemed to bring with it a new spirit of enthusiasm, optimism and cultural unity in Europe.

The feudal system

Society in the Middle Ages was organised according to the feudal system, a pyramid structure in which the king was the highest in command. Society was grouped around a lord (such as a knight) who ruled over isolated manors in the countryside and rented land to peasants.

This social class included craftsmen, peasants and some serfs who had almost no freedom and were in fact little more than slaves.

The triumph of the Church

The Roman Catholic Church was the one large international unifying structure in 11th-century Europe. Even before the end of the Roman Empire it had become a powerful institution, but in the Middle Ages it grew in strength and influence until eventually it completely dominated Europe politically as well as spiritually. As all levels of society were gripped by intense religious fervour:

- **Monasteries** grew in strength and numbers (fig 11.2).
- Millions of people undertook great **pilgrimages** across Europe to visit locations holding religious relics.
- Christian knights went on **crusades** against the Muslims in the East to stop the spread of Islam.

Church organisation

- **Bishops** ruled in their own diocese, but worked directly as part of an international papal system.
- **Bishops and archbishops** frequently came from wealthy noble families, so they often sat on the king's council, playing leading roles in government.
- **The Church was outside of the feudal system** and was basically a democratic institution. Clever men could therefore rise to positions of great power and influence.

FIG 11.2 Le Mont Saint Michel, Normandy, France

- **The Church was supported by heavy taxes**, but large and generous donations were also made to the Church and monasteries. As a result it became very wealthy, giving it the power to influence kings and rulers.

The **Church laid the ground rules** and guided everyone's life from the richest king to the lowest serf from birth to death. Life was hard and poverty and disease were widespread. For many, light and warmth came only from the sun because firewood and candles were expensive, but fire was an ever-present danger.

The magnificently decorated and well-lit churches must have had an extraordinary effect on the ordinary people of the early and late Middle Ages. For them, pictures of any kind existed only in monasteries and the only music they heard was the simplest of songs. Living quarters were crude and not even the lower nobility had much in the way of comfort.

The average life expectancy was about 35 years, so it is little wonder that people had such a deep belief in an afterlife that promised comfort and happiness in return for prayer and penance.

Strong papal authority

Church reforms took place during the 11th century and the Pope established strict rules for the clergy. Celibacy was strictly enforced to avoid the problem of divided inheritance and the appointment of bishops by secular rulers was forbidden. This led to conflict with the kings, but the Pope emerged even more powerful and the influence of the Church became even stronger on the way of life in every European nation.

Monasteries

Religious orders played one of the most crucial roles in the medieval Church. Monasteries were independent, self-supporting communities. They had three main functions: they were places of prayer, locations for the storage of sacred relics and centres of learning. Despite their closed nature, however, they were also intimately connected with and highly influential on society.

There were two prominent orders:
- **The Benedictines** are associated with education, music and art.
- **The Cistercians** favoured a more austere life of manual labour and self-denial.

Most monks were drawn from the aristocracy and it was customary for them to enter Benedictine monasteries as children. Here they could become very wealthy and live comfortable lives. The monastery was often established on well-to-do estates and some became enormous establishments. Covering many acres and surrounded by massive walls, they had the appearance of fortified towns. The abbot in charge was a powerful figure and had huge political influence.

Crusades

Crusader knight

The Church called upon the feuding knights (fig 11.3) to turn their fighting spirit to more profitable ends and encouraged them to form a Christian army. They set off on crusades or holy wars to recapture Jerusalem and other former Christian sites from the Jews and Muslims. Today it is generally accepted that the Crusades were

FIG 11.3 Medieval crusaders

RELIQUAIRE DE LA VRAIE CROIX BORDÉ DE PERLES ET ORNÉ DE PIERRERIES,
CONSERVÉ A LA CATHÉDRALE DE TOURNAI. (VI⁵ siècle.)

FIG 11.4 Relic of The True Cross

brutal campaigns of violence and self-interest, but they enabled Europe to expand its borders eastwards and it profited greatly from new trade opportunities with the Islamic world. The Church also benefited as areas associated with the Crusades grew wealthy and prosperous.

Relics and pilgrimages

Relics

Relics (fig 11.4) were objects associated with Jesus, such as pieces from the cross of the crucifixion or the Crown of Thorns, or with a saint, such as fragments of clothing or bones. As the Crusaders returned, an enormous influx of relics flooded into Europe and were distributed to monasteries across Europe. Devout Christians travelled miles to pray at them because they believed these objects of contact with a holy person had curative powers.

Pilgrimages

Church leaders encouraged people to make these journeys. The most important pilgrimages for Christians were to Rome and Jerusalem in the Holy Land, but these journeys were long and very dangerous for people travelling on foot due to bandits and pirates.

Santiago de Compostela

During the early 11th century, a crusade had driven the Muslim Arab Moors out of northern Spain. At the same time, the tomb of St James was rediscovered at **Santiago de Compostela** (fig 11.5) and pilgrims began to travel there instead of to Rome and Jerusalem.

When the abbot of the highly influential Cluny Abbey promoted Santiago de Compostela as a destination, it quickly became the most famous Christian pilgrimage of all time. It drew unprecedented crowds of people from all over Europe, including Britain and Ireland, who made their way on foot slowly through France into Spain and all across to the furthest edge of the north-western coast. Such were the numbers that it is said that at any time, one-tenth of the population of Europe was either at, on its way to, coming back from or looking after those who were travelling to Santiago de Compostela to pray at the shrine of Christ's apostle.

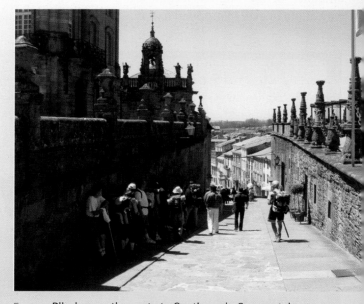

FIG 11.5 Pilgrims on the route to Santiago de Compostela

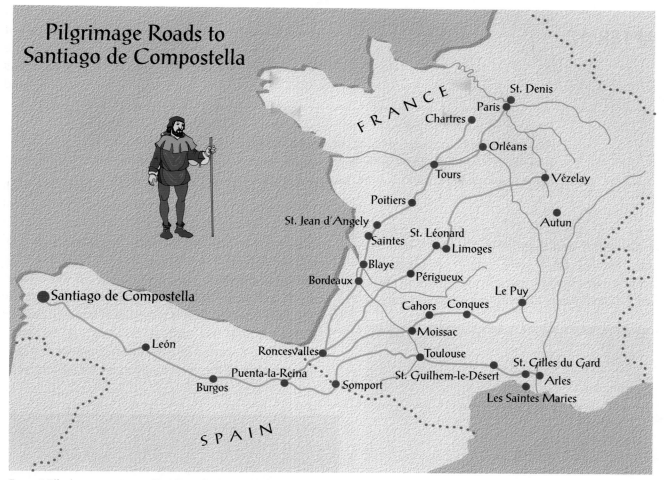

FIG 11.6 Pilgrimage routes to Santiago de Compostela

Pilgrimage routes

There were four traditional routes to Santiago de Compostela through France that joined together to form one route at the Pyrenees in northern Spain (fig. 11.6). This generated a massive building boom resulting in hostels, hospitals, bridges and – most dramatic of all – churches. These churches each had a relic and many became pilgrimage destinations in their own right.

Conclusion

The development of the style known as Romanesque in Europe was influenced by social prosperity and in particular by the strength and dominant position of the Roman Catholic Church. The enormous surge in building was due mainly to the need for churches along the main pilgrimage routes to Santiago de Compostela.

Questions

1. What is the origin of the term 'Romanesque'?
2. Outline the social reasons that influenced the development of the Romanesque style.
3. Write a short paragraph on medieval society in the 11th century.
4. Write a brief account of the organisation and influence of the Roman Catholic Church in medieval Europe under the following headings: dominant position, organisation, wealth, influence on daily life, papal authority.
5. Write a short paragraph on monasteries in medieval Europe.
6. What was the purpose of the Crusades?
7. Give a brief outline on the important consequences of the Crusades that affected medieval art.
8. Write a brief paragraph on medieval pilgrimages.
9. Make a drawing of the main pilgrimage routes through medieval France and Spain.
10. Why was Santiago de Compostela such an important pilgrimage destination in medieval Europe?

CHAPTER 12

ROMANESQUE ART AND ARCHITECTURE

Because of the dominant role of the Church, most Romanesque art is religious. Architecture was the main focus of the period and the 11th and 12th centuries saw a frenzy of church-building activity. Many examples of Romanesque architecture can be seen today around Europe, but some of the finest are detailed below.

- **Pisa Cathedral and Baptistry** (fig 12.1), with its famous leaning tower, was begun in 1063 and developed over the next 300 years when the city was one of the most powerful maritime centres in Italy.

FIG 12.1 Pisa Cathedral and Baptistry

- **Durham Cathedral** (fig 12.2) in northern England is renowned as a masterpiece of Romanesque architecture. It was begun in 1093 and largely completed within 40 years. It is a superb example of Norman building and craftsmanship and is the only

FIG 12.2 Durham Cathedral

cathedral in England to have survived with its original design almost intact.

- **Speyer Cathedral** (fig 12.3) is one of the most significant of the many Romanesque monuments in Germany. The church was a symbol of imperial power in stone and the largest building of its age. Construction started in 1030 under Emperor Conrad II and remained the royal burial place for around 300 years.

FIG 12.3 Speyer Cathedral

Cluny III

Cluny's great power was reflected in its vast abbey church, known as Cluny III, which unfortunately is now in ruins (fig 12.4) This was the third church built on the same site and for many years it remained the largest and most beautiful in all of Christendom.

Its main features were its great nave of 187 m with four aisles, crossed over by two huge transepts, all of which was arched over by a broad stone pointed barrel roof vaulting system over 30 m high.

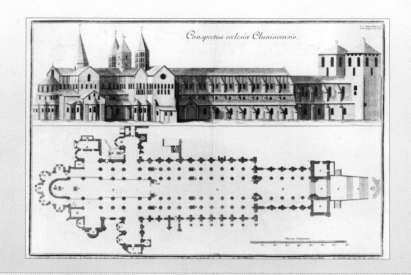

FIG 12.4 Plan and elevation of Cluny Abbey

Cluny Abbey

Cluny Abbey in east-central France is of paramount importance to Romanesque art. By the end of the 11th century Cluny had become extremely influential and powerful and was famous far and wide for its splendour and great wealth.

Art and music

The Cluniac order placed great emphasis on elaborate religious services. Singing and music were essential parts of its liturgy and the vaulting system was designed to enhance the sound. It also had an extremely high regard for art, particularly architectural sculpture, using it both as ornament and as a means of spreading the message of Christianity.

Accounts describe not only the splendour of its beautiful carved capitals but also its arches, windows and cornices, which were surrounded by sculptured ornament. In addition, there would certainly have been murals, carpets, huge chandeliers, figures of saints, golden liturgical vestments and gleaming ornaments set with precious stones.

In terms of splendour, no castle or palace of the period would have compared with this abbey in any way because secular rulers had to invest most of their money in soldiers and military equipment and also because the Church forbade the faithful to accumulate wealth or display it ostentatiously.

The demolition of Cluny

The church and the surrounding monastic buildings were destroyed, so the only remaining part of the abbey church is the majestic Clocher de l'Eau-Bénite ('Holy Water Belfry') (fig 12.5).

Churches on the pilgrimage routes

The style of building first explored at Cluny soon became common throughout France, Spain, Italy and England.

FIG 12.5 Clocher de l'Eau-Bénite, Cluny

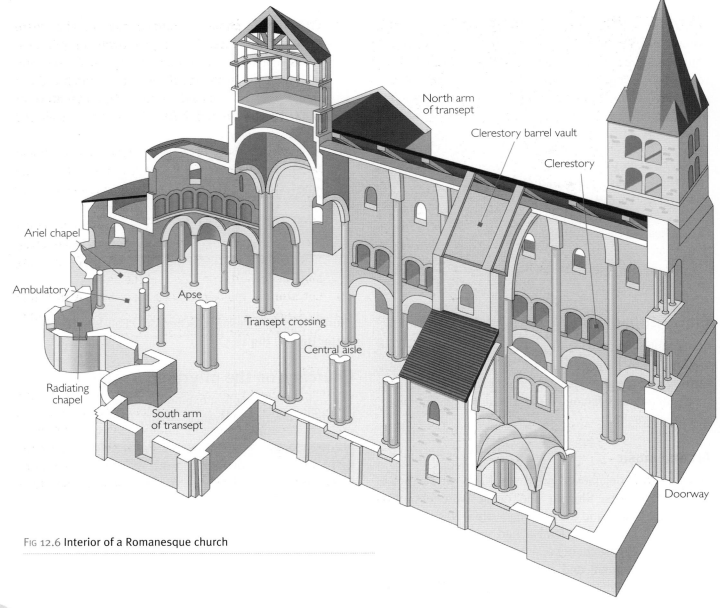

Ariel chapel

Ambulatory

Apse

Radiating chapel

South arm of transept

Transept crossing

Central aisle

North arm of transept

Clerestory barrel vault

Clerestory

Doorway

FIG 12.6 Interior of a Romanesque church

The churches built along each of the four main pilgrimage routes in France were remarkably similar in design.

Characteristics

The characteristics of a typical **Romanesque pilgrimage church**:

- **Blocky in shape** (fig 12.6) – They had a solid geometric appearance.
- **Rounded arches** – Roman arches were used extensively for doors, windows, on the towers and even ornamental arcades on walls.
- **Stone roofs** – The Romanesque building boom went hand in hand with a number of technological innovations, but the supreme achievement was the development of the stone vault, which not only insulated against fire but also greatly improved acoustics (sound quality).

- **Massive walls** – A huge amount of stone was needed to construct high stone roofs, and in order to carry this weight, walls and pillars had to be **strong and thick** (fig 12.7).
- **Interiors** – They had a **dark and solemn aspect** because there were few window openings (which would have weakened the walls).
- **Roman basilica** – Early Christian churches were based on the **Roman basilica** rather than the Roman temple (fig 12.8). The basilica served a general community purpose in Roman towns and this model was chosen over the round Roman temples, which had a pagan association. Romanesque builders continued using this model.

FIG 12.7 Romanesque church

- **Cruciform in shape** – Romanesque churches were designed to cater for large crowds of pilgrims. Crosswise transepts broke up the long nave and pilgrims could walk about the entire church without interrupting the monastic liturgy. An **ambulatory** or walkway around the back of the altar facilitated viewing the relics.
- **Radiating chapels** – A ring of smaller chapels called radiating chapels (fig 12.9) extended from the ambulatory and each one of these contained a minor relic.
- **Lighting** – A **tower or cupola** (dome) on the roof over the central crossing of the transept and nave lit up this central area and had the effect of drawing pilgrims towards the altar and the choir.
- **Cut stone** – Many churches were built with ashlar masonry, that is, even, regularly cut blocks of stone, suitable for monumental architecture.

Vaulting

Stone vaulting was absolutely essential in Romanesque churches because fire was a constant problem and there had been many catastrophes. Romanesque masons were able to vault the entire width of the church using the Roman model, but the exact technical knowledge developed by the Romans had been lost. As problems

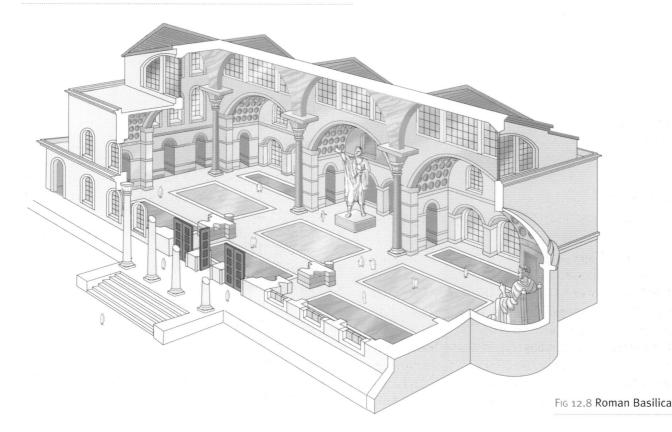

FIG 12.8 **Roman Basilica**

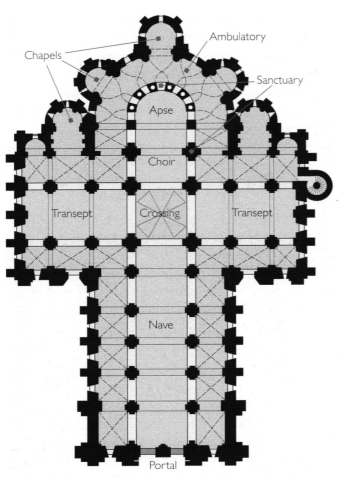

FIG 12.9 **Romanesque church floor plan**

developed, architects could only solve them by experimentation.

- **Barrel vaulting** was the first method tried, but the heavy stones pressed out as well as down, causing the semi-circular arches to flatten, the walls to push outwards and the roof to collapse. This problem is known as **outward thrust**.
- **Broken barrel vaulting** was an improvement as it used **pointed transverse arches**, but the problem of outward thrust remained (although it took longer to develop).
- **Groin vaulting** was a further experiment in finding a solution. This consisted of two barrel vaults intersecting at right angles. For a while it seems as if this approach provided a solution, but the problem of outward thrust continued to plague builders for a century after.

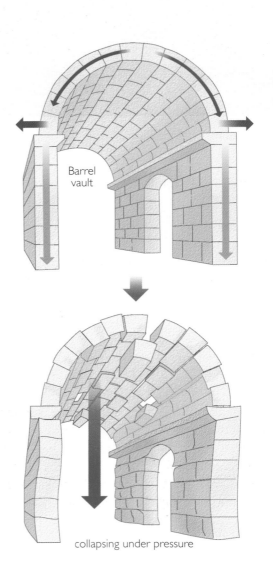

collapsing under pressure

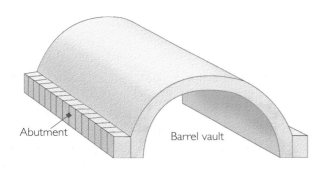

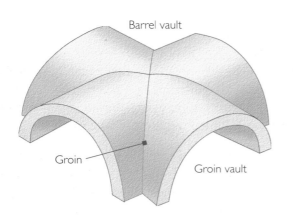

FIG 12.10 Sainte-Foy de Conques

FIG 12.11 Sainte-Foy de Conques, western façade

Notable pilgrimage churches

Sainte-Foy de Conques

Sainte-Foy de Conques (fig 12.10) is a well-preserved example of a Romanesque abbey church in France.

Plan

Built on the foundations of a smaller, earlier basilica, it was completed around the year 1120. Its cruciform shape, large-aisled nave, transepts and five radiating chapels extending from the ambulatory make it a typical pilgrimage church.

Design

Sainte-Foy has the classic Romanesque look – it is massive, blocky and geometric in appearance. Rounded arches are found on its windows, doorways and supporting piers and thick walls support a high stone barrel-vaulted roof. Small windows make the interior quite dark, but a very large dome over the crossing that originally brought good light into the central area was replaced in the 15th century after it collapsed.

Sculpture on the west front

The main western façade is large, simple and geometric in design (fig 12.11). Over the main doors, a splendid semi-circular tympanum illustrates the Last Judgement. Christ in Heaven occupies the central position, and on his left is a particularly grotesque depiction of Hell and devils. The sculpture was originally painted in full colour and some of this is still visible on sheltered spots.

Pilgrimage stop

Conques became a popular stop for pilgrims after a monk from Conques stole the skeleton of Sainte Foy (French for 'holy faith'), a young woman martyred for her faith in the 4th century, from a nearby monastery in order to draw travellers (and wealth) to Conques.

The relic of Sainte Foy is still on display in the church today in a magnificent gold reliquary statue that depicts the little martyred girl sitting on a throne wearing a Roman crown glittering with gold and gems.

FIG 12.12 St Sernin, Toulouse

St Sernin of Toulouse

The route to Santiago taken by pilgrims coming from Italy, Switzerland or central Europe passed through Toulouse and its typical Romanesque church, St Sernin (fig 12.12).

Paray-le-Monial

The architect of Notre Dame in Paray-le-Monial (fig 12.13) was the Abbot Hugo of Cluny. This is a miniature version of Cluny III with many of the same architectural features, but it lacks the space and elegance of its inspiration.

FIG 12.13 Notre Dame in Paray-le-Monial

Saint-Lazare of Autun

Cathédrale Saint-Lazare in Autun is one of the most important Romanesque churches in France. Dating from

FIG 12.14 Saint-Lazare of Autun

the mid-12th century with some later Gothic additions, it is especially famed for its splendid sculptures by the Romanesque master sculptor Gislebertus.

Saint-Lazare held relics of Lazarus (the man whom Jesus raised from the dead) that were discovered in Autun in the early 12th century. The church was built on a grand scale shortly afterwards in the hopes that it would become a major pilgrimage destination like nearby Vézelay.

The Bishop of Autun was a great admirer of Cluny and the interior of Saint-Lazare of Autun (fig 12.14) is closer to the elegance of Cluny III than any other building. He was also inspired by classical Roman decoration, which is not surprising considering the amount of important Roman remains at Autun.

Gothic additions were made to the exterior, including the spire, after a fire in the 15th century, but the main core of the church and its sculpture remain firmly Romanesque.

St Mary Magdalene in Vézelay

The Basilica of St Mary Magdalene (fig 12.15, fig 12.16) in Vézelay is the largest Romanesque church in France. The Benedictine abbey was overseen by Cluny and first came

FIG 12.15 Basilica of St Mary Magdalene in Vézelay

to fame after it acquired relics of Mary Magdalene in 1037. News of miracles associated with the relic soon spread and it was officially designated by Cluny as a major stop on the Compostela route.

The church was rebuilt around 1150, after a devastating fire in which 1,200 pilgrims lost their lives. It suffered quite an amount of damage during the French Revolution when its façade and one of the towers were destroyed, but it was saved from near collapse during the 19th

FIG 12.16 St Mary Magdalene in Vézelay, central nave from the southeast and the Tour Saint-Michel

century. This restoration was somewhat clumsily executed on the exterior but the superb sculpture inside the narthex (entrance or outer porch) has survived almost unscathed. The interior is also well preserved and the impression conveyed on entering this perfect gem of 12th-century architecture is one of stately Romanesque dignity.

Rhythm and light

Semi-circular arches (fig 12.17) divide the nave into groin-vaulted bays, creating balance, rhythm and light in a soaring upward structure. One of Vézelay's most notable characteristics is ochre and white stone on all its arches, which makes a chequered effect and shows the influence of Islamic architecture, possibly from Spain, and pilgrims travelling to and from Santiago.

Supporting the arches are square piers with engaged (attached) pillars on each side, surmounted by beautifully decorated carved capitals.

FIG 12.17 Interior of St Mary Magdalene

Conclusion

Romanesque churches were specifically designed to cater for the needs of pilgrims. Designs became more sophisticated in the 12th century and many pilgrimage churches were influenced by Cluny, but Roman and Islamic influences can also be found in the architectural features.

Questions

1. Name some important Romanesque churches in Europe.
2. Write a brief account of the importance of Cluny in the development of Romanesque art.
3. What were the important characteristics of Romanesque architecture?
4. Why did Romanesque churches need stone roofs?
5. How did Romanesque builders respond to the challenges presented by the vaulting system?
6. Name a typical Romanesque pilgrimage church and describe its main features.

Essay

1. Discuss the influences of medieval society and the Christian Church on the development of Romanesque architecture in Europe in the 11th and 12th centuries. Make reference in your answer to one important named example of a Romanesque church and describe its important architectural features.

Colour picture studies

1. Examine the photo of the interior of the Basilica of St Mary Magdalene in Vézelay (fig 12.17). Describe the architectural features and atmosphere created by these. Compare this to the interior of the Cathédrale Saint-Lazare in Autun (fig 12.14). Mention the influences that contributed to the overall design of both these interiors.

CHAPTER 13

ROMANESQUE SCULPTURE

A fundamental change

The most fundamental change in art during the Romanesque period was a return to monumental stone carving on buildings.

In the early Middle Ages, classical sculpture was regarded with great suspicion, especially free-standing figures of pagan gods. This was to change, however, when the nobility in France began to appreciate them as works of art and to display Roman statues in their own castles.

Sculptors at Cluny were the first to pick up on this and use art on architecture. For the first time since the Roman Empire, the human figure appeared in Western art and the idea soon spread to other pilgrim churches.

Teaching the word of God

Architectural sculpture gave the Church a new and powerful medium for teaching the word of God. Most people were illiterate, but now they could 'read' the stories of Jesus and the saints over and over in the form of sculpture on the churches.

Some Romanesque façades (fig 13.1) were modelled on Roman triumphal arches and had life-size figures of saints on either side of the door. Many, however, had chilling images of God the Father in dramatic Last Judgement scenes sculpted on a monumental scale and placed on the great tympanum (semi-circular shape) over the doors for pilgrims to see as they entered the church.

Death and the grotesque

Death in medieval times was understood in a very different way. In Christian religious teaching, death was a passage to the next, more important, life, and every dying person faced the question of whether they would receive mercy from God or face the eternal damnation of Hell (fig 13.2, fig 13.3).

For this reason, Romanesque art produced a greater wealth of images of death in all its forms than any other period in the history of Western art. At a time of deep religious faith, a medieval believer entering the house of God was faced with the most terrible images that imagination could conjure up of the end of the world and a God of vengeance sitting in judgement. The grotesque

Fig 13.1 Door of the Abbey Church of Saint-Gilles, France

Fig 13.2 Death of Dives

FIG 13.3 Death of Lazarus

images of devils, demons and tormented souls were intended to create a fear of Hell in people's minds and serve as a reminder to them to be prepared for death at all times by repenting their sins.

Abstract imagery

Romanesque art was quite abstract. Realism was completely avoided not only in the case of demons and other fantastic creatures, but also in the representation of the human figure. No attempt was made to portray God or the saints in a natural way. Instead they were blocky, dignified and unreal or depicted as strange, elongated beings in a swirl of limbs and drapery.

Sculpture on Romanesque churches

Some of the most impressive Romanesque sculpture, both on capitals and tympanums, is found at the cathedrals of St Mary Magdalene in Vézelay and Saint-Lazare of Autun.

St Mary Magdalene in Vézelay

Inside the western portal over the doorway in the narthex (entrance or outer porch) is the great tympanum (fig 13.4) of the Pentecost (Christ bringing the holy spirit to his apostles in the form of fire). A massive Christ sits serenely inside a mandorla (oval-shaped halo) with his arms thrown open, symbolising the glory of his resurrection. His beautifully pleated robe is arranged in whirling patterns, and from his hands the flames of the Holy Spirit fall to the apostles' heads, giving them the strength to teach the word of God to all races depicted above and below.

Carved capitals in the nave

None of the sculptors who created the wonderful saints, angels and devils carved into scenes on the capitals of the pillars at each intersection of the nave of Vézelay signed their work, so they remain anonymous works of art. Many display imagery typical of the Romanesque fascination with the grotesque, but the church's most interesting as well as beautiful capital is its most famous: The Mystic Mill, which shows Moses pouring

FIG 13.4 Tympanum at St Mary Magdalen in Vézelay

FIG 13.5 THE MYSTIC MILL

grain into a mill while St Paul the Apostle gathers the flour. The grain represents the law given to Moses and the mill symbolises Christ (fig 13.5).

Saint-Lazare in Autun

The tympanum

Pilgrims entering the church of Saint-Lazare at Autun passed beneath the great tympanum (fig 13.6) on the west-facing doorway. As they ascended the steps, the dramatic scene that met them was calculated to inspire hope, but it also put fear into the hearts of sinners. The Weighing of Souls at Autun is probably the most famous Romanesque Last Judgement scene, particularly as the artist chose to sign it.

The Last Judgement

A huge figure of an impassive Christ sits on his throne in the centre of a world filled with tiny figures of souls rising from their tombs as angels sound the last trumpet. St Peter, with a large key, welcomes the saved to Paradise while the damned are dragged in dramatic fashion to Hell by grotesque demons.

In the lintel below the feet of Christ are pilgrims, easily identified as having travelled to Jerusalem and to Santiago de Compostela by the cross for Jerusalem and the shell for St James on their satchels (fig 13.7).

The Weighing of Souls

On the lintel below Christ's feet on the left, the damned are driven from him, naked, by an angel with a flaming sword, while giant hands grip a tormented soul (fig 13.8). Various forms of sin are depicted here – a miser has his heavy money bags and an adulteress is being gnawed by snakes. Above their heads, an impassive

FIG 13.6 Tympanum at Autun: The Weighing of Souls

FIG 13.7 Detail tympanum: pilgrims

Archangel Michael weighs the souls while terrified figures hide beneath his robes. A grotesque devil tries to pull down the scale and another sits in it to make it

FIG 13.8 Detail tympanum: The Weighing of Souls

heavier, before a laughing demon pours those condemned forever down a chute towards the gaping jaws of Hell and the fires below.

Gislebertus

It was a rare occurrence in medieval art for an artist to sign his work, but the sculptor of Autun has placed his name – GISLEBERTUS HOC FECIT ('Gislebertus made this') – beneath Christ for all to see (fig 13.9).

FIG 13.9 Detail tympanum: GISLEBERTUS HOC FECIT

It is known that Gislebertus trained at Cluny and probably worked as an assistant at Vézelay, but he was by now a mature artist and this was his crowning glory. The unique style of elongated figures and exaggerated expressions is particularly and very distinctly his own.

The Last Judgement theme has an intensity not seen before and the scale and drama of the imagery could not have failed to inspire awe in an impressionable pilgrim visitor, particularly as it would have been painted in full colour. Gislebertus, like all good storytellers, seems to have had a taste for horror, and the gruesome scene conveys the impression that the artist relished the opportunity to portray this one in all its horrific detail.

Carved capitals at Autun

The capitals on the supporting piers inside the cathedral were all carved by Gislebertus himself and also show his skill as a sculptor and storyteller. Some of the best are from the pillars of the choir. On these, fine ornamental foliage is combined with figures in expert fashion. However, their key element is the story itself and the simplicity of its telling.

Surviving the French Revolution

The west tympanum of Saint-Lazare at Autun was lucky to have survived when so many others were damaged or destroyed during the French Revolution. This happened because the Church had grown ashamed of the grotesque and dramatic imagery used in the Romanesque period. It was considered crude and slightly vulgar. In 1766 the sculpture was covered with a thick layer of plaster and a more contemporary design was painted over it.

The sculpture was saved but other parts of the church were ruined, including another tympanum over the north door, which was smashed to bits by revolutionaries. The west tympanum was rediscovered in 1837 when a local priest began chipping away at the plaster. As he worked, he was surprised to find the original tympanum almost perfectly preserved underneath. Christ's head had been sticking out, so it had been hacked off and cast aside. It survived in a local collection before being given to a local museum. It was returned to the tympanum in 1948.

Fig 13.10 THE SUICIDE OF JUDAS

Fig 13.11 THE DREAM OF THE MAGI

The Suicide of Judas

Judas, having betrayed Christ, despairs and hangs himself from a tree. Hideous devils pull on the rope and the viewer is spared none of the details of the horrific death that shows the hanging figure with tongue protruding and head lolling grotesquely (fig 13.10).

This contrasts with a beautifully depicted ornamental tree, which is skilfully composed along with three figures to fit neatly into the shape of the capital.

The Dream of the Magi

This charming scene of the sleeping Magi is told with the minimum of detail, yet it conveys the message clearly and directly. The three kings are all wearing their crowns and share a cosy bed under a magnificent semi-circular bed cover. In the simplest of gestures, the angel points to the star and gently touches the hand of a sleeping king, who opens one eye. The star is a reminder of the one that led the kings to Bethlehem, but now the angel is warning them not to return to Herod after the visit (fig 13.11).

The Flight into Egypt

Having been warned in a dream that Herod seeks to kill Jesus, the holy family leaves for Egypt on a donkey. Joseph leads and in the traditional manner Mary's lap forms a throne for the serene figure of the Christ child. All are dignified and solemn, except for the donkey, who is naturally portrayed and looks quite content with maybe even a hint of a smile (fig 13.12).

FIG 13.12 THE FLIGHT INTO EGYPT

Discovering Santiago

After Christ's crucifixion, St James, one of Christ's apostles, journeyed to Spain to preach the word of Jesus. Later he returned to Jerusalem, where he continued baptising Jews even after Herod, King of Judea, forbade him to do so. Eventually the king had him beheaded, making him the first apostle to be martyred. It is thought that the apostle's followers then took his body back to Spain and, after they landed at Galicia on the north-west coast, they buried his body in a field.

By the 11th century, a story emerged that angels had informed a hermit of the burial site of St James in Galicia.

214

The local bishop led his congregation in search of the burial site. As they followed a strange brightness in the sky, they came upon an ancient marble tomb hidden in thick brambles.

The remains were identified as those of St James, and when the king of Galicia had a church built on the site, it was named Santiago de Compostela (Sant Iago de Campus Stella, or St James in the Field of the Star) (fig 13.13). Almost immediately, the tomb and its new church became the most famous pilgrimage site of the Middle Ages.

FIG 13.13 Santiago de Compostela

Cluny

Founded in 910, the abbey at Cluny was the seat of the Benedictine order and had very close ties with the Papacy. When Cluny III was constructed in 1095, it was the largest church in Christendom (and remained so until the building of St Peter's Basilica in Rome in the 16th century). Consecrated by the Pope in 1130, the new church had five altars, a narthex (entrance or outer porch) and several towers. The church, with its spectacular sculpture, was regarded as one of the wonders of the Middle Ages.

Cluny was demolished almost completely during the French Revolution because of its long association with the ruling aristocracy. The abbey was sold as a stone quarry and systematically dismantled over 20 years.

One tower remains intact and the monumental staircase, which once led to the entrance, has been reconstructed. Column bases of the vast narthex have been excavated, but the entire nave of this most magnificent of churches is gone (fig 13.14).

The light of the world

Before Cluny, most monasteries were independent institutions, but over 2,000 smaller monasteries (or priories) were associated with Cluny. Cluny's great success was mainly due to a succession of very capable abbots. These were well-educated men drawn from the highest aristocratic circles and, as head of a giant monastic organisation, were almost as powerful as popes. Four went on to become popes and, in 1098, Pope Urban II (himself a Cluniac) declared that Cluny was the 'light of the world'.

Fig 13.14 Drawing of Cluny Abbey (left) and photo of Cluny today (right).

Conclusion

Architectural sculpture was designed as part of the overall design of the building and its function was to teach, but many Romanesque sculptured scenes are strong and powerful works of art in themselves and are much more than merely decorative.

Questions

1. In what way and why was stone carving a change in art during the Romanesque period?
2. What was the role of Romanesque sculpture for society?
3. Name some of the themes found in Romanesque sculpture.
4. Describe the style of Romanesque sculpture.
5. Write a brief paragraph on the relationship between sculpture and architecture in a Romanesque church.

Colour picture studies

1. Examine the Last Judgement scene on the tympanum at Sainte-Foy de Conques (fig 13.6), The Weighing of Souls on the tympanum at Saint-Lazare in Autun (fig 13.8) and the scene of the Pentecost from the tympanum at the Basilica of St Mary Magdalene in Vézelay (fig 13.4). Compare the style and imagery in these scenes and describe the methods used by the artists to portray the narrative. Use sketches in your answer.
2. Examine the following capitals at Saint-Lazare Cathedral in Autun.
   - The Suicide of Judas (fig 13.10)
   - The Dream of the Magi (fig 13.11)
   - The Flight into Egypt (fig 13.12)

Make a drawing and describe each. Comment on the methods used by the artist to compose the scenes in the space and to convey emotion as well as the narrative.

CHAPTER 14

THE GOTHIC PERIOD

The purpose of medieval art was to teach. Everything the faithful needed to know about the truths of their religion and the lives of the saints, they learned by looking at the windows in Gothic cathedrals and the statues around the church door. The simple peasant and the weary pilgrim of the time found messages they could understand, but later scholars were able to search the imagery in order to uncover the deeper and more symbolic meanings they carried.

Background

A sacred science

Intellectual ideas and the deepest thoughts of learned theologians were all expressed through the medium of art. This was, however, governed by the fixed laws of the Christian Church and its presentation **was treated as a sacred science**. This could not be broken by any individual imagination of a sculptor or painter.

The age of the great cathedral

The 13th century was the age of the great cathedral. Their silhouettes were visible for miles around, dwarfing all other buildings in their shadow and drawing numerous visitors. These visitors must surely have been impressed (just as we are today) with the sculptured architecture bringing life to religious scenes (such as the Coronation of the Virgin) or the rows of stone figures painted in full colour (as was the practice). Progressing inside the building, their every turn would have been marked by images in stone or wood and brilliantly coloured glass. Small wonder if they thought themselves in Heaven.

The beginnings of Gothic

In the mid-12th century, France was no more than a small kingdom with the royal city of Paris at its centre. At the Benedictine Abbey of St Denis, Abbot Suger had a dream of restoring his abbey to its former glory. The old church was completely dilapidated, but Suger set about building a new façade with two towers and three doors before moving to the other end to build a new choir. The result was a major event in the history of architecture. Gothic was born.

Architecture of light

Suger had a very close association with the king of France and a deep love of art, but his work had a profound philosophical basis. For him, art and beauty were ways of honouring God, and he argued that one could only come to understand absolute beauty – which is God – through the effect of beautiful things on our senses. He was fascinated by the religious implications of light and his new concept was for 'an architecture of light'.

The 'creator of Gothic'

This was the beginning of far-reaching developments in architecture, sculpture and stained glass. At St Denis, Abbot Suger took elements of Romanesque architecture – like the cross-ribbed vault and the pointed arch – and united them. These had been used in Burgundy and Normandy, but by bringing the features together in a completely new way, he became, in effect, the 'creator of Gothic'.

The 'French style'

Suger's concept of sacred architecture soon spread around the Île-de-France (the area around Paris) and several great Gothic cathedrals were created there in a very short time. The style later spread to other parts of France, and as Gothic architecture represented the latest in building technology, in time other countries in Europe adopted the 'French style'.

Destruction of St Denis

St Denis suffered very badly during the French Revolution, so to fully appreciate the beauty of a Gothic

FIG 14.1 Chartres Cathedral

cathedral one has to look at Chartres (fig 14.1). Here the same harmonious scheme for the new façade has been used. It also has three doorways sculpted with a series of column statues on both sides of the entrance and a round (or 'rose') stained glass window is flanked by twin towers.

13th-century Gothic cathedrals of France

Culturally and intellectually, France was the most important country in Europe in the mid-13th century. Paris was its shining light, but other large towns like Chartres, Tours, Orléans and Reims were also renowned centres of learning with their own universities and great cathedrals.

The purpose of the cathedral

The cathedral had a dual purpose:
- It was the most important status symbol of the town.
- It served to educate the faithful.

Features of the Gothic style in France

The features of Gothic architecture were:
- The pointed arch.
- The ribbed vault.
- The ambulatory with radiating chapels.

- The clustered columns supporting ribs spreading in different directions.
- Flying buttresses, which enabled the insertion of large clerestory (upper level) windows.
- Large stained glass windows.
- Tracery and window moulding.

These features contrasted with Romanesque architecture because:
- **Pointed arches** were stronger than the rounded Romanesque arch.

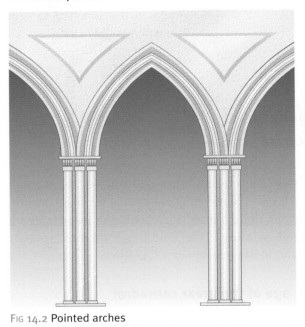

FIG 14.2 Pointed arches

- **Rib vaulting** (crosswise vaulting) was a far more effective system of supporting stone roofs than either barrel or groin vaulting.

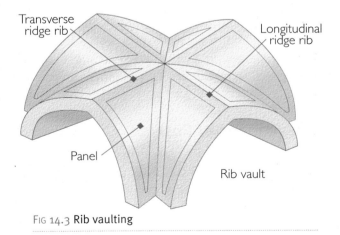

FIG 14.3 Rib vaulting

- **Buttresses** and external arches on the higher parts of the wall, called **flying buttresses**, supported the walls and eliminated the problem of outward thrust.

FIG 14.4 Flying buttresses

FIG 14.6 Window filled with coloured glass

- **Slender pillars** were sufficient to support the vaulting system as outward thrust was eliminated. (Pressure from the vaults was now concentrated only in small areas at the end of the ribs.)
- **Thinner walls** allowed for buildings of much greater height and elegance than the Romanesque style (fig. 14.5). Solid walls were no longer a structural part of the building, so it instead became a skeletal structure supported by flying buttresses and filled with coloured glass (fig. 14.6).

- **Large windows** let in light, in contrast to the dark Romanesque interiors.
- **Tracery** – Ornamental stonework was used to support the glass in the round and tall lancet windows, giving them a light and delicate appearance (fig. 14.7). (The word may have come from the tracing floors on which the complex patterns of Gothic windows were laid out.)

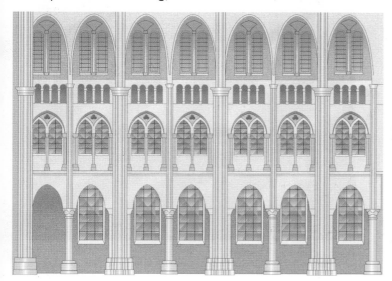

FIG 14.5 Romanesque wall

FIG 14.7 Gothic tracery

FIG 14.8 Notre-Dame de Chartres

Heavenly light

These splendid places of worship must have had an extraordinary effect on ordinary people of the Middle Ages. Coming as they did from small, dark, cramped dwellings, it is easy to imagine how the space and beautiful coloured light filtering through the magnificent stained glass windows and falling on the heads of rich and poor alike was seen as God's grace.

Chartres Cathedral

220

Chartres Cathedral, or Notre-Dame de Chartres (fig 14.8), about 50 miles from Paris, is considered to be one of the finest examples of the high Gothic style and is one of the greatest of all French Gothic cathedrals. It is visible from miles away, but it is only when the visitor draws closer that the buildings of the town clustered at the end of the hill come into view.

The Sancta Camisia

Dedicated to Our Lady and regarded as the 'Seat of the Virgin Mary on Earth', Chartres was a major pilgrimage site and its most sacred relic was the Sancta Camisia (fig 14.9), the gown worn by the Virgin during childbirth. When the old Romanesque church fell victim to a fire in 1134, the opportunity for the building of a new church was presented – but it was not long before disaster struck again.

FIG 14.9 The Santa Camisia

Disaster

On 10 July 1194, another even more terrible fire overwhelmed not just the cathedral but also the town. For three days the inferno raged and the people of the town could only watch in horror as the lead in the cathedral roof melted and poured down in hot streams, making it impossible to go near the building. Eventually it was possible to see that the west front, with its two towers, had survived, but that the rest of the building was damaged beyond repair. To the people's great despair, their precious relic had also perished.

Divine intervention

Some days later, however, the Sancta Camisia was found in the crypt, unharmed beneath the charred embers. To the people of Chartres this was a miracle and there was great rejoicing. The fire came to be seen as a divine intervention from the Virgin herself, who clearly desired a new and even more magnificent cathedral. Huge sums of money were quickly pledged to the rebuilding, and as donations poured in from all over France, rich and poor alike helped by bringing cartloads of building materials up the hill. Miracles were often reported by those who contributed.

A new cathedral

Chartres Cathedral today is the best preserved of the major French cathedrals, with its sculpture and most of its original stained glass still intact. Numerous restorations have not altered its elegant beauty (nor, indeed, a plan to demolish it during the French Revolution that happily never materialised). It remains as it was when it was rebuilt over 800 hundred years ago – a triumph of Gothic art.

Structure

The cathedral is essentially a 13th-century building, for such was the enthusiasm for its rebuilding that it was nearly complete by 1220, a remarkably short time for the construction of medieval cathedrals. Much of the original 12th-century structure still exists on the west front, but 300 years separate the spires, which is immediately obvious from their irregular appearance. The south spire is the original, plain, early Gothic pyramid dating from the 1140s, but the north tower was replaced following a lightning strike in 1506 with a taller tower and spire in the late Gothic (Flamboyant Gothic) style (fig 14.10).

Flying buttresses

Chartres was one of the first large buildings to utilise the full potential of flying buttresses (fig 14.11). There are

FIG 14.10 Chartres north tower

three levels of them along the nave. At the first level they take the form of a simple arch; the next level is connected by small columns arranged like spokes of a wheel; a third layer of arches stretch from the top of the buttresses to just below the gutter of the upper nave (fig 14.12).

FIG 14.11 Flying buttresses at Chartres

FIG 14.12 Flying buttresses

Interior

The interior is built in the shape of a cross, with a central aisle and transepts forming the arms. The sheer size is breathtaking. The spacious nave is the widest in France and offers an unbroken view from the western door towards the magnificent apse in the east (fig 14.13). Clustered slender columns soar dramatically upwards to support the rib vaulting (fig 14.14) and direct the eye to the massive upper-level clerestory windows within them. These, in combination with the three large rose windows over the west door and both transepts, further intensify the feeling of light and space (fig 14.15).

FIG 14.13 Floor plan Chartres

0   50   100 ft

0   30 metres

FIG 14.14 Chartres Cathedral ceiling vaulting

FIG 14.15 Rose window

FIG 14.17 The Royal Portal, Chartres

The Royal Portal

The west front, with its two towers and three tall lancet windows above, is the earliest part of the cathedral. Most of this façade survived the fire of 1194. The main doorway, called the Royal Portal (fig 14.16, fig 14.17) is

FIG 14.16 Chartres Cathedral west façade

one of the three great entrances that make Chartres so unique. Its three doors are framed on both sides by rows of tall figures of kings and queens. These column statues are some of the most famous sculptures in Western art.

Notre Dame, Paris

Notre Dame Cathedral (fig 14.18) was rebuilt in the 13th century, when Paris was developing as the main centre of political power and commerce. No expense was spared in creating a cathedral with impressive new architectural features that would surpass those of all the towns nearby, and the construction was supported and encouraged by King Louis VII himself.

Different styles

The aim of the Paris builders was to push the limits of the new style, and construction of the west front, with its distinctive two towers, began around 1200, before the nave had been completed. During the construction period, however, numerous architects worked on the site, resulting in differing styles at different heights of the west front and towers. The towers were finished around 1245 and the cathedral was finally completed around 1345.

During the reigns of Louis XIV and Louis XV at the end of the 17th century, the cathedral underwent major alterations, during which many tombs and stained glass windows were destroyed. It also suffered during the French Revolution in 1793, when many of its sculptures and treasures were destroyed or looted.

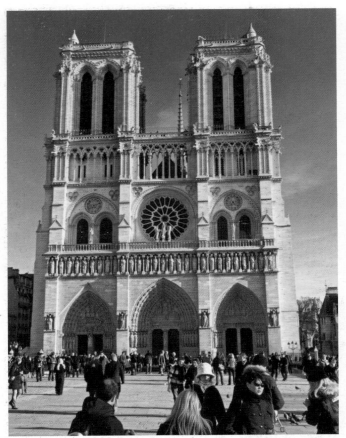

FIG 14.18 Notre Dame Cathedral, Paris

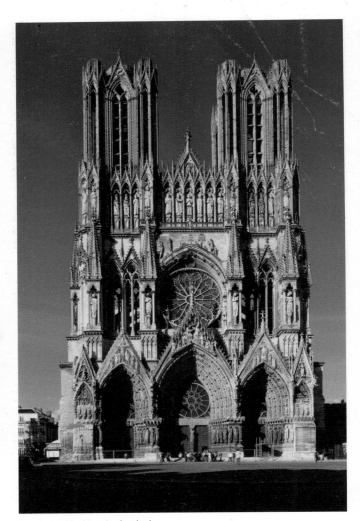

FIG 14.19 Rheims Cathedral

Rheims Cathedral

Built in 1210 after a fire destroyed the original, Rheims Cathedral (fig 14.19) has many of the finest Gothic architectural features: flying buttresses, very thin walls and complicated delicate tracery on its windows. The cathedral was badly damaged during World War I, but much of its sculpture survived and although the façade has been greatly restored, the statues on the sides of the doorways are original.

There were to have been seven towers, but only the two on the western façade were completed and the spires for these were never completed.

Dedicated to the Virgin Mary

The three portals of the west front have a profusion of sculpture and are second only to Chartres in sculpted figures. The central portal is dedicated to the Virgin, but instead of the traditional tympanum it is surmounted by a rose window framed by a triangular sculptured arch (fig 14.20).

Coronations of kings

Rheims is famous for its association with royalty and all the kings of France from the 9th century to the 19th were crowned here. Clovis, the first king of the Franks, was baptised here in 496 AD, and this event is represented in a central position in the 'gallery of the kings' on the main façade among the statues of his successors.

Rouen Cathedral

Rouen has been called the 'City of a Hundred Spires' because of its numerous churches, but towering above them all is the highest spire in France, erected in 1876. This cast iron masterpiece rises 490 ft above the **Cathedral of Notre-Dame de Rouen** (fig 14.14), making it the tallest building in the world for some time.

It was built mostly in the 13th century but there were several later additions, so it has a mixture of styles, including early Gothic, high Gothic and late or Flamboyant Gothic.

FIG 14.20 Tympanum Rheims Cathedral

FIG 14.21 Cathedral of Notre-Dame de Rouen

Flamboyant Gothic

Flamboyant is the name given to a florid style of late Gothic architecture dating to the 15th century. The main portal of Rouen Cathedral, as well as the steeple on the right, are built in this style.

Rouen has even greater attention to decoration and its highly ornamental tracery with dramatic lengthening of the supporting stonework creates an almost lacelike effect (fig 14.22).

Impressionist paintings

Rouen's decorative façade can be seen at its best in some of the most famous images painted by French Impressionist artist Claude Monet. He immortalised the cathedral in the late 19th century by painting a series of scenes in full sunlight or varying degrees of shadow at different times of the day (fig 14.23).

Other important cathedrals of France include those in Amiens, Beauvais, Strasbourg and Laon. The Gothic style also spread to other parts of Europe and there are a number of very fine cathedrals in Germany, England, Italy and Spain. Notable among them are the cathedrals of Cologne and Milan.

Conclusion

The development of Gothic was a major event in the history of architecture. The style began as a deeply intellectual concept as developed by Abbot Suger of St Denis of honouring God through art and beauty. It led to the building of many soaring cathedrals that are as impressive today as when they were first constructed.

FIG 14.22 Tracery, Rouen Cathedral

FIG 14.23 Rouen Cathedral in Full Sunlight: Harmony in Blue and Gold by Claude Monet

Questions

1. How did Gothic architecture begin?
2. What purpose did a Gothic cathedral serve?
3. List the architectural features of a typical Gothic Cathedral.
4. Describe the function of the following.
   - Ribbed vault
   - The buttress and flying buttress

Essay

1. Compare the architecture of a typical Romanesque church with that of a typical Gothic cathedral. Make detailed references to specific examples of the style in your answer. Illustrate with diagrams.

Coloured picture study

1. Compare Chartres Cathedral (fig. 14.1), Rheims Cathedral (fig 14.19) and Rouen Cathedral (fig 14.21) with reference to the development of Gothic architecture over the period of the 13th to the 15th century.

CHAPTER 15

GOTHIC SCULPTURE

A light in the dark

One of the most important developments during the 12th century was a change in the ordinary person's attitude to God. A new humanism had come into religious discussion in the universities and, like light piercing the darkness, this filtered down to the level of ordinary people, breaking through the layers of fear and ignorance. Gradually it banished the vivid but terrifying vision of death and its aftermath that had so long obsessed the medieval mind.

Transition from the Romanesque

Hope was the new message. The Church now preached salvation rather than damnation, and nowhere are these changes seen more clearly than in the imagery and art of the new Gothic cathedrals. In a typical Romanesque scene, like that found in Saint-Lazare in Autun or Sainte-Foy de Conques, an impassive God sits in judgement with the blessed to his right and the damned to his left, who deserve nothing better than eternal torment with grotesque devils in Hell.

These grotesque scenes are in complete contrast to the new Gothic imagery. Mary the mother of God occupies a very prominent position and her story appears in many ways on most of the cathedrals. The emphasis is also more on Christ as the saviour of mankind. Final Judgement scenes have not disappeared, but they tend to be far less obvious. They still show an awesome and all-powerful God, but Hell is smaller and far less gruesome and the inclusion of the Virgin Mary and St John with Christ offers further hope.

The saints

Numerous images of saints are found all over in Gothic sculpture and stained glass. Medieval people loved their saints and prayed in times of sickness or distress for them to intercede with God for them. Stories of the saints and their miracles were completely familiar to the average person, so these were easy to 'read'. Traditionally, saints were identified by their symbols, but as the artists of the 13th century became more skilled, they depended less on symbols to show the sanctity of saints and concentrated instead on facial expressions.

Column statues

Column statues of kings and queens were a feature of early Gothic imagery. These were originally found around the doorway of the façade at St Denis and may have been associated with the French royal family. These were rapidly followed by the west front of Chartres Cathedral

FIG 15.1 Column statues, Chartres

FIG 15.2 Column statues, Chartres

FIG 15.3 Column statues at Chartres

and became common on cathedrals throughout the Île de France.

The statues at St Denis were destroyed during the French Revolution, but drawings show they were free-standing figures carved into the columns. A very group is found at Chartres (fig 15.1, fig 15.2 and fig 15.3).

As Gothic sculpture developed, these groups of carved figures on doorways became more free-standing and adopted more naturalistic poses as they relied less on the supporting architecture. Expressions also tended towards realism, with some even smiling, like those found at Rheims (fig 15.13).

Chartres

The Royal Portal (early Gothic, 12th century)

The theme of the Royal Portal (west portal, main entrance) (fig 15.4) is salvation. The tympanum over the centre door presents a peaceful and calm vision of eternity with Christ in Majesty, welcoming the visitor. The scenes on either side are that of the Virgin Mary and the Ascension of Christ.

FIG 15.4 Christ in Majesty, the Royal Portal, Chartres

FIG 15.5 North Portal, Chartres

The doorway gets its name from the so-called kings and queens on either side. Nobody is quite sure who they are, but they probably represent the kings and queens of Judea, or Christ's royal ancestors from the Old Testament. These tall column statues are related in style to the Romanesque, but they also show a clear advancement in that they are no longer a minor addition to a building but an important part of the overall design of the doorway, blending with and enhancing the architecture.

They vary in height, but all the heads are at the same level and folds in the drapery tend to emphasise their tall, linear quality. Some of the patterns are similar to that used in the sculpture at Autun and Vézelay, but they are much more refined, as is evident in their serene and dignified facial expressions and more accomplished body proportions. Great delight appears to have been taken in portraying the finest detail of their crêpe-like garments, especially those worn by the queens on either side of the central door, and their plaits, long, flowing

sleeves and girdles are carved with great attention to detail.

The master sculptor

Differences in quality can easily be seen between the figures of the three doors, but this is because the master sculptor is credited with those on the central doorway, while assistants may be responsible for the work on the doors to the right and left.

The North Portal (high Gothic, 13th century)

The North Portal is dedicated to the Virgin Mary (fig 15.5). The figure of St Anne holding her baby daughter, Mary, stands in the central trumeau (fig 15.6), and in the central tympanum above she is crowned Queen of Heaven. She is the link between the Old and New Testaments. Ranged along both sides of the doorways are the prophets who foretold the coming of Christ, standing beside the apostles.

Old Testament and New Testament figures

The Old Testament high priest Melchizedek carries a chalice and opposite him on the other side is St Peter,

FIG 15.6 St Anne

FIG 15.7 Abraham and Isaac

the successor of Christ. Abraham, the Old Testament patriarch who was willing to sacrifice his beloved son, Isaac, anticipates the sacrifice of Christ and faces John the Baptist, who points to the Lamb of God.

Individual personalities

The most dramatic aspect of these figures is the way they are treated – very much as individuals with defined gestures. This kind of naturalism is seen in the depiction of Abraham (fig 15.7), who, in the very act of sacrificing his son, turns to look up at the angel sent by God to stop him. This approach was quite new and had not been seen in sculpture in France before this.

Women

The portal dedicated to Mary was paid for by Blanche of Castille, a strong and powerful figure in medieval France. This explains the presence of so many women on this doorway. Several Old Testament heroines appear in the arches, but undoubtedly the finest sculpture on the portico is the graceful image of St Modeste (fig 15.8), a local saint, standing at the corner.

FIG 15.8 St Modeste

Modesta and Potentian

Modesta was the daughter of the governor of Chartres in Roman times, but drew her father's wrath when she was converted to Christianity by Potentian, a preacher reputed to have been sent by St Peter himself to Chartres. She begged her father to spare the life of Potentian when he was tried by her father, but both were

FIG 15.9 The South Portal at Chartres

martyred and her body was thrown down the sacred well in the crypt at Chartres. Potentian is depicted on the opposite corner to Modesta, dressed in bishop's clothing.

St Modeste

Many scholars have commented on the superior quality of the statue of St Modeste, considered a beautiful portrayal of maidenly sweetness and purity. The young woman with a veil over her unbound hair lifts her mantle while holding a book in one hand and raises the other in blessing as she turns her head in a gesture of gentle refinement.

The South Portal (high Gothic, 13th century)

The whole of the South Portal (fig 15.9) is dedicated to the glory of Jesus Christ. His church and apostles are on either side of him in the central doorway.

The teacher

Jesus stands on the central trumeau with book in hand, the other lifted in blessing, and behind his head is his defining symbol – the cruciform halo (fig 15.10). His feet rest on a lion and a dragon, but he is very far from the Romanesque judge of sinners. This is a loving Christ – the teacher of mankind or the shepherd who laid down his life for his flock. The gentle expression on the finely carved face portrays that image.

FIG 15.10 Jesus Christ blessing

Fig 15.11 St Peter

Fig 15.12 St John

Christ's apostles

On either side of the door on beautiful twisted columns, the 12 apostles stand barefoot. St Peter (fig 15.11), as head of the Church, stands on Christ's right and is recognisable by his curly hair and beard. He is carrying a key – the symbol of his power on earth. Nearby, St Andrew has a

cross and St John (fig 15.12), the beardless youth, carries a book. The other apostles have no special symbol; instead they carry the instruments of their deaths, and beneath them are the crowned figures of the Roman Empire who persecuted them.

Last Judgement

In the tympanum above the central doorway a Last Judgement scene is presented, according to the Gospel of St Matthew. The familiar images of Michael weighing

Fig 15.13 THE ANNUNCIATION, Rheims cathedral

Fig 15.14 Virgin Mary and Saint Elizabeth, Rheims Cathedral

the souls with devils fighting for the souls are all present. Even though the damned are led to eternal fire by these demons, once again this image is far less graphic and grotesque than earlier representations on Romanesque churches.

Rheims Cathedral

Sculpture

Devotion to Mary was very popular in the 13th century. This was the era of chivalry, with its ideals and virtues of honour and courtly love. The knightly code of behaviour included great respect for women and the honour accorded Mary was highest of all. Many cathedrals were dedicated to her and at Rheims she is seen in the gable above the central doorway with her son, who is crowning her Queen of Heaven. She appears again on the central pier of the main doorway, welcoming the faithful. Among the surrounding statues are some (fig 15.13) representing the Visitation and the Annunciation.

Figures inspired by Rome

The figures of Mary and Elizabeth are clearly inspired by Roman statuary, with lifelike bodies and flowing garments (fig 15.14). Near them, the angel Gabriel has a

delicate, smiling face, graceful movement and an elegantly draped body. This famous smiling Angel of Rheims has become the emblem for the city (fig 15.15).

Germany

As the Gothic style spread from France during the 13th century, many new and magnificent cathedrals were built in neighbouring countries, including England, Spain and the German Rhineland. Artists who had learned their craft on the first Gothic cathedrals in France also often travelled to other countries, bringing their skills to local artists. One of these was a talented sculptor known only as the Naumburg Master. He is thought to have trained in France, where his sculpture is found in several cathedrals, including Chartres, but his most famous work is in Naumburg in an impressive 13th-century Gothic cathedral.

Ekehard and Uta

Naumburg lies along the Saale River, in east-central Germany, and here the sculptor produced a cycle of 12

Fig 15.15 The smiling Angel of Rheims

FIG 15.16 Ekehard and Uta

exceptionally fine figures around the choir of the Cathedral of St Peter and St Paul, representing its founders. The most famous of these are Count Ekehard and his wife, Uta (fig 15.16), who are so convincing that one could believe they were portraits from life if one did not know that they had been long dead at the time of carving. With amazing attention to detail of clothing, faces and, most of all, in the subtle nuances of pose and gesture, the artist has conveyed an astonishingly real human quality.

Walt Disney influence

Ekehard holds the strap of his shield and Uta, seemingly feeling the cold, pulls her heavy ermine cloak to her face. The hands are particularly finely depicted and are treated with great sensitivity. Both figures still retain a good deal of their original bright colours and the figure of Uta, with her veil and golden crown, is said to have influenced Walt Disney in the creation of some of his cartoon queens.

Conclusion

Humanism in religious thinking found its way into art, making the imagery used in Gothic sculpture far gentler than the terrifying visions of the Romanesque era.

Questions

1. How did new religious thinking affect Gothic sculpture?
2. How did the medieval person identify the saints in sculpture?
3. What is meant by a column statue?
4. Outline some of the elements of Gothic sculpture that indicate a more naturalistic approach to the human figure.

Essay

1. Looking at some of the sculpture on the three portals of Chartres and figures on other cathedrals, discuss the development of Gothic sculpture from the 13th to the 15th century. Indicate the changes in style, with reference to some named figures in your answer.

Colour picture study

1. Examine the Royal Portal at Chartres (fig 15.4) and describe the figures. Why do you think these are some of the most famous figures in the history of art?
2. Examine the figures of Uta and Ekehard (fig 15.16) in the Cathedral of St Peter and St Paul in Naumburg and describe them in you own words. Do you think the sculptor has made a convincing likeness of the two people? In what way do their gestures convey emotion?

CHAPTER 16

LATE GOTHIC SCULPTURE (14TH CENTURY)

A time of changes

The 14th century brought many changes. Towns that had grown up around the great cathedrals were by now teeming with trade and people were living far more independently of the power of the Church and the feudal lords. Church building continued, but it was no longer the focus for all branches of art. Wealthy members of the nobility commissioned large amounts of art and those that were living in luxurious homes in the cities preferred smaller works of art that were never intended for public display. Their taste was for refined and delicate works, and artists were now widely employed by individual wealthy patrons to produce statuettes in precious materials like silver and ivory for private chapels rather than great works in stone for large spaces.

Curved poses

A curved, slightly swaying posture in these statuettes was very fashionable. This may have reflected the kind of mannerisms seen at court in this age of great chivalry or it may have come about simply in relation to the natural curve in ivory, which comes from an elephant's tusk. The most noticeable change in sculpture of this time, however, was the humanisation of the portrayal of religious figures.

The Virgin of Notre Dame

The large statue of the Virgin in Notre Dame Cathedral in Paris (fig 16.1) was sculpted for a small church in the centre of Paris in the middle of the 14th century, but it was transferred to Notre Dame in the 19th century to replace one destroyed during the Revolution.

It stands on the spot of an altar dedicated to the Virgin since the 12th century, but its exaggerated S curve posture is typical of a much later Gothic style. The Virgin is long and elegant, the folds of her garments falling gracefully away from her outstretched hip. At the same time it is also a very tender portrayal of a mother smiling at the baby on her arm while he plays with the fastening of her cloak. This Mary is not solemn or aloof like earlier images, but is more of a worldly queen, dressed in royal garments, wearing a heavy, gem-encrusted crown.

Burgundy

We do not know much about most medieval artists, but the life of Claus Sluter, a Dutch artist from the late 14th century, has been very well documented.

Claus Sluter

Claus Sluter was one of the many Netherlandish artists who benefited from the wealth of France. Having left his

Fig 16.1 The Virgin of Notre Dame

The duke's own tomb was later reassembled in the Musée des Beaux-Arts of Dijon and his most famous work is the Well of Moses fountain (fig 16.2) which, although damaged, shows the real excellence of his work.

The Well of Moses (late 14th century)

This fountain is a tall, hexagonal pillar covered with six lifelike figures and weeping angels. All were originally richly painted and gilded, and traces of paint can still be seen in parts. It was originally surmounted by a crucifix and the figures of the Virgin Mary, St John and Mary Magdalene, but this was destroyed during the French Revolution when the monastery was badly damaged.

Luckily, the base with the prophets of the Old Testament survived. Their faces in particular show enormous strength and character, with skin texture and hair rendered to perfection. Moses is a grand and noble figure, dressed in a long, flowing garment. His beard, divided into two long strands, is so convincingly real that under the wrinkled brow and god-like horns one would not be surprised to see the eyes flash.

Conclusion

Curved statues in elegant poses are classic examples of 14th-century sculpture. These small works in precious materials like silver and ivory indicate changes in society as the wealthy built their own smaller chapels for private worship.

FIG 16.2 The Well of Moses fountain, Dijon, France

native town of Haarlem in Holland, he worked for the dukes of Burgundy at the Carthusian monastery of Champmol located just outside Dijon. This magnificent monastery was the burial place of the dukes and attracted many artists. Sluter was the greatest of these and although the monastery suffered much destruction during the Revolution, some of his sculpture survived. His very realistic depictions of the monastery's founders (Duke Philip the Bold and his wife, Margaret of Flanders) are among these. These portraits were apparently very good likenesses, but they also represented a radically new departure for sculpture. Not only was it the first time that living people were given a space normally reserved for religious imagery, but they were also carved fully in the round.

Questions
Essay

1. Trace the development of Gothic sculpture from the 13th to the 15th century. Indicate the changes in style with reference to named works in your answer.

Colour picture studies

1. Examine the Well of Moses fountain (fig 16.2) and make a drawing of it, adding the colours you think might have been used by the artist.

CHAPTER 17

STAINED GLASS

Stained glass windows were not a Gothic invention. They had been used before, but with the great Gothic cathedrals they evolved to become translucent coloured walls. Sunlight pouring through the coloured glass filled the interiors with glorious mosaics of colour, creating the impression of a carpet of transparent rubies, emerald and gold covering the floor and falling on the heads of the faithful.

The origins of stained glass technique are not fully known, but it may have come from the East and possibly developed from jewellery-making and mosaics. St Denis was the first to fully explore its possibilities and Abbot Suger brought in craftsmen to do the work. He kept a journal, so we know from what he wrote that he truly believed its beauty would lift men's souls closer to God.

Technique – making a stained glass window

The same basic method for making stained glass windows has been in use since medieval times.

Step 1: The artist makes a coloured design on a small scale. A full-size drawing called a cartoon, which emphasises the leading (see Step 3), is made on paper. In medieval times a whitewashed board or table was used for the cartoon. Pieces of glass (white or coloured) are cut to shape and laid on the cartoon.

Step 2: Black or dark brown enamel paint is used to paint details and textures. The glass is then fired in a muffle kiln to fix the painting.

Step 3: Leading in a variety of cross-sections is very flexible.

Step 4: The painted glass is laid back on the cartoon and the leading is fitted around it and cut to size.

Step 5: In larger windows, iron bars are set in the frames and wired onto the leading to provide additional strength and support against wind pressure.

Step 6: The joints in the leading are soldered.

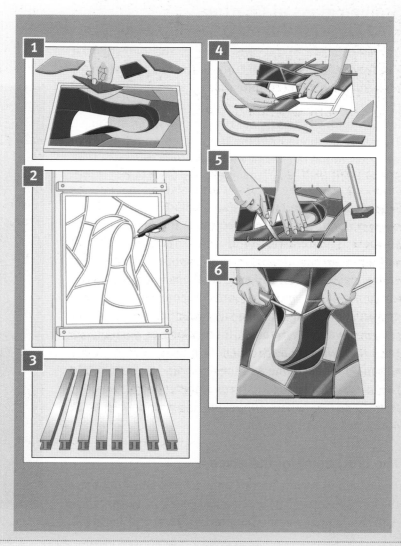

FIG 17.1 Stained glass windows at Chartres

Stained glass at Chartres

The windows of Chartres Cathedral (fig 17.1), dating from as early as the 1140s, are some of the oldest, most extensive and beautiful in Europe. The fact that so many have survived intact is quite unique. It represents one of the most complete collections of medieval stained glass in the world. Of the original 183 windows, 145 still exist. They vary in shape from the three large round (or rose) windows to the tall lancet windows along the nave. High above are the huge, ornate clerestory windows.

238

The windows were created as the church was built and many different artists contributed to their construction, so there is quite a variety of styles. The cathedral was designed to have the maximum amount of space for stained glass, and the fact that these windows would have been the most expensive component in the construction of the building suggests that the chapter of Chartres was very wealthy. Inscriptions or portraits on the lower window panel identify individuals or groups who paid for each one and these provide an insight into the role of royalty, the aristocracy and guilds of everyday tradesmen like bakers or bankers, all of whom helped to adorn this great cathedral.

The blackening of the glass

The windows have suffered from a build-up of patina, a thick crust caused by a chemical reaction of the glass with the normal weathering process. Over the years this caused the windows to blacken, which had the effect of darkening the interior considerably. In recent times the windows have been removed one by one and each individual pane has been painstakingly cleaned. This

FIG 17.2 The life of St Martin window at Chartres

process has allowed the modern visitor to experience the cathedral like the medieval pilgrim and fully appreciate the magnificence of the coloured light falling around them in all its original brilliance.

Stories in the glass

Abbot Suger promoted the idea of stained glass as a narrative medium and a ready source of instruction for the illiterate population, so each window in the cathedral has a story to tell. Some are relatively easy to 'read', like those featuring Christ and Mary, and others tell detailed stories of popular, well-known saints. Each of these many saints has an entire window dedicated to them. The life of St Martin (fig 17.2), for example, in which he shares his cloak with a freezing beggar and dreams that Christ appears to him wearing the same cloak, is told in 33 panels.

Medieval heroes like Roland of Roncevalles or Charlemagne, the emperor of the Holy Roman Empire, also have a window each, but unfortunately the meaning of some of these wonderful medieval works of art has

FIG 17.4 South rose window, Chartres

become obscure. This is because after the Reformation the Church grew ashamed of some of the old popular legends and they disappeared from Church teaching. New generations with a different view of the world no longer understood them and their complex symbolic references are virtually a mystery nowadays.

Rose windows

Chartres has three large circular windows known as rose windows because of their shape. They are found over the entrance door on the western front and over the doorways on both transepts. The northern rose (fig 17.3) is dedicated to the glorification of the Virgin and the southern glorifies Christ (fig 17.4).

The Blue Virgin window

The most famous window at Chartres is known as the Blue Virgin (fig 17.5). The large figure of the Virgin of Chartres is in four panels of blue glass on a ground of ruby. This masterpiece of 12th-century workmanship belonged to the former cathedral before the fire in 1194. Similar to the imagery found in the sculpture of the period, she is portrayed as a queen, with her lap forming a throne for her child. She is Queen of Heaven, with angels all around, and Queen of Earth, with authority over demons.

FIG 17.3 North rose window, Chartres

Fig 17.5 The Blue Virgin of Chartres

Fig 17.6 Church of Sainte-Chapelle, Paris

14th-century stained glass

Sainte-Chapelle

The church of Sainte-Chapelle in Paris (fig 17.6) was built by King Louis IX (St Louis) in 1246. The king was a renowned patron of the arts and was responsible for a good deal of the innovation in Gothic art and architecture. For him, Sainte-Chapelle had to be perfect. It was to house his most precious relic – a fragment of the crown of thorns worn by Jesus during the crucifixion.

Sainte-Chapelle is a jewel of Rayonnant Gothic architecture and consists of two churches, one above the other. The lower chapel is quite plain – it served as a parish church for the inhabitants of the palace – but the upper chapel holds a very special place among the monuments of Paris due to its beautiful stained glass windows (fig 17.7).

The windows – colour and light

Structural supports on the exterior walls were reduced to a minimum to make way for a complete wall of tall and narrow lancet windows (fig 17.8). The effect is a wondrous atmosphere of fragile beauty and a feeling of being enveloped in light and colour. Part of the reason for this is the blending of deep reds and blues to form a purplish haze. This gives the windows a certain unity, but it does make the individual scenes, which feature over 1,130 figures from the Bible, quite difficult to make out.

Destruction during the Revolution

During the French Revolution, the choir stalls and interior furniture were destroyed when the chapel was converted to offices.

Enormous filing cabinets were placed against windows, which all but covered them – but luckily, they also protected the windows from vandalism.

Most of the interior statues were placed in storage and were later recovered (fig 17.9), but the sculpture outside was hacked off the tympanum, the spire of the church was pulled down and most of Louis IX's precious relics were scattered.

Stained glass in the 13th century

The stained glass workshop at Chartres in the 13th century was highly influential and its craftsmen were very skilled. They made sure that the colours in the glass were well separated so that bright colours did not clash and outshine each other. When Paris became the centre of stained glass around 1240, however, its manufacture became less delicate. Production was on such a large scale that it was almost industrial and the standards of craftsmanship were less rigorous. The same motif tended to be repeated over and over and, more importantly, far less care about separating blues and reds was taken so that the brightness of the one overwhelmed the other. However, the resulting violet hue was much appreciated in its day and led to the phrase describing good wine: 'wine the colour of the windows in the Sainte-Chapelle'.

FIG 17.7 **Stained Glass Windows in Sainte-Chapelle**

FIG 17.8 **Rose Window in Sainte-Chapelle**

FIG 17.9 Statue at Saint-Chapelle

Restoration to the chapel took place between 1837 and 1838, when Sainte-Chapelle was returned to its earlier splendour.

Some fragments of the relics survived and are today kept in the treasury of Notre Dame Cathedral.

Conclusion

Although stained glass was not a new art, it evolved during the Gothic era to a level of great sophistication. The great new cathedrals filled with the 'heavenly' light created by stained glass windows undoubtedly supported Abbot Suger's conception of artistic beauty that would lift men's souls closer to God.

Questions

1. Describe the process of making a stained glass window.
2. What makes the windows of Chartres Cathedral so special?
3. What is the name given to the tall, pointed windows found in Chartres and other cathedrals?
4. Outline how a story is told in a typical window.
5. Make a drawing of a rose window in a Gothic cathedral.

Essay

1. Discuss the impact of the stained glass windows on the interior of Chartres Cathedral and compare this to Sainte-Chapelle in Paris. Compare the styles of both and briefly describe the methods used in the production of stained glass windows.

Coloured picture study

1. Examine and describe in detail the Blue Virgin window in Chartres Cathedral (fig 17.5), referring to the overall plan/design, theme, composition and use of colour.

CHAPTER 18

THE INTERNATIONAL STYLE

The Gothic style that developed in the late 14th century and early 15th century spread widely across western Europe, creating the name for the period – the International style.

In this period, artists and ideas moved from one country to another. They took smaller, easily carried works of art like illuminated manuscripts with them and travelled widely around the Continent, creating a sophisticated style that became common among the royalty and higher nobility. The main influences on the style were northern France, the Duchy of Burgundy, Bohemia and Italy.

The *Wilton Diptych*

The little painting known as the *Wilton Diptych* (fig 18.1) in the National Gallery in London is a particularly fine example of the International style.

It is one of the most beautiful, yet most mysterious, paintings ever made, with its intricacy of detail, varied techniques and rich colours. Its exquisite gold tooling and its remarkable state of preservation from the late Middle Ages make it quite unique.

The word 'diptych' comes from the Greek and refers to two panels hinged together. The *Wilton Diptych* takes its name from Wilton House, near Salisbury, Wiltshire, where it was housed from 1705 until 1929, when it was bought by the National Gallery in London. The name of the artist and where it was painted are unknown.

It is painted on two wooden panels in frames and its function was that of a portable altarpiece that could be set up on altars of different churches but closed like a book to protect the inner painting. The inner paintings are in excellent condition, but some of the paint on the outer faces has been lost over the years.

Private devotion

The *Wilton Diptych* was probably made for the private devotion of King Richard II. Its jewel-like appearance means it would have been one of the royal treasures along with the king's jewels and golden robes. Richard II was crowned king of England at the age of 10 in 1377,

and he was deposed (and probably murdered by his cousin, Henry IV) in 1399.

In the left-hand panel he is presented to the Virgin and Child by his patron saint, John the Baptist, and two English royal saints, Edward the Confessor and Edmund.

On the right, the Virgin and Child stand in a meadow strewn with flowers, indicating the gardens of Paradise. The heavenly nature of this apparition is further stressed by the Virgin's brilliant blue robes and those of the angels surrounding her (fig 18.2).

Portrait of the king

The *Wilton Diptych* is the first painting to record a real historical person and at first glance it is a straightforward portrait. It is, however, full of symbolism that nobody today can precisely explain. For example, why is one of the angels carrying a white banner with a red cross of the type normally carried by Christ in scenes of the Resurrection? Why is there a crown of thorns and three nails symbolising Christ's Passion inside the child's halo area (fig 18.3)?

Despite its religious theme, the real focus of the *Wilton Diptych* is the king himself. Every figure either gestures towards or looks at him, and every detail on both panels ensures that the viewer looks first not at the Virgin and Child, but at the kneeling king. Richard wears his own emblem (a white hart, or stag) in a gold-and-white enamelled brooch and the angels surrounding the Virgin Mary also wear badges featuring white harts.

FiG 18.1 THE WILTON DIPTYCH, National Gallery London

The king is portrayed as the youth he was when he came to the throne in his eleventh year. He kneels before the Virgin and the child leans towards him in what appears to be a playful gesture, but the hands in fact are raised in blessing.

Painted books

It was the custom in the Middle Ages to illustrate calendars with the labours of the month. These were attached to prayer books and were called books of hours.

Les Très Riches Heures du Duc de Berry

Jean de France, Duc de Berry, was the son of King John II (Jean le Bon/John the Good) and was related to many other princes and queens of the Burgundy region, all of whom were collectors of books like himself. His most

famous book, *Les Très Riches Heures* (fig 18.4), is regarded as the finest manuscript of the 15th century and the supreme example of painting in the International Gothic style.

As patron of the arts, the duke sought out and encouraged new artists. Among these were the Limbourg brothers from the Netherlands, who brought with them some of the new realism prevalent in northern Europe.

A book of prayer

The book was produced as a book of prayer, but as the rich illustrations show, it is less about the glory of the Lord and far more about the duke himself.

He obviously appreciated the beauty of artworks and delighted in the realistic portrayal of his own person. His

FIG 18.2 **THE WILTON DIPTYCH** - detail of the Virgin

courtiers are depicted in splendid costume (fig 18.5) and all his prized possessions as well as his beautiful castles, unfortunately mostly destroyed after his death, are shown in precise detail.

Real space

This depiction of real space and action was a completely new departure for miniature painting in France. The artists were the first to paint the intricate details of fairy tale castles, sweeping landscapes, birds, animals and even insects with incredible accuracy. In stark contrast to the hardships of everyday life at this time of the plague in Europe, the illustrations depict only harmony and peace. The most famous of these images of splendour and grace are the calendar months.

FIG 18.4 October, *LES TRÈS RICHES HEURES DU DUC DE BERRY*

FIG 18.3 **THE WILTON DIP TICH** – detail of the Child

FIG 18.5 APRIL, LES TRÈS RICHES HEURES DU DUC DE BERRY

FIG 18.6 January, LES TRÈS RICHES HEURES DU DUC DE BERRY

The months

January (fig 18.6) was the traditional month of giving New Year's gifts and in this scene Jean de Berry himself can be seen on the right, wearing a brilliant blue velvet robe decorated with gold and a fur hat. Behind him, the fire screen that guards the open fire encircles his head from behind like a halo. On the table, some of the duke's treasured possessions are depicted in detail. Small dogs eat the scraps on the table and elegant courtiers gather around in their colourful clothing.

In contrast, February (fig 18.7) shows the winter chill and the land is cloaked in a blanket of snow as peasants go about their chores. The realism of the picture gives a real indication of what a medieval farm looked like, with its sheep pen, beehives, barrels, bales of straw and even the hooded crows pecking at the straw on the ground. The farmer's house has been opened up so that we can

see a woman with her skirt lifted to warm herself at the fire. She turns her head from the servants behind her, who have less delicately lifted their garments, clearly showing one as male and the other as female.

In May (fig 18.8), the courtiers don leaves and garlands and go riding, and in the heat of August they ride out with the falcons while the workers toil in the background, some taking a moment to swim in the river.

In September (fig 18.9), the workers on the estate gather in the grapes in front of the great chateau of Saumur.

March to December each depict one of the great castles and the estates surrounding them, but if the duke ever worried about the plight of his tenants, there is no account of it at a time when society was structured in an ordered fashion and everybody had their place.

FIG 18.7 February, LES TRÈS RICHES HEURES DU DUC DE BERRY

FIG 18.8 May, LES TRÈS RICHES HEURES DU DUC DE BERRY

FIG 18.9 September, LES TRÈS RICHES HEURES DU DUC DE BERRY

Conclusion

As artists moved from one court to another developing a sophisticated style, works became smaller for practical reasons. Many have undoubtedly been lost, but those that have survived are exquisite in finish and detail.

Questions

1. What was the International style?
2. What is a diptych?
3. What is a book of hours?

Colour picture study

1. Examine the *Wilton Diptych* (fig 18.1) and describe the event taking place and the style of the work. Why is this a good example of the International Gothic style?
2. Examine January and February from Les *Très Riches Heures du Duc de Berry* by the Limbourg brothers (fig. 18.6, fig 18.7) and discuss what makes this book so special. In your answer, describe the details of both scenes and compare the characters depicted in each.
3. Examine May and September from Les *Très Riches Heures du Duc de Berry* (fig 18.8, fig 18.9) and explain why these can be described as images of splendour and grace. Draw attention to some of the fine details of the costumes and lifestyles depicted in the scenes and say why this may have been in sharp contrast to everyday life.

CHAPTER 19

Cimabue and Giotto

The Florentine artist Cimabue is often regarded as the last great painter working in the Byzantine tradition, but he had also made quite a move towards naturalism. Cimabue enjoyed a widespread reputation in his time, but today he is much better known as the teacher of Giotto.

The Byzantine tradition

Byzantine art refers to the art of the Byzantine Empire (or Byzantium), the Greek-speaking Eastern Roman Empire of the Middle Ages, centred around its capital of Constantinople. It is highly stylised and looks solemn, unreal, abstract and flat in appearance. The most famous Byzantine painting is the Hodegetria icon (meaning 'image'), which was widely copied. St Luke the apostle was believed to have painted the original of the Virgin Mary from life (fig 19.1).

FIG 19.1 The Hodegetria icon

St Francis and realism in art

St Francis of Assisi lived in the 13th century. He urged people to picture Christ's life and meditate on his Passion. His sermons were delivered in the plain speech of the people and he felt that realistic art should explain the scriptures to ordinary people, the vast majority of whom could not read. This brought about an entirely new kind of piety and an awareness of the importance of a narrative or story in art.

Assisi

The Franciscans persuaded the Pope to employ artists to paint in a real and lifelike manner. Pope Nicholas III, who had a great liking for the art of classical antiquity, commissioned **Cimabue**. He worked in Rome and then on the little Church of St Francis in Assisi, where he executed a grand scheme of decoration based on the life of Christ, Mary and the apostles. The frescos in this magnificent cycle are in the style of ancient Roman wall paintings, with lifelike figures, proportions and shading. It was very famous in its own day, but today it is unfortunately in a very poor state due to lead in the paint that has made all the whites turn black.

Giotto di Bondone

Giotto di Bondone (c. 1267–1337) was apprenticed to Cimabue and learned all the elements of the new art alongside him in his workshop in Florence. He followed him to Rome, where he studied classical painting and in time surpassed his master to become the most famous artist in his day. He worked for rich Florentine families and other patrons who valued his painting for its intellectual qualities and its ability to imitate nature.

Giotto's innovations

Giotto created the illusion of real space in his paintings and they featured real people set against real backgrounds, almost like a drama on a stage.

He achieved reality by using **correct proportions**, **foreshortening** and **light and shade**, but the real novelty of Giotto's work was his extraordinary ability to convey **human emotion** through **facial expressions** and **lifelike gestures**.

An important technical improvement in Giotto's fresco painting was his use of **wet plaster**, which bonded with the colour to make it firm and lasting.

Giotto's work

Giotto became very famous in his own lifetime and demand for his services took him all over Italy. Many stories were told about him, but the most famous was recounted by Giorgio Vasari, the biographer of famous Italian artists. Vasari relates that Giotto was a shepherd boy who was discovered by Cimabue. The boy was drawing pictures of his sheep on a rock and they were so lifelike that Cimabue took him back to Florence to be his apprentice. Vasari suggests that Cimabue called Giotto to join him in Assisi, and so it is thought that Giotto is responsible for the great fresco cycle of St Francis there.

The Madonna Enthroned

Painted images of the Virgin were reputed to have performed many miracles of healing. The *Madonna Enthroned with Angels and Prophets* (fig 19.2), or *Ognissanti* ('all saints'), was a particularly popular image. Although only 20 years separate Giotto's version from those by Duccio di Buoninsegna (fig 19.3) and Cimabue (fig 19.4), the difference is astonishing. Like them, Giotto includes traditional symbols, but he depicts the scene as a real space with depth and perspective and gives the figures lifelike movements. He maintains the Virgin's dignified expression and large size in the traditional manner, but she is portrayed as a real woman in a naturalistic pose.

Fresco painting

Fresco is a type of mural painting. (In Italian, *fresco* means 'fresh'.) Giotto was the first painter to change from working with the traditional *secco*, or dry technique, to *buon fresco*, using wet plaster. In *secco*, the paint is applied to a dry surface, but it is not permanent. In *buon fresco*, or 'pure' fresco, the colour fuses with a layer of wet plaster to create a permanent image. The surface cannot be too wet, however, or the brush will not slide over it properly. Working with wet plaster meant there was only a short period of time available to the artist to complete the work. Traditionally a section was completed in a single day. These sections are known as the *giornata* (meaning one full day). Evidence of *giornata* can be seen in many frescos and they are distinguishable by a characteristic outline and slight difference in colour.

Buon fresco required less plaster, since plaster was only applied to the area of one session. Compositions were planned well in advance and then sketched in *sinopia* – red chalk. A layer of plaster called *intonaco* was applied over the section of the *sinopia* about to be painted. Assistants worked collaboratively with the master under his supervision and design. If the wall was large, they worked on scaffolding, beginning at the top and working downwards.

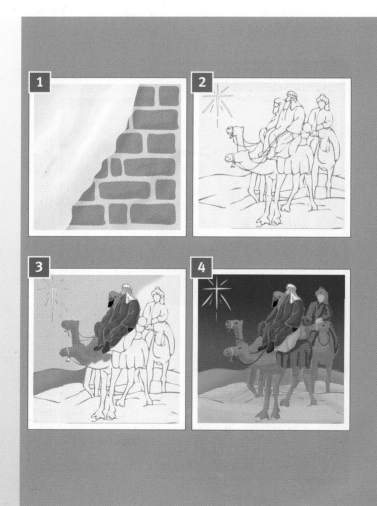

FIG 19.2 OGNISSANTI MADONNA ('MADONNA ENTHRONED'), Giotto, Uffizi Gallery, Florence

FIG 19.3 MADONNA ENTHRONED (RUCELLI MADONNA), Duccio, Uffizi Gallery, Florence

Giotto's career

Information on Giotto's career is scarce, but it is certain that he worked in the church of St Anthony Padua, where he painted scenes from the life of St Francis. This was the first time the new style had been seen in northern Italy and it caused a sensation. He was soon employed by a wealthy Paduan merchant and patron of the Franciscans called Enrico Scrovegni to decorate the small family chapel. In the Last Judgement scene, Scrovegni himself is included, kneeling before Mary and dressed in the purple of penitence, offering a small model of the chapel as retribution for sins committed by his father (fig 19.5).

The scenes

In one of the most famous scenes, *The Lament for Christ* (fig 19.6), the artist used foreshortening, flowing lines of drapery and light and shade to create lifelike figures with real expressions of deep human grief. All the gestures lead the eye to the lifeless figure of Christ and Mary, who holds her head close to her dead son and encloses her arms around him.

The Kiss of Judas (fig 19.7) is a tense dramatic scene and a powerful image of good versus evil. As Judas reaches out to embrace Jesus, his great yellow cloak sweeps forward to cover him and the two faces, one serene and dignified, the other evil and repellent, look intently at each other.

In contrast, two faces again confront one another in *Joachim and Anne at the Golden Gate* (fig 19.8), but this time in a moving and tender manner. The Virgin's parents, Joachim and Anne, meet and she tells him she is to bear a child. The gentle scene is emphasised by the circle of halos that enclose the couple.

The Arena Chapel

Enrico undertook the project of decorating the chapel attached to the Scrovegni Palace to make up for the sins of his father. His father had made his money in banking, but lending money for interest was considered the sin of usury at that time.

Giotto covered the walls of the small chapel with frescoed scenes from the life of Jesus, but the chapel was

FIG 19.4 MADONNA ENTHRONED, Cimabue, Uffizi Gallery, Florence

FIG 19.5 Arena Chapel Padua interior, looking towards THE LAST JUDGEMENT

FIG 19.6 THE LAMENT FOR CHRIST, Giotto di Bondone, Arena Chapel, Padua, Italy

dedicated to Our Lady of the Annunciation, so the first scenes are dedicated to Mary's life and that of her parents, Joachim and Anne. The corrupt influence of money is highlighted by Jesus chasing the moneychangers out of the temple and the despair of Judas, who hanged himself, having accepted money from the enemies of Jesus.

FIG 19.7 THE KISS OF JUDAS, Giotto di Bondone, Arena Chapel, Padua, Italy

FIG 19.8 JOACHIM AND ANNE AT THE GOLDEN GATE, Giotto di Bondone, Arena Chapel, Padua

FIG 19.9 THE FLIGHT INTO EGYPT, Giotto di Bondone, Arena Chapel, Padua

Blue in fresco painting

In *The Flight into Egypt* (fig 19.9), the blue of Mary's mantle and parts of the sky have disappeared because Giotto used azurite rather than the more expensive lapis lazuli to make blue. Azurite was not compatible with lime in the wet plaster, so he painted this colour *a secco*, or when the plaster was dry.

Frescos in Sante Croce

Following his work for the wealthy and influential Scrovegni family, Giotto was constantly in demand by secular patrons. The wealthy Florentine Peruzzi and Bardi banking families commissioned him to decorate adjoining private chapels in Sante Croce, but these were executed *a secco* fresco and have suffered badly over the years.

Lapis lazuli, or blue stone

This deep blue gemstone (fig 19.10) became very important in the world of art. The word comes from *lapis*, the Latin word for 'stone', and *azul*, the Arabian word for 'blue'. In Europe, the colour was called ultramarine, meaning 'from beyond the seas'.

The gemstones were ground down to make a bright blue paint so powerful that other colours seemed dull in comparison. The only source of the stone was in the rough mountains of Afghanistan, so it was extremely expensive. As a result, artists usually quoted prices for using the colour blue separately.

FIG 19.10 Lapis lazuli

Altarpieces

Altarpieces, or pictures of religious subjects, were placed on the altar in churches or sometimes were free-standing behind the altar. The back was often painted. An altarpiece with two separate panels was called a diptych, one with three panels was a triptych, and if it had more it was a polyptych. In some cases, these panels are hinged together so that they could be closed over the painting when it was not in use and then opened again for special occasions. After the Reformation, altarpieces were replaced with tabernacles to hold the Blessed Sacrament on the altars of Roman Catholic churches.

FIG 19.11 THE MAESTÀ ALTARPIECE, Duccio di Buoninsegna

Conclusion

In his lifetime, Giotto raised painting to a position of high respect among the arts and in so doing changed the course of European art dramatically. Within 10 years of his death, however, Europe was swept by the plague, or Black Death, creating a sense of terror and pessimism. The plague was viewed as a punishment from God and, perhaps in an effort to appease his wrath, painting returned to the remote and rigid style of the Byzantine style in use before Giotto. The population of Florence was halved by the Black Death and it was to be another 100 years before painters of that city – and in particular the painter Masaccio – began to look again at Giotto's warm and real human scenes and learn from them.

Questions

1. What were altarpieces?
2. Describe Giotto's method of fresco painting.
3. Why was lapis lazuli better than azurite for making blue in painting?
4. What is meant by the term '*buon fresco*'?
5. What was the role of the patron in the Arena Chapel?

Essay

1. Discuss the influences on Cimabue that were in turn passed on to his pupil, Giotto. Make detailed reference also to the innovations in painting that made Giotto so famous and his style so unique.

Colour picture study

1. Compare and discuss the versions of *The Madonna Enthroned with Angels and Prophets*, or *Ognissanti,* by Giotto (fig 19.2), Duccio (fig 19.3) and Cimabue (fig 19.4). Make reference to style, composition, subject matter and the period in which they were produced.
2. Examine *The Lament for Christ* (fig 19.6) by Giotto and describe the scene. Draw attention to details that show Giotto's innovative techniques and describe how he conveys emotion.
3. Compare *The Kiss of Judas* (fig 19.7) and *Joachim and Anne at the Golden Gate* (fig 19.8) by Giotto and describe the different emotions depicted by the artist in both scenes.

The Renaissance was one of the great periods of creative and intellectual achievement in world history. (The word *renaissance* means 'rebirth' in French.) It was an extraordinary upsurge of learning and artistic activity that spread throughout Europe in the 15th and 16th centuries, and it was inspired by the literature, language, culture and art of classical Greece and Rome. Although the Renaissance is today mostly associated with the visual arts, it began in Florence as a literary movement when old Latin and Greek manuscripts were rediscovered.

New learning

After the fall of the Roman Empire, manuscripts containing the accumulated literary, historical and scientific knowledge of the ancient Greeks and Romans were tucked away in libraries of medieval monasteries. When European scholars began to study them many centuries later, they were inspired by the knowledge and ideas of the ancient world. Latin was the language of the Church, so they were easily translated, but the secrets of the ancient Greeks were not so readily revealed.

Learning Greek

The Florentine poets had long inspired a love of classical Latin poetry, but in the last years of the 14th century the Chancellor of Florence persuaded a Greek scholar, Manuel Chrysoloras, to teach Greek in the schools. This opened the way to entirely new thinking among Christians, as Greek philosophy led to a fuller appreciation of human life.

Humanism

Traditional Christian belief had always regarded life on earth as merely a preparation for the real destiny of man, which was to spend eternity with God in Heaven, but the Greek philosopher Plato believed in the dignity of man. This led to Neo-Platonism and a new philosophy called **humanism** that valued human achievements as God's creations and became widespread among intellectuals throughout Europe.

Antiquity and beauty

The highest point of human intellectual achievement was considered to have taken place in ancient Greece and Rome. Appreciation of beauty was also one of the key elements of the new Renaissance. Beauty in all things was thought to have deep inner virtue and was therefore essential in the path towards God.

The 'new learning' spreads

New ideas and learning spread quickly with the discovery of printing. More people could read humanist literature as well as translations from antiquity of learned works on science and astronomy.

The city

The amazing growth of European cities also contributed to the spread of learning. By the mid-14th century, Europe's countryside was greatly changed after plague had wiped out more than a third of the population. The power of the landlords had weakened, so wealth shifted to towns and cities and, in a continent linked by commerce and shipping, education became a more valued commodity. The main centres of wealth, education and culture were London, Amsterdam, Paris, Vienna, Venice and, of course, Florence (fig 19.12).

'A city made to the measure of man'

A title given to Florence in the 16th century – 'a city made to the measure of man' – reflected the importance of the city. It was a busy and thriving commercial centre and its people enjoyed a standard of living unknown in other great European cities. Its citizens also had a high regard for all things cultural and intellectual. With its academies, churches, great houses and wealthy citizens, Florence provided the perfect intellectual conditions for humanist scholars to promote their vision of the dignity and importance of man.

Becoming an artist

In the Middle Ages and early Renaissance, art was a trade like any other and the terms 'art' and 'artist' did not really exist. Craftworkers were goldsmiths, painters or stone- or woodworkers, and the idea of artistic ability as a specific gift was simply unknown.

On completion of an apprenticeship, a young artist entered the guild that certified their competence to work professionally. Sculptors belonged to the stoneworkers' guild, goldsmiths to the silk guild and painters often formed associations or companies.

FIG 19.12 City of Florence, Italy

Patronage and art

Almost all art was commissioned and artists had to promote themselves by writing flattering letters to possible patrons or by entering competitions. The subject and theme of an artwork were agreed by written contract and the price took account of materials and workmanship.

Patrons usually had very specific goals in mind. Altarpieces or other such works were offered as gifts to the Church so that God and the saints would reward the patron in the next life, while rulers often commissioned art to beautify their city and to promote their image as generous and caring leaders.

Patrons had complete direction of the work and it was simply unheard of for individual artists to have ideas of their own.

The artist as genius

By the mid-15th century, the old ways were changing and the very concept of art was transformed. Painting, sculpture and architecture were now given the same dignity as the liberal arts of poetry and music. Social conditions and the training of Florentine artists altered greatly as they came to be respected for their intellect and ideas as much as their craft. Leonardo da Vinci and Michelangelo, for example, were regarded as geniuses and were sought after by princes and wealthy patrons, for whom it became a status symbol to have such a great artist work for them.

CHAPTER 20

THE BAPTISTERY DOORS IN FLORENCE

Patrons of art

The guilds were major patrons of art in Renaissance Florence. Each participated in the celebration of religious holidays of the city and organised events for their own patron saint's feast day. They also had financial responsibility for the city's major churches, hospitals and charitable institutions.

As associations of master craftsmen, the guilds set standards of apprenticeship, qualification and good workmanship. Members of important guilds, such as the Arte de Cambrio (bankers) and the rich Arte dei Mercanti di Calimala (wool and cloth merchants), were extremely powerful politically and virtually controlled the city's government. Well educated in humanist ideas, they were interested in the revival of the classical style. In Florence, the many exceptionally fine craftsmen were more than happy to meet their needs.

Competitions

The building of a new cathedral in the centre of Florence had continued throughout most of the 14th century. No final plan existed, so in order to make decisions as to its eventual structure, the guilds instigated a series of competitions for its construction and decoration that became one of the main driving forces of artistic development in the city.

The Florence Cathedral

Florence Cathedral and the octagonal-shaped Baptistery of San Giovanni (St John) (fig 20.1) opposite were traditionally the responsibility of the Calimala (wool and cloth merchants' guild). Dedicated to St John the Baptist, the patron saint of the city, the baptistery was restored around 1200 by the Calimala with green and white marble cladding. It then commissioned the sculptor

FIG 20.1 Florence Cathedral and Baptistery of San Giovanni

Andrea Pisano to make bronze doors to replace the heavy wooden ones on its south face.

The 1st baptistery doors (Andrea Pisano)

The baptistery doors were made of bronze and Andrea Pisano sculpted gilded (thinly layered gold) figures in 28 relief scenes from the life of St John the Baptist. Each scene was enclosed within a quatrefoil, a shape commonly used in medieval architecture, which consisted of four arcs placed together (fig 20.2).

The scenes relate to the theme of baptism and when the doors are closed they read like open pages of a book. Fourteen scenes on the left illustrate the life of John the Baptist and 14 on the right tell the story of his death.

Sculpture for a new century

The competition for the 2nd baptistery doors

Florence welcomed the 15th century with one of the most famous competitions in art history. In 1400 the Calimala instigated a competition for new bronze doors to match the style of Andrea Pisano's. The finalists were two bitter rivals, 23-year-old Filippo Brunelleschi and 20-year-old Lorenzo Ghiberti. Both submissions were judged to be of equal merit, so the commission was awarded jointly. Brunelleschi, however, was bitterly disappointed by this outcome, refused to collaborate and left Florence shortly

FIG 20.2 Baptistery of St Giovanni, south door, Andrea Pisano, Florence

quatre foil: meaning "four leaves", a quatrefoile is a symmetrical shape which was often used in Gothic & Renaissance architecture it form the overall outline of four circles of the same diametre that over laps slightly

258

FIG 20.3 THE SACRIFICE OF ISSAC panels, baptistery doors competition. Ghiberti (left) and Brunelleschi (right), Museum of the Bargello, Florence

FIG 20.4 Baptistery of St Giovanni, north door, Lorenzo Ghiberti, Florence

FIG 20.5 THE FLAGELLATION OF CHRIST, panel from the north door, baptistery of St Giovanni, Lorenzo

afterward. Ghiberti worked on the baptistery doors for the rest of his life.

The competition reliefs

The competition required the artist to submit a model relief sculpture in gilded bronze on the subject of the sacrifice of Isaac (fig 20.3). They had to maintain the quatrefoil framing shape of Andrea Pisano's panels and show the biblical scene in precise detail. Models from both finalists are today hanging side by side in the Bargello Museum in Florence.

The 2nd baptistery doors (Lorenzo Ghiberti)

The subject of the new east-facing doors was changed to the life of Christ and they took Ghiberti 27 years to complete (fig 20.4). During that time he made considerable artistic progress. Even though his development was somewhat limited by the quatrefoil shape, the 28 panels are fuller and more adventurous than Pisano's earlier work. He made full use of the new art of perspective, developed by his rival Brunelleschi,

and in *The Flagellation of Christ* the classical spirit of the Renaissance is evident in Jesus' gently curved pose against an architectural background of classical Corinthian columns (fig 20.5).

The 3rd baptistery doors (Lorenzo Ghiberti)

The doors were in place less than a year when the Calimala agreed a further contract with Ghiberti for a third pair of doors for the north portal. Ghiberti had advanced by now from craftsman to architect and was overseeing some of the construction work on the cathedral. As a master, he was on a par with scholars and could decide on the design of the work himself. This kind of independence represented a turning point in the history of European art and had major implications for the new doors.

A new design scheme

Under the influence of recent work by Donatello, a former assistant and contemporary sculptor, Ghiberti cut the number of panels to 10 and introduced an entirely new framing system. He replaced the quatrefoil shape and placed five fully gilded panels, one above the other on each side, giving the doors a more overall unified appearance and allowing greater freedom to relate the stories. The Old Testament scenes are far clearer and the artist included several episodes of each story within one panel, completely transforming the flat surface into

FIG 20.6 A copy of the east doors, or 'Gates of Paradise', of the baptistery of St Giovanni, Lorenzo Ghiberti, Florence. The original gold panels have been removed for safety to the Museum of the Cathedral.

three-dimensional spaces with perspective and three-dimensional figures (fig 20.6).

Jacob and Esau

In the story of Jacob and Esau, Esau loses his birthright to his brother Jacob. His hunger is so great after his work in the fields that he gives up his inheritance in exchange for food, and in his blindness Isaac mistakenly blesses his younger son, watched by his wife Rebecca, who has set up this deceit. Single-point perspective leads the eye to the central architectural arch and the various groups of figures involved in the story (fig 20.7).

Art takes priority

The doors were finished in 1452 and Ghiberti considered them his finest achievement. The Calimala were so impressed by their splendour that they made an extraordinary decision. Although Old Testament scenes were considered inappropriate to face a Christian cathedral, the Calimala decided to move the second

FIG 20.7 THE STORY OF JACOB AND ESAU, panel from the east doors of the baptistery of St Giovanni, Lorenzo Ghibert

doors to the north side and place the new golden doors on the east, facing the cathedral.

The 'Gates of Paradise'

Ghiberti's golden doors are also known as the 'Gates of Paradise'. Legend has it that Michelangelo called them that because of their beauty, but it is more likely that the name relates to the space between the cathedral and the baptistery, which is known as Il Paradiso in Florence because it was once a cemetery.

Conclusion

Placing such imagery in front of the cathedral represented a major change in attitude and a radical departure from traditional thinking. For the first time, **art** and **not its subject matter** had been given priority.

Questions
1. Why was the decision to place Ghiberti's second set of doors opposite the door of the cathedral so unusual?
2. Give a brief account of the competition for the new doors of the baptistery.

Essay
1. Describe Ghiberti's doors for the baptistery in Florence and the innovations he made on Pisano's original doors. In your answer, compare the themes, style and technique of his early panels with those on his later 'Gates of Paradise'.

CHAPTER 21

Donatello

Rilievo schiacciato

While Ghiberti was working on the babtistery doors he came under the influence of one of his former students, Donatello, who had overtaken his master to become the most prominent sculptor in Florence.

St George and the Dragon

Donatello's method of relief sculpture was based on the rules of perspective and was first seen on a relief panel below the statue of St George in the centre of Florence. Called *rilievo schiacciato* (meaning 'squashed' or 'flattened relief'), it was the first example in sculpture of the use of single-point linear perspective, which had been invented by his friend Brunelleschi.

Perspective in sculpture

Up to this point, perspective was only used in painting and drawing, but Donatello's image of the saint fighting the dragon is set against a landscape in a very clever illusion of space (fig 21.1).

The *Feast of Herod*

Donatello's first relief in bronze was a scene from the life of John the Baptist on one of six panels around the base of the baptismal font in the baptistery in Siena. Donatello's *Feast of Herod* (fig 21.2) depicts the king's birthday feast after he asked the beautiful Salome to dance for him and she agreed, but only if he gave her the head of John the Baptist on a platter. The highly emotional scene shows Herod recoiling in horror as the severed head is presented to him, but each figure reacts intensely to the ghastly sight. Only Salome in classical dress continues to dance and her mother tries to explain the deed to Herod.

Episodes of the story

The gruesome drama is split into several episodes in a complex set of spaces created by clever perspective set between classical arches. Food and knives can clearly be

FIG 21.1 ST GEORGE AND THE DRAGON, pedestal of St George, Donatello, Museum of the Bargello, Florence

FIG 21.2 THE FEAST OF HEROD, Donatello, baptismal font in the Baptistery of Siena

FIG 21.3 BEHEADING OF JOHN THE BAPTIST, panel from the south door of the Baptistery of Florence

seen on the table in the foreground as the scenes move from the banqueting hall through the musician's gallery to the executioner at the back.

This must have amazed Donatello's contemporaries, who were more used to scenes like Andrea Pisano's neat and almost gentle *Beheading of John the Baptist* on the south door of the baptistery (fig 21.3).

Conclusion

The development of perspective in sculpture – and in particular in Donatello's *Feast of Herod* – was highly influential on other artists. Its impact can especially be seen in Ghiberti's later designs for the doors of the Florence Baptistery.

Colour picture study

1. Examine the *Feast of Herod* (fig 21.2) by Donatello and describe the scene. What new and unusual techniques did the artist use in this panel?

CHAPTER 22

THE FREE-STANDING FIGURE

Breathing statues

In the early years of the 15th century a radically new and very public sculpture appeared in Florence. This happened long before any similar changes in painting or architecture and was unlike anything that had been created before. Statues on Gothic cathedrals had stood in solemn rows of unreal figures around the doorways. In complete contrast, huge new sculptures were erected in Florence that stood in public places at street level and were completely lifelike. The people of the city interacted with the figures in the traditional belief that 'sculpture hovers somewhere between flesh and stone' and saw them as 'breathing statues in which only the voice is lacking'.

Orsanmichele

Examples of the new sculpture appeared on the Church of Orsanmichele, a former grain store that had been destroyed by fire (fig 22.1). An image of the Virgin painted on one of the pillars that survived the flames was taken as a sign to build a new church on the ruins, and the resulting building included two extra floors for the grain store.

The patron saints of the guilds

The Signoria (city governors) decreed that each of the guilds in Florence should place a statue of its patron saint in niches around the exterior walls of the new church, but by 1400 only three were in place. Growing impatient, the Signoria gave the guilds 10 years to complete the work.

The **Arte del Calimala** (wool and cloth merchants' guild) chose **Lorenzo Ghiberti** to create the statue of their patron saint, **John the Baptist**. This was the first life-sized bronze figure and undoubtedly Ghiberti's expertise and experience with the Florence Baptistery doors was the deciding factor, because bronze was a difficult and extremely expensive material. Only the major guilds could afford it, but they needed a master artist.

The **stonemasons' guild** chose a young sculptor, **Nanni di Banco**. His ***Four Crowned Saints*** is the only group sculpture on Orsanmichele. It represents four early Christian sculptors who were executed after they refused to carve an image of a Roman god (fig 22.2). Various professions of architects, sculptors and stonecutters at work are depicted on the pedestal (fig 22.3).

The **linen workers' guild** commissioned **Donatello** to sculpt **St Mark** and the **armourers' guild** also chose him to sculpt **St George**.

FIG 22.1 The Church of Orsanmichele, Florence

FIG 22.2 FOUR CROWNED SAINTS, Nanni di Banco, Orsanmichele, Florence

Classical influence

Leading artists in Florence were always in competition, but in the small city where everyone knew everyone else, ideas were constantly exchanged and the artists learned from each other. Ghiberti was the most important sculptor for a time, but very soon Donato di Bardi (better known as Donatello) took over the position. Donatello's remarkable work completely changed the approach to sculpture for generations to come. He greatly admired the classical works of ancient Greece and Rome. No longer content to follow the established medieval formulas, he learned from the artists of ancient times and, like them, used live models for his studies of the human figure.

Donatello (1386–1466)

The biggest impression on Donatello's training was his time spent in Ghiberti's studio working on the Florence Baptistery doors. Ghiberti was only eight years older than his student, but from him Donatello learned to make smooth, clear-cut surfaces, mould figures and treat drapery with harmonious curved rhythms.

After some time Donatello moved to the workshop of the cathedral, where he met Nanni de Banco and together they developed a new style of free-standing sculpture. He also worked very closely with Filippo Brunelleschi, learning the rules of proportion and perspective and spent some time in Rome with him studying antiquities. This influenced Donatello above all and gave him the creative and intellectual stimulation to develop his own unique artistic style.

FIG 22.3 Stone cutters at work from the base of FOUR CROWDED SAINTS

FIG 22.4 ST JOHN THE BAPTIST, Ghiberti, Orsanmichele, Florence

FIG 22.5 ST MARK, Donatello, Orsanmichele, Florence

Donatello's *St Mark* and Ghiberti's *St John the Baptist*

Ghiberti's *St John the Baptist* (fig 22.4) in Orsanmichele is a beautifully composed work and is very much in keeping with the late Gothic style popular in Florence.

The linen workers' guild may have expected something like it when they commissioned the young Donatello to sculpt their patron saint, St Mark (fig 22.5), but what they got was a stunning contrast. Ghiberti's saint is clothed in crescents of folded drapery, but is lacking in real human form and facial expression, while Donatello's figure has a physical as well as psychological presence and oozes with life. Even the hands convey energy as he stares out with furrowed brow and deep-set eyes. Examining the statue later, Michelangelo is said to have remarked, 'If this saint looked like this during his lifetime one would have to believe anything he wrote.'

St Mark's weight is placed over the right leg and the upper body and head are turned *in contrapposto* (placed opposite), a pose first developed by classical Greek sculptors as a means of avoiding the stiffness that tilts the body from hip to shoulder.

St George

A couple of years later Donatello produced an even more lifelike figure. *St George* (fig 22.6), commissioned by the armourers' guild, is a younger and leaner version of *St Mark* and full of strength and courage. His gaze is also on his audience in the street, but it is more urgent and is fixed presumably on the ferocious dragon that has come to ravage the maiden. With a hand resting upon his shield, St George is firm and ready to do battle as if, in the words of the artist's biographer, Vasari, 'Life itself seems to be stirring within the stone.'

The figure fits into the tradition of medieval chivalry, but the treatment is completely new and the warrior knight in his classical armour is a convincingly real person standing with his feet resolutely apart, tense but determined. His face is a study of concentrated energy.

The original marble sculpture is in the Bargello Museum in Florence and a bronze copy stands in the niche of

FIG 22.6 ST GEORGE, Donatello, Orsanmichele, Florence

FIG 22.7 DAVID, Donatello, Museum of the Bargello, Florence

Orsanmichele. The figure originally held a real sword and wore a real metal helmet, but these have long since disappeared.

David

Donatello had achieved his ambition to free sculpture from its traditional role as merely architectural decoration, but he was also the first artist since classical times to dare to produce a life-sized, fully three-dimensional nude figure. The bronze statue of David (fig 22.7), which is nude (apart from his hat and leggings), is one of the most important sculptures of the early Renaissance. The gentle S shape echoes classical statues, but here the similarity ends because this slim adolescent boy is no Greek god or in any way like the powerful idealised nudes of antiquity. Donatello's interpretation of the young hero of the Old Testament is quite unique, representing the victory of youth over age and suggesting that youth is pure and incorrupt. The sleek, sensual portrayal of the effeminate young boy is gentle yet lifelike, and the bronze surface is treated in a naturalistic way with a highly polished blue-black shine over the body to emphasise the smooth, adolescent skin and to provide a contrast with the rougher finish of the hair and hat.

The bronze figure stood in the courtyard of the Palazzo Medici for many years and the youth resting his foot casually on the severed head of the giant Goliath can perhaps be interpreted as symbolic of the Medici family's struggle to fight off threats to the small city-state of Florence from its powerful enemies.

Mary Magdalene

Of all Donatello's later works the most haunting is surely the tragic figure of Mary Magdalene (fig 22.8) in painted wood. Sad blue eyes stare from hollow sockets, partially opened lips show broken white teeth, bones protrude from gaunt cheeks and the yellow-streaked hair is matted and twisted in tangled curves.

Fɪɢ 22.8 MARY MAGDALENE, Donatello, Museo del Opera del Duomo, Florence

The penitent prostitute stands with one knee slightly bent over the long, veined feet in a pitiful gesture of grace that evokes memories of her legendary youthful beauty. Long, bony fingers are held together in prayer and the flesh is tanned and eaten up from fasting, but Donatello's masterpiece is much more than clever realism. The harrowing figure 'lives' with unseen energy pulsating throughout the body and has the power to touch the emotions of the viewer. Hers is a timeless presence, representing all human suffering and her pain is all human pain.

Fame in his own lifetime

Donatello lived a long life working in Florence, Siena, Padua and other cities. In his biography, Giorgio Vasari said of the sculptor, 'The world is so full with Donatello's works that it may be said that no artist produced more than he,' and his writing ends: 'He possessed invention, design, skill, judgement and all the other qualities that one may reasonably expect to find in an inspired genius.'

Conclusion

Sculpture changed radically during the early 15th century in Florence. This happened long before any similar changes in painting or architecture and was highly influential on the artistic developments that followed.

Questions

1. Who commissioned the statues around Orsanmichele?
2. Identify some of the classical aspects of these statues.
3. Why did the *Four Crowned Saints* represent the stonemasons' guild?
4. How did the statues interact with the people on the street?

Essay

1. Identify Donatello's break with the traditional portrayal of the human figure in sculpture and discuss the influences that led the artist to this. Refer to specific examples of the artist's work in your answer.

Colour picture study

1. Examine the statue of Mary Magdalene by Donatello (fig 22.8) and in your own words describe why you think it appeals to the emotions. In your opinion, does it in any way resemble modern sculpture? Do you know of any contemporary work that might be comparable?

PATRONS AND ARTISTS IN RENAISSANCE ITALY

Artists of the Italian courts

At the time of the Renaissance, the Italian peninsula was a series of independent states ruled by dukes and princes (fig 23.1). These states often had lavish courts and there was considerable competition among them in displays of splendour. Three important Italian courts were those of the Sforza dukes of Milan, the Gonzaga family of Mantua and Federico da Montefeltro, duke of Urbino, but the city-states of Venice, Siena and Florence were remarkable political entities that maintained their independence in spite of enemies on all sides.

There had always been a strong tradition of competitive patronage, but during the Renaissance – when a humanist education was considered essential for those in authority – artistic patronage became increasingly important. Humanist thinking revived the classical notion of demonstrating one's right to rule by spending generously on fine buildings and works of art.

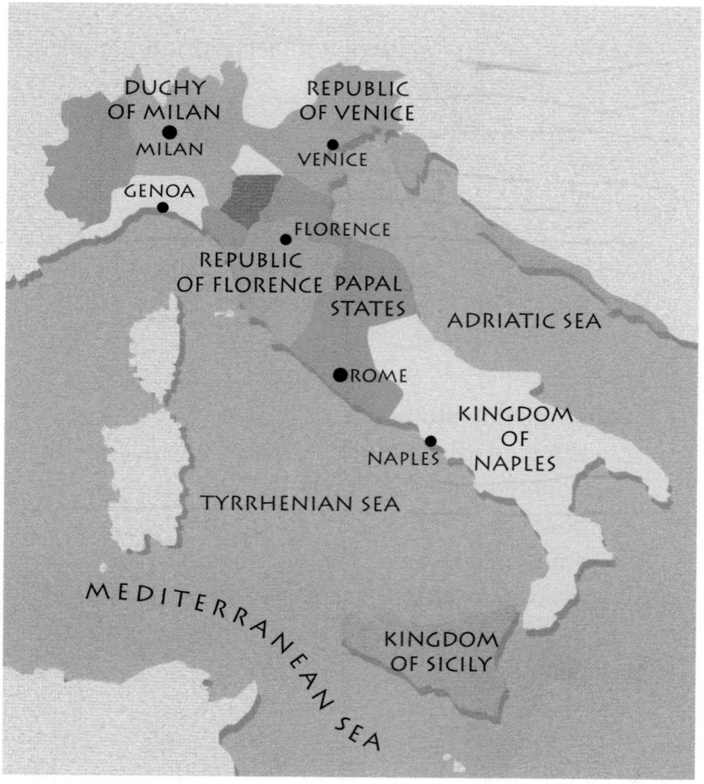

Fig 23.1 Renaissance Italy

Florence

The Republic of Florence was one of the most powerful and prosperous states in Europe. It had a particularly strong woollen industry. It also had its own currency, the florin, which was the first European gold coin to play a significant commercial role. As many Florentine banks had international branches, the florin quickly became the dominant trade coin of western Europe.

Renaissance Florence was a major centre of artistic activity and while the guilds commissioned art for public places, there were also many private patrons. Religion pervaded all aspects of life and wealthy families often commissioned religious works of art. The family best known for its artistic patronage was the Medici – Cosimo, his son, Piero, and his grandson, Lorenzo.

The Medici – rulers of Florence and patrons of art

The Medici family made their fortune by being the bankers of the papacy. Cosimo il Vecchio inherited his wealth from his father and worked his way into the politics of Florence. Although banished from the city for a time, he returned in 1434 to become its ruler. Florence prospered under the Medici, but in reality Cosimo, followed by his son and grandson, governed with an iron hand. The arts flourished, however, and ruling dukes and princes of nearby states looked towards Florence and its artists for inspiration (fig 23.2).

Cosimo il Vecchio

Cosimo de' Medici lived quite simply but spent a considerable amount of his vast fortune on charitable

acts, education, literature and the arts. He collected the largest library in Europe. He was also deeply religious and funded the construction, restoration and decoration of ecclesiastical sites. Cosimo's artists included Ghiberti, Brunelleschi, Donatello, Alberti, Uccello and Fra Angelico.

San Marco in Florence and Fra Angelico

Cosimo de' Medici's personal places of worship and devotion were the nearby Church of San Lorenzo and the Dominican Monastery or Convent of San Marco. He put a great deal of money into its renovation and chose one of the monks to paint the walls. For 10 years or so, Fra Giovanni and a team of assistants worked on a series of frescoes in a simple, restrained style that was completely devoid of ornamentation or detail.

Fra Angelico (1395–1455)

Fra Giovanni acquired the reputation of 'an inspired saint' and after his death he was given the name Fra Angelico (angelic), by which he is now better known. Fra Angelico was in fact a highly professional artist who ran a very efficient workshop, but his work reflects the serenity and discipline of communal religious life. In *Lives of the Artists*, Vasari recounts that Fra Angelico's life was lived in holiness and that tears would stream down his face as he painted the crucifixion.

The San Marco frescoes

The artist and his assistants painted a sacred scene in the 45 cells occupied by the monks of St Marco. The simple compositions convey a deep sense of serenity. *The Annunciation* (fig 23.3) is the best known and most

FIG 23.3 THE ANNUNCIATION, Fra Angelico, fresco in a cell at San Marco, Florence

FIG 23.4 The Virgin with Saints, detail from the ANNALENA Altarpiece, Fra Angelico, Musuem of San Marco, Florence

for the cultural and artistic events of 15th-century Italy). Its subject was the Virgin and Child with saints (fig 23.4), but it was dedicated to Saints Cosmas and Damian, who kneel before her. It is assumed that the figure of St Cosmas is the likeness of his namesake, Cosimo de' Medici.

Divine intervention saved the saints from execution on several occasions and their story was told in nine small pictures in the predella (the decorative base of an altarpiece). It was later taken apart and the pictures in the predella removed. Two pictures remained in Florence and the others are in museums in Washington, Munich, Paris and the National Gallery of Ireland.

Scene from the predella in the National Gallery of Ireland

The Martyrdom of Saints Cosmas and Damian (fig 23.5) from the predella of the San Marco altarpiece depicts one of the attempts to execute the saints along with three of their brothers by fire. Behind them on the balcony is the proconsul of Syria, who has condemned their burning at the stake. The flames have spread outwards, however, and have forced the executioners to flee, leaving the saints untouched.

Although it appears simple, the composition – even in such a small work – has been carefully planned by Fra Angelico. By using perspective lines he creates a clever illusion of spatial depth.

captivating of the series. Masaccio's influence is evident in the use of perspective and the lack of all unnecessary detail.

The main altarpiece of the chapel at San Marco

Cosimo de' Medici commissioned an altarpiece for the high altar in the church of San Marco that was one of the most grandiose of the Quattrocento (the collective name

FIG 23.5 THE ATTEMPTED MARTYRDOM OF SAINTS COSMAS AND DAMIEN, Fra Angelico, National Gallery, Dublin

The Brancacci family chapel

The rich and powerful Brancacci family were another of Florence's patrons of the arts. In 1423 Felice Brancacci commissioned a fresco decoration in their small family chapel in Sante Maria del Carmine that was to be a source of inspiration to artists for over a century.

The artists

He engaged a well-established painter, Masolino da Panicale, to undertake the work. His young assistant, Masaccio, joined him. Together, they frescoed the panels of the upper walls until Masolino left to work elsewhere, whereupon Masaccio continued the work on the lower panels until his own untimely death left it unfinished for many years.

FIG 23.6 THE TEMPTATION OF ADAM, Masolino, Brancacci Chapel, Florence

Masaccio (1401–28)

Masaccio was a remarkable painter, but he died at age 27. In his brief life he became a highly acclaimed artist, creating some of the most monumental works of the early Renaissance in a classical style but also in a restrained, exact, scientific and highly innovative manner.

The Brancacci Chapel frescoes

The paintings in the Brancacci Chapel are based on episodes from the life of St Peter, but overall they represent the story of the salvation of mankind. The choice of Peter, the first Pope, underlines the Church's position as mediator between mankind and Christ the Saviour.

The Expulsion of Adam and Eve from the Garden of Eden

The cycle of frescos begins with Adam and Eve because their sin against God was the first need for mediation between God and man. Masolino and Masaccio painted Adam and Eve on the entrance columns of the chapel opposite each other. It is interesting to compare them.

Masolino's *Temptation of Adam* (fig 23.6) is painted in the late Gothic style and its courtly, elegant manner is strikingly different to Masaccio's *Expulsion of Adam and Eve from the Garden of Eden* (fig 23.7), which is in the early Renaissance style. Masolino's long, slender figures have gently modelled faces and stand quietly in the garden, while the serpent in the form of a woman hovers above. Masaccio's figures, on the other hand, are simple but dramatically expressive as they stumble forward in misery and nakedness. Adam and Eve have been cast from Paradise forever into a world of sorrows and all the emotion of the moment is concentrated in their gestures and faces. Eve lifts her head to cry out in anguish and Adam covers his face, stumbling forward as he weeps bitter tears of shame and regret.

In spite of this clumsy yet very human despair, Masaccio managed to convey the beauty of the body – even in sin, man is not degraded nor has he lost his dignity. Eve's gestures echo those of a classical statue well known at the time named *Venus Pudica* (fig 23.8), so called because of way she attempts to cover her nakedness with her hands. Masaccio's work is, however, much more than simply a copy of ancient forms and has a fresh realism, making it special and new.

FIG 23.7 EXPULSION OF ADAM AND EVE, Masaccio, Brancacci Chapel, Florence

Giotto's influence on Masaccio

Masaccio had learned a good deal from Brunelleschi's development of perspective and Donatello's impressive free-standing muscular figures, but the greatest influence on his painting was Giotto. Masaccio became the real heir to Giotto's discoveries 100 years earlier and he revived the style to create three-dimensional space and solid, sculptural, realistic figures with naturalistic expressions and gestures. His work created a sensation and inspired many artists of the early Renaissance.

The Tribute Money

Masaccio's famous fresco *The Tribute Money* (fig 23.9) is a huge scene on the upper level of the fresco cycle and is located next to *The Expulsion of Adam and Eve from the Garden of Eden*. It relates to the yearly tax payment for the maintenance of the temple in Jerusalem and is based

FIG 23.8 VENUS PUDICA (The Medici Venus), Uffizi Gallery, Florence

A giornata

In Masaccio's *Expulsion of Adam and Eve from the Garden of Eden,* in one section around Adam's head, the blue azurite applied to the dry plaster has completely faded. Only the grey blue primer under the colour applied to the wet plaster has remained. The outline is evidence of a *giornata*, or one day's work in fresco.

Jesus

FIG 23.9 THE TRIBUTE MONEY, Masaccio, Brancacci Chapel, Florence

Tax collector

Sc. Peter

on the account in St Matthew's gospel. Jesus and his disciples have just arrived at the gates of the city of Capernaum and the tax collectors asks Peter: 'Does your master not pay the half shekel?' Peter is reluctant to pay, but Jesus says to him: 'However so as not to offend these people go to the lake and cast a hook; take the first fish that bites, open its mouth and there you will find a shekel. Take it and give to them for me and for you' (Matthew 17:24–27).

This small and relatively unimportant biblical event was a very unusual choice of subject matter for such a large art work and has been interpreted over the years in several ways. It probably refers to a proposed increase in taxation in Florence and, as a banker, Felice Brancacci would appreciate the importance of money and the duty of every inhabitant of the state to pay taxes.

A narrative in three parts

The story has three separate moments within the one scene. Christ is the focal point and he is pointing towards the left, where Peter hesitates. The second episode shows Peter crouched at the lakeside, taking money from the fish's mouth, and in the third scene Peter gives the coin to the tax collector at the gate.

Masaccio's strong and monumental figures are carefully modelled to accentuate the smooth roundness of the flesh and the light catching the folds of the drapery leaves dark pockets of sculpture-like shadow, which contribute greatly to the dramatic impact of the story. Masaccio was highly influenced by classicism and was certainly working closely with other artists involved with this new style. For example, the group of disciples stand in poses similar to

the semi-circle of figures seen in Nanni de Banco's *Four Crowned Saints* (see Chapter 22, fig 22.2) and are dressed in similar classical Greek tunics.

Peter's pose is an exact replica of Christ's. Both have one knee bent with arm outstretched, suggesting that both had equal authority – possibly underlining the importance of papal authority. Similarly, on both occasions when Peter is confronted by the tax collector the bodies are mirror images of each other. This has the effect of locking the main characters of the story into a single unit within the composition.

Perspective

A fire in the chapel many years ago blackened the frescoes. While there were various attempts at restoration, none was successful until recently. Only in the recent past has it been possible to fully appreciate the original detail, such as the luminous blue sky streaked with white clouds, the farmhouses and hedges that dot the hills and the snow-capped mountains receding into the distance in perfect perspective.

Crisp architectural outlines also serve to frame Peter and the tax collector, but the artist has also cleverly used the lines of perspective to take the eye to the central point in the picture, which is the head of Christ.

The Trinity

Masaccio used perspective with great emphasis and this can be seen in another famous fresco on the wall of St Maria Novella in Florence. *The Trinity* (fig 23.10) was one of the first paintings where all the lines of perspective converge to a single vanishing point at eye level.

FIG 23.10 THE TRINITY, Masaccio, St Maria Novella, Florence

The painting was covered at a later stage with a tabernacle, but this was removed during the 19th century. The fresco was removed from the wall at this time, causing considerable damage, but it is now back on the wall near its original position. It creates the image of the real space of a small chapel with the three members of the Trinity and was probably a substitute for a real building that the patron and his wife could not afford to build.

A huge figure of God the Father supporting the arms of the cross dominates the scene. He solemnly presents his son while Mary and John stand at the base of the cross and below our line of vision the image of a sarcophagus tilts towards us, revealing a skeleton and the words of an ancient warning in Latin translated as 'I was what you are and what I am you shall be'.

To construct the perspective lines of the picture, Masaccio first drew a rough sketch of the scene, which was then covered by plaster. In order not to lose the central point, he knocked a nail into the wall just below the base of the cross then drew strings out from it, pressing them into the plaster. These marks can still be seen.

Urbino

The celebrated court of Urbino was largely the creation of one person, Federico da Montefeltro, duke of Urbino (fig 23.11). The town is situated in quite an isolated position, so the duke had to search widely for artistic

FIG 23.11 Court of Urbino

talent. Fortunately, because of his career as a military captain and diplomat, he had numerous contacts and was able to employ artists and architects from all over Italy as well as northern Europe.

His artists reflected his refined taste and his main focus was his ducal palace. He believed that architecture was the greatest of the arts and, influenced by Cosimo de' Medici's palace in Florence, he took great care with its design. He also followed the guidelines outlined in humanist scholar Leon Alberti's book, *On Architecture.*

A Renaissance man

As a typical Renaissance man the duke set a high standard of leadership and Urbino became a renowned centre of learning and good manners. Deeply religious, he lived a quiet life but was interested in philosophy, Latin and Greek, and mathematics. His wife, Battista Sforza of Milan, was highly regarded for her intelligence, but she died at age 25, shortly after the birth of her ninth child. The duke greatly mourned her loss.

The duke of Urbino and his wife

One of the most renowned of the duke's artists was Piero della Francesca, who shared many of his patron's intellectual interests, particularly mathematics. His double portrait (fig 23.12) of Federico and his recently deceased wife depict them in profile. This was probably because the duke's face was badly disfigured during a jousting tournament, but it was also in keeping with the new art of portraiture that imitated the medals of ancient Rome. It was, however, highly original to place Federico and his dead wife facing each other together in a poignant, never-ending partnership.

Piero della Francesca (1416–92)

Piero della Francesca is now considered to be one of the greatest of all Italian painters, but his name was all but forgotten by the end of the 16th century. This neglect may have been due to the fact that he worked in small, little-known towns or it may have been his austere, intellectual style of painting. It shows his interest in geometry and perspective and is completely lacking in frivolous detail. It is, however, harmonious and graceful, with a calm, remote quality, which is possibly why it appeals to the modern eye.

Piero absorbed a good deal of the artistic discoveries of his predecessors and contemporaries in Florence; the monumental quality of his figures certainly owes much to Masaccio. He would undoubtedly have been greatly interested in Leon Battista Alberti's new theories.

Almost all of Piero's works are religious in nature and the undisputed high point of his career was the series of large frescoes he created for the Church of San Francesco in Arezzo entitled *Legend of the True Cross.* Despite the damage these frescoes have suffered over the years, they are scenes of astonishing beauty and luminous freshness. This, together with the silent, stately figures fixed in clear, crystalline space, is still extremely impressive (fig 23.13).

Fig 23.13 Fresco LEGEND OF THE TRUE CROSS at San Francesco, Arezzo, Italy

characters' costumes it is now thought that it may symbolise reconciliation between the Roman Catholic and the Eastern Orthodox churches. The man in the centre of the three on the right wears a Byzantine robe, the bearded man may be a Turkish emperor and the man in the turban watching the flogging of Christ may represent the Muslim threat to the Church.

The picture is divided into two separate scenes, each with its own source of light. The understated, quiet and solemn atmosphere is typical of Piero and emphasises the dignity of Christ in contrast to the brutish torturers who surround him.

The artist's love of fine detail is seen in the fashionable blue and gold costume, while the painted architecture of the palace shows his grasp of mathematically perfect perspective. The checkerboard patterns on the floor are absolutely correct and can be completely worked out. Christ and those around him are placed at the exact centre, and the lines of perspective converge at a crucial point to the left of the man with the whip, leading the eye directly to him.

The Flagellation of Christ

Piero's *Flagellation of Christ* (fig 23.14) is one of his most mysterious paintings. A superb masterpiece of perspective, its meaning has been a source of discussion among scholars for years. At one time it was thought to represent contemporary figures, but because of the

Baptism of Christ

The *Baptism of Christ* (fig 23.15) was painted for a church in Piero's native town of Borgo Santo Sepolcro. This is one of his early paintings and the figures have a mixture of grace and serenity with a gentle, coloured light and delicate colours combining with perfect perspective to convey a deeply spiritual atmosphere. The sky is mirrored in the water and not a ripple disturbs the

Fig 23.14 FLAGELLATION OF CHRIST, Piero della Francesca

Fɪɢ 23.15 BAPTISM OF CHRIST, Piero della Francesca

stillness as the Holy Spirit hovers over St John. Fine lines of gold suggest heavenly light falling on Christ's head.

The figures are bathed in full light with only a subtle translucent shadow, and in the background, details of Borgo Santo Sepolcro are clearly visible.

Piero was a significant influence on later painters, such as Perugino, whose own pupil was Raphael, the great master of the High Renaissance.

Mantua

The members of the ruling Gonzaga family of Mantua were very progressive and one their most important decisions was to found a school that taught classical studies. The family members were also renowned for their artistic patronage and when Ludovico Gonzaga became marquis in 1444, he surrounded himself with humanist thinkers. He sought advice from Leon Battista Alberti on many occasions.

Andrea Mantegna (1431–1506)

When Ludovico invited Andrea Mantegna to enter his services in 1460 as a court artist, the event proved to be a turning point in the career of this inventive and versatile painter. He settled quickly and worked for three

Fɪɢ 23.16 LUDOVICO GONZAGA AND HIS FAMILY, Andrea Mantegna, Palazzo Ducale, Mantua, Italy

Gonzaga rulers in succession as a famous and respected artist until his death in 1506. His most celebrated work is the superb series of frescoes in the Palazzo Ducale in Mantua that include portraits of the duke and his family (fig 23.16).

Mantegna was raised in Padua, the intellectual centre of northern Italy. He had a sound knowledge of archaeology and a passionate interest in classical antiquity, but Donatello's influence can also seen in his solid, expressive and anatomically correct human figures.

The Lamentation over the Dead Christ

Mantegna's mastery of perspective is possibly best displayed in the most unusual of his paintings, the amazingly foreshortened figure of a prone Jesus in his *Lamentation over the Dead Christ* (fig 23.17). In this picture, Mary and John are very much in the margin as the eye of the beholder is drawn immediately to the feet of Jesus as though personally involved in the scene. Because of the unusual use of perspective, the painting has a dramatic impact, one that reflects the sad and emotional atmosphere of a tomb. It is clear that the artist wished to emphasise the tragedy and grandeur of the sacred theme. The use of the illusionist technique means that the dead figure appears to 'follow' the spectator around the room. The painting was shown at the head of Mantegna's own coffin when he died, which may have been what he intended.

278

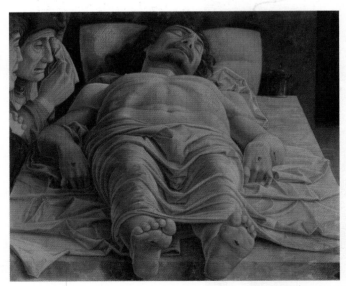

FIG 23.17 THE LAMENTATION OVER THE DEAD CHRIST, Andrea Mantegna, Pinacoteca di Brera, Milan

Conclusion

Humanist education during the Renaissance revived the classical notion of demonstrating one's right to rule by spending generously on art. Because religion pervaded all aspects of life, most works of art were religious in theme. The primary purpose of religious art was to glorify God, but it also enhanced the status of the patron and his family.

Questions

1. Name some of the Italian courts and identify the patrons of art and the artists associated with them.
2. Who were the Medici family and what was their contribution to early Renaissance art?
3. Describe some of the features associated with a typical Piero della Francesca painting.
4. What does the term '*giornata*' mean in reference to fresco painting?
5. What is a predella? Describe any work of art from a predella.

Essay

1. Masaccio is considered to be a very innovative and influential painter. Discuss the reasons for this, with particular reference to his work in the Brancacci Chapel. Compare his style to Masolino's and to other artists working at the same time in Florence.

Colour picture study

1. Examine *The Tribute Money* (fig 23.9) by Masaccio and describe the narrative as depicted by the artist.
2. Examine Mantegna's *Lamentation over the Dead Christ* (fig 23.17) and explain why, in your opinion, this painting might have been planned to be placed over the artist's tomb.
3. Examine the *Flagellation of Christ* by Piero della Francesca and indicate the possible meaning behind this mysterious painting. Draw attention to areas of fine detail and the artist's clever use of perspective (fig 23.14).

CHAPTER 24

CIVIC RIVALRY

Religious art

The primary purpose of religious art was to glorify God, but it also enhanced the status of the patron and his family. There was considerable rivalry among wealthy families and patrons commissioned buildings, sculpture and paintings to reflect glory upon themselves, their families and their cities.

Preference for a style of painting was part of the rivalry. Some preferred the classical style associated with humanism and others the Byzantine style from the Siennese school, but the exceptionally elegant International style or International Gothic was associated with the rich courts of northern Europe and this made it very sought after.

Civic rivalry and styles of painting

The Strozzi and Medici families were members of opposing factions in Florence, and when the Medici came to power in the city one of their first action was to exile Palla Strozzi and his family. The result was that paintings in the International style favoured by the Strozzis are less well known and the classical works in the more statuesque style, based on the rules of perspective favoured by patrons during the Medici period, is now the accepted early Renaissance style.

Gentile da Fabriano and the *Adoration of the Magi*

Palla Strozzi was a wealthy and educated man who was a great lover of the antique, but the *Adoration of the Magi* (fig 24.1) (the three kings or wise men who attended the birth of Jesus) by Gentile da Fabriano is not a classical painting. Gentile da Fabriano was internationally recognised as one of the foremost artists of his day and had carried out important commissions in several major Italian cities. This celebrated altarpiece is his major surviving work and while it is a typical example of the International style, it is also part of the early Renaissance style and it represents quite a new departure for Florentine painting.

The 'courtly style'

Richly painted with gold decoration, splendidly patterned costumes and surrounded by an elaborate gold frame, the painting is a lavish expression of the Strozzi family's enormous wealth.

FIG 24.1 THE ADORATION OF THE MAGI, Gentile da Fabriano

Detail

The artist's love of fine detail is seen in the magnificent horses and elegantly dressed figures. The painting has used the traditional Gothic flat gold-leaf background in the distant sky behind the hills, but the exceptional splendour and novelty of treatment makes it truly remarkable.

Treatment of the surface

It must have looked quite sensational in its original setting, where its only source of light in the chapel would

FIG 24.2 Detail from THE ADORATION OF THE MAGI, Gentile da Fabriano

have been candles or oil lamps. The irregular flickering light would have emphasised different surface areas, which Gentile treated in different ways. In some areas he placed a layer of gold or silver beneath the paint and engraved relief patterns into it. He raised the surface of other features using plaster and glue. This technique (seen on the kings' gold crowns and the dog's collar) was

commonly used in Venetian paintings, but the artist introduced it to Florence (fig 24.2).

Paulo Uccello (1397–1475)

Cosimo de' Medici had many artists and among them was Paulo Uccello. Highly regarded in his own time, Uccello became obsessed by mathematical principles in painting and a rather negative image of him has persisted over the years. Vasari wrote that when his wife pleaded with him to come to bed, his reply was, 'Oh, what a lovely thing is this perspective.'

Cosimo fully appreciated how art could promote subtle messages to underline his authority and Uccello's three panels depicting the Battle of San Romano showcase a military victory for the Florentines against the combined forces of Lucca, Siena and Milan. The battle itself, however, was of little or no significance and would have been quickly forgotten but for the paintings.

The Battle of San Romano panels

The panels originally decorated the large hall on the ground floor of the Medici Palace, but they are now in the Louvre in Paris, in the Uffizi Gallery in Florence and in London's National Gallery. They indicate a profound interest in weapons and warfare on the part of both the artist and the patron. Every feature is accounted for: knights, foot soldiers, shields, lances, crossbows, trumpets and horses, with the detail even showing the rivets in the armour and the nails on the horseshoes. Cosimo was a connoisseur of warfare and *The Battle of San Romano* (fig 24.3) appears to have been important to him, probably because of his friendship with the battle's victor, Niccolò da Tolentino.

FIG 24.3 THE BATTLE OF SAN ROMANO – General Niccolò da Tolentino leading the Florentine troops, Paulo Uccello, National Gallery, London

General Niccolò da Tolentino

General Niccolò da Tolentino was a mercenary soldier. In the painting he is idealised beyond belief as he is shown in his parade outfit and on a lovely white charger, a creature of almost geometric perfection balanced carefully on a tuft of grass while by his side a page carries his ceremonial helmet, completely unaffected by the battle.

Uccello's preoccupation with single-point linear perspective is apparent in the foreshortening of shapes, broken lances and the posture and proportions of the horses. He was probably aiming for a high degree of realism, but the horses have a stiff cardboard cut-out or wooden appearance and the whole effect is quite theatrical, as though the battle was taking place on a stage. The painting is certainly more of an ornament than an historical account, but is nonetheless interesting for its symbolic significance. For example, on the trees are bright, orange-coloured fruit known at this time as *mala medica*, or 'medicinal apples'. Since the name 'Medici' means 'doctors', it was natural for them to choose this fruit as their symbol.

<small>Fig 24.4 MADONNA AND CHILD, Fra Fillipo Lippi, Uffizi Gallery, Florence</small>

Uccello falls out of favour

Apart from *The Battle of San Romano*, few other works by Uccello are still in existence. His popularity declined due to his eccentric solitary nature and his obsession with perspective as other artists emerged with fresh ideas.

Lorenzo the Magnificent

Lorenzo de' Medici took over as ruler of Florence with his younger brother Giuliano when he was only 21 after their father's death. He was a poet and a generous patron of the arts, but this skilled politician was a harsh ruler, especially after his brother was stabbed to death in a conspiracy to overthrow the Medici.

The Golden Age

Lorenzo ruled during the 'Golden Age' of the Florentine Renaissance, when the city surpassed even the superb cultural achievements of the earlier period. Like his father and grandfather, he supported artists and funded education. The people of Florence thanked him by granting him the title 'The Magnificent', but during the Renaissance, 'Il Magnifico' was a common title of respect in Italy.

Botticelli in the Medici Palace

Piero de' Medici had first spotted the teenage artist Botticelli in the late 1460s and gave him studio space inside the Medici Palace. Only five years older than Lorenzo, Botticelli quickly became friends with him and his brother Giuliano and shared their great interest in humanistic literature and philosophy. His most famous paintings – **Primavera** and **The Birth of Venus** – hung in the Medici Palace for many years.

Botticelli (1445–1510)

Botticelli's art became the most recognisable works of the Florentine Renaissance, but the artist himself was born to a poor family living in the back streets of the city. Alessandro Filipepi was brought up by his brother, who gave him the nickname *botticelli*, meaning 'little barrel', and the name stuck.

He learned his most recognised characteristic – the idealised, slightly melancholic image of feminine beauty – from his master, Fra Filippo Lippi. This wistful delicacy is also found in Lippi's work, whose *Madonna and Child* (fig 24.4) is a charming portrayal of a young and beautiful mother with a chubby Christ child and a most appealing young angel. Fra Fillipo worked for the Medici and here Piero met and was impressed by his young

FIG 24.5 THE ADORATION OF THE MAGI, Botticelli, Uffizi Gallery, Florence

apprentice, offering him patronage and intimacy with the most powerful family in Florence. This proved to be critical to Botticelli's career.

Adoration of the Magi

A prominent tax collector in Florence commissioned Botticelli to paint the *Adoration of the Magi* in an effort to impress the Medici. This painting (fig 24.5) includes portraits of Medici family members placed right at the heart of the Nativity itself. Cosimo il Vecchio, Piero, Lorenzo and Giuliano are all gathered around the holy family and nearby are friends, allies, scholars, politicians and businessmen. A self-portrait of Botticelli, staring at the viewer from within the group, is a powerful statement of alliance with the family that would not have gone unnoticed in a city like Florence.

Classical inspiration

Like other artists, Botticelli painted religious subjects, but he also created an entirely new genre of art as a result of his association with Lorenzo's intellectual friends. Through them, he was introduced to classical poetry and was inspired to paint mythological themes related to it.

Neo-Platonism

Primavera (fig 24.6) is one of the all-time great Renaissance paintings, but it is still surrounded by controversy. This much-discussed work was painted for a younger cousin in the Medici family also called Lorenzo. Lorenzo di Pierfrancesco de' Medici was a very learned member of a group of intellectuals known as

FIG 24.6 PRIMAVERA, Botticelli, Uffizi Gallery, Florence

Neo-Platonists after the Greek philosopher Plato, whom they greatly admired. This influential group of humanists believed that there was a hidden agreement between Christianity and pagan mythology, so the painting's true meaning has probably long been suppressed because it was contrary to mainstream religious teaching.

Primavera – the coming of Spring

Venus, ancient goddess of beauty and fertility, celebrates the arrival of Spring, surrounded by allegorical figures representing the virtues and gods of the ancient world. The mysterious, golden-haired goddess is lost in daydream as she stands in a niche like a Madonna. Her expression of melancholic purity is similar to that found on Botticelli's religious figures. All the women in the picture are pregnant. It reads from right to left, beginning with Zephyr (the wind) pursuing Chloris (the wood nymph), with flowers (a sign of fertility) falling from her mouth before she transforms into Flora, scattering blossoms before her. Overhead, Cupid (the blindfolded son of Venus) shoots his arrow towards the girls dancing in an endless circle of life,

while on the extreme left, Mercury (the messenger of the gods) holds up his staff to remove the cloud, which hides the truth. This figure has been identified as a likeness of Giuliano, Lorenzo de' Medici's murdered younger brother.

Once again, laurel bushes behind Venus make reference to Lauro – a reminder of the rebirth of a golden age under the patronage of Lorenzo de' Medici.

The Birth of Venus

Inspired by the Medici collection of classical sculptures, Botticelli later took his radical style to a new extreme with *The Birth of Venus* (fig 24.7), painted as a wedding present for Lorenzo di Pierfrancesco.

This was unlike any other painting of its time and was so controversial it was kept behind closed doors for half a century. The legend of Venus' birth and arrival from the sea was well known at the time, but instead of following the text of the classical poem, Botticelli developed his own form of visual poetry. The elegant figure of Venus may refer to the creative power of love.

FIG 24.7 THE BIRTH OF VENUS, Botticelli, Uffizi Gallery, Florence

Venus is delicately posed on her shell and although she is unnaturally elongated with a very long neck and sharply sloping shoulders, she is a perfect image of graceful elegance with hair blowing in the wind and hands in the classical pose of Venus pudica. Her face is considered one of the most beautiful in art, but Botticelli used this perfect oval and expression of melancholic purity again in *The Madonna of the Pomegranate* (fig 24.8). The model for this and for both the mythological paintings was probably Giuliano de' Medici's mistress, Simonetta Vespucci.

Truth is beauty

The Birth of Venus may have been designed as a celebration of human desire, but in humanist thinking Venus was the personification of beauty and to the philosopher Plato, truth was beauty. Botticelli's Venus is neither a temptress nor an object of lust, but is a symbol of untouched innocence, which, in Neo-Platonist Christian thinking, was the soul purified by baptism.

A linear artist

Botticelli has been described as 'the greatest linear artist Europe ever had' because he painted almost entirely

FIG 24.8 THE MADONNA OF THE POMEGRANATE, Botticelli, Uffizi Gallery, Florence

with line and with little or no light and shade. He also reduced all surfaces to a minimum, such as using elements like the decorative little Vs to form the waves on the sea in *The Birth of Venus*.

Savanarola

Botticelli remained close to Lorenzo the Magnificent, but he became a follower of the Dominican monk Savonarola, who preached fiery public sermons against the 'paganism' of the Medici and the lifestyle followed by the people of the city. The Florentines responded with a frenzy of religious intensity, making 'a bonfire of their vanities' (in which they burned valuable possessions), as Savonarola suggested, and Botticelli, fearing for his own everlasting salvation, even went so far as to hurl many of his early 'pagan' paintings onto the fire. He became deeply religious, concentrating only on religious painting for the rest of his life, some of which reflected the apocalyptic themes from Savonarola's sermons. Savonarola was eventually burnt as a heretic and Botticelli fell out of favour with his patrons. He died in 1510, neglected and forgotten.

Conclusion

A preference for a particular style of painting was part of the rivalry among ruling families. The elegant International style or International Gothic associated with the rich courts of northern Europe was favoured in Siena and by some families in Florence. The Medici, however, favoured the classical style and because they were the rulers of Florence this became the dominant style of the Renaissance.

Questions

1. What was the International Gothic or 'courtly' style?
2. What movement influenced Botticelli's mythological paintings?
3. Why did Botticelli destroy some of his early works in later life?

Colour picture study

1. Examine *The Battle of San Romano* (fig 24.3) and describe Uccello's use of perspective.
2. Examine *Primavera* (fig 24.6) and *The Birth of Venus* (fig 24.7) by Botticelli and describe the composition and treatment of the human figure in both works. What was the subject matter of these paintings?

CHAPTER 25

ARCHITECTURE

A dome for the Cathedral of Santa Maria del Fiore

Filippo Brunelleschi's name first came to prominence with the competition for the new doors for the Baptistery of San Giovanni (St John) in Florence in 1400. He was by all accounts extremely upset to have lost to his rival, Lorenzo Ghiberti, but the history of the Renaissance would have been very different had he not done so because many years later he returned to Florence to take part in an equally bitterly fought competition.

A new competition

In 1418 a competition was announced for models and designs for the construction of a dome for the Cathedral of Santa Maria del Fiore. Many engineers and architects participated, but Brunelleschi was determined to win this commission.

Building the cathedral

The city's new cathedral (fig 25.1) had been under construction for more than a century. Designed as a vast space to hold the entire church-going population of Florence, it was to be one of the most sumptuous and magnificent cathedrals in Christendom. Frequent

changes were made to the design as the building took shape, but by 1418 most of it was completed, including the massive drum to hold the dome. All that remained was the construction of the dome.

Designing the dome

Discussions, plans and competitions for the design of a dome had raged back and forth through Florence for several years, but nothing like it had been built in Italy since Roman times. There was not an architect in Europe – let alone Italy – who had the relevant expertise or experience. So as the building progressed, no one had the least idea how to solve the structural problem of constructing a huge cupola over the gaping open space

FIG 25.1 Cathedral of Santa Maria del Fiore, Florence

FIG 25.2 Model for the cupola of St Maria del Fiore, Filippo Brunelleschi, Museum of the Cathedral, Florence

of the crossing. Brunelleschi, however, enlisted the help of two of the most innovative sculptors of the day, Donatello and Nanni di Banco, and produced a model (fig 25.2) that so impressed the judges that they immediately awarded him the commission.

Filippo Brunelleschi (1377–1446)

Born in Florence the son of a notary, Brunelleschi was expected to follow in his father's footsteps, but eventually he was allowed to study his real interest: art and design, including mechanics. He began in a goldsmith's workshop, where he learned embossing, engraving in silver and casting small figures in metal. He eventually became a sculptor, architect, painter and scholar. An ideal Renaissance man, he linked theory and practice to formulate the laws of perspective and bring about a revolution that has effects to this day. He also learned a great deal from the surviving buildings of ancient Rome.

Brunelleschi's dome

Brunelleschi's design for a self-supporting cupola was unique. Other designs included wooden scaffolding that would have required the use of timber strong enough to support the weight of the dome, thereby creating enormous technical problems. Brunelleschi's technically brilliant and innovative system solved this problem.

A double-shell cupola

First, he invented a form of scaffolding that could be started at the top of the drum (rather than the ground), and in another master stroke he designed a double-shell cupola that included an access walkway and steps between the walls. Massive stone ribs ensured that the inner and outer shells were bound together for strength and stability. To prevent the dome from buckling under its own weight, he included a series of stone chains buried within the masonry, which stiffened each of the eight faces.

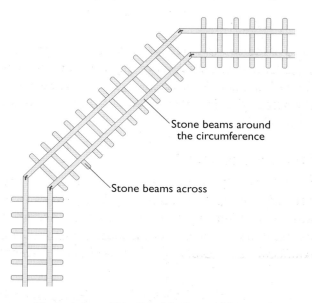

Stone beams around the circumference

Stone beams across

FIG 25.3 Stone chains within the eight faces of the cupola. A series of chains were set in the walls for strength, with four stone chains and one of wood encircling the dome at regular intervals upwards.

A self-supporting vault

Brunelleschi's expertise at mathematics and geometry and his knowledge of mechanics, combined with his study of classical buildings in Rome, helped him to realise that an inward-facing circular vault had to be self-supporting, so he included a particularly clever technique, which he copied from the Pantheon in Rome. The brickwork of the walls was in a herringbone pattern,

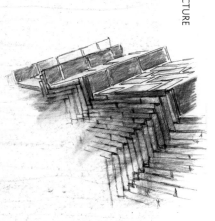

FIG 25.4 Brickwork in the walls of the cupola.

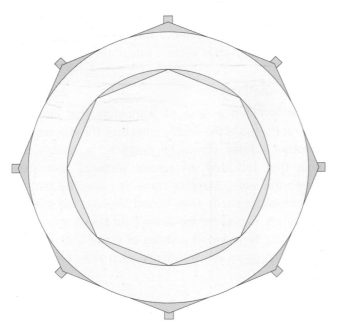

FIG 25.5 The inner wall of the dome was constructed as a circular vault within the thickness of the walls but cut away to form an octagonal shape.

FIG 25.7 The lantern of St Maria del Fiore, Filippo Brunelleschi

ensuring that as it was laid, each ring would be supported by the one below. To prevent the dome from collapsing in on itself, Brunelleschi invented the idea of a circular ring within the thickness of the octagonal wall (fig 25.5).

The lantern

The cupola was such an overwhelming success that Brunelleschi won first place in another competition – this time to design the lantern for the top. He did not, however, live to see it in place. He died in 1446, the year construction began. His design not only capped the entire composition of the dome, but also included some novel architectural elements mixed with classical features (fig 25.7). In full daylight, white is the only colour to convey a sense of weightlessness, but by shaping the marble to pick up shadow, he cleverly created variations in the pure white. The russet tiles on its eight great faces make a striking colour contrast with the white of the powerful ribs converging upwards to the lantern and the great ball that supports the cross.

FIG 25.6 The Dome of St Maria del Fiore, Filippo Brunelleschi

Classical influences

This combination of an original style and a blending of the antique became a characteristic of Brunelleschi's architectural designs. He studied the proportions of monuments of classical antiquity and followed the system of architectural orders from ancient Greek and Roman public buildings.

The classical order

Greek temples were built with very strict rules (orders) and the Romans used these for their own buildings. The basic design had a central block surrounded on all four sides by a columned portico with the capitals (tops) on the columns. The columns conformed to one of three basic types: Doric, Ionic or Corinthian (fig 25.8). The rules also applied to the details of the upper parts of the building, or entablature, carried by the columns.

Conclusion

The vast curved silhouette of Brunelleschi's dome stands out huge and magnificent against the sky as the great landmark of Florence. Like a great umbrella over the city, it relates to the hills of the surrounding Tuscan countryside as much today as it did in Brunelleschi's time.

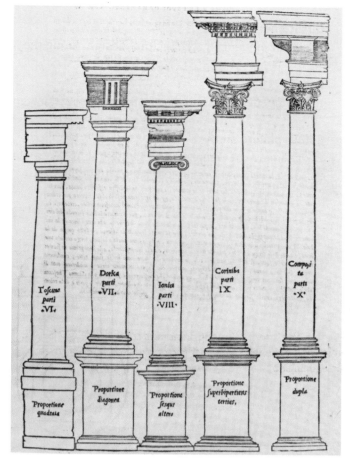

FIG 25.8 The classical orders of architecture

Leon Battista Alberti

Leon Battista Alberti's wealthy banking family had been exiled many years before. An expert humanist, he had spent some time at the papal court, but when he returned to Florence in the late 15th century and observed the intense artistic activity going on there, he was by his own admission 'astonished by what he saw'. What he saw was Brunelleschi's great dome almost complete, Donatello's lifelike sculpture and Masaccio's frescos still fresh. It all inspired him to write the first Renaissance book about art.

On Painting

Alberti's treatise, *De Pitura* (*On Painting*), was neither a history of art nor a manual on techniques. Instead, it put forward new and revolutionary theories on why artists deserved to be recognised as intellectuals and their position in society be stronger. He singled out the sculptors Donatello, Ghiberti and Luca della Robbia for special praise, as well as the painter Masaccio (who had recently died at the age of 27), but he was deeply impressed by Brunelleschi and dedicated the book to him.

On the Art of Building

Alberti published another book, *De Re Aedificatoria* (*On the Art of Building*), which brought a new view to the subject of architecture and proposed the idea of a planned city designed to accommodate the various classes of the population in harmony and elegance around state buildings, temples and palaces.

It is partly based on a Roman manuscript by the ancient architect Vitruvius, but it is also a study based on his own careful examination of ancient Roman classical buildings. Alberti became an architect and like Brunelleschi, his new classical style became extremely popular in Italy.

Questions

1. What influenced architectural design during the Renaissance?

Essay

1. Name, describe and discuss two buildings designed by Brunelleschi in Florence.

Colour picture study

1. Examine the dome for the Cathedral of Santa Maria del Fiore in Florence (fig 25.1) and describe how it relates to its surroundings.

CHAPTER 26

A GOLDEN AGE

⬚ = important

Rome and Florence

The period of Italian art known to us today as the High Renaissance was a Golden Age in its own time. Florence was the source of the inspiration, but Rome and the Papacy made a very significant contribution. The Popes had always taken an interest in what was happening in Florence, but Rome's economy was poor and later in a tumbledown state following the years of papal exile in France. Two Popes set out to change this: Pope Julius II, of the important de Rovere family, and later, Pope Leo X, son of Lorenzo de' Medici of Florence. Although very different in character, political views and culture, the two Popes had one thing in common: both were determined to restore the city to its former position of cultural and political glory under papal leadership and were prepared to pay for it on an unprecedented scale. From 1503 to 1521 they employed craftsmen and artists to rebuild St Peter's Basilica, refurbish the streets, build bridges, construct churches and create some of the world's most treasured works of art, making this period one of exceptional splendour for the Eternal City.

✳ Innovations in painting

There were some very important artistic innovations during this period. There was a far greater degree of realism within painting, a new sensitivity towards portrayal of facial features and expressions and a much greater range in the depiction of human movement. Figures within the compositions also related to each other in a far more natural fashion.

✳ From craftsman to genius

Before the Renaissance, artists were considered mere craftsmen, but writers like the influential humanist Leon Battista Alberti claimed that the successful artist must also be well educated and his opinions respected. Leonardo da Vinci also wrote that painting was a science worthy of comparison with other complex intellectual activities.

Alberti's *De Pitura*

Alberti's treatise *De Pitura* (*On Painting*), published in 1435, presented quite revolutionary theories on why artists deserve intellectual recognition and improvement of their position in society. He cleverly associated painting with geometry and speech-making, two of the liberal arts, but by relating its importance to princes and leading citizens of classical times, he suggests that this was an activity suitable for educated men. In this book we see, for the first time, an image of the artist as a man of culture rather than an unlearned craftsman. Alberti began a discussion on artistic theory that was to continue through the next two centuries.

The book was written in Latin, but Alberti immediately translated it into Italian for the artists of Florence. He compares the structure of painting to Euclidian geometry and takes up the idea of perspective drawing developed by Brunelleschi, but further expands the theory based on mathematics and optics.

He urged painters 'to remember their link with the artists of classical antiquity' and to turn away from gold and represent reality with colour, basing human figures on the study of anatomy by starting with the bones and adding flesh and clothing. He also advocated the interplay of emotions between the figures with natural gestures and facial expressions.

As these ideas became accepted in society, the professional and social situation of artists changed radically. By the early 16th century, artists were recognised as having their own ideas and they could share their thoughts with other educated people, including their patrons. Artists had become more like the sort of person we think of today when we use the word 'artist' and expect someone who is special, creative, intellectual and perhaps even a genius.

A new status for the artist

In his *Lives of the Artists*, Vasari refers to **three phases of revival** in the arts in Italy. The first was in the 13th century with the members of the **'first generation'** (artists such as Giotto). The **second** came in the early 15th century with advances in **perspective and natural portrayal of the human figure**. The third phase began with Leonardo da Vinci and was a time when **drawing, proportion and grace were brought to a new level of art** and **beauty**. It culminated in the 'divine' Michelangelo, whose genius was considered nothing less than a gift from God.

High Renaissance artists

Leonardo da Vinci and Michelangelo were regarded as geniuses in their own time and it gave them freedom to pick and choose their commissions. Patrons were so honoured to receive any work from the hand of a great man that Leonardo's habit of leaving work unfinished was tolerated and Michelangelo could dare to argue with a Pope. Even Raphael is said to have had followers as if he were a prince.

Leonardo da Vinci (1452–1519)

Leonardo da Vinci was the oldest and most famous of the great Renaissance masters. He was the originator of a new movement that marked fundamental changes and set him apart from other artists. A good deal of his time and energy were devoted to scientific interests that anticipated many developments of modern science. This was combined with his unique artistic ability to make him exceptional. His innovations in painting influenced the course of Italian art for more than a century after his death.

He believed that painting was one of the highest vocations to which a man could be called and he spent much of his life attempting to prove that it was an intellectual activity. His theories were highly influential in changing attitudes towards the artist and went a long way towards shattering the widely held view that painting was simply a low form of manual labour that required no sophisticated mental skills.

Early life

The son of a Florentine lawyer and a servant girl, Leonardo came from the little town of Vinci in the Tuscan hills. At school, he excelled at drawing and was even then interested in all things to do with nature.

He was apprenticed to the painter and sculptor Andrea del Verrochio. Leonardo's talent was so great that he soon outstripped his master. His earliest known painting is of a beautiful young angel in Verrochio's *Baptism of Christ* (fig 26.1). Legend has it that when Verrochio saw how much nicer Leonardo's work was than his own, he put down his brush forever to concentrate only on sculpture.

Leonardo made quite a mark in Florence, but he was restless and wrote a long and now famous letter to Ludovico Sforza, the duke of Milan, offering his services as an engineer, canal builder, designer of war machines and – almost as an afterthought – a painter.

FIG 26.1 BAPTISM OF CHRIST, Andrea del Verrochio, Uffizi Gallery, Florence

Milan

Ludovico Sforza was one of the wealthiest and most powerful princes of Renaissance Italy, and he spent immense sums of money furthering the arts and sciences. Known as 'Il Moro', or 'the Moor', because of his dark complexion, he and his wife, Beatrice d'Este, held a brilliant court in the city-state of Milan. It is thanks to 'Il Moro' that Milan has the good fortune to possess one of the greatest works of Italian painting. Ludovico

Sforza paid for the rebuilding of the church of Santa Maria delle Grazie and, in the monastery nearby, for *The Last Supper*, the famous fresco by Leonardo da Vinci.

The Last Supper

The subject of conversation had long been of interest and debate among artists who wanted to depict not just actions but also communication. Leonardo solved this problem with *The Last Supper* (fig 26.2) by using

FIG 26.3 THE LAST SUPPER, Domenico Ghirlandaio, Church of Ognissanti, Florence

gestures and facial expressions, making the painting one of the most famous and important works in the history of Western art. It influenced artists forever afterwards and presented new opportunities in depicting human interaction. Unfortunately, Leonardo's search for perfection has meant that the painting has come down to us in a state of near ruin.

Experimentation with new techniques in fresco

Leonardo decorated the walls of the monk's refectory (dining room), but was dissatisfied with the fast-drying fresco. This prevented him using the kind of fine detail he liked, so he searched for new technical solutions and experimented with mixed media. He mixed oil with tempera paints, like that used for panel painting, but this, combined with plaster and the damper climatic conditions of northern Italy, spelled disaster and in less than 20 years the great painting began to disintegrate. Since then, every generation has worked hard to preserve it.

A break from tradition

Even in its semi-ruined state, the picture is majestic. Even in its own day the quality was recognised and numerous copies were made. Artists had long vied with each other to perfect the theme of the Last Supper, but Leonardo broke new ground. In no way does his work resemble older versions. Traditional representations of the scene (fig 26.3) depicted the apostles seated next to

Jesus as he solemnly blesses the bread, with Judas always segregated from the group on the opposite side of the table. Leonardo's picture, however, tells the story in a silent yet highly dramatic language of gestures and expressions (fig 26.4).

Leonardo's story picture

Leonardo studied the passages relating to the Last Supper in the Bible and imagined the chaos that would have followed when Jesus announced, 'One of you will betray me.' In a superb psychological study of human emotion, the apostles reel in horror, each one full of self-doubt and confusion and reacting with denial or disbelief (fig 26.5).

To solve the problem of the long composition, Leonardo arranged the apostles in groups drawing away from Christ or leaning towards him. They are connected by a series of hand and facial gestures communicating their fear, anger or even sorrow. One lifts his hands as if to say, 'Lord, is it I,' and clasps his hands to his breast, while Peter, with a knife clutched in his hand, leans forward to John, seated on the right of Jesus, and whispers in his ear. This action has the effect of pushing Judas aside and isolated from the group. He recoils in an opposite pose from Jesus, his hand clenched, with Peter's knife at his back. The central figure of Jesus remains serene and dignified, alone in the knowledge of what is about to befall him.

FIG 26.4 Detail of the apostles from THE LAST SUPPER, Leonardo da Vinci

FIG 26.5 Detail hand gestures from THE LAST SUPPER, Leonardo da Vinci

discovered in Restoration nail hole found in chriss forehead was used to pinpoint the prespective lines that helpd create the paintings remarkable illusion of space

Thomas points upward with the finger, that he would later place into christ wound when he doubted the apperence of the resserected christ

Clever perspective

The picture is cleverly arranged to give the impression of the wall receding back and the group has the appearance of sitting at the top table in the room. The painted window forms a natural halo behind the central figure of Christ, with all the perspective lines converging on his face. This – and his blue and red garments – draw the eye immediately to him.

A Renaissance man

Leonardo is regarded as the ultimate Renaissance man because of his wide-ranging talents. His inventions and scientific interests made him a master in every discipline, from natural science, engineering and architecture to philosophy and art, and during his time in Milan he wrote a huge work, *A Treatise on Painting*, which was to influence artists for centuries.

Court artist

As court artist, he organised elaborate festivals to celebrate special occasions, but he also designed buildings, drainage systems, weapons of war and, of course, his famous flying machine (fig 26.6).

Scientific interests

Leonardo's reflections on mathematics, geology, the human body and other scientific subjects were recorded in thousands of manuscripts pages that were preserved

FIG 26.6 Flying machine sketch from Leonardo da Vinci's notes

after his death. These enabled historians to piece together the wanderings of this unique mind that grappled with such a huge range of problems. It was typical of him to explore in great detail whatever he worked on or whatever interested him.

Observations of nature

He studied anatomy, which was very controversial at the time, by managing to get dead bodies and dissecting them. He secretly discovered many human anatomical features long before they became common knowledge. He sketched continually (fig 26.7).

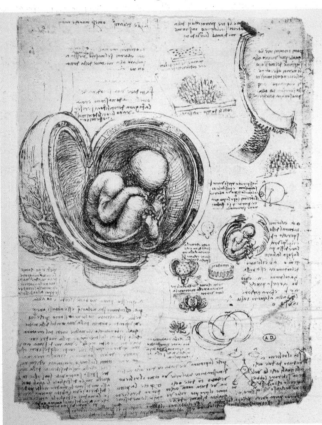

FIG 26.7 The babe in the womb, page from Leonardo da Vinci's notes, Windsor Castle Royal Library

Very few paintings

Very few artists drew as much and painted as little as Leonardo. Only 15 paintings and one fresco have survived, but there are hundreds of drawings of places, people, plants and other natural phenomena as well as animal studies – particularly of horses.

He was, in fact, working on a great monument to Francesca Sforza in the form of a 26-foot-high sculpture of a rearing horse that was to be the first of its kind, but due to technical difficulties the clay was never cast in bronze and so it no longer exists.

The invasion of Milan

Leonardo had to leave Milan quickly when the French invaded, but not before he had witnessed drunken French troops destroy his great clay horse by using it for target practice.

Technical developments

Atmospheric perspective

Perspective and atmospheric defects such as rain and dust were also of interest to Leonardo. He studied the effect of these on colour and distance and was one of the first artists in Italy to use atmospheric perspective.

Virgin of the Rocks

In *Virgin of the Rocks* (fig 26.8), his close observation and study of nature can be seen in the plants and flowers as well the in the strange landscape of water and rock formations in the background.

He painted two versions during his time in Milan. The first is now in the Louvre and a later version is in the National Gallery in London. The scene is set in an

FIG 26.8 THE VIRGIN OF THE ROCKS, Leonardo da Vinci, Louvre, Paris

imaginary enchanted grotto. The Virgin and Child with St John are treated with great tenderness, but Leonardo's love of the mysterious shows through. The gentle light and rugged shadowy background create an air of mystery in the earlier version, but the later version is a little more formal.

Sfumato

He was constantly playing with light and shade and developed a technique called *sfumato* (the Italian word for 'smoke'). This softens outlines, allowing a smooth passage from light to shade. *Sfumato* was particularly effective on faces, both in his religious works and in his portraits.

Portraits

Portraiture competed with religious painting as the main subject of Leonardo's work. He painted women, and his wonderful range of techniques gives these works a peculiar quality of secret wistfulness.

Ginevra de Benci

Traditionally, Renaissance portraits of women usually showed them at the time of their marriage and in profile. As such, these women generally lack any great sense of inner character. In contrast, Leonardo presents *Ginevra de Benci* (fig 26.9), his earliest portrait, in a three-quarters pose and calmly meeting the viewer's gaze. A Renaissance wife would normally not engage the artist's (a man's) eye, but Ginevra was a member of the wealthy and educated Benci family, which had considerable cultural influence. A woman of renowned beauty, she was 17 years old and shortly to marry a man twice her age when Leonardo painted her with that haunting, almost unearthly beauty that is so peculiar to his work.

Lady with an Ermine

Cecilia Gallerani is the subject of the wonderfully graceful portrait known as *Lady with an Ermine* (fig 26.10). She was a prominent lady at the court of Milan and was known for her beauty, but she was also a poetess and a lover of Latin. She was the duke of Milan's mistress and gave birth to his son. Although Ludovico's wife, Beatrice, was very jealous of her, Leonardo painted her with an ermine, which was one of Ludovico's emblems. (The Greek word for ermine is *galen,* a pun on Cecilia's surname.) Once again, instead of the conventional pose, Cecelia turns gracefully towards the left and her face, throat and curve of her shoulders are fully displayed, while her elegant hand – with its long, tapering fingers so typical of Leonardo – strokes the

FIG 26.9 GINERVA DE BENCI, Leonardo da Vinci, National Gallery, Washington, DC

FIG 26.10 LADY WITH AN ERMINE, Leonard da Vinci, Czartoryski Museum, Cracow

FIG 26.11 MONA LISA, Leonardo da Vinci, Louvre, Paris

animal's sleek coat. The painting became instantly famous for its *grazia* (grace) and created a new ideal for courtly female portraiture.

Mona Lisa

Leonardo's most famous portrait, *Mona Lisa* (fig 26.11), dates from the unsettled period of his life after he had returned from Milan to Florence. All his portraits combine *sfumato* with *chiaroscuro* (the balance of light against dark), and the barest touch suggests that the subjects are dissolving into their backgrounds, but these are seen to perfection in *Mona Lisa*.

No painting in the history of the Renaissance has inspired so many interpretations and so much disagreement. Her smile, which has been described as mysterious and unfathomable, has made her more famous than any other of Leonardo's works and it is probably the most extreme example of an expression that cannot be defined.

Leonardo has combined clever devices with skilful brushwork, exact rendering of living flesh and folds of cloth to make it a work of art that will continue to fascinate viewers for many years to come. He is said to have worked on it over several years, constantly returning to it and touching it up before taking it with him when he left for France. It is now in the Louvre in Paris, but is in poor condition, and because of the materials Leonardo used it is very difficult to restore.

Later life

Rome

Before going to France, Leonardo went to Rome, hoping to get commissions from the newly elected Pope Leo X. He remained in Rome for two years, but the Pope had little time for an artist with a series of unfinished commissions and spectacular failures behind him. He considered him yesterday's man and was far more impressed with the artists who had produced some stunning works of art for Pope Julius II. The new Pope preferred Raphael Sanzio, the young artist from Urbino, and Leonardo's old rival from Florence, the great Michelangelo Buonarroti.

France

Neither was the Church all that happy with Leonardo's work. It was seen as anti-Christian, so in the end he was forced to leave Italy and seek refuge at the more liberal court of the king of France, where he died in 1519.

Conclusion

Discussions on artistic theory took place for the first time during what became known as the High Renaissance. This led to a change in the status of the artist from craftsman to an intellectual whose education and ideas were respected. Artists like Leonardo da Vinci were now considered geniuses and the quality and beauty of works of art produced during this Golden Age of Italian art have remained unsurpassed.

Questions

1. What were the three stages of revival according to Vasari?
2. What contribution did Alberti's treatise *De Pitura* make to the Renaissance?
3. Why is Leonardo's *The Last Supper* in such a poor state?
4. List some of Leonardo's technical developments.
5. What is *sfumato*?

Essay

1. Discuss the innovations in painting and the status of the artist during the High Renaissance.
2. Leonardo da Vinci has often been described as 'the ultimate Renaissance man'. What made this artist so special?

Colour picture study

1. Examine Leonardo's *The Last Supper* (fig 26.2) and describe how he solved the problem of conversation.
2. Examine Leonardo's painting of Cecilia Gallerani, *Lady with an Ermine* (fig 26.10), and describe his unusual depiction of women in portraiture. Compare it with some of his other portraits of women.

CHAPTER 27

MICHELANGELO — SCULPTURE

A new genius

Towards the end of the 15th century a new name emerged in Florence. This was Michelangelo Buonarotti, who was 17 years old and living in the Palazzo Medici under the protection of Lorenzo the Magnificent. Lorenzo facilitated the flowering of this genius and treated him with respect and warm-hearted familiarity.

Lorenzo had recognised Michelangelo's talent when he was 13. He supported him financially and gave him a room at the *palazzo*, allowing the young sculptor to eat at the table with his sons and other distinguished people.

Unfortunately, Lorenzo died in 1492, at age 43, and his son, Piero, had little or no time for the arts or culture and lacked his father's political abilities. The population soon revolted against him and Florence was re-established as a republic. Michelangelo had, however, already left the city to seek out patrons who would better appreciate his unique talent.

Michelangelo Buonarroti (1475–1564)

As an infant Michelangelo had been given to a wet nurse in a family of stonecutters and his childhood was spent among them. He always said this determined his career and it certainly gave him a familiarity with stone.

He spent a short time in the studio of the artist Ghirlandaio before going on to a school set up by Lorenzo the Magnificent in the Medici gardens, with the sculptor Bertoldo di Giovanni as teacher. He studied the Medici collection of classical statues as well as Masaccio's frescoes in the Brancacci Chapel.

Rome

By 1496 Michelangelo was in Rome, working for Jacopo Galli, a wealthy banker with a fine collection of antique sculpture. He put the young sculptor in touch with an elderly French cardinal who wanted a statue for his tomb. Galli promised the cardinal would get 'the most beautiful work in marble that exists in Rome today' and Michelangelo certainly fulfilled that promise.

The *Pietà*

In Italian, the word *pietà* means 'pity', but its specific meaning in religious art is the Virgin grieving over the dead Christ. The theme was far more common in northern European art, but 23-year-old Michelangelo took the subject and presented it as never before. He returned to the theme in later life but this first *Pietà*

FIG 27.1 PIETÀ, Michelangelo, St Peter's Basilica, Rome

FIG 27.2 DAVID, Michelangelo, Accademia, Florence

FIG 27.3 APOLLO BELVEDERE, The Vatican, Rome

(fig 27.1) is probably the most beautiful, elegant and harmonious of all and is the only work he ever signed. The youthful Madonna with downcast eyes is dignified in her grief and the drama of the event is treated in a restrained classical manner. While the figures are completely realistic, they are idealised beyond the mere human to the divine.

A technical solution

The problem of stretching a grown man over the lap of a seated woman was solved by building up the drapery in a pyramid of support and transforming cold marble into folds of cloth.

The *Pietà* established Michelangelo's name in Rome, but by 1500 he was preparing to return to his native Florence.

The republic as patron

Florence was once again a republic, and to celebrate this the Signoria had embarked on a number of commissions. The cathedral-building committee asked Michelangelo to make a statue of David for one of the buttresses. They gave him a gigantic block of marble which belonged to the board of works of the cathedral and with it he produced a figure that symbolised the restored republic and established him as the leading artist in Florence without rival.

David

The great statue of *David* (fig 27.2) was executed in the true tradition of Donatello, dating back nearly 100 years. Carved from that single block of fine marble, the 4-metre-high statue represents the young boy who killed the huge Goliath with one shot from his sling. This symbolises the strength of Florence, a small city-state pitched against its stronger enemies. The resolve is expressed in David's frowning, preoccupied features, but he has all the appearances of a classical statue, with a dreamy lack of urgency and one hand relaxed at his side. This great stone giant rests somewhere between the real and the ideal, a distant figure rising above the human to an elevated, divine level in the shape of a perfectly proportioned and flawlessly beautiful male.

Classical influence

The turn of the head echoes the pose of the so-called *Apollo Belvedere* (fig 27.3) that was discovered near Rome in the late 1400s, but it also reflects the blend of classical poetry and Neo-Platonism, or *poesie*, that had been prevalent in the Medici household when Michelangelo lived there as a youth. He would have known Botticelli at that time and the resemblance between the pose and gesture in the older artist's *The Birth of Venus* and *David* is so striking that one is almost a mirror image of the other.

David took one year to complete and the Signoria of Florence were so impressed that instead of placing it on the cathedral as originally intended, it was put in the Piazza del Signoria outside of the Palazzo Vecchio in 1504, where it remained for many years until it was given a special room in the Accademia and a copy replaced it in the Piazza.

A tomb for Pope Julius

Less than a year after the completion of *David*, Michelangelo was summoned again to Rome. The newly elected Pope Julius II wanted him to work on a grand scheme that should have been the most prestigious commission of his career, but in reality was one of the most frustrating experiences of the artist's life. Julius wanted a free-standing, grandiose tomb over 15 metres high, which he envisaged as the focal point of the new St Peter's, covering an area of over 200 square metres. It occupied him on and off for the next 40 years and became, in the words of Michelangelo's biographer, the 'tragedy of the tomb'.

302

The tomb

Michelangelo spent almost a year at the Carrara marble quarries in Tuscany selecting marble for the tomb, which he had transported by sea to Rome at his own expense, but in the meantime Julius ran out of money and postponed the project. The tomb was never completed and was dragged through six disputed contracts, having to be redesigned each time. Even after the Pope's death in 1513, the contract was redrawn. Although Michelangelo made numerous attempts to finish it, successive Popes refused to pay for it and wanted the artist to do other work. Michelangelo eventually got out of the contract completely and it was finished in 1545 by assistants, in the church of San Pietro in Vincoli, in a highly unsatisfactory form that was described by one writer as a 'miserable object'.

Apart from Michelangelo's great figure of Moses, the sculptures are little short of disastrous, so it is not surprising that the Della Rovere family were extremely unhappy with the result and felt that they had been cheated.

FIG 27.4 THE DYING SLAVE, Michelangelo, Louvre, Paris

FIG 27.5 SLAVES, Michelangelo, Accademia, Florence

Figures imprisoned in marble

There were to have been about 40 large figures, most of them nude males, but they mostly remained in the early stages of cutting. The only finished figure, *The Dying Slave* (fig 27.4), is in the Louvre in Paris, and four unfinished slaves are now in the Accademia art gallery in Florence (fig 27.5). It is unclear what they may have symbolised, but they do reveal Michelangelo's sculptural process of outlining the figure on the front of the marble block and working inwards, or, as he said, 'liberating the figure imprisoned in the marble'. He would bring the exposed parts to quite a finished state and leave the rest rough, giving the figures the appearance of struggling to be free of the marble block.

Moses

Four prophets were to have adorned the tomb, but *Moses* (fig 27.6), one of Michelangelo's greatest sculptures, was the only one to be finished. Frowning and majestic, the more than life-sized superhuman figure has a ferocious stare made all the more tense by the left hand being intertwined in the folds of his mighty beard. One leg is pulled under the seated figure, the other is strong and tense as a tree trunk. Moses' massive, muscular, veined arm holds the tablets of law, which he received on Mount Sinai. With horns on his head, or rays indicating a halo, his face expresses the supreme authority given to him by God as his messenger. Michelangelo's contemporaries described his severe, forbidding air as *terribilità* (a sense of awe-inspiring grandeur).

A figure on the tomb

Moses occupies the central ground level in the present tomb, but it had been intended for high up and to be seen from below. There the powerful, dominating figure, no doubt related to the personality of Julius and even Michelangelo himself, would have been even more impressive than it is now.

FIG 27.6 MOSES, Michelangelo, tomb of Pope Julius II, San Pietro in Vincola, Rome

FIG 27.7 The tomb of Giuliano de Medici, Michelangelo, New Sacristy, San Lorenzo, Florence

FIG 27.8 The tomb of Lorenzo de Medici, Michelangelo, New Sacristy, San Lorenzo, Florence

The Medici funerary chapel

When Giovanni de' Medici became Pope Leo X he commissioned Michelangelo to work on a new scheme for the Medicis' tombs in Florence. The chapel was to accommodate four tombs, but only two were finished and the sculptural decoration of the chapel, intended to be an integral part of the architecture, was never completed. The partially complete Madonna holding the Christ child on her lap was to be the focal point, but the seated Medici figures on the tombs are among Michelangelo's finest creations.

Giuliano and Lorenzo

Pope Leo's younger brother, Giuliano (fig 27.7), and his nephew, Lorenzo (fig 27.8), both died at an early age. Beneath them, reclining figures of Day and Night and Dawn and Dusk represent Time and Mortality through the passage of time. It is not certain what exactly Michelangelo intended to symbolise with these figures, but Giuliano and Lorenzo are highly idealised figures and are certainly not portraits.

The last *pietàs*

Mother and child groups were a constant theme in Michelangelo's art. A deep religious faith dominated his work and his last *pietàs* are intense, almost desperate statements of the mother-and-child theme.

FIG 27.9 THE FLORENCE PIETÀ, Michelangelo, Museum of the Cathedral, Florence

The *Florence Pietà*

The *Florence Pietà* (fig 27.9) is one of Michelangelo's most moving creations. It was most certainly intended for his own tomb, but is now in the museum of the cathedral in Florence. It remained in his studio for many years because the artist himself had damaged it when he broke the leg in a moment of frustration and would have destroyed it had his pupils not intervened. The contrast with the Rome *Pietà* of half a century earlier could hardly be greater.

A tormented figure

A troubled spirit now permeates his work and the deliberately awkward pose and lack of beauty relate more to the tormented religious intensity of the Middle Ages. The hooded figure standing at the rear has the unmistakable features of the aged Michelangelo and shows him to be tired, sad and utterly disillusioned with the world.

Pope Julius II (1503–13)

When Cardinal Giuliano della Rovere was elected Pope (fig 27.10) in 1503, he already had a long history as a generous patron of the arts and had quite a collection of antique sculpture. He chose the name Julius and soon humanists began to refer to him as the second Julius Caesar.

The warrior Pope

By his own admission, he was happier with a sword than a book in his hand, and he almost immediately initiated a series of military campaigns to enlarge the Papal States and asserted his authority over dissident clerical movements. Like his ancient predecessor, however, he was determined to leave his mark on Rome and he turned his attention to the rebuilding of the city and pursued it with the same intensity as his military campaigns.

Rome in ruins

When Julius took over the papacy, Rome was a mess. The spiritual capital of Christendom was little more than a shanty town in a series of tumbledown villages clustered around the River Tiber. The new Pope set out to realise his vision of making it the greatest Renaissance city with the most magnificent court of all.

Raising taxes

To do this he needed money. Taxes were levied in the expanding Papal States. In addition, an alum mine had been discovered within his new territory. Alum was an essential ingredient in the dyeing of textiles (the main Italian industry), but it was in short supply and had to be imported from Muslim Turkey. The discovery meant that the Pope was virtually the sole Christian supplier of alum, so he could charge what he liked.

Building Rome

Julius called in Donate Bramante as his chief architect and town planner, but neither Pope nor architect were too fussy about the ruins of Rome's classical past and the Roman Forum as well as the Coliseum served as a stone quarry for the construction of new buildings. Equally devastatingly, the huge new St Peter's Basilica meant the complete demolition of the most venerated ancient religious building in Rome. Despite a widespread belief that St Peter was buried beneath the basilica constructed in 330 AD by the first Christian emperor, Constantine, it was razed to the ground in 1506, earning Bramante the nickname 'Bramante *ruinante*' (wrecker).

FIG 27.10 POPE JULIUS II, Raphael, Uffizi Gallery, Florence

The *Rondanini Pietà*

To one last marble composition, however, Michelangelo entrusted his most dramatic message. He kept the *Rondanini Pietà* (fig 27.11) in his studio and continued to work on it even up to his 89th year, the year of his death. He started it several times, but the final version presented the mother and son in a new revolutionary *pietà* composition, one that interprets the theme psychologically rather than realistically.

An expression of anguish

The son appears to be supporting the mother even after his death and with it Michelangelo declares that the bond between mother and child is like that of the artist with his creation. It has lost all elements of classical restraint and is reduced to its absolute essentials. It is almost modern in its abstract expression of anguish.

FIG 27.11 THE RONDANINI PIETÀ, Michelangelo, Castello Sforzesco, Milan

Conclusion

The perfectly proportioned and flawlessly beautiful male figure of *David* established Michelangelo as the leading artist in Florence without a rival. To this day he remains the most revered sculptor of the Renaissance period.

Questions

1. Why was the tomb of Pope Julius II never finished?
2. Describe Michelangelo's relationship with his patrons.
3. Describe the intended layout of the Medici chapel in San Lorenzo.
4. Why was the statue of *David* placed in the square in Florence rather than in the cathedral, as planned?
5. What method of work did Michelangelo use in carving his figures?
6. Describe the figures in the Medici funerary chapel.

Essay

1. Classical art as well as the work of earlier artists were a significant influence on Michelangelo's sculpture. Discuss this influence and make comparisons, using specific examples.
2. Michelangelo's *David* (fig 27.2) 'rests somewhere between the real and the ideal'. Discuss what is meant by this statement.
3. Michelangelo returned to the subject of the *pietà* many times throughout his lifetime. Compare several examples of the theme and discuss their significance to the artist.

Colour picture study

1. Examine the figure of *Moses* (fig 27.6) from the tomb of Pope Julius II and describe the character that it portrays. Why do you think this figure might have been more impressive if the tomb had been finished according to Michelangelo's plan?

CHAPTER 28

MICHELANGELO – PAINTING

An inferior art form

When Michelangelo first heard that payment for the marble for the tomb of Pope Julius was diverted towards the construction of the new St Peter's, he left Rome in a fit of temper. It seemed that any agreement between the two proud and obstinate men was at an end.

Return to Rome

Pope Julius eventually succeeded in enticing Michelangelo back to Rome, but he informed him that the tomb was not to be finished. Instead, he was asked to paint the ceiling of the largest chapel in the Vatican, the Sistine Chapel (named after the Pope's uncle, Sixtus IV).

With great reluctance and protesting that he was a sculptor and that painting was an inferior art, Michelangelo was eventually persuaded to undertake the project that proved to be his greatest achievement. He turned the vault of the chapel into a huge architectural illusion in imitation white marble decorated with sculpture-like figures that could be described as the realisation of Julius's tomb in paint instead of stone.

The ceiling of the Sistine Chapel

Michelangelo began work in 1508 on nine narrative paintings from the Book of Genesis in alternate larger and small panels (fig 28.1). These represent the opening

FIG 28.1 The ceiling of the Sistine Chapel, Michelangelo, The Vatican, Rome

FIG 28.2 THE SEPARATION OF THE WATERS FROM THE EARTH, detail of the Sistine Chapel, Michelangelo, The Vatican, Rome

passages of the Bible, but the general meaning of the design is unclear and it is not certain why precise subjects were chosen or how the artist imagined the scenes relate to each other.

Creation and Fall

Beginning at the altar wall, the ceiling is divided into three groups that tell the story of the creation of the world, the creation and fall of Adam and Eve and the story of Noah – in other words, the stages of the human race from its inception to its fall. All around are the prophets and sibyls, the Jews and pagans who foretold the coming of Christ and, in the corners, the *Ignudi*, or idealised nude youths, with the ancestors of Christ below.

A change in style

The artist took a break between *The Creation of Eve* and *The Creation of Adam*. The scaffolding was removed so he could see the effect from the ground, and when he returned he simplified much of the detail in the second half. The later scenes of the Creation are far more original and the figures stronger and more monumental.

The scenes

Creating an image

The great scenes of the Creation had rarely been attempted in Christian art and Michelangelo created an entirely new imagery. His commanding God the Father remains the accepted image to this day. This stern and athletic figure reaches upwards to the heavens to create light before wheeling around to form the planets with a mere gesture (fig 28.2).

The Creation of Adam

The ceiling's most famous scene is *The Creation of Adam*. God surges across the empty sky, his great cloak billowing around him filled with angels, and reaches out to the reclining figure of Adam (fig 28.4). They do not quite touch, but a spark of life passes between their outstretched fingers.

The artist

God gives and Adam receives in the same way that God gives the artist the ability to create from nothingness. This is Michelangelo's way of giving praise to God.

Adam and Eve

The Temptation and Expulsion (fig 28.5) represents a decline from beauty to distortion. Before the Fall, Adam and Eve are idealised figures, perfect in all ways. The scene is separated by the Tree of Knowledge twined round with a sly, feminine serpent, and on the other side Adam and Eve are expelled from the Garden of Eden as a mean and graceless image of their former selves. In comparison to Masaccio's figures (see Chapter 23, fig 23.7) in the

Fig 28.3 CREATION OF EVE, detail of the Sistine Chapel, Michelangelo, The Vatican, Rome

FIG 28.4 CREATION OF ADAM, detail of the Sistine Chapel, Michelangelo, The Vatican, Rome

adam (handwritten)

Brancacci Chapel, Michelangelo's faces lack any real character, but they are a reminder that the artist's primary interest was the portrayal of the body and an idealised version of the scene rather than dramatic reality.

Classical sculpture

The ceiling is full of references to classical sculpture. *painted on* (handwritten) Noah resembles a Roman river god and the figure of

Adam is reminiscent of a fragment known as the *Belvedere Torso* (fig 28.6), while several others have unmistakable links to the Roman statue *Laocoön and His Sons* (fig 28.7), which was found not long before in a vineyard near Rome and which Michelangelo helped to unearth.

FIG 28.5 THE TEMPTATION AND EXPULSION OF ADAM AND EVE, detail of the Sistine Chapel, Michelangelo, The Vatican, Rome

FIG 28.6 BELVEDERE TORSO, Vatican Museums, Rome

FIG 28.7 THE LAOCOÖN AND HIS SONS, Vatican Museums, Rome

Michelangelo's techniques

Dissatisfied with traditional methods of fresco painting and mistrustful that his assistants could not keep up with his changing methods, Michelangelo dismissed them all soon after beginning and worked on it entirely alone. To have accomplished such a huge task was absolutely amazing, but he did it in a great burst of energy and the painting of the whole ceiling took him just four years to complete. However, in a poem written by the artist himself, he recounts the effort of painting, bent over backwards, his neck permanently arched to look up while his arm aches as it stretches upwards.

The Last Judgement

Pope Julius II died within one year of the completion of the Sistine Chapel ceiling and for some time after Michelangelo divided his time between Rome and Florence, working for the two Medici Popes, Leo X and Clement VII. Over 20 years later, Michelangelo returned to the Sistine Chapel to paint the largest single fresco of the century.

Shortly before his death, Pope Clement had commissioned a fresco of the Last Judgement (fig 28.8) for the altar wall, but it was his successor, Paul III Farnese, who finalised the project and put Michelangelo under pressure to complete the work in the shortest time possible.

The composition

Placing such a scene on the east rather than the traditional west was highly unusual, but the scheme is quite traditional. The figures are far from traditional, however. Christ is the focal point (fig 28.9) and towers over all the composition. Looking more like a Greek god than the usual image of Jesus, he waves the damned from his presence and calls the saved towards him. Mary, the traditional intercessor, sits by his side.

There is no perspective or landscape, so the swirling mass of figures is carried in a void. On either side of Christ and the Virgin are the saints who have been martyred for their faith. They press forward, holding out the instruments of their gruesome deaths. Among them, St Bartholomew clutches the knife with which he was skinned alive and in the other hand holds his skin. Here Michelangelo has imprinted his own face.

Hell

At the bottom right a boatman ferries the damned across

FIG 28.9 Christ in Judgement, detail of THE LAST JUDGEMENT, Michelangelo, Sistine Chapel, Rome

the river to Hell and raises an oar in a threatening gesture. The people are hurled into the arms of the demons, who drag them down into a bottomless pit. A figure with the ears of a donkey and a serpent entwined around his body is Minos, prince of Hell, and legend has it that Michelangelo painted his face as one of the Pope's assistants because he had objected to the nude figures.

The position of the artist in society

Michelangelo worked with his patrons, despite the difficulties, because they were the ones with enough money to facilitate his grand designs. He established his power and independence as no artist before him had and was fundamentally different from artists of earlier periods. He had a personal vision and was determined to express it, but this was possible for two reasons only.

The position of the artist was hugely improved in the 15th century due to:
- A change in the popular understanding of the artist, fostered by Alberti's writings.
- The development of an open, tolerant, art-loving atmosphere among patrons and high society.

This situation was soon to change, however, as the Reformation and Counter-Reformation rekindled the Church's rigid control of imagery in religious art.

The 'reform' of the nude figures

The Last Judgement was criticised after its completion in 1541 and as time went on opposition to Michelangelo's interpretation of the theme became larger. Objection to the nude figures continued to grow and eventually the scene was 'reformed' in accordance with the artistic policy of the Council of Trent, which had decreed an almost total ban on nudity in religious art. NB

'Dressing' the figures

One of Michelangelo's pupils, Daniele da Volterra, was given the job of making *The Last Judgement* 'decent', thereby earning himself the nickname 'the Breeches-maker'. The figures have remained clothed despite the extensive cleaning of recent years.

Colours

Cleaning has revealed Michelangelo as a brilliant colourist. Traditionally art historians had thought he was more suited to sculpture because his colours were so subdued and dull, but the removal of years of grime has seen the frescos restored to wonderfully vivid lemons, lime greens, pinks and intense blues.

Conclusion

Despite the fame and beauty of the fresco painting in the Sistine Chapel, Michelangelo always considered himself to be a sculptor.

Questions

1. Why did Michelangelo work alone on the ceiling of the Sistine Chapel?
2. What was the significance of the nude male figures in the scheme?
3. Where did Michelangelo place his self-portrait in *The Last Judgement*?
4. Why were the nude figures painted over in *The Last Judgement*?

Essay

1. Examine the scheme for the decoration of the ceiling for the Sistine Chapel and discuss the compositional devices used by Michelangelo to unify the whole work.
2. Discuss the more unusual aspects of Michelangelo's *The Last Judgement* on the altar wall of the Sistine Chapel.

Colour picture study

1. Examine Michelangelo's *The Creation of Adam* from the Sistine Chapel ceiling (fig 28.4) and discuss his treatment of the figures.
2. Examine *The Temptation and Expulsion* (fig 28.5) and make a comparison between it and Masaccio's *Expulsion of Adam and Eve from the Garden of Eden* (see Chapter 23, fig 23.7) from the Brancacci Chapel.

CHAPTER 29

façade (front)

Architecture and sculpture

Medici family power in Florence was dramatically restored thanks to the support of Cardinal Giovanni de' Medici. Lorenzo the Magnificent's son became Pope Leo X in 1513 after the death of Pope Julius and, having known Michelangelo from boyhood, commissioned him to complete the façade for San Lorenzo, the Medici parish church in Florence. The commission came to nothing and the façade remains unfinished to this day, but it led to one of Michelangelo's architectural masterpieces, the Medici Chapel (or New Sacristy), attached to San Lorenzo. The chapel was intended as a blend of architecture and sculpture, but was never fully completed after the Medici family were again expelled from Florence.

The Medici Chapel (the New Sacristy)

The Medici Funerary Chapel in the New Sacristy was intended as a blend of architecture and sculpture but was never fully completed. During its construction the Medici family were again expelled from Florence.

A new expression in architecture

Michelangelo's design explored new possibilities in expression for architecture. He transformed wall surfaces into sculpture and included a completely novel use of classical orders. Like Brunelleschi, he used grey stone, the famous *pietra serena*, to outline the main architectural features and its dark colour contrasted with the white plaster and marble. The sculpture was planned as an integral part of the architecture and if the chapel had been completed, the priest turning from the altar would have seen the tombs of all four of the Medici family members for whom he was praying. He would have followed the gaze of the two Medici dukes on the side walls towards the Virgin and Child, with the Medici saints Cosmas and Damian that should have stood over the double tomb of Lorenzo the Magnificent and his father, Cosimo il Vecchio.

St Peter's Basilica

Pope Julius II was determined to leave a lasting memorial to himself. His grandiose tomb never came to be, but in 1506 he ordered the Basilica of St Peter, built by the Emperor Constantine in the 4th century, to be demolished. The construction of a new basilica began soon afterwards

and building continued – with many alterations to its original design – for almost a century and a half.

FIG 29.1 The dome of St Peter's Basilica, Rome

The dome of St Peter's

Several architects were involved over the years, but in 1546 Pope Paul III asked Michelangelo to be its chief architect. At 81, Michelangelo was reluctant but it was a position of utmost importance, so he accepted the assignment and, as was characteristic, became deeply involved in the project. He is regarded as the principal designer of a large part of the building as it stands today and he centralised the entire space with a huge dome.

An egg-shaped cupola

The dome of St Peter's is not quite as Michelangelo designed it, however. His design was for a spherical (half-circular) cupola, but when he died only the drum (the base on which the dome rests) had been completed. The dome itself was modified to a more egg-shaped design, mainly for structural reasons (fig 29.1).

The drum

Michelangelo's design can still be appreciated nonetheless with its giant order of paired Corinthian columns that appear to be part of the drum, but which, in fact, stand away from it like buttresses. The whole effect creates a strong vertical upward movement that culminates in the dome above.

Conclusion

It had long been an ambition of Michelangelo's to combine the skills of architecture and sculpture. With his work in the Medici Chapel he realised that ambition, but

NB

the great sculptor, painter, poet and architect dedicated the last years of his life to the dome of St Peter's in Rome. He refused payment for the project, considering the work to be for the greater glory of God.

Questions
1. What aspects of the dome of St Peter's were adapted after Michelangelo's death?

Essay
1. Michelangelo's design for the Medici Chapel, or New Sacristy, attached to San Lorenzo, explored new possibilities for architecture. Discuss this statement with reference to the colour scheme, and the artist's plan to use sculpture as an integral part of the overall design. Describe how the chapel would have looked had it been completed.

Colour picture study
1. Study the dome of St Peter's in Rome (fig 29.1) and compare its architectural features with Brunelleschi's dome of Santa Maria del Fiore in Florence (see Chapter 25, fig 25.3).

CHAPTER 30

RAPHAEL

A sweet-tempered genius

After Leonardo and Michelangelo, the third great name associated with the High Renaissance is Raphael. He did not create an independent new style, but instead learned from both of the older artists. He developed their techniques and brought Renaissance art forms to their most complete expression in a classical, serene and long-lasting manner.

Raphaello Sanzio (1483–1520)

Born in Urbino, Raphael was initially trained by his father, a man of culture at the court of Urbino. He introduced the boy to the advanced artistic ideas and humanist philosophy that formed the basis of his extraordinary talent.

He was already an expert painter, but as yet little known, when he arrived in Rome in 1504. Almost immediately he made such a deep impression on Pope Julius that he was given a commission to paint four large rooms in the papal apartments in the Vatican.

An easy personality

Raphael's personality greatly helped his success and although he had neither Leonardo's cleverness nor Michelangelo's powerful drive, he was sweet tempered, easy to work with and completed commissions quickly and without fuss or disagreement.

Death at a young age

Raphael's talents were recognised and fostered by the two Popes, Julius II and his successor, Leo X, but his remarkable career was unfortunately short and he died on his 37th birthday.

Influences

Perugino

Raphael absorbed influences from many artists. After his father died, he worked as an assistant in the large and thriving workshop of the artist Perugino, where he gained extensive professional knowledge. He mastered Perugino's calm, exquisite style and the sweet, lyrical expressions so associated with Raphael's figures came directly from him. In fact, in the beginning, the painting

Fig 30.1 MARRIAGE OF OUR LADY, Perugino, Musée des Beaux-Arts, Caen

styles of Perugino (fig 30.1) and Raphael (fig 30.2) were so similar that it is sometimes difficult to determine which is which.

Leonardo and Michelangelo

Raphael is best known for his many images of Madonnas. These were mostly painted during his time in Florence and Leonardo's influence is very clear. In *La Belle Jardinière* (fig 30.3) (also known as *Madonna and Child with Saint John the Baptist*), Raphael has adopted

FIG 30.2 MARRIAGE OF OUR LADY, Raphael, Pinacoteca di Brera, Milan

FIG 30.3 LA BELLE JARDINIÈRE, Raphael, Louvre, Paris

the pyramidal shape used so often by Leonardo, as in *Virgin of the Rocks* (see Chapter 26, fig 26.8), and softened the edges with *sfumato*.

There is also evidence of Michelangelo's influence in *Madonna of the Goldfinch* (fig 30.4). This is very similar in composition to a relief sculpture by Michelangelo of the Virgin and Child called *Pitti Tondo* (fig 30.5). Michelangelo's children are lively and climb on their mother's knee, but Raphael's child Jesus stretches in a gentle, almost languid manner towards the young St John, who offers him a goldfinch, a symbol of Christ's Passion.

The *Madonna della Sedia*

The *Madonna della Sedia* (*Madonna of the Chair*) (fig 30.6) was painted during the artist's time in Rome and is the most popular of all Raphael's Madonnas. The Virgin's face is the same as that in *La Velata*, or *Portrait of a Veiled Lady* (fig 30.7). No one knows exactly who this was, but there are theories that she may have been

FIG 30.4 THE MADONNA OF THE GOLDFINCH, Raphael, Uffizi Gallery, Florence

FIG 30.5 PITTI TONDO, Michelangelo, Museum of the Bargello, Florence

FIG 30.7 PORTRAIT OF A VEILED LADY, Raphael, Palatina Gallery, Pitti Palace, Florence

Raphael's mistress or fiancée. Certainly he seems to have been fascinated by her beauty, because this is the same face seen in other key works, such as the *Sistine Madonna* (fig 30.8).

The tondo

During the Renaissance, the tondo, or circular shape, was popular. It is a difficult shape to work with because there is no top or bottom, but Raphael cleverly adapted the figures to the outline. The Virgin protectively cradling the infant Christ follows the curve so they become more closely entwined together, making the little Christ into the spiritual centre of the picture. The interlocking arms and legs emphasise the circular composition and the baby's elbow forms the pivotal point.

Raphael was working in Rome when Michelangelo was painting the Sistine ceiling and it had a strong influence on his receptive imagination. The unusual combination of strong red, blue, orange and bright green in the *Madonna della Sedia* may be related to this.

The *Stanze Raphael*

Raphael was still in his early twenties when he began work in the Vatican on his most celebrated work for Pope Julius II. The Pope had chosen this suite of rooms as part

FIG 30.6 MADONNA OF THE CHAIR, Raphael, Piffi Palace, Florence

FIG 30.8 SISTINE MADONNA, Raphael, Gemäldegalerie, Dresden

over the next decade with the assistance of his pupils, and after his death the work continued according to his design. They are now known simply as the *Stanze Raphael*.

The most famous of these compositions, *The School of Athens* (fig 30.9), representing the concept of philosophy, is in the first of the rooms and is called *Stanza della Segnatura* because important papal documents were signed there. This was Julius's personal library and its decoration celebrates the importance of books and learning.

The School of Athens

The ancient Greek philosophers Plato and Aristotle are at the centre of the composition and along with other masters of natural science they are placed in an imaginary architectural setting that may refer to the new St Peter's but may also relate to ancient buildings in Rome. Like Leonardo's *The Last Supper*, all of the architectural perspective lines lead to the main figures standing against the daylight of the arched doorway.

Portraits of the artists

Many portraits of well-known figures are included in the scene and Plato, at the centre of the composition, is thought to have Leonardo da Vinci's face. Aristotle beside him may be Bramante and seated in front, his head propped on one elbow, Michelangelo, representing the Greek philosopher Heraclitus, appears to be

of his own residence and painting had already begun, but Raphael outshone all the other artists so the work was given completely over to him. He frescoed the walls

FIG 30.9 THE SCHOOL OF ATHENS, Raphael, Stanze Raphael, The Vatican, Rome

Aristotle

Raphael

michelangelo

consumed with melancholy. Groups everywhere are engaged in lively debate and to Plato's left, men of all ages listen attentively to Socrates as he emphasises points on the fingers of his left hand. One of the group calls urgently for pen and paper, and a young man laden with parchment – his orange cloak formed cleverly to look like a rolled document – rushes in to record the words of wisdom. In a touch of humour, Pythagoras, in the bottom left-hand corner of the picture, is so wrapped up in his theorems that he does not notice the figure at his elbow, stealing his ideas even as they are formulated.

A position of influence

Leo X became Pope when Julius II died. He appointed Raphael chief architect for the new St Peter's and made him Director of Antiquities. He now had overall responsibility for the conservation of all antiquities as well as excavations in and near Rome. Added to this, the Pope commissioned him to design a set of 10 tapestries for the Sistine Chapel.

Portraits

Raphael's portraits are some of his most compelling works. *Baldassari Castiglione* (fig 30.10) is a particularly sensitive rendition of the well-known Renaissance humanist and courtier, writer and friend of Raphael. Raphael's famous portraits also include impressive images of the two great Renaissance Popes.

Portrait of Pope Julius II

Not only was Raphael court painter, but by all accounts was also a friend and his *Portrait of Pope Julius II* (see Chapter 27, fig 27.10) defined the art of portraiture from the Renaissance onwards. As well as establishing the ideal shape of a portrait and that a painter must know his subject on a personal level, Raphael's psychological insight into the character of his sitter marked a new departure in the history of portraiture.

This is a quiet and pensive moment for this aggressive and impatient man, but the artist has fully grasped the strength of character of his sitter in the deep emotional intensity in Julius's deep-set eyes. As he grips the arm of his throne, this lean and spare man seems filled with a restless energy.

Portrait of Pope Leo X

Raphael's greatest masterpiece is his *Portrait of Pope Leo X* (fig 30.11). The painting created a sensation and captured the character of this much-criticised pontiff.

FIG 30.10 BALDASSARI CASTIGLIONE, Raphael, Louvre, Paris

FIG 30.11 PORTRAIT OF POPE LEO X, Raphael, Uffizi Gallery, Florence

cardinals (also said to be Pope Leo X nephew)

Illuminated manuscript

Bell shows the interest the Pope had in the arts

The Medici Pope was a pious man, but because of his failure to deal with the Reformation he is remembered as an incompetent ruler, more interested in the arts than in the Church. Recent studies have been a little kinder to him and have drawn attention to some of his better qualities. A report by the Venetian ambassador in March 1517 says:

> The pope is a good-natured and extremely free-hearted man, who avoids every difficult situation and above all wants peace; he would not undertake a war himself unless his own personal interests were involved; he loves learning; of canon law and literature he possesses remarkable knowledge; he is, moreover, a very excellent musician.

The portrait is certainly no idealised image, but the beautiful painting has an underlying sense of power and splendour. Lost in thought, the learned Pope has just glanced up from his examination of one of the beautifully illuminated manuscripts in his collection and the finely carved bell on the table alludes to his support for the arts.

In keeping with other representations of his family in Florence, the delicately brocaded cassock and lush velvet cape are depicted with the greatest care, while the subtle handling of the rich red tones adds to the harmonious composition, making it one of Raphael's most admired and significant works.

Along with the Pope, the group portrait features two cardinals, Luigi de' Rossi and Giulio de' Medici (who later became Clement VII), both of whom were related to him.

Perfect and sweet

Raphael's art is sometimes criticised for being too perfect and sweet. Some art historians believe his work lacks Leonardo's or Michelangelo's dynamic power, but Raphael was a great artist who exemplified the tastes of

Pope Leo X

Giovanni de' Medici, son of Lorenzo the Magnificent of Florence, succeeded Julius II to become Pope Leo X in 1513. At 37 years of age, the new Pope was the personification of Renaissance ideals. As the second son, Giovanni was always destined for religious life. He even had his head shaved with the tonsure to indicate this at a young age. Growing up in one of the most sophisticated households of Europe gave him the refined manners and tastes that suited him to the calm and peaceful life in Rome that everyone wanted after 10 years of warlike papacy under Julius II.

Leo devoted much of his papal career to the arts, scholarship and building Rome up as the cultural centre of Europe. He greatly expanded the Vatican Library to house some of his father's collection of fine manuscripts and, like him, supported poets and scholars. He continued the Vatican Stanze and the construction of St Peter's Basilica, making Raphael chief architect as well as giving him responsibility for the conservation of Rome's classical past and commissioning him to design tapestries for the Sistine Chapel. Tapestries were the most expensive of all the arts and as such are probably a fitting monument to a papacy so strongly committed to the arts.

A consistent rumour attributes the phrase 'God has given us the papacy so let us enjoy it' to him, and as part of this enjoyment he travelled around Rome at the head of a great parade featuring panthers, jesters and his own pet white elephant called Hanno. Unfortunately, his lavish expenditure exhausted the savings Julius II had so carefully managed in just two years and brought about a financial crisis from which he never recovered. It also led him to raise money in ways described by his critics as 'shameless'. Clerical positions were sold and money borrowed in large sums, but the most controversial was the practice of giving indulgences (remission of time in Purgatory as penalty for sins) in exchange for financial contributions for the construction of St Peter's. Selling indulgences was one of the main abuses cited by Martin Luther when he nailed his 95 Theses to the door of the Church in Wittenberg, Germany, in 1517, but Leo had no appetite for the reforms so badly needed in the Church and failed to take the growing Lutheran movement seriously. By the time he had condemned Martin Luther as a heretic and excommunicated him, the new movement for reform had the support of influential figures in Germany and was going from strength to strength.

In December 1521, Leo X died suddenly and this led to the ruin of several banking firms as well as many individual creditors. He also left behind political turmoil in Italy and religious turmoil that was spreading rapidly across northern Europe.

his time. He was as famous in his own lifetime as the great Michelangelo, and he received so many commissions that he had a difficult time keeping up with them. Particularly significant is the tremendous effect the artist had on those who followed, given the shortness of his life.

Conclusion

Along with Michelangelo and Leonardo, Raphael became one of the three greatest masters of the High Renaissance. His skilled compositions formed the basis of training successive generations of artists. He died at the early age of 37, but by that time he was a famous, wealthy and very popular personality.

Questions

1. Why did Raphael's personality contribute so much to his success?
2. What was Raphael's position in the papal court?

Essay

1. Raphael's Madonnas represent an image of ideal beauty. Discuss the concept of 'the ideal' or 'godlike beauty' with reference to Raphael's work.
2. Raphael was famous for his perfect compositions. Discuss this aspect of his work and outline the influence of other artists in this.
3. Discuss the importance of portraiture in Renaissance art with specific reference to the work of Raphael and those who influenced him.

Colour picture study

1. Examine Raphael's *The School of Athens* (fig 30.9) and describe the composition of the figures set against architecture. What is the meaning of such a scene and how has Raphael organised the groupings of figures?
2. Examine the *Portrait of Pope Leo X* (fig 30.11) by Raphael and discuss how, with the image of the Pope not idealised in any way, the artist manages to convey an image of a powerful yet cultured man.

CHAPTER 31

RELIGIOUS PAINTING

In early-15th-century Flanders a movement in painting was taking place that was separate to – but equally important as – the developments occurring in Florence.

Flanders was part of the Duchy of Burgundy, which covered a large area of northern France and what is today Belgium. The cities of Ghent and Bruges were also thriving due to a booming trade and the strength of the wool industry. There was a strong demand for religious painting among wealthy urban populations, but the absence of the driving force of humanism meant that the Church was far more influential. Like their Italian counterparts, artists were concerned with realistic space and the human figure, but their depiction of naturalism was very different.

Flemish painting

Solemn facial features and awkward figure postures make Flemish paintings appear medieval in style. Sacred scenes were often placed in ordinary domestic interiors and perspective was less advanced than in Italy (space was often distorted), but Italian artists were very influenced by northern artists. They made clever use of little devices like mirrors to reflect hidden sides of a room and naturalistic landscapes were often glimpsed through open windows. Their careful observation of nature and their portrayal of detail in flowers, jewels and elaborate fabrics greatly impressed the Italians, as did the lustre and brilliance of shiny metal, glass, fur or velvet. This rich detail was possible because Flemish artists mixed traditional paint pigment with oil instead of water for painting on wood panels. In the damp climate, this produced more successful results than fresco. Oil paint gave the paintings a smooth, shiny, velvety surface that dried to a hard, opaque, enamel-like finish. The technique of using thin layers of paint, unknown outside of Flanders, gave the artist the freedom to capture subtle detail.

Jan van Eyck (1390–1441)

Oil painting was known long before the early 15th century, but the artist Jan van Eyck brought this practice to an extraordinary level of refinement and skill. Van Eyck was one of the main founders of the Flemish School and worked with his brother, Hubert, in their native city of Ghent at the same time as Masaccio in Florence. He

developed another key element in painting called atmospheric perspective, which means that objects not only get smaller but colours fade and shapes blur in the atmosphere of a distant landscape.

Although little is known about the artist, it is known that van Eyck worked for Philip the Good, duke of Burgundy, from 1425 to his death in 1441. The duke appears to have held van Eyck in high regard, as much for his intellectual and scientific accomplishments as for his artistic ability.

Van Eyck was the first northern painter whose personality comes through his work. His use of oil paint meant that his work had quite a different finish to Italian paintings in tempera. Slow-drying oil paint allowed the artist to blend the colours and gave him more freedom to make changes than would have been the case with the difficult, quick-drying egg tempera that often resulted in a dry, powdery look. This versatile medium has a tinted translucent look and van Eyck could paint microscopic detail in striking realism infused with a glowing inner light by using layer upon layer of thin oil paint and subtle glazes over the highlights.

The Ghent Altarpiece

One of his earliest and largest surviving paintings is the Ghent Altarpiece. Both of the van Eyck brothers are thought to have worked on this. It is a polyptych (many painted panels) of painted doors that are quietly coloured that when opened have both a spiritual and an intellectual significance. It reveals 12 panels of

Grace

FIG 31.1 THE ADORATION OF THE MYSTIC LAMB, central panel from the Ghent Altarpiece, St Bavo Cathedral, Ghent

splendidly coloured figures in minute detail representing the communion of saints and the 'new heaven and earth' (St John) in its central panel, *The Adoration of the Lamb* (fig 31.1). The saints are gathered around the altar in the heavenly garden to witness the sacrifice of the lamb, which has sprung from Christ's blood, and angels hold the emblems of his Passion. Processions of Old and New Testament characters face one another and members of the Church wear the bright red clothing of martyrdom, while overhead a dove symbolises grace. The landscape of Paradise runs across all five lower panels and the fairy-tale buildings of the heavenly Jerusalem can just be made out in the distance.

The Madonna of Chancellor Rolin

It was very common to include the patron in a prominent position in paintings and this can be seen in one of Jan van Eyck's (nearly) mystical compositions, *The Madonna of Chancellor Rolin* (fig 31.2). It was painted in 1422 for Nicholas Rolin, chancellor of Burgundy, whose position was similar to that of a prime minister.

Kneeling in piety and silent meditation in his magnificent palace, he has become aware of a divine presence and looks up to see the Queen of Heaven crowned by an angel and the infant raising his hand in blessing. Symbols such as lilies in the centre of the terrace

represent the Virgin, but the overall message of the picture suggests that Christ has appeared on earth to redeem humanity from sin.

Van Eyck's mastery of linear and atmospheric perspective are seen in the splendid robes and stunning

FIG 31.2 THE MADONNA OF CHANCELLOR ROLIN, Jan van Eyck, Louvre, Paris

FIG 31.3 THE ARNOLFINI MARRIAGE, Jan van Eyck, National Gallery, London

FIG 31.4 Mirror detail of THE ARNOLFINI MARRIAGE, Jan van Eyck, National Gallery, London

detail, which shows in areas like the floor tiles and the panoramic view seen through the arches and stretching past the town to the hills fading into the distance.

The Arnolfini Marriage

324

The commercial connection between Italy and Burgundy meant that wealthy Italians working in northern cities often patronised the Netherlandish painters. One of these is the subject of *The Arnolfini Marriage* (fig 31.3), van Eyck's most famous work and one of the best-known paintings in the world. The Italian merchant Giovanni Arnolfini and his fiancée, Giovanna Cenami, lived in Bruges. The painting celebrates their betrothal, showing them solemnly holding hands in their elaborate ceremonial costumes. He wears a fur-trimmed cape and large, strange-looking hat, and she an elaborate green velvet gown, the details of which (like the fur and lace on her dress) are painted in minute detail. The room is a model of middle-class prosperity, but the deceptively simple scene is full of symbolic detail, such as the shoes on the floor indicating a holy place to be used for a sacred ceremony. The dog (representing faithfulness) symbolises fidelity in marriage, the fruit on the window

refers to man's innocence in the Garden of Eden and the crystal beads and the spotless mirror indicate Mary's purity. The single burning candle denotes the presence of Christ and also signifies the taking of an oath. The peculiar stance of the bride suggests pregnancy, or it may represent the possibility of children in the future.

The mirror

The painting of the mirror (fig 31.4) on the wall behind the pair is a remarkable piece of miniature technical brilliance. Surrounded by 10 small circles, each containing a tiny scene from the Passion, the centre shows not only reflections of the bed and window curved in the convex glass but also the backs of the figures with the painter facing them as he works.

The inclusion of the artist in the painting in this manner suggests that he is possibly a witness at the ceremony and – as if to emphasise this – he has signed his name on the wall just above in the formal, decorative handwriting associated with legal documents, stating 'Johannes van Eyck Fuit Hic 1434' ('Jan van Eyck was here 1434').

The Portinari Altarpiece (*The Adoration of the Shepherds*)

Jan van Eyck was greatly admired by the Italians, but other Netherlandish painters also impressed them. Tommaso Portinari worked in a branch of Lorenzo de' Medici's commercial bank in Bruges and he commissioned Hugo van der Goes to paint *The Adoration of the Shepherds* (fig 31.5). Portinari brought the triptych back to a church in Florence, where it caused a sensation. The central panel is a very elaborate depiction of the Nativity with angels and saints surrounding the Virgin and Child. It is a strange scene and is filled with all manner of symbolic details. The solemn, stylised religious figures make an interesting contrast to an extremely lifelike group of shepherds kneeling at the side and as the crude but enthusiastic labourers lean over each other to gaze on the scene, their wonder is clear from the expressions on their simple faces and hand gestures. They in particular influenced patrons and artists in Florence.

The Adoration of the Shepherds hangs in the Uffizi Gallery in the same room as *The Birth of Venus*, which was painted at more or less the same time.

FIG 31.5 THE ADORATION OF THE SHEPHERDS, Hugo van der Goes, Uffizi Gallery, Florence

Portraiture

V. important

This portrait is famous for its realism and attention to detail, but it was also the first full-length painting involving real people in a real-life event and it lifted portraiture to a new and more important position.

Conclusion

Jan van Eyck brought a new realism to painting as well as perfecting the skills of oil painting, and his *Arnolfini Marriage* remains one of most famous works in the history of art. It is one of the greatest celebrations of human empathy and an image of a true marriage.

Questions

1. What were the technical advances in painting made by van Eyck?
2. What is the lesson of *The Adoration of the Lamb*?
3. What was atmospheric perspective?

Essay

1. Compare the northern early Renaissance style to that of Italian artists and give the reasons for the differences.

Colour picture study

1. Examine the scene presented in *The Madonna of Chancellor Rolin* (fig 31.2) and comment on it. Make reference to perspective and the fine detail included in the work.
2. Examine *The Arnolfini Marriage* (fig 31.3) and describe the symbolic references included in the work.

Queen of the Adriatic

Florence and Rome suffered as a result of war in the 16th century, but Venice, the 'Queen of the Adriatic', prospered to become the most splendid city in Italy. This city, serving as the crossroads of East and West, was characterised by luxury and an exotic mix of cultures. A powerful and independent city-state, it was the only one to have an overseas empire, so its commercial fleet dominated Eastern trade with Europe for centuries.

Second only to Florence as one of the great Italian Renaissance centres, Venice was slow to adopt the Florentine model of classical architecture. Venice's unique style of building, however, made it the spectacular city we know today.

Painting in Venice

In many ways, Renaissance Venice was the polar opposite of Florence. Sculpture was the important artistic element in Renaissance Florence, but for Venice it was painting. Painters in Venice used vibrant colours in their work. They applied it directly to the canvas and even on rough sketches. Added to this, a loose style of brushwork gave their paintings a smooth, velvety texture and a distinctive style.

Light and colour

In a city built on water, reflections on the blue lagoons tended to blur all sharp outlines and bathed everything in a soft, radiant light. This light played an important role for painters and helped them create atmosphere and mystery, particularly in landscape painting.

Painting on canvas

The most significant contribution that Venice made to the visual arts was the development of oil painting on canvas, which to this day is still widely used by artists.

Oil paint suited the Venetians particularly well because of the damp atmosphere that made fresco painting on plastered walls impossible. Instead, artists stretched canvas over a wooden frame and primed it with white gesso so that the light glowed through the oily paint and glazes.

Giorgione (1477–1510)

Giorgione (meaning 'Big Giorgio') developed the use of more opaque paint that opened up the painting process and relieved the artist of the laborious preparatory tasks involved in making preliminary drawings. This also meant corrections could be made more easily.

Little is known of Giorgione's life – and his early death deprived the Venetian School of its most promising master – but his dreamlike and mysterious painting brought the new word 'poesie' (meaning 'visual poetry') to Renaissance art. Titian, his pupil, probably finished

FIG 32.1 THE TEMPEST, Giorgione, Gallerie del' Accademia, Venice

FIG 32.2 SLEEPING VENUS, Giorgione, Gemäldegalerie, Dresden

several of his paintings – indeed, only a few can be ascribed to him with certainty – but the ones we have are filled with a strange, hazy light and an atmosphere of moody romance.

The Tempest

Giorgione's technique is best seen in a fascinating painting known as *The Tempest* (fig 32.1), one of his few genuine surviving works. Its meaning has been greatly debated and no one knows exactly what it represents, but the painting certainly marks a transformation in the Venetian style of painting.

The meaning of this atmospheric landscape remains a mystery, but the mood stems from the vibrant brightness of a single flash of lightning just before a storm that creates a series of contrasting tones of light and shadow. The man with a staff and the architecture in ruins behind him possibly symbolise construction and destruction, while a mother cradling her child under the trees may represent shelter.

Sleeping Venus

Most Venetian paintings were religious in theme, but there was also a demand among certain wealthy patrons for 'Venuses', or paintings of nude female figures. Giorgione established this motif and so, not surprisingly, his *Sleeping Venus* (fig 32.2) is one of the most perfect Renaissance accomplishments. The mythological goddess of love slumbers beneath a tree in the peace of

the countryside, seemingly unaware of her nakedness. In true Giorgione style, the soft afternoon sunlight brings the landscape and girl together in a picture of poetic beauty.

Arcadia

Giorgione's painting was inspired by a popular type of pastoral poetry that drew on the ancient notion of the rural landscape as a place where urban dwellers might retire to dream of love and contemplate the meaning of life. It remained one of the most popular genres of European literature for generations, with its theme linked – both in the classical and the Renaissance mind – to a vision of a lost golden world of a mythical landscape. This untroubled secular paradise peopled by serene and wise shepherds and shepherdesses was known as Arcadia.

Venus of Urbino

Giorgione influenced his young assistant and friend, Tiziano Vecelli, or Titian, who is said to have completed his *Sleeping Venus* after his master's death. Titian dealt with the Venus theme in a number of later works, the best known of which is the *Venus of Urbino* (fig 32.3).

The similarities are immediately obvious between both paintings, but Giorgione's silent and untouched landscape has now become a private room and although the pose is almost the same, Titian's is a much more erotic image. Titian's girl is awake, quite aware of her audience and conscious of her charms.

FIG 32.3 VENUS OF URBINO,
Titian, Uffizi Gallery, Florence

The picture was painted to celebrate a marriage and has many symbolic references, including a little dog curled up on the bed (symbolising fidelity). In the background, the maids can be seen with an open 'marriage' chest.

Concert Champêtre

Titian worked as Giorgione's assistant until his death in 1510. Some works once attributed to Giorgione are now considered to have been by Titian. *Concert Champêtre* (*Pastoral Concert*) (fig 32.4) is one contentious work. For

years this strange painting was considered to be the pinnacle of Giorgione's creative career, but now it is believed to have been painted, or at least finished, by Titian.

Titian (1485–1576)

After Bellini's death, Titian became the painter to the Republic. He had acquired all his technical skill and innovations from Giorgione and was the most expressive painter of his time. He remained one of the great names

FIG 32.4 CONCERT CHAMPÊTRE, Titian, Louvre, Paris

in European art. His rich colours and painterly technique were widely imitated.

Assumption of the Virgin

Titian's *Assumption of the Virgin* (fig 32.5), the altarpiece in the Basilica of Santa Maria Gloriosa dei Frari in Venice, broke with tradition with its bold colour and innovative composition. Some at the time were uneasy, however, with the painter's novel portrayal of the Virgin, clothed in vibrant red and positioned in a dramatic twisting movement, rising above the dynamically gesticulating apostles.

Bacchus and Ariadne

The *Assumption of the Virgin* marked the first monumental work of the High Renaissance in Venice, but Titian was also commissioned by Alfonso d'Este, duke of

FIG 32.6 BACCHUS AND ARIADNE, Titian, National Gallery, London

Ferrara, to paint a number of mythological compositions. One of these was an exuberant scene depicting a dramatic moment when the wine god Bacchus falls in love with Ariadne, daughter of the king of Crete.

Bacchus and Ariadne (fig 32.6) illustrates a theme from classical mythology, but the real theme of this picture is the idea of love at first sight. Ariadne fell in love with Theseus, and for him she helped to kill the Minotaur at the palace of Knossos on the island of Crete – but then he abandoned her. Now, as she wanders along the shore in search of her lover's ship, she is surprised by Bacchus, the wine god, and, startled by his noisy group of followers, she looks up with a mixture of shock and fear. Bacchus immediately asks her to marry him, offering her the sky as a wedding gift. The promised crown of stars can be seen in the sky above Ariadne's head.

Colour

The picture is famous for its spectacular colours and unusual pigments, such as the intense ultramarine blue and the deep reds. To complement these primary colours, Titian chose a rare and beautiful gold-orange pigment for some of the clothing.

Classical references

The composition forms a triangular shape with Bacchus as the central element, and there are various references to classical sculpture. The wine god's dramatic leap

FIG 32.5 ASSUMPTION OF THE VIRGIN, Titian, Venice

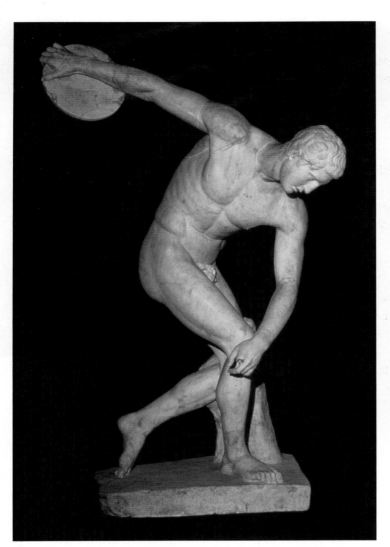

Fig 32.7 THE DISCUS THROWER, Myron, Victoria and Albert Museum, London

Fig 32.8 ECCE HOMO, Titian, National Gallery of Ireland, Dublin

 330 recalls the pose of an antique Greek sculpture, the *Discus Thrower* (fig 32.7), and among his group of rowdy followers, the snake-wrestling satyr relates to the famous classical statue, *Laocoön and His Sons* (see Chapter 28, fig 28.7).

Spiritual response

Titian created one of his most moving and deeply spiritual paintings when he was almost 80. He painted the subject many times, but *Ecce Homo* (fig 32.8) (in the National Gallery of Ireland) is perhaps the finest rendition of this pathetic subject. The bright yellow glow of the halo places this 'Man of Sorrow' face in shadow with downcast eyes, but its soft, painterly tones serve only to enhance this deeply moving image of a gentle Christ bound, tortured, beaten and crowned with thorns.

Unlike many other great artists of the Renaissance whose talents spread over a range of activities, Titian was only a painter, but he left a huge body of work on almost every subject. When he died at about 90 he was a rich man and the most famous artist in Europe.

Conclusion

Because of its unique location, Venice was less susceptible to outside influences and its paintings are quite distinctive. Maybe something about the light coming off the Adriatic contributed to this because long before the Impressionist artists in France became fascinated by the effect of light on water, Venetian painters were exploring the interplay between light and colour.

Questions

1. What was the most significant aspect of Venetian painting to the world of the visual arts?
2. What does the term 'poesie' suggest in relation to Venetian painting?
3. Describe the concept of Arcadia.
4. Who were the main painters of Venice?

Essay

1. Who was Giorgione and what particular aspects of his work have made it so famously mysterious?
2. The painter Titian left a huge body of work on almost every subject. Discuss some of these works and comment on the changes of concept and style that occurred over his lifetime.

Colour picture study

1. Examine the *Sleeping Venus* (fig 32.2) by Giorgione and compare it to the *Venus of Urbino* (fig 32.3) by Titian. Draw attention to symbolic detail and discuss the similarities and the obvious differences of both works. Suggest for whom these might have been painted.
2. Examine Titian's *Bacchus and Ariadne* (fig 32.6) and describe the scene. Identify some of the colours for which the painting is so famous.

The Renaissance spreads

Intellectuals in northern Europe had long been suspicious of the pomp and majesty of the Roman Church. Piety in these countries was far more austere, so a revolt against the authority of the Pope was threatened long before the Reformation fully took hold. Towards the end of the 15th century there was a widespread belief that the end of the world might be near, and this was combined with a deep feeling of pessimism with the state of the world.

This notion that the world was in deep spiritual peril emanated mainly from the German writer Desiderius Erasmus. Erasmus was a humanist scholar, but northern humanism was unique in that unlike its Italian counterpart, it was coloured from the beginning by a strong spirit of religious reform. Although Erasmus remained a devout Catholic, his writing sowed the seeds for religious upheaval and influenced a generation of thinkers and clerics to speak openly of their discontent. These ideas spread rapidly among intellectuals due to the new technology of the printing press.

Albrecht Dürer (1471–1528)

The artist Albrecht Dürer was similar to Erasmus in many ways. A learned and well-travelled man, he too had been inspired by Italy after he visited there. Italian art had a strong influence on his work and he noted with envy the far higher status of the artists in Italy than in his own land. Even though he absorbed many Italian ideas, Dürer remained very much his own man.

Dürer's works include a series of self-portraits. His first painted self-image was painted when he was 22 (fig 33.1). At 26 he produced another showing him to be slender and aristocratic in a self-confident pose, proclaiming his success in wealth and status (fig 33.2). With his hair artificially curled, he is dressed according to Venetian fashion in an elegant jacket edged with black, beneath which he wears a white pleated shirt, embroidered along the neckline. His striped hat matches the jacket and the artist completes the luxurious costume with fine leather gloves that are intended to distance himself from a manual worker. The Germans' view of the artist as a craftsman was bitterly unacceptable to Dürer, so he created an image of an

artist of high standing. The dramatic mountain view seen through the window refers to his Italian travels, indicating that this is no limited provincial but a man sure of his own genius.

Self-portraits

The third and most striking of his self–portraits, at age 28, shows the artist full-face, with flowing hair, staring

Fig 33.1 SELF-PORTRAIT AT 22, Albrecht Dürer, Louvre, Paris

FIG 33.2 SELF-PORTRAIT AT 26, Albrecht Dürer, Museo del Prado, Madrid

FIG 33.3 SELF-PORTRAIT IN A FUR-COLLARED ROBE, Albrecht Dürer, Alte Pinakothek, Munich

coldly out at the viewer (fig 33.3). This is a sombre image of a wise man, or even a German Leonardo Da Vinci, but there the connection with Italy ends for this is a picture of distinctly northern piety.

For the first and only time in art history the face is clearly portrayed in imitation of the head of Christ. In late medieval art, Jesus was traditionally presented looking straight ahead with brown hair parted in the middle and falling over the shoulders. Dürer deliberately set out to create a Christ-like image, with his hand raised in blessing, but this was no gesture of arrogance or blasphemy. It was a statement of faith: Christ was the son of God and God had created man, so this was an acknowledgment that artistic skills were a God-given talent and that it is man's duty to think and meditate on Christ's example.

Woodcuts

Like Erasmus, Dürer was a master of the new printing technology and woodcuts formed a large part of his work. He responded to the wave of apocalyptic (end of the world) feeling in a series of 15 woodcuts illustrating scenes from the Apocalypse and based on the Book of Revelation. These large, imaginative prints with their

terrifying visions of the horrors of Doomsday and the signs preceding it were an immediate success. Never before had they been visualised with such force and power. The Four Horsemen of the Apocalypse arrive after the opening of the first four seals (Rev. 6: 1–8), bringing plague, war, hunger and death to mankind (fig 33.4).

The first horseman is the Conqueror and holds a bow, next comes War with a sword, then Famine with a pair of scales and finally Death, on a sickly pale horse, closely followed by Hades, a hideous Leviathan. Urged on by an avenging angel in the sky, the pitiless riders descend upon the Earth to trample all unfortunate humans beneath their hooves and Hades swallows everything in his enormous jaws.

Dürer also made numerous pencil sketches. He treasured his own sketches and signed many of them with his famous monogram and dated them, even though they were generally not intended for sale, but to be gifts for close friends. Approximately 1,000 of his sketches have survived.

Conclusion

As well as a painter, Albrecht Dürer is considered one of the greatest printmakers of all time. Working with both woodcuts and engravings, he attained a level of detail that is virtually unsurpassed.

Questions

1. Describe some of Dürer's woodcuts and outline the reasons for their popularity.

Essay

1. 'Dürer was a learned and well-travelled man whose work was inspired by Italian art but who remained very much his own man.' Discuss this statement with reference to his series of self-portraits.

Colour picture study

1. Examine the self-portrait Albrecht Dürer made at age 28 (fig 33.3) and discuss this as an image of piety. Describe the unusual aspects of the work and its references.

CHAPTER 34

ART, POLITICS AND REVOLUTION

French Impressionist painting is today one of the most popular of all the European art movements. The museums that house Impressionist paintings are constantly crowded with admiring onlookers, but they were mocked and ridiculed when they were first shown to the public. The artists were regarded with deep suspicion and even considered to be dangerous revolutionaries. This reaction seems rather strange since Impressionist paintings have no political or social overtones. Indeed, they are for the most part colourful, cheerful in mood and easy to understand (fig 34.1).

To appreciate the difficulties experienced by the Impressionists, it is important to know something about the level of insecurity that existed in French society in the years leading up to the 20th century as a result of political upheavals.

FIG 34.1 THE BRIDGE AT ARGENTEUIL, Claude Monet Musée d'Orsay, Paris. Claude Monet's delightful summer picture of reflections in the water was painted near the bridge at Argenteuil where he lived at the time.

Political turmoil in 19th-century France

Revolution to republic

Society in France was ripped apart by the revolution of 1789. The monarchy was overthrown and France was declared a republic. The execution of King Louis XVI and his wife, Marie Antoinette, with the guillotine in 1793 was followed by the bloody and chaotic Reign of Terror, during which other members of the nobility were beheaded.

Republic to empire

Napoleon Bonaparte brought stability and reassurance to France with the **First Empire**, but his reign was short lived and he was defeated at Waterloo in 1815 by the English and Austrian armies. The Bourbon Restoration brought with it a sharp conservative reaction when the dead king's brother took over the throne, becoming Louis XVIII, and then followed on his death by another brother, Charles X. He was deposed in a revolution in 1830 and a distant cousin, Louis-Philippe, was proclaimed the French king. He abdicated in 1848 and Napoleon's nephew, Louis-Napoléon Bonaparte, took control. Within a year he became **Emperor Napoleon III** and transformed France into the **Second Empire**.

Empire to republic

This government was quite successful, but in 1870 the emperor led the country into a disastrous war with Prussia. A humiliating defeat ended the Second Empire almost overnight and France was once again declared a republic. It remains so to this day.

Changes in society

The Industrial Revolution

The Industrial Revolution brought even more divisions to French society. As well as creating a rich, new middle class (or bourgeoisie), it also produced a social class that lived and worked in appalling conditions.

The Commune

Workers became more and more resentful until the defeat in the Franco-Prussian War presented an opportunity for them to organise a revolutionary government (or **Commune**) to fight for social justice. Young men erected barricades around Paris, but the fighting lasted only a very short time and it was ruthlessly and bloodily suppressed.

Revolution and art

Revolution and empire

All of this had an influence on art. Revolutionaries saw themselves almost as Greeks and Romans reborn. During the patriotic fervour of the revolution, an austere form of art known as **Neo-Classicism** was the favoured style. This was later adapted to suit the stately dignity of **Napoleon's empire**.

Romanticism

The Romantic movement that followed continued to glorify contemporary events and scenes. For example, *Liberty Leading the People* by **Eugène Delacroix** commemorated the July Revolution of 1830 that brought Louis-Philippe to the French throne.

The Academic system and the art movements that challenged it

The Academy

The government-controlled Academy (École des Beaux-Arts or Académie des Beaux-Arts) rigorously trained students in a rigid standard of artistic taste and exhibited the work of artists once a year at the Salon, which was the greatest annual art event at the time. The system, of course, did not suit all artists and towards the end of the 19th century artists searched for other ways to express their ideas.

Realism

Several movements emerged to challenge the system. In the first of these movements the artist Gustave Courbet aimed to shock society out its complacency and to protest against the accepted conventions of the day with his **Realism**.

The *Plein Air* painters (the Barbizon school)

As part of the Realist movement, artists worked near the **village of Barbizon** and from them **Claude Monet and Pierre-Auguste Renoir** learned to appreciate the subtlety of nature and work directly on canvas out of doors, or *en plein air*.

Paris during the Second Empire

Emperor Napoleon III commissioned the redevelopment of Paris and during the 1860s **Édouard Manet** represented the prosperous modern city with scenes of entertainment and fashionably dressed people. His work was regarded with great suspicion by the public.

The Franco-Prussian War and the Commune

The return of famine and siege to the streets of Paris during the Franco-Prussian War of 1870 as well as the new 'Terror' of the Commune deeply upset an already insecure society and made its members fearful of revolution again.

Impressionism

A group of artists began painting nature in a completely new manner. Their work was rejected by the Salon (the official art exhibition of the Academy), so they held their own private exhibitions. They were considered dangerous and revolutionary.

Impressionism to modern art movements

The artists persevered until Impressionism became one of the most popular styles of all times. It brought lasting changes to French painting and the Academic system. It can be considered the first of the modern art movements of the 20th century.

Questions
1. List the regime changes that took place during the 19th century in France.
2. What effect did the Industrial Revolution have on 19th-century French society?
3. List the art movements that took place during 19th-century France.

CHAPTER 35

TOWARDS IMPRESSIONISM

Classicism and Romanticism

The Academy maintained strict order in its teaching and its grades and prizes were the first honours an aspiring young artist sought to receive. During the years following the French Revolution, the art favoured by the Academy embraced the 'noble and 'ideal' in the classical style, which had first been introduced to France in the 17th century by Nicolas Poussin.

Nicolas Poussin and Classicism

The French artist Nicolas Poussin (fig 35.1) spent most of his artistic career in Rome, where he was heavily influenced by the classical ideals of Italian art. This in turn greatly influenced French art because of his many patrons in France. The Royal Academy of Painting and Sculpture, was established in 1648 based on his concepts. The official teaching at the Academy followed his theory that drawing was the fundamental basis of painting and that history painting ranked highest in artistic value.

Neo-Classicism

Poussin's influence remained strong, and in the late 18th and early 19th centuries a new imitation of classicism and Roman art became popular. Jacques-Louis David, the

FIG 35.1 THE TRIUMPH OF PAN, Nicholas Poussin, Louvre, Paris

leading painter of the Neo-Classical movement, passed on his passion for the style to his students and, in particular, to Jean Auguste Dominique Ingres.

Classicism at the French Academy

Jean Auguste Dominique Ingres

Ingres spent many years developing his skills and achieving success in Italy. He returned to France after the fall of Napoleon, where he found that his traditional and classical approach to painting was well received by the new regime. He was appointed director of the French Academy, a position he held for over 40 years, and he became an influential member of the Salon jury that upheld the 'noble and ideal' standard of the classical style, which valued historical painting above all else and considered drawing to be the basis for all painting. The problem with the classical style was not that it or the theories it embraced were in any way faulty in themselves, but the fact that over the years they changed from ideals to a rigid set of formulas that guaranteed success and respectability for any artist who conformed to them and rejection and accusations of mediocrity for any who chose another path. As a result, Ingres's name has become associated with Academic art at its most sterile, which is unfortunate.

Formulas in art

With advancing age, Ingres's own polished style hardened into a dogma that he imposed on others. He believed that the 'inner form' could be expressed through line alone and he often chose to portray his figures in profile in the Greek fashion, using a sinuous, unbroken line. He firmly believed that line was far superior to colour in painting. His personal view became a set academic rule that opened the way for a disagreement that became one of art history's most memorable controversies in a 'battle of styles' among artists.

The line or colour debate

The battle lines were drawn, with Ingres on one side as the fearless defender of line, ideal beauty and classical tradition, against **Eugène Delacroix**, representing the colour and passion of **Romanticism**. The press reported on the debate with enthusiasm, writing numerous articles, while caricaturists made drawings and more and more people entered the dispute on one side or the other. The real debate was political, however. The Academic establishment had a good deal of influence over public opinion and it favoured 'safe' classical subjects derived from the history or myths of ancient Greece and Rome. Ingres therefore represented the establishment, and those who were against him were seen as rebellious and dangerous.

Ingres's career as a painter

Ingres's own paintings are a peculiar mixture of convention and contradiction, making it quite difficult to classify them within a particular style. He adored Italian art and favoured the traditional method of Academic study from the nude and classical art. His technique as a painter was academically flawless and his own view was that paint should be as smooth 'as the skin of an onion', but his vision of ideal beauty also led him to distort the proportions of his figures and the critics roundly attacked him for this.

The *Valpinçon Bather*

In 1808, while still in Italy, Ingres sent some paintings to Paris for submission to Salon. One was the now-famous *Valpinçon Bather* (fig 35.2), which got its name later on from the person who bought it in 1822. Ingres had a

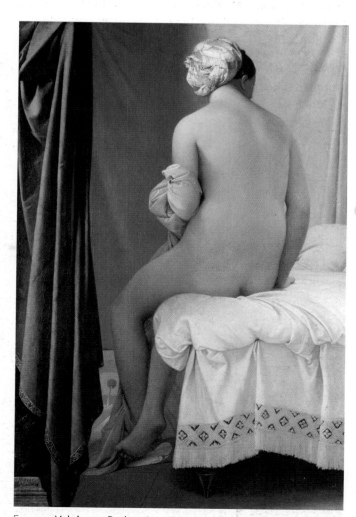

FIG 35.2 Valpinçon Bather, Jean Auguste Dominique Ingres, Louvre, Paris

lifelong love of painting women, but compared to the nudes painted by his contemporaries this small, hushed image of an exotic bather in a fantasy oriental setting is highly unique.

The Valpinçon Bather is generally regarded today as one of Ingres's finest works, but it was not well received in its day. Devoid of classical trappings and appealing directly to the senses, the critics found it hard to comprehend and were disturbed by elements such as the deliberately distorted proportions in the model's right leg and the bed supported by just one carved wooden point. The back view was also considered highly unusual, but was in fact very clever in that it had the effect of gently drawing the spectator into the tranquil and almost poetic mood created by the small setting. The subtle light and hidden face added to the mystery of the scene.

Inspired by Renaissance artists

Ingres was inspired by the freely distorted and elongated figures of the late, or Mannerist, works by Michelangelo and other artists that he saw in Italy to produce his own unique vision of ideal feminine beauty. However, his sketches for these paintings are often completely naturalistic. A study in pencil for the painting *Vénus à Paphos* (fig 35.3) is an example of his superb draughtsmanship and his skilled use of line captures the elegance and grace of the figure.

Fig 35.3 VÉNUS Á PAPHOS, Jean August Dominique Ingres, Musée d'Orsay, Paris

Eugène Delacroix

Like other artists of the time, Eugène Delacroix had begun his art career by entering the Academy of Arts but acquired much of his education and skills by copying works of the Old Masters at the Louvre.

Influences on the artist

Delacroix spent time in England and was impressed by English watercolour paintings. He came to appreciate the potential of outdoor, or *en plein air*, painting that was soon to become such an important part of the study of art. Delacroix also found inspiration in the subject matter of the new music and poetry. He was also greatly inspired by the Orient and Eastern costumes and colour.

Influence from Morocco

Delacroix took a trip to Morocco and was overwhelmed by what he saw there. It was one of the most important journeys of his career. He spent six weeks in Tangiers and visited the sultan's palace, where the French party were given gifts of Arab horses as well as exotic animals, including lions and tigers. While there, he filled notebooks with drawings of local details and gathered facts that he would use in the many paintings on Oriental subjects that he would produce over the next 30 years (fig 35.4). These pictures were always far more than observational studies because Delacroix believed imagination was an essential element of painting.

The power of colour

The light and colour in Morocco inspired Delacroix to experiment. Rejecting the teachings of the Academy on the supreme importance of drawing, he chose instead to work with colour. He discovered the power of colour relationships by placing complementary colours together. Creating vibrant colour harmonies, he avoided black completely and relied on reflected violet and green to intensify the richness of shadow and make flesh tones brighter. He also studied the work of scientists on colour and famously wrote, 'One must be bold to extremity; without daring, and even extreme daring, there is no beauty.'

Liberty Leading The People

Delacroix's best-known work was inspired by the July Revolution of 1830, in which King Charles X was deposed from the French throne in favour of the 'Citizen King', Louis-Philippe. In *Liberty Leading The People* (fig 35.5), the figure of Liberty (personified as a woman) wears the

FIG 35.4 LION HUNT, Eugène Delacroix, Art Institute of Chicago, USA

red hat of the revolutionaries and is followed by a ragtag mob. She runs forward, her naked breasts symbolising the social virtues of republicanism, with a bayonet-fitted rifle in one hand and the flag in the other. The message is mixed, though, and Liberty is not absolutely the leader. A Parisian urchin runs ahead of her, and her own followers include a top-hatted bourgeois who may indeed be the artist himself.

FIG 35.5 LIBERTY LEADING THE PEOPLE, Eugène Delacroix, Louvre, Paris

The government's reaction

This first modern political composition marked a turning point in Romanticism's ability to find inspiration in contemporary life. The painting was not well received at the Paris Salon of 1831, however. It was bought by the state but kept from view because Louis-Philippe was afraid of its power. It was only in 1848, after new revolution swept away his government, that *Liberty Leading Her People* was displayed.

The line versus colour debate

A somewhat artificial divide between Classicism and Romanticism continued to dominate artistic debate. The rivalry between these two painting styles centred on the virtue of line (favoured by Ingres) versus colour (favoured by Delacroix). It was as much about the intense personal dislike of the artists for each other as anything else, but their followers took up the debate and for years the cafés and studios buzzed with heated discussions. The press, of course, enjoyed printing the disparaging remarks made by the artists but Delacroix lost the battle to Classicism, failing completely to capture the Academy, and was not elected to membership until he was an old man close to death.

Influence on later artists

Delacroix's artistic output was enormous and he prided himself on the speed at which he worked. His long letters and journals provide a marvellously rich source of information on his opinions, but his real influence was to come later when artists finally accepted his liberation of colour. Among those he inspired were Renoir, Seurat, Cézanne and van Gogh.

Conclusion

The Academy favoured 'noble' and 'ideal' art in the classical style and during the years that Jean Auguste Dominique Ingres was head of the establishment, his own polished style hardened into a fixed dogma. Eugène Delacroix challenged the position of drawing in Academic teaching when he discovered the power of colour harmonies, but his real influence was to come much later when artists like Seurat, Cézanne and van Gogh eventually accepted his theories on colour and began to explore its possibilities.

Questions

1. Name some of the characters in drawings by Jean Auguste Dominique Ingres.
2. Describe the techniques Ingres used to achieve a fine finish on his paintings.
3. What was the colour–line debate?
4. How did the artist Eugène Delacroix influence later artists?

Essay

1. Outline the importance of art of the past as an influence on classical painting with reference to the work of Jean Auguste Dominique Ingres.

Colour picture study

1. When *The Valpinçon Bather* was first exhibited, it was considered 'irrational, awkward and impossible to understand' by the critics. Examine the painting (fig 35.2) and discuss whether or not you agree with these criticisms. Compare the work to another painting by Jean Auguste Dominique Ingres and describe your own reaction to the artist's 'vision of ideal beauty'.

CHAPTER 36

LANDSCAPE AND THE BARBIZON PAINTERS

Background

Traditionally, artists made sketches out of doors but finished paintings in the studio.

Influence of John Constable

When the English artist John Constable exhibited his picture *The Haywain* (fig 36.1) at the Paris Salon of 1824, it created a remarkable impression. Eugène Delacroix was particularly affected by it and began to imitate its shifting light, flickering brushwork and broken colour in his own work.

But while Constable's painting shone a new light on ordinary, everyday subjects from the countryside, he was more concerned about conveying a moral through his work rather than realism for its own sake. He sketched a great deal and observed atmospheric effects out of doors, but his large paintings were always done in the studio.

The collapsible painting tube

At this time oil painting on canvas required a good deal of cumbersome equipment, so it was really only possible to paint indoors in a studio. In 1842 Winsor and Newton invented the collapsible tin painting tube and this was one of the things made it easier to paint outdoors.

FIG 36.1 THE HAYWAIN, John Constable, National Gallery, London

FIG 36.2 LANDSCAPE WITH BRIDGE, Jean Baptiste Camille Corot, Russell-Cotes Art Gallery and Museum, Bournemouth

The Barbizon painters

When a group of painters chose to specialise only in landscapes, they were moving considerably away from traditional art practice. This group of artists chose to live outside of Paris in the village of Barbizon and sketch directly from nature out of doors (or *en plein air*) on the edge of the forest of Fontainebleau where the peasants, houses, the trees and the plain near the village became an endless source of inspiration.

The Barbizon painters set out to make a realistic record of nature without historical or mythological interpretations. There were nonetheless certain romantic overtones of gloom, grandeur or melancholy in their works, which was probably because paintings were finished in the studio, where the painter tended to add meaning or emotion to the work.

In contrast, when the Impressionists began to work completely out of doors in the 1870s, their aim was to make an 'on-the-spot record' of what they saw, with little or no inclusion of ideas or feelings. The first painter to work regularly at Barbizon was Théodore Rousseau. He was followed by others, including Jean-François Millet and Charles-François Daubigny, and they were joined on a regular basis by Jean-Baptiste-Camille Corot.

Camille Corot

By the 1860s Jean-Baptiste-Camille Corot and the Barbizon painters had acquired a certain status. Although not yet accepted by the Academy, their work was shown regularly at the Salon.

Gentle landscapes

In line with the Salon tradition, Corot's work frequently included classical or literary figures. His landscapes are characterised by a gentle, still silvery-toned mood of slightly overcast days, often with twilight approaching (fig 36.2, fig 36.3).

FIG 36.3 GUST OF WIND, Jean Baptiste Camille Corot, Pushkin Museum, Moscow, Russia

Critical of Impressionism

Corot is a transitional figure in this period. He strongly influenced younger painters through his constant praise of nature. He urged his followers to hold fast to the first impression they received from a scene, even though he often added features like trees or even nymphs to 'improve' his paintings and please the Salon. In the end, he criticised the Impressionists and condemned their work, but he was a helpful influence on Pissarro, Monet, Renoir, Berthe Morisot and other younger painters, and his own works have a fresh, country air feeling unmatched by any French painter of his generation.

Conclusion

It was a considerable move from tradition for the Barbizon painters to work out of doors (or *en plein air*) and specialise in landscape painting. Camille Corot was highly influential within the group, but even though he encouraged younger painters in their efforts to study nature, in the end he remained quite conservative and was willing to 'improve' his work to please the Salon.

Questions

1. Why did artists choose to work *en plein air*?
2. Why was it easier to work out of doors than in earlier times?

Essay

1. Who were the Barbizon painters and how did landscape painting become an important subject in its own right?

Colour picture study

1. Look at *Gust of Wind* (fig 36.3) by Camille Corot and describe the mood achieved by the artist in this painting.

CHAPTER 37

REALISM

Academic art was challenged again in the 1850s. This time Gustave Courbet painted scenes from his own farming background and his work reflected his own staunch socialism. He chose subjects that avoided everything that had previously been thought suitable for fine art.

Gustave Courbet (1819–77)

Courbet was a farmer's son from Ornans in south-eastern France near the Swiss border. He was a larger-than-life character and was often at the centre of controversy because of his bull-like appearance and reputation as an arrogant, beer-swilling peasant. In fact, under this imposing public image was an intelligent and sensitive man.

The 'Temple of Realism'

Courbet became involved with a group of intellectuals who met in a Paris café, the Brasserie Andler, which they renamed the 'Temple of Realism' because it was here that they discussed their theories on art and literature. The Realist group criticised Academic art and felt that art should be based on real situations. Rejecting traditional subjects, they favoured ordinary scenes of modern life over historical, mythological and religious subjects.

'Truth, not prettiness'

Courbet said he wanted 'truth, not prettiness' and was determined to portray the world as he saw it. He aimed to shock society with straightforward images of contemporary rural society and accurate representations of farmers, gravediggers, woodsmen and poachers in paintings that glorified their hard work. He and his followers objected to smooth, slick, 'false surface' paintings that had no real texture and they experimented with rough, unfinished textures in their paintings.

Exhibiting at the Salon

The Salon was the only opportunity for young and aspiring artists to exhibit their work, but Courbet found it very difficult to get his paintings shown there. In 1848 another short-lived revolution in Paris brought Louis-Napoléon Bonaparte to power as president of the French Republic. That year the Salon opened without a selection

FIG 37.1 BURIAL AT ORNANS, Gustave Courbet, Musée d'Orsay, Paris

committee and Courbet had 10 works displayed, one of which was purchased by the government and won a gold medal. As a result, he was exempt from subsequent selection processes and free to present Realist scenes from his beloved home town of Ornans, which he visited regularly.

A Burial at Ornans

The first of his great masterpieces created a storm of outrage when it was exhibited at the 1850 Salon. *A Burial at Ornans* (fig 37.1) proclaimed the dignity of an ordinary life and death in a highly dramatic fashion, but it shocked contemporary French critics. They said it was 'too big and the figures were too ugly'.

In the Academic tradition, large paintings were reserved for historical, religious or mythological subjects and workers and peasants were suitable only for smaller genre scenes. But Courbet's painting was huge, some 21 feet by 10 feet, and the effect of its nearly 60 life-sized figures standing around the open grave was stunning. It may have been Realism at its most powerful, but the raising of this scene to the status of an historical painting deeply offended observers used to a more romanticised and idealised image of peasant life. It was seen as a 'glorification of vulgarity'.

Political statements

From then on Courbet's paintings were interpreted as political statements intended to provoke and were refused by the jury of the Universal Exhibition of 1855 in Paris. Courbet responded by setting up a one-man show and opened his own pavilion close to the site of the official exhibition, advertised under a single heading, 'Realism'. The enterprise failed, but it was to be the turning point of Courbet's career. Less reliant on the Salon to advance his career, from then on he received increasing support from outside Paris until by 1859 he was the undisputed leader of the Realist movement.

Bonjour, Monsieur Courbet

His paintings offended the Academic notions of dignity and grandeur. He represented himself in *Bonjour, Monsieur Courbet* (fig 37.2) with no graceful poses but as a simple representation of the artist walking across the country to visit the home of Alfred Bruyas, a distinguished collector in Montpellier. He portrays himself in his shirt sleeves with a stick and painting equipment strapped to his back. This direct, anti-bourgeois gesture must have outraged those who expected an image of the 'respectable' artist. The

Fig 37.2 BONJOUR, MONSIEUR COURBET, Gustave Courbet, Musée Fabre, Montpellier, France

painter, however, holds his head high and meets his patron as an equal, while behind the servant stands with head bowed. The pose was based on a popular print, *The Wandering Jew*, an image that would have been associated with the outsider in 19th-century thinking. Courbet is, of course, identifying himself with this figure, cursed and condemned to walk the earth.

Conclusion

Realism was a further challenge to the Academic system. Gustave Courbet's paintings were interpreted as political statements intended to provoke, but the modern movements that followed Realism were also strongly influenced by Courbet's philosophy, and this went a long way towards ridding artistic practice of some of its stale and worn-out models.

Colour picture study

1. Examine *A Burial at Ornans* by Gustave Courbet (fig 37.1). Describe the event taking place and explain what was new in presenting such a scene of ordinary life. Why did this painting create such controversy?

Essay

1. Discuss the ways in which Gustave Courbet endeavoured to convey a social message in his painting. Describe how such paintings were received in the 19th century.

CHAPTER 38

JEAN-FRANÇOIS MILLET

Jean-François Millet and the Barbizon School

Jean-François Millet also depicted French rural life and human situations with insight and compassion. He too was accused of socialism in what came to be known as the Realist Salon of 1851, and although not attracting as much attention as Courbet, his work was often considered crude.

Social concerns

Peasant life had long been a subject in European painting, but uplifting them to such a noble status was an entirely new concept. Millet presented a reassuring sentimental image of the noble peasant at work on the land, but the reaction to his paintings reflected some of the fears of the Paris bourgeoisie (middle classes) towards male rural labourers, who had just gained the right to vote. Furthermore, with the Industrial Revolution of the 19th century, a steady stream of men from French farms began to come to the city in search of work and Millet's art was interpreted as a socialist protest about the peasant's plight. Millet himself, though, never set out to cause controversy. He came from a family of peasant farmers near Cherbourg in Normandy. He wrote, 'I have never seen anything but fields since I was born, so I try to say as best I can what I saw and felt when I was at work.'

The Barbizon school of painters

Millet moved to the small village of Barbizon on the outskirts of the forest of Fontainebleau near Paris. He remained there for the rest of his life, painting peasant life and country scenery. His real love remained depicting peasants at work and he struggled with pure landscape painting. His success, when it came, probably stemmed from the fact that although he was a Realist, he showed the human side of life in a kind of idealised manner. In addition, the religious overtones in his work made his paintings more acceptable.

FIG 38.1 THE GLEANERS, Jean-François Millet, Musée d'Orsay, Paris

FIG 38.2 THE ANGELUS, Jean-François Millet, Musée d'Orsay, Paris

The Angelus

That same year he began work on *The Angelus*, showing a dignified, hard-working couple labouring in the fields with their heads bowed and wearing an expression of devotion in the face of nature. The man holds his cap reverently and the woman, in a white cap and a long blue apron over her dress, clasps her hands as they stop to pray near the end of the work day. The evening sky is flushed pink over the expanse of the fields and one can almost hear the bells that peal from the church steeple in the distance. The scene is apparently reminiscent of those that Millet would have seen in his childhood – his father standing bare-headed like this, cap in hand, and his mother with bowed head and folded hands at the sound of the evening Angelus bell.

His first real observations of the countryside and the immensity of the spreading Barbizon harvest fields came with *The Gleaners* (fig 38.1) in 1857, followed by *The Angelus* (fig 38.2) the year after. These are Millet's best-known works and both distinctively personal scenes show peasants working in the fields in a low-keyed, almost melancholy (but deeply emotional) atmosphere.

The Gleaners

The Gleaners was shown at the Salon in the summer of 1857 to a hostile, conservative response. It shows three women bending forward to glean (pick up) the leftovers from the harvest. This was regarded as one of the lowest jobs in society, but Millet places them in the central focus of the picture that in Academic works would have been reserved for heroes – servants would only have appeared as part of a noble household. The composition is clear and sculptural and under a wide, magnificent sky the scene is bathed in a golden light that falls on their shoulders as well as the field that stretches into the distance behind them. The silhouetted figures have an air of quiet nobility and their labour is presented as worthwhile and beautiful.

Success by the end of the century

Unfortunately, Millet did not live to see the status of these two paintings grow to such an extent that by the end of the century they had both sold for huge sums.

Conclusion

Millet's treatment of landscape and his perception of light and weather conditions had a profound impact on his artistic contemporaries. His influence on later artists was also considerable. Among his particular admirers were Degas, Seurat, Pissarro, Gauguin and especially van Gogh, who imitated many of his themes and considered him a father figure. He once described an exhibition of Millet's work as 'holy ground'.

Colour picture study

1. Examine *The Gleaners* (fig 38.1) and *The Angelus* (fig 38.2) by Jean-François Millet and describe the way in which you think the artist was sympathetic to both the landscape and the people working in the fields in both works.

CHAPTER 39

ACADEMIC ART AND THE SALON

The Royal Academy

The Royal Academy of Painting and Sculpture was founded under Louis XIV in the 17th century. It was a strictly organised system and consisted of societies of learned men who instructed students in literature, painting and sculpture, music, dance and architecture.

The Salon

To become a member of the Academy, an artist had to exhibit in the Louvre's *salon carré* (square room) every two years. This became known simply as the Salon. It later moved to larger premises when it opened the submission process to all artists and a jury selected works for inclusion. It also awarded prizes.

The jury

The jury was made up of carefully selected artists, academicians and important officials who more often than not reflected government policy and, by the mid-19th century, conservative, middle-class values. The Royal Academy was abolished during the French Revolution, but it was re-established after Napoleon as the Académie des Beaux-Arts.

The Academy in the 19th century

The Salon exhibition

By the 19th century the Salon exhibition had become one of the year's biggest public events and was believed to show the best works of contemporary art from around the world. It was the only way for an artist to advance their career and it attracted hundreds of thousands of people from all walks of life in Paris who queued for hours to see the works.

The selection process

The selection process took several weeks as the jurors worked their way through thousands of entries. After this, a separate hanging committee decided on the placement of the selected works for exhibition. Thousands of artworks were selected, so the choice to locate a work at eye level was really important if the artist was to have success with buyers or patrons. Works

placed near the ceiling (where the light was poor) meant less recognition for the artist. After 1861 reforms were introduced to reduce some of the obvious signs of favouritism and paintings were arranged alphabetically in the exhibition's huge galleries.

Art and society in 19th-century France

By the late 19th century, the Academic system had hardened into a set of formulas to which successful artists had to conform. Any who took a different path found it very difficult to work as artists because the Academy held such influence over public opinion.

The artistic patronage that had originally come from a monarch or a wealthy, cultivated aristocracy no longer existed. Instead, wealthy members of the industrial and commercial classes had become the buying public for art.

Subjects

Given the troubled history of France throughout the century, it is easy to see why there was so much trust in the 'experts' of the Academy. Story pictures with historical or moral content were favourite subjects, but others included images of roses, pets, children and elegant ladies (sometimes classically draped in semi-undress). Pictures of the rural poor or hunting scenes were popular if presented with sentimental realism, but anything related to sexuality was completely taboo, as were subjects that highlighted any of the less glamorous realities of life.

Classical nudes

One of the most popular subjects with the buying public derived from the classical myths and legends of ancient Greece and Rome. This was considered serious and respectable and in this context images of nudity were

Academic teaching and training

Academic artists believed that art, like science, could be governed by unchanging rules. The approach to truth and beauty in art was therefore structured in a technical manner. Appropriate types of subject matter were identified and ranked in three levels of importance.

Subject matter

Level 1:

- **History painting** – This was the noblest station to which an artist could aspire and involved morally elevating scenes on large canvases that illustrated important factual events like battles, coronations, religious themes and episodes from **ancient history**, **mythology** or **religion**.

Level 2:

- **Literature** – Subjects from the classics as well as contemporary writing.
- **Portraiture** – Portrayals of significant people.

Level 3:

- **Landscape** – Outdoor settings and suitable backgrounds for historical scenes.
- **Genre scenes** – Ordinary people engaged in common activities, which were realistic, imagined, or romanticised by the artist but which carefully reflected attitudes of nobility or virtue.

Training

To become an artist a student had to enter the studio (fig 39.1) of a recognised master and study according to the Academic system. Drawing was the basis of this system and was taught as an exact science in a series of repetitive exercises.

Drawing from the antique was considered essential practice for learning the human figure and students in the studios drew from white plaster copies of antique statues. Later they progressed to drawing from male nude life models.

After four to five years, students would study 'higher' art forms such as painting and sculpture, but they had to follow strict rules of **composition.** Figures and objects had to be pleasing and placed in a harmonious manner within the picture using **perspective** to make sure they were realistic and three-dimensional.

Surface

In addition to an appropriate subject matter, one of the most easily recognisable characteristics of Academic painting is surface. This was smooth and polished like enamel, with colours and brushstrokes fully blended together.

FIG 39.1 THE STUDIO OF JAQUES LOUIS DAVID, Jean Henri Cless, Musée Carnavalet, Paris

acceptable. It was popular, too, for artists because they had learned to be artists by drawing unclothed models.

The female nude

Painting the unclothed figure also provided an outlet for the erotic that was safely bound up in titles such as *The Birth of Venus* or *The Greek Slave*. Under the strict rules applied to the depiction of nude women, nymphs or figures from ancient history were perfectly acceptable, even when they were obviously sensual. Body hair was never included and breasts were depicted with only the barest hint of nipple. Skin tones were pale and rosy,

conveying very little in the way of detail, but often the outlines of the female shape were unmistakably voluptuous and even graceful poses could be quite seductive.

Example of Academic painting

Romans in the Decadence of the Empire (fig 39.2) is today considered an example of the worst type of pretentious Academic history painting. Impeccable in every detail, the painting was one of the most praised 19th-century paintings and caused a sensation at the Salon of 1847. Thomas Couture was the artist of this vast 'orgy'

FIG 39.2 THE ROMANS OF THE DECADENCE, Thomas Couture, Musée d'Orsay, Paris

picture and the scene is one of drinking, nakedness and overindulgence in a feverish mix of eroticism and sentimentality. Noble Roman statues look on in disgust, standing in poses that indicate their disapproval.

FIG 39.3 THE BIRTH OF VENUS, Alexandre Cabanel, Musée d'Orsay, Paris

Fig 39.4 LA SOURCE, Jean Auguste Dominique Ingres, Musée d'Orsay, Paris

Images of innocence

The Birth of Venus by Alexandre Cabanel (fig 39.3) was the hit of the 1863 Salon exhibition. The painting has all the refined eroticism expected by Salon-goers of the time. She is idealised, sexually passive, characterless

and yet perfection itself. She represents the ultimate male fantasy with masses of luxuriant hair that tumbles beneath her as she skims across the surface of the waves, voluptuous yet chaste and accompanied by her little *putti* and in a pose of pure surrender.

Similarly, *La Source* by Jean Auguste Dominique Ingres (fig 39.4) shows a young woman standing at the edge of a rock pool with arms stretched languidly over her head to empty a water jar over her shoulder. One leg is seductively placed forward in a classical pose as she gazes at the viewer with lips apart. At the same time, however, she has a pure, virginal quality that is quite beyond reproach.

Conclusion

By the late 19th century the rules of the Academy had hardened into a rigid set of formulas, but because of its strong influence on public opinion it was extremely difficult for any young artist to go against it.

Questions

1. List the levels of importance given to appropriate subject matter in Academic training.
2. What kind of subject was considered appropriate for paintings?
3. Name some of the main features associated with Academic paintings.
4. How were exhibitions at the Salon organised?
5. Why was the antique considered so important?
6. How was the nude figure portrayed?

Essay

1. Outline the Academic tradition of artistic education and discuss why artists had come to believe that art, like science, could be governed by unchanging rules.

Édouard Manet – art for a democratic age

Édouard Manet was a student of art in the 1850s when Gustave Courbet's work was causing controversy and outrage. He was deeply influenced by the Realist artist's energy and independent spirit, but the dark, provincial, earthy paintings were not to the young Manet's taste.

A modern revolution

Manet dreamed of a different kind of revolution in art. His ambition was to become an established artist working in all the Academic categories of painting accepted by the official Paris Salon, but in a truly modern style. He greatly admired 17th-century Dutch and Spanish painting as well as Italian – particularly the Venetian art of the Renaissance – and had a clear vision of how to modernise these grand traditions in a specifically French context. Unfortunately, this did not fit with the accepted manner.

A well-to-do background

The son of a wealthy lawyer, Manet was born into a prosperous, upper-middle-class family with aristocratic connections. He went to a good school and when his father opposed the teenage Manet's wish to become a painter, he joined the navy. By the time Manet reached age 18, however, his father allowed him to enrol as a pupil in the studio of respected painter Thomas Couture. Manet remained with the artist for six years and although he found his teacher's harsh criticism of Delacroix and Courbet difficult to accept, he had a great deal of respect for Couture.

Manet acquired a high regard for the art of the past, but the Academic system of instruction, with its reliance on artificial studio light and the affected poses of life models, frustrated him. Manet said, 'I paint what I see, and not what others choose to see.'

A new direction in art

After he left Couture's studio, Manet's art took a new direction. Rejecting the Academic tradition of using a light source from one side and creating a smooth, rounded finish, Manet chose to use natural light sources (such as

Fig 40.1 THE ABSINTHE DRINKER, Édouard Manet, Ny Carlsberg Glyptothek, Copenhagen

sunlight) that resulted in strong colour contrasts and exaggerated lights and darks. Critically, this excluded the in-between grey tones and tended to 'flatten out' the figures, so when Manet exhibited his work, it was greatly criticised and even ridiculed by the critics.

Spanish influence

Manet's earlier paintings were created using thick paint with dark backgrounds and drew on elements of Spanish 17th-century artists such as Diego Velázquez. Spanish influence had just become fashionable because Empress Eugénie, the wife of Napoleon III, was herself from Spain. Manet's first submission to the Salon (in 1859) was *The Absinthe Drinker* (fig 40.1), which had a definite Spanish influence, but – much to his disappointment – the painting was rejected by the jury because this aspect of Parisian life was considered to be unacceptable to society.

Manet and the Paris Salon

Manet had the highest regard for the Paris Salon and his goal was to gain recognition there. This ambition never changed throughout his life, even though he suffered rejection and ridicule over the years. In 1861 *The Spanish Singer* (fig 40.2) earned him an honourable mention, but this success was short lived and for the next 20 years the Salon became his battleground. He worked relentlessly

FIG 40.2 THE SPANISH SINGER, Édouard Manet, Metropolitan Museum of Art, New York

on major compositions and although some work was accepted from time to time, none created the impact he

FIG 40.3 LE DÉJEUNER SUR L'HERBE, Édouard Manet, Musée d'Orsay, Paris

Fig 40.4 FÊTE CHAMPÊTRE, Titian, Louvre, Paris

wanted and many more were completely rejected. This upset him greatly, but at least he had no money worries because after his father died in 1862, Manet inherited a considerable fortune.

Salon des Refusés

In 1863 the Salon jury rejected an unusually large number of paintings. This caused Emperor Napoleon III to intervene and the result was the now famous Salon des Refusés (French for 'exhibition of rejects'). People mostly came to laugh and jeer at the paintings, but Manet's works created a particular furore.

The scandal of *Le Déjeuner sur l'Herbe*

Manet had taken some well-known Renaissance paintings and had adapted the figures to a modern setting. One of these was *Le Déjeuner sur l'Herbe*

(fig 40.3), which was a modern interpretation of *Fête Champêtre* (fig 40.4) by the great Venetian artist, Titian. It completely outraged the moral guardians of France and caused an immediate outcry. Had the scene been portrayed in the respectable classical tradition, it would have been perfectly acceptable, but Manet's painting featured everyday men in modern dress seated alongside a nude female. It became one of the most talked about works at the exhibition and made Manet a celebrity, but critics accused him of only trying to shock people. His own reply was that he 'obviously should have painted the men in the nude as well as the woman, and then it would be in an Old Master painting'.

The scandal of *Olympia*

That same year Manet created another painting based on *Venus of Urbino* (see Chapter 32, fig 32.3), also by Titian. He named it *A Modern Olympia* (fig 40.5), but did not at first submit it to the Salon, worried no doubt about the reaction of the critics. His friends persuaded him to put it forward for the next Salon in 1865 and the jury, more lenient following the experience of the Salon des Refusés, accepted the painting. Manet's fears were confirmed, for its reception by the public was one of real hatred. There was no appreciation of his fine painting methods, splendid colour harmonies and subtle simplification of light and shade. Instead, the critics savaged it. The reaction was so intense that the jury ordered it moved to the top corner of the wall.

A modern woman

Like *Le Déjeuner sur l'Herbe*, the woman is nude, but she is far from the demure classical figure depicted in Titian's painting. This modern young woman wears a neck-ribbon and bracelet, a ribbon in her hair and one satin slipper, all of which emphasise her nakedness. She fixes the spectator with a cool, confident gaze that is neither inviting nor provocative, but simply neutral. A large area of light tones is contrasted by a flat, dark background that is broken only by a dark-skinned servant holding flowers and a black cat has taken the place of the gently sleeping little dog at the foot of the bed in *Venus of Urbino*.

What the critics said

One critic remarked with regard to *Olympia*, 'I do not know whether the dictionary of French aesthetics holds expressions to characterise her... Her face is stupid, her skin cadaverous.' Finding the subject extremely disturbing, another said:

> The model is puny, the bed covered with cat's footprints, the general effect ugly, but that could be forgiven if it were truthful; even the least beautiful woman has bones, muscles, skin and some sort of colour, whereas on this woman the flesh colour is dirty and the modelling non-existent.

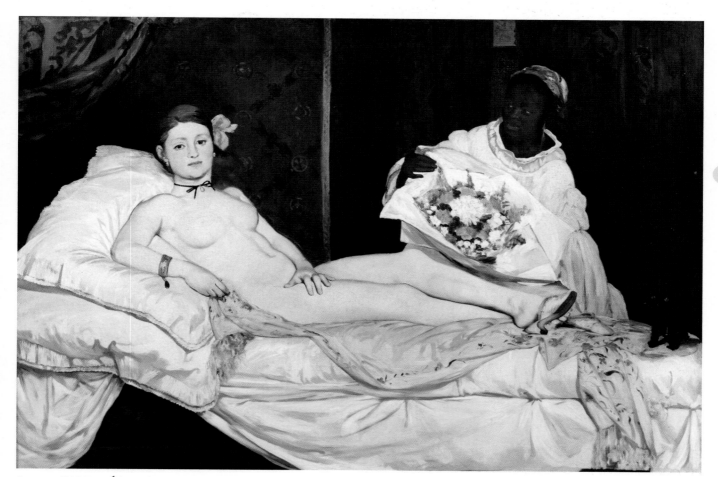

FIG 40.5 OLYMPIA, Édouard Manet, Musée d'Orsay, Paris

Manet was referred to in another article as 'a brute that paints green women with dish brushes' and young girls and pregnant women were advised to stay away.

The critics agreed that the painting had a 'childish ignorance of drawing', its arrangement of forms had little or no depth and the artist had ignored the time-honoured conventions of perspective, detail and illusionist modelling.

Manet was shattered by the criticism and said, 'The attacks directed against me broke me in the mainspring of life. No one knows what it is to be constantly insulted. It disheartens you and undoes you.' He never repeated the powerful imagery and bold colour of *Le Déjeuner sur l'Herbe* and *Olympia*, but his work continued to cause controversy.

A man of 'agreeable character and correct appearance'

With all the outrage and bad publicity surrounding his works, people naturally assumed that Manet was a rough, almost revolutionary type. In fact, nothing could have been farther from the truth. He was known for his elegance and charm, even if he could be sharp tongued and impatient. He had a cutting wit, but his friends all spoke of his goodness and generosity of spirit. Indeed, those critics who on rare occasions wrote favourably about his art were always at pains to stress his 'agreeable character and correct appearance'.

Exhibition in the gallery of Louis Martinet

Manet exhibited his work at private galleries and in March 1863 held an exhibition of his paintings in the gallery of art dealer Louis Martinet. One of these was *Music in the Tuileries* (fig 40.6), which depicts a gathering of sophisticated people in the gardens of the Tuileries Palace. The emperor held court in the palace and concerts were held twice weekly in the gardens, which became an attractive centre for the fashionable people of Paris to meet and be seen. In 1862 Manet made numerous sketches before returning to his studio to complete the painting. It contains many portraits of his friends and acquaintances as well as one of himself (on the extreme left). The painting could be considered a snapshot in more ways than one because it shows the influence of the new art of photography in the way some of the figures are cut in half by the framing edge of the canvas.

FIG 40.6 MUSIC IN THE TUILERIES, Édouard Manet, National Gallery, London

reviews as they did. He suffered this rejection painfully, but remained happy to play the part of modern master to the younger artists.

A medal of honour at last

Finally, in 1880 the recognition he had been waiting for came with a one-man show. Manet was awarded medals of honour (which carried with them automatic acceptance in the Salon), but it was too late and the Salon of 1882 was to be his last. He was by now a very sick man and his leg was so bad he had to sit to finish *A Bar at the Folies-Bergère*. The leg was amputated the following spring but he never recovered and died in April 1883, aged 51. After his death, Manet's work was exhibited at the École des Beaux-Arts and five years later, at the International Exhibition held in Paris, his works were greatly admired.

Women in Manet's paintings

Berthe Morisot married Manet's brother, Eugène, but she and Édouard remained close friends, sharing a passion for painting. She features in several of his works, but most notable is the group portrait entitled *The Balcony* (fig 40.7), exhibited at the Salon of 1869. This painting concentrates very much on her seated figure as her intense, dark eyes stare out of the picture. Manet had only recently met Berthe and her sister Edma, but this picture shows his fascination with her. The painting was poorly received and Manet suffered under the harsh criticism.

The artist's model

Manet's favourite model was Victorine Meurent. She was a girl from a poor Parisian background who would normally have had little opportunity to mix with people like Manet. Meeting her by chance in 1862 when she was 18 years old, he was captivated by her striking red hair and fair complexion. He admired her original and distinctive appearance and for the next 13 years or so used her as a model for many of his best-known paintings, including *Olympia* and *Le Déjeuner sur l'Herbe*. He said that in her face he found 'truth' and it was his mission to paint 'the real truth'.

A Bar at the Folies-Bergère

A Bar at the Folies-Bergère (fig 40.8) is probably the best known of all Manet's paintings. The stage entertainment at the Folies-Bergère attracted a wide audience that included prostitutes and men of all classes on the look-out for casual relationships.

Fig 40.7 THE BALCONY, Édouard Manet, Musée d'Orsay, Paris

Association with the Impressionist group

Manet mixed in the artistic circles that gathered in the cafés of Paris. He discussed art with the younger painters who looked up to him as leader of the revolt against the traditions of French art. Claude Monet and other members of the Impressionist group tried to get him to join them, but although Manet admired and encouraged them he steadfastly refused to exhibit with them. He was, however, influenced by the group's innovations in painting and especially by Berthe Morisot, a young woman who had broken with convention to become a successful artist. It was she who encouraged Manet to use colour instead of grey or black – particularly in shadow – and to observe the effect of light on water.

The 1870s began well for Manet with the sale of his large painting *Music in the Tuileries*, but his name was linked with the Impressionists and he received the same hostile

He persuaded the barmaid who worked there to pose in his studio for the picture, which combines novelty and tradition. A blurred, Impressionist effect blends with the solid, strong and stable. Every detail in the painting has been rendered with meticulous realism and a huge mirror in the background reflects the crowd of people gathered together, talking and drinking.

Conclusion

Manet's efforts to bring the art of the past into a modern, specifically French, context met with disapproval and ridicule. He was a great inspiration to the younger group of Impressionist artists, and he was in turn influenced by their innovations, but he continued to have the highest regard for the Paris Salon. To the end, Manet sought recognition there.

Questions
1. What was Manet's relationship with the official Salon?
2. List some of the contemporary subjects that Manet chose for his painting.
3. What was Manet's relationship with the Impressionist artists?
4. Where did these artists discuss their work?
5. When did Manet achieve the success he had worked so hard for?

Essay
1. Manet's ambition was to work in a truly modern style while establishing himself as an artist of high regard. In what way did he try to do this and how were his efforts frustrated by the reaction of the critics to his work?

Colour picture study
1. Examine *Le Déjeuner sur l'Herbe* (fig 40.3) and *Olympia* (fig 40.5) by Édouard Manet. Compare these works to these Renaissance paintings: *Venus of Urbino* (see Chapter 32, fig 32.3) and the *Sleeping Venus* by Giorgione (see Chapter 32, fig 32.2) and *Concert Champêtre* (*Pastoral Concert*) (see Chapter 32, fig 32.4) by Titian. From your studies, outline the modern aspects of Manet's painting compared to these Renaissance works.

CHAPTER 41

The origins of Impressionism

In April 1874 a group of young artists mounted their own independent exhibition.

Having had little success with the Salon, they came together to present their work to the public, but society was shocked and the paintings were ridiculed and rejected. The artists – including Edgar Degas, Claude Monet, Paul Cézanne, Pierre-Auguste Renoir, Camille Pissarro, Alfred Sisley and Berthe Morisot – soon came to be known as the Impressionists. Over the next 12 years the group held seven more exhibitions, during which time the buyers gradually accepted the new style.

The first exhibition

Visitors who came to the exhibition found the paintings with their short, slapdash brushstrokes impossible to understand. They wondered why the artists didn't take the time to finish their canvases. Critics wrote that the artists couldn't draw, their colours were vulgar and their compositions strange.

What is Impressionism?

The term 'Impressionism' derives from a painting entitled *Impression, Sunrise* that Monet included in the first exhibition (fig 41.1). This depiction of a sunrise over the sea at Le Havre near Monet's home in Normandy clearly shows the artist's interest in colour affected by light on water. His aim was to create an impression of the rapidly

FIG 41.1 IMPRESSION: SUNRISE, Musée Marmottan, Paris.

changing, shimmering orange light of the morning sun as reflected on the water. He wanted to capture the intense brightness by implementing a colour theory that held that contrasting complementary colours make primary colours brighter.

Monet was in a hurry to give this painting a title to put in the catalogue of the exhibition, so he came up with the name 'Impression' for the sketchily painted work. The editor of the catalogue, Renoir's brother, Édouard, added the word 'Sunrise'. They were not to know that the critics would seize upon the word and thereby give the movement its famous name.

The most widely read review of the first exhibition was by the journalist Louis Leroy. His article, entitled 'The Exhibition of the Impressionists', took the form of a funny story in which he visits the exhibition with a respectable landscape painter who suffers one traumatic experience after another in front of the dreadful, scrappy 'impressions'. Leroy's harshest criticism was levelled against Claude Monet. Making fun of *Impression, Sunrise*, he described the work as an 'impression' of nature, nothing more, and that 'Wallpaper in its preliminary state is more finished!' 'Who,' he wondered, 'were these "Impressionists"?'

A group of friends

These 'Impressionists' were merely a group of friends who had a shared approach to painting and had established a particular style. As artists, they were in fact quite a diverse group, but they had in common a spirit of independence and reaction against the system. They met regularly in the Café Guerbois in Paris to discuss their art, along with Édouard Manet, who was of considerable influence on them.

Impressionist style

The paintings were mostly simple scenes of landscapes, cityscapes and everyday life worked directly from nature, out of doors. They were rendered quickly with loose brushstrokes because the artists felt that this method best captured the life, character and play of light on the subject. In fact, many of the techniques used by the Impressionists had been used by painters throughout history, but they were the first to use all of them together and with such boldness.

A break with tradition

Quick outdoor sketching with loose brushstrokes had long been part of the Academic process – indeed, oil sketches called *esquisses* were very similar to Impressionist paintings – but finished paintings in the approved Academic style had very smooth surfaces. Impressionist artists broke almost every rule of the Academy of Fine Arts and went against the accepted manner of 19th-century French painting that favoured historical, religious and mythological subjects and dark, earthy colours. As a result, the work of the Impressionists was considered to be a dangerous protest against the establishment.

Innovations of Impressionist painting

The main characteristics of Impressionism were achieved by:

- **Working out of doors (*en plein air*)**
  - Painting subjects – including figures – directly from nature and out of doors.
- **Using colour in place of black or grey**
  - Artists became aware that shadows are not grey or brown, but coloured. They avoided using black and instead mixed complementary colours to achieve grey and dark tones.
  - They examined the effects of bright sunshine or light on water and snow and noticed, for example, the blue of the sky reflecting on surfaces like snow, making blue and purple shadows.
- **Observing the effects of light**
  - Artists noticed how subjects change colours when placed in different positions or light.
  - They used slabs of unmixed primary colours and small brushstrokes to simulate reflected light.
  - They used the law of optics to create optical mixing. In other words, they placed small brushstrokes of unmixed, vivid colour directly onto the canvas and allowed the mixture of colour to form in the spectator's own vision.
- **Working with loose brushstrokes**
  - Artists worked quickly, using short, thick brushstrokes of paint to capture the essence of the subject rather than its details; they used loose brushstrokes to capture a feeling of movement or quivering light.
- **Painting with flat brushes – the *tache***
  - Impressionist paintings have become known for the *tache* (which means 'patch') and refers to a coloured brushstroke achieved by the use of a brush (newly available at that time) that was flat rather than round.

- **Applying thick, wet paint on the surface**
  - Impressionist paintings were typically opaque, with wet paint often placed onto wet paint to produce a unique, soft-edged effect and an intermingling of colour. (Earlier painters had built up the surface slowly in thin layers or transparent glazes.)
- **The influence of photography and Japanese prints**
  - Impressionism was influenced by two cultural trends in the late 19th century: the rise of photography and the European discovery of the Japanese decorative arts, especially print-making, a trend known as *Japonisme*.

Impressionist artists

Claude Monet (1840–1926)

Claude Monet is the best-known member of the Impressionist group. He was one of its most dedicated members and is considered the leader because he pushed the possibilities of *en plein air* painting and the use of pure colour most enthusiastically. He was obsessed with capturing fleeting moments in the atmosphere of time and light on canvas. When the other artists turned their attention to more substantial subjects, Monet continued steadily in his pursuit of these momentary sensations. In time his painting came close to abstraction in its depiction of swirling shapes of colour that dissolved in light.

Early influences

Monet started painting close to his home near the port of Le Harvre in Normandy before going to Paris. There he met Camille Pissarro, a painter 10 years his senior and also interested in landscape painting. Through Pissarro he met the artist Camille Corot and the Barbizon painters and learned to appreciate the benefits of working out of doors (*en plein air*).

Paris

Under pressure from his father, Monet enrolled in Charles Gleyre's studio and it was here that he met fellow students Frédéric Bazille, Alfred Sisley and Pierre-Auguste Renoir. This friendship proved to be one of the most significant for the future of art. Every evening after leaving their studies, the students went to the Café Guerbois, where they met other young artists like Paul Cézanne and Edgar Degas, and engaged in lively discussions on art.

FIG 41.2 WOMEN IN THE GARDEN, Claude Monet, Musée d'Orsay, Paris

Monet continued to work on landscape paintings for the next couple of years and in 1865 the Salon accepted two seascapes. Unfortunately, the critics confused his name with that of the notorious Édouard Manet.

Financial difficulties

Life for Claude Monet was very difficult during the late 1860s. He had little success at the Salon and his father withdrew his support after his girlfriend, Camille, became pregnant. When a large work called *Women in the Garden* (fig 41.2) was rejected by the Salon, he abandoned his ideas of figure painting. In spite of his financial problems, he spent the summer of 1869 painting with Renoir and produced some wonderful riverside pictures that were to mark the real beginning of Impressionism.

Monet and Impressionism

The history of Impressionism is bound up in Monet's progress over the next decade. Monet painted with Renoir at La Grenouillère (the Frog Pond) on the banks of the Seine just outside Paris, where the people of the city came to swim and enjoy boating. No longer content to sit on the riverbank, Monet devised a floating studio,

painting both the boat itself and scenes from it. The work of Renoir and Monet from this period is almost identical, but Monet was the more adventurous of the two, leading the way in painting as the friendship turned into a full working relationship and marking a turning point for Impressionism.

In Monet's *Bathers at La Grenouillère* (fig 41.3), the whole scene is constructed with detached brushstrokes. Long brushstrokes represent the jetties, tree trunks, bathing sheds, distant boats, oars and seats of the rowing boats and emphasise the sunlight-filled water and foliage. Brushstrokes applied as flat patches with dabs and curls of paint indicate patterns of light on water. This came about as a result of *en plein air* painting, but could also have been inspired by Japanese prints (fig 41.4).

FIG 41.4 Japanese woodblock print STONE BRIDGE OVER THE AJI RIVER AT MOUNT TENPO, Yashima Gakutei

FIG 41.5 GARE ST LAZARE, Claude Monet, Musée d'Orsay, Paris

Japonisme

Monet had quite a collection of Japanese woodblock prints, which had become widely available in 19th-century France at affordable prices. These often used flat planes of bright colour and irregular shapes and were very influential on the Impressionists, offering them an alternative approach to traditional landscape painting.

Colour and light

People enjoying themselves in the sunshine continued to dominate the Impressionist mood of the 1870s, but their paintings were moving towards studies in colour. Painting snow scenes in winter had taught them to see colours in white and blues and purples rather than grey or black in dark shadow, and their observations also led them to perceive that surrounding colours and atmosphere equally influenced light and shade. For the first time they explored the possibilities offered by the use of bright colours instead of dividing a picture into dark and light areas in the traditional manner. They became interested in the new scientific investigations into light and colour. They realised, for example, that colours had an effect on each other if placed together, especially complementary colours like red and green. Devising their own experiments, they developed the technique of optical mixing – in other words, applying small brushstrokes of vivid colour side by side on canvas so that they blended together in the mind's eye to form one colour.

London

Monet and Camille were married in 1870 and left Paris for London during the Franco-Prussian War. In London, good fortune led Monet to meet up again with Pissarro, who introduced him to the art dealer Paul Durand-Ruel, who took a keen interest in his work and later became a champion of Impressionism.

In London, Monet made some paintings of the Thames and, fascinated by the thick fog of the city of that time, made a series of eight paintings of the Houses of Parliament. On his return to Paris, Monet painted the railway station at St Lazare in Paris (fig 41.5), where his aim was to capture the effect of the steam shooting from the engines towards the light filtering through the grimy glass roof.

Life in Argenteuil

After the war, Monet and his family settled outside Paris in Argenteuil, where he was enthralled with the loveliness of the countryside. One of his best-known works of this time is the scene entitled *Poppy Field at*

FIG 41.6 POPPY FIELD AT ARGENTEUIL, Claude Monet, Musée d'Orsay, Paris

Argenteuil (fig 41.6) in which his wife and son are seen walking through the flowers. He painted his wife on many occasions but the *Poppy Field*, which was shown at the first Impressionist exhibition, typifies the mood associated with Impressionism. *Regatta at Argenteuil* (fig 41.7) is also from this time and is a splendid study of reflections in which the artist uses slabs of pure colour to suggest the shimmering effect of the reflections of sails and the buildings on the water.

FIG 41.7 REGATTA AT ARGENTEUIL, Claude Monet, Musée d'Orsay, Paris

Camille's death

Monet's second son, Michel, was born in 1878, but his wife remained seriously ill after the birth and so he came to an unusual arrangement with the family of his former patron, Ernest Hoschedé. Both families lived in the one house until Camille died, and afterwards Monet and Alice Hoschedé continued to live together. They married in 1892, after Ernest Hoschedé died.

Giverny

Monet's fortunes gradually improved and he moved to Giverny, a small village on the Seine, in 1883 with Alice and her own family of six children. He created a beautiful garden where he painted continuously. Some years later he bought another section of land on the other side of the road and by diverting a stream from a small river developed a magnificent water garden with its now-famous water lily pond and Japanese bridge.

Monet lived in Giverny for 43 years, painting almost until his death in 1926 at the age of 86.

Camille Pissarro (1830–1903)

Camille Pissarro's role in the Impressionist movement was of considerable importance. He was about 10 years older than the other artists involved, who regarded him as their teacher. He constantly advised and encouraged

them. Pissarro organised the exhibitions and was the artist who exhibited at all eight Impressionist shows.

A teacher

Pissarro was unique in that he could both teach and learn from younger artists. He was a good friend and advisor to Claude Monet and Alfred Sisley, but Paul Cézanne benefited particularly from his encouragement and support. Cézanne, a moody and touchy personality, eventually left Paris to work in solitude in his hometown of Aix-en-Provence, but he continued to have the highest regard for Pissarro and later said, 'He was like a father for me – someone like God.'

Mary Cassatt, a young American artist who joined the Impressionist group for some time, painted beside him and said, 'He could teach the stones to draw.'

In spite of this, Pissarro was deeply uneasy about his own ability and it was only late in life that he was in any way satisfied with his work.

Meeting with Claude Monet

'The first Impressionist', as Cézanne referred to Camille Jacob Pissarro, spent his childhood in the Virgin Islands. His father was French, however, and he came to Paris to pursue a career in art.

FIG 41.8 VERSAILLES, Camille Pissarro, Walters Art Museum, Baltimore

Pissarro arrived in Paris during the time of the great Universal Exhibition of 1855 and was impressed by Camille Corot's landscapes. He introduced himself and became a pupil of Corot, but he also took lessons at Gleyre's studio, where he met Claude Monet. Pissarro's early submissions to the Salon were successful, but as the influence of his younger contemporaries led him towards Impressionism, his early success diminished and he suffered great financial problems trying to support a quickly growing family.

Working with the Impressionists

Pissarro worked with the Impressionists, but he always strove to maintain a solid structure in his work. The places where he lived all put their mark on his work. In the mid-1860s he settled in Louveciennes, located along the River Seine, not far from Paris. Pissarro worked consistently outdoors making landscapes, but he also kept a studio in Paris, where he met regularly with Monet, Renoir, Sisley, Bazille and Cézanne in the Café Guerbois to discuss art. He often worked with Claude Monet and the two painted winter scenes together, such as the *Road to Versailles* (fig 41.8).

London

The outbreak of war on 19 July 1870 forced the Pissarro family to move to London for safety. Here he made contact with the art dealer Durand-Ruel.

Return to Louveciennes

After the war, the family returned to Louveciennes, but what they saw horrified them. The Prussians had commandeered the house and had used his paintings as a walkway on the ground for the soldiers. Only about 40 of the original 1,500 were left intact. Refusing to be discouraged, Pissarro worked as diligently as ever.

Impressionist exhibitions

During the 1870s Pissarro combined work with organising the Impressionist exhibitions and patching up disagreements and personality clashes among the group. He even persuaded them to include Cézanne in the first Impressionist exhibition in 1874, but, of course, the critics condemned his landscapes as much as the others. As a result, all the artists who participated in the exhibition suffered considerable financial losses.

The search for perfection

Many of Pissarro's landscapes included riverbanks or views of winding roadways, but one of his favourite subjects was houses half-hidden by trees to make a broken design over the canvas. *The Red Roofs* (fig 41.9) shows a cluster of houses seen through the bare winter trees at Côte des Bœufs, near where he lived. The dense screen of trees against the roofs is all the more effective due to its rich surface, formed by small, thick brushstrokes.

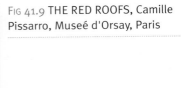

Fig 41.9 THE RED ROOFS, Camille Pissarro, Museé d'Orsay, Paris

Throughout his career, Pissarro relentlessly searched for the perfect method of expressing himself and his ideas, and although he remained in more or less permanent dire financial straits until his early 60s, he never begrudged anyone advice and encouragement.

Artistic crisis

Durand-Ruel supported Pissarro when he could, and somehow he had managed to get by, but by the time of the last Impressionist exhibition in 1886 the great teacher was himself in an artistic crisis.

Neo-Impressionism

This dissatisfaction led him in the direction of Neo-Impressionism with two young artists, Paul Signac and Georges Seurat. The format developed by Seurat involved placing dots of colour in tiny brushstrokes side by side and allowing the colours to mix in the eye of the spectator. After a short time, Pissarro found the method too laborious and abandoned it just in time, as the reputation of his Impressionist work had begun to rise.

Success at last

In 1892, 50 of his works sold at a major retrospective exhibition and Pissarro was at last in a position to offer his wife and seven children the security she had always yearned for. He bought the house at Eragny and painted some of his finest works in the countryside near his home. *Landscape at Eragny* (fig 41.10) is painted in a freer style compared to Pissarro's earlier works, but it has not lost its structure. A study of warm, diffused sunlight, its colours are warmer and the light more dissolved, but the artist has remained faithful to the realistic origins of Impressionism.

In later life he could no longer work out of doors and so rented hotel rooms from where he painted splendid street scenes. Pissarro died in 1903 at age 73.

Pierre-Auguste Renoir (1841–1919)

In 1862 Pierre-Auguste Renoir entered Charles Gleyre's studio, where he met Pissarro and formed a lasting friendship with Claude Monet, Alfred Sisley and Frédéric Bazille. (Bazille was a talented young painter who would have undoubtedly become as successful as the other Impressionists had he not been tragically killed at age 29 in the Franco-Prussian War of 1870.) The small group of friends continued to paint together even after Gleyre retired. Monet then persuaded them to travel to Fontainbleau and paint out of doors. Together, they came to appreciate the benefits of painting *en plein air* under the influence of Camille Corot.

Pretty children

For a while Renoir shared Monet's fascination with the effects of light on water, but over time the human figure became his chief interest. Some of his most enduring with pearly flesh tones and said, 'I never think I have finished a nude until I think I could pinch it.' He also said, 'Why shouldn't art be pretty? There are enough unpleasant things in the world.'

Conflict of style

Like the other Impressionists, Renoir endured much hardship early in his career, but he achieved success quite quickly. By the late 1870s he was freed from financial worries when the art dealer Paul Durand-Ruel found regular buyers for his work. Around this time, Renoir felt he had taken Impressionism as far as he could and a visit to Italy in 1881–82 to study the work of the Old Masters confirmed his view that he should seek greater solidity in his own work. The inner conflict he endured – between tradition and innovation – caused a noticeable irregularity in his painting, but gradually he came through the crisis to produce work that was stronger than before.

Influences and early career

Renoir came from Limoges and his grounding in painting began when he was a commercial artist painting figures and scenes on porcelain. After his studies in Paris, Renoir deepened his friendship with Monet and both painters spent the summer of 1869 at Bougival, an exclusive upper-class retreat near Paris, developing a technique of small brushstrokes and vibrant colours at La Grenouillère (fig 41.12), a popular bathing area. After the

FIG 41.11 YOUNG GIRLS AT THE PIANO, Auguste Renoir, Musée d'Orsay, Paris

images are of people enjoying themselves with smiling faces. Above all, his pretty children (fig 41.11) and lovely women have instant appeal. He painted nude figures

FIG 41.12 LA GRENOUILLÈRE, Auguste Renoir, Kunstmuseum Winterthur, Switzerland

Franco-Prussian War of 1870, Monet rented a house at Argenteuil and Renoir stayed with him, painting riverside regattas and the surrounding countryside (fig 41.13). Renoir's paintings from this time are remarkably similar to Monet's.

Impressionist exhibitions

Renoir's technique was firmly defined by the time he exhibited his work in the first Impressionist exhibition.

He made many studies using models and friends for the figures, often working on the same canvas for weeks or even months, changing, adding or removing figures. His favourites were models from Montmartre, dressed in the latest Paris style, as seen in *Bal du Moulin de la Galette* (fig 41.14), described later as the most beautiful picture of the 19th century. Public dances had become very popular in the 1870s and the painting shows a gathering in Montmartre at Moulin de la Galette, a well-known

FIG 41.14 BAL DU MOULIN DE LA GALETTE, Auguste Renoir, Musée d'Orsay, Paris

establishment with an outdoor dance floor and that served red wine and *galettes* (a kind of waffle).

In this masterful rendering of facial expression and movement, Renoir has successfully gathered numerous figures into the frame while capturing the fleeting effect of light and colour. The sunlight filtering through the trees casts shadows on the dancing figures and ground alike, creating a unified dappled effect.

Aline Charigot

Around 1880, Renoir met Aline Charigot, whom he later married in 1890. In 1885, their first son, Pierre, was born, followed by Jean (who grew up to be the well-known filmmaker) in 1894 and Claude in 1901. Aline features among other friends in one of his most famous works, *Luncheon of the Boating Party* (fig 41.15). The scene is set in the Maison Fournaise, a restaurant on a little island in the Seine. Everyone in the painting appears to be enjoying themselves following a boating expedition and a nice lunch. The picture is linked by the interchange of glances among the people in the group and the girl in the centre, leaning on the rail, leads our eyes to the three on the right. Aline is the woman on the left-hand side with the dog. As his model, she featured in many of his scenes, such as in *Dancing in the Country* (fig 14.16, fig 14.17), one of two nearly life-sized pictures of dancing couples that Renoir painted for Durand-Ruel. The differences in both are quite marked. Relaxed and happy, Aline Charigot's plump figure sways merrily with her partner as she smiles in response to the dance. The other more composed and

FIG 41.16 DANCE IN THE COUNTRY, Auguste Renoir, Musée d'Orsay, Paris

FIG 41.17 DANCE IN THE CITY, Auguste Renoir, Musée d'Orsay, Paris

elegant woman is the young model Marie-Clémentine Valadon, who later became the artist Suzanne Valadon. In both pictures, strong colour combinations are set off against darker backgrounds.

Later, Renoir also painted his wife nursing their first-born child, and after she died he made a small bronze sculpture of this happy scene.

Departure from Impressionism

In the 1880s, Renoir abandoned Impressionism and no longer exhibited with his former colleagues. He said that he 'had wrung Impressionism dry' and had 'come to the conclusion that he neither knew how to paint nor draw'. Seeking new inspiration, he travelled to Italy with Aline and rediscovered the works of the Old Masters. Changes in his painting style can clearly be seen in *The Umbrellas* (fig 41.18). The figures on the right are painted in the bright colours and loose brushwork of Renoir's Impressionist style, whereas the two figures on the left are more 'finished' and subdued in colour.

The nude figure

A solo exhibition at the Durand-Ruel Gallery in Paris in 1883 fully established Renoir's reputation and Durand-Ruel exhibited his work in New York in 1886, as the American market opened for Impressionism. Painting nudes in sunlight, Renoir returned to the rich colours and free brushwork of his earlier days and in 1887 completed *The Bathers*, a series of nude female figures with the soft and pearly skin texture for which he has become so well known.

FIG 41.18 THE UMBRELLAS, Auguste Renoir, National Gallery, London

A world-renowned artist

Renoir was afflicted by arthritis and moved to the south of France, where he continued to paint, even when the brush had to be placed in his hand by the nurse. After the Louvre had acquired some of his paintings, Renoir travelled to Paris in 1919, where he was honoured as a world-renowned artist and wheeled through the galleries. He died shortly after.

Alfred Sisley (1839–99)

Another member of the group that met in Gleyre's studio was Alfred Sisley. He was quite a docile student and if not for his association with Monet he might never have challenged the system.

Sisley tends to be overlooked in the history of Impressionism, yet his was a quiet, steady talent. His work is quite dramatic and powerful and his snowscapes especially have a gentle, almost poetic quality.

His style did not appeal to the public, however, so Sisley's only real source of encouragement throughout his lifetime was his immediate group of friends. He worked in all the places whose names are associated with Impressionism – Bougival, Argenteuil and Louveciennes – and his depictions of the Seine in flood and the snow-bound suburbs of Paris constitute 'pure' Impressionism, but unlike Pissarro or Renoir, his landscapes had no social or political aspect whatsoever.

A life of leisure

Sisley was born in Paris to wealthy English parents and later spent some time in London, where he saw and admired works by Constable and Turner. He settled in Louveciennes and painted in the neighbouring district of Marly-le-Roi, along the River Seine.

He worked only from a very limited number of motifs, but these have the kind of insight and vision that were the very hallmarks of early Impressionism.

Impressionist years

Sisley exhibited with the Impressionists and although Monet's influence was quite evident, he did not attract the same scornful criticism as the others.

He produced a series of paintings of villages overrun by floods. These convey a peaceful image of nature rather than scenes of distress caused by flood damage (fig 41.19, fig 41.20). Many consider these his finest paintings.

Struggles for success

With the help of a few friends and dealers, Sisley found a modest outlet for his painting, but working out of doors in winter caused him severe rheumatism. He died from cancer in 1899.

FIG 41.19 THE BOAT IN THE FLOOD, PORT-MARLY, Alfred Sisley, Musée d'Orsay, Paris

FIG 41.20 THE FLOOD AT PORT-MARLY, Alfred Sisley, Musée des Beaux-Arts, Rouen

Conclusion

As acceptance of Impressionism grew, the painting style became popular with buyers. The artists who formed the movement did more than just achieve success in their own careers. Their innovation had a huge impact on art and was the most significant of the modern art movements.

Questions

1. What are the main characteristics of Impressionism?
2. What colour theories influenced the artists?
3. What was the Salon des Refusés?
4. How did the Barbizon school influence the Impressionist movement?
5. Where did the name 'Impressionism' come from?
6. What did the critics say about the first Impressionist exhibition?
7. Why did the public not accept the art of Impressionism?
8. Who were the main supporters of the Impressionist painters?

Essay

1. What particular innovations of technique, colour and light made the work of the Impressionist painters so controversial when compared with the work of the Academic painters?
2. Give a detailed account of the work of two Impressionist painters of your choice and make a comparison between the subject matter and style of both, with reference to two or more key works by both.

Colour picture study

1. Examine *Bathers at La Grenouillère* (fig 41.3) by Claude Monet and *Luncheon of the Boating Party* (fig 41.15) by Pierre-Auguste Renoir and compare the approach by both artists to colour, composition, light and the human figure.
2. Examine *The Red Roofs* (fig 41.9) by Camille Pissarro and *Flood at Port-Marly* (fig 41.20) by Alfred Sisley and discuss the artists' treatment of the landscape in both works.

CHAPTER 42

From rejection to success

The Impressionists had eight exhibitions in Paris and one in New York City.

Support from Durand-Ruel

The art collector and dealer Paul Durand-Ruel became interested in Impressionism after he met some of the artists in London during the Franco-Prussian War of 1870. He returned to Paris in 1871, which was a difficult time to buy and sell art, but his support gave them the confidence to mount an independent exhibition.

'The Anonymous Society of Artists'

For their first exhibition in 1874, the group chose 'The Anonymous Society of Artists' as their title. Edgar Degas had argued consistently that as wide a group as possible should exhibit to prevent them being identified only as a group of Salon failures. He insisted that the public would accept a mixed show better than a concentrated exposure to an advanced form of modern art.

The exhibition was a failure and incurred such huge losses that the artists had to disband. Two years later, their next exhibition was even less well attended and the reviews were no better.

'The Exhibition of the Impressionists'

The group had, however, achieved a certain notoriety with the name 'Impressionists'. Degas detested this title and continued to argue vehemently that the group should have no particular identity. The other artists overruled his objections and in April 1877 a third exhibition, entitled 'The Exhibition of Impressionists', took place in a rented apartment. It was their most important show to date, with 230 works by 18 painters on show. Monet exhibited several of his Gare St Lazare paintings, Sisley a remarkable series depicting the flood at Port-Marly and Renoir's contribution included *Bal du Moulin de la Galette*. Cézanne had been scorned until now, but his new landscapes and still lifes so impressed his colleagues that they gave him one full wall. In a separate room, Degas showed 25 paintings and pastels of dancers, café-concerts (musical establishments) and women washing.

Lack of commercial success

The public remained largely unimpressed with the painters' work, and although the exhibition had done marginally well, the lack of real commercial success was creating fundamental disagreements among the artists. Ironically, it seems that the style was actually on the verge of public acceptability, but at that time the movement was in crisis. Some of the artists were thinking of breaking away on their own or even going back to the Salon.

The break-up of Impressionism

In 1879 Degas had his way and the group's fourth exhibition was entitled 'Exhibition of a Group of Independent Artists'. Monet and Pissarro's work once again dominated the show, but Renoir, Sisley and Cézanne did not take part.

Degas organised the fifth show as he wanted, but the only other members of the original group to exhibit with him were Pissarro and Morisot. The break-up was even more apparent by the sixth exhibition in 1881, and once again only Pissarro, Degas and Morisot contributed with other new and unknown artists.

Degas leaves the group

The artists met near the end of 1881, and, after a long discussion, Degas left the group. Monet, Sisley, Pissarro and Morisot then exhibited in a seventh Impressionist exhibition.

376

The death of Manet

That year Manet's great work, *A Bar at the Folies-Bergère*, was shown to great acclaim at the Salon, but he died soon after. Morisot organised a large retrospective exhibition, but Manet's death profoundly affected his colleagues and marked the effective break-up of the Impressionist group, whose exhibitions he had followed so fondly.

Conclusion

Durand-Ruel assumed control of the business arrangements of the group and took Impressionism to America. The American artist Mary Cassatt had been a substantial contributor to the eighth and last Impressionist group exhibition in Paris and her American contacts were vital. With her help, a huge Impressionist exhibition was organised in New York in 1886. The willing American buyers brought long-awaited financial success to the Impressionists. By now, however, the artists had gone their separate ways.

Questions

1. Discuss Edgar Degas's role in the Impressionist group.
2. Outline the progress of Impressionism from 1874 until the break-up of the group.

Art and the city

Impressionist paintings were not just modern in style, but also in subject matter, and they were influenced in this by Édouard Manet. Unlike the Barbizon painters, who focused on rural scenes and peasants, the Impressionists painted modern life in Paris and its suburbs filled with fashionably dressed people involved in leisure and entertainment activities.

Paris redesigned

Paris in the 1860s was undergoing a fundamental change. Emperor Napoleon III (nephew of Napoleon Bonaparte) had hired civic planner Baron Georges-Eugène Haussmann in 1853 to 'modernise' the city. Many well-loved old buildings were pulled down as Paris was transformed into a stylish capital city featuring the wide boulevards and intersections that have been admired ever since.

New streets

The improvements meant that the River Seine and its banks were opened to increased commercial activity. It was the replacement of the narrow streets with wide boulevards, and the consequent improvement in the city's light and the quality of the air, that made Paris more attractive to tourists. In the booming economy, the addition of railroads and gas lamps allowed for a more convenient and leisurely lifestyle to be pursued, with open spaces for the bourgeois population to flaunt their new wealth.

The Franco-Prussian War

Not all Parisians welcomed the changes and some predicted they would bring trouble. They were proved right when siege and famine returned to the streets of Paris in 1870 with the disastrous Franco-Prussian War. The Second Empire ended almost overnight and was followed by a short but bloody uprising of a small group of communists. However, normality returned to Paris in 1873, although the war and the Commune continued to dominate politics and people's memories for a long time.

After the war

Haussmann lost his position, but his projects continued, including the Opéra Garnier, the huge building designed to house the Paris Opera and that Napoleon III had intended to be the set piece of his empire. It opened in 1875, five years after his fall, and as newcomers continued to flood into Paris they found a steady increase in the number of large department stores, hotels, cafés, café-concerts (musical establishments), restaurants and theatres.

Impressionist imagery

The new streets and squares, cafés, restaurants and theatres of the new Paris and its suburbs along the River Seine formed the basis of Impressionist imagery.

The *flâneur*

In 19th-century France a certain type of wealthy and fashionable city dweller acquired the description *flâneur*, a term based on the French verb *flâner*, which means 'to stroll'. The word was first used by the writer Charles Baudelaire and refers to a particular kind of man who spent a good deal of his time strolling purposefully along public thoroughfares. The *flâneur* had exquisite manners and modelled himself on the English dandy in his British top hat and formal clothes. Édouard Manet was a perfect example in his style of dress, exquisite manners and devotion to shocking the bourgeoisie. He depicted himself in *Music in the Tuileries* on the extreme left and several other friends, including Baudelaire, are also included in the work (see Chapter 40, fig 40.6). Degas, too, shared many of the *flâneur*'s qualities and represented this type of city dweller often in his

FIG 43.1 SELF PORTRAIT, Edgar Degas, Musée d'Orsay, Paris

paintings. (Degas was not a *flâneur*, however, as he was something of a loner and so did not quite fit the type.)

Edgar Degas (1834–1917)

Degas (fig 43.1) took part in all but one of the Impressionist exhibitions between 1874 and 1886, but there were aspects of his work and personality that always set him apart from the other painters. He was never comfortable with the title Impressionist – he preferred to call himself a Realist or Independent – but he remained one of the Impressionist group's core members. Degas, too, sought to capture fleeting moments in time, but he had little time for outdoor, or *en plein air*, painting. He admired the solid traditions of the Old Masters, but his complex compositions featured scenes of modern life, including racecourses, theatres and cafés.

Early life

Hilaire-Germain-Edgar Degas came from an aristocratic family background. He attended an elite boarding school for boys, where he formed friendships that lasted all his life. His father, who was half-French, came from Naples,

and his mother from New Orleans. She died in 1847 and with the loss of his mother at such a young age, his father, Augustin de Gas, and grandfather, Hilaire de Gas, became the most influential figures in his early life.

Degas studied art in Paris in the traditional manner and admired the painter Ingres above all other artists. His Academic training had a powerful impact on his sensibilities and he always regarded drawing and line as fundamental to painting.

Portraiture

Degas painted many portraits. His father urged him to continue with this line of work, insisting that it would be 'the finest jewel in his crown'. These portraits were mainly of the members of his family and himself and his aim was to capture not only appearances, but also personality traits. His first great masterpiece, *The Bellelli Family* (fig 43.2), is a disturbingly frank portrayal of his Aunt Laura with her daughters and husband. The family is pictured not so much posing as preparing to pose, but his aunt stands upright, staring ahead, with her hand on the shoulder of one daughter, Giovanna. Arranged in a triangle and dressed in black and white, the mother and daughters form a strong, united group, even though the father, Baron Gennaro Bellelli, is shown apart from them, seated next to the desk and in front of the fireplace. Laura Degas Bellelli's father had just died, which explains the black clothing that the mother and daughters are wearing. There is a baby cradle in the background because she was pregnant, so the white candle on the mantel, waiting to be lit, may well suggest the new life.

Degas enjoyed spending hours talking about art in the Café, but was shy and awkward with an aloof manner and sharp tongue. He had very few close friends, apparently no love affairs and was intensely private, particularly about his studio. He was famous among the other young artists for his cantankerous personality and constant complaining, but his colleagues always fully recognised his spectacular talent for drawing and painting.

The influence of Édouard Manet

In the 1860s Degas came to know Manet, and his painting turned to contemporary themes. He, too, became interested in Japanese prints and this led him to experiment with unusual visual angles and asymmetrical compositions. Because of this, his subjects are often cropped at the edges.

FIG 43.2 THE BELLELLI FAMILY, Edgar Degas, Musée d'Orsay, Paris

Media

Degas worked in a wide range of media, including oil, watercolour, chalk, pastel, pencil, etching and photography.

Modern subjects

380

Degas urged his fellow artists to join him in a 'realist' endeavour, by which he meant selecting subjects related to contemporary life and actual experiences. He became most famous for his countless images of dancers, but he also painted many other subjects, such as milliners (hat shop assistants) and performers at the café-concerts. He focused on the dancers' gestures and poses as they practised, waited and stretched in the rehearsal room. During the latter part of his career, he painted several controversial scenes of women bathing.

The opera

Degas was a frequent visitor to the Salle Le Peletier, the home of the Paris Opera until it was destroyed by fire in 1873. When the new building to house the Paris Opera – the Opéra Garnier (fig 43.3) – opened in 1875, it in turn became the focus of his attention.

Horses

In his early years, Degas drew and painted all kinds of horses, but in the 1860s he concentrated on racehorses and the racetrack. Organised racing in France was linked to the rapid expansion of Paris and was based on the British model. While horses had always been a major part of French social life, racing on a fixed track, with well-defined rules, was hardly known in France before the 1830s. The expansion of the French economy and the arrival of large numbers of British investors in France changed this, resulting in major innovations in social life. Racing in Britain was an aristocratic sport, and the British dandy (or Le Dandy) who liked to talk horse all day and all night long was greatly admired.

Exclusive clubs were established in Paris based on the British model and in 1833 the Society for the Encouragement of the Improvement of Horse Breeding in France was established. (The name was shortened to the Jockey Club.) Manet and Degas favoured the subject for painting because both had many friends among the upper classes.

FIG 43.3 OPERA GARNIER, Paris

Longchamp

A racetrack for the Jockey Club was included on a large plain behind the newly developed park of the great forest of the Bois de Boulogne and the Longchamp Racecourse (Hippodrome de Longchamp) immediately became one of the fashionable sites in Paris. Manet painted the horses in action on the track in *Race course at Longchamp* (fig 43.4), but Degas chose to portray the scene before the races began with *At the Races Gentlemen Jockeys* (fig 43.5) and *Racehorses in Front of the Stands* (fig 43.6), and instead of portraying the stands in their exact location he cleverly changed around the space to give an impression of swiftness.

FIG 43.4 RACECOURSE AT LONGCHAMP, Édouard Manet, Howard University Art Museums

FIG 43.5 AT THE RACES, Edgar Degas, Musée d'Orsay, Paris

Café scenes

Café scenes feature prominently in paintings by Manet and Degas. The café was the meeting place for members of Parisian society and it offered them an opportunity for eating, drinking, resting and being with friends in a city where recent arrivals were often young and single and living in rented accommodation.

Cafés now spilled onto the widened pavements, taking the form that we associate with Paris to this day. They provided the perfect amenity, serving meals at all hours or catering for those who only wanted a beer or a coffee. Cafés also provided excellent spots from which to watch

FIG 43.6 RACE HORSES IN FRONT OF THE STANDS, Edgar Degas, Musée d'Orsay, Paris

FIG 43.7 IN THE CAFÉ, Édouard Manet, Oskar Reinhart Collection, Winterthur, Switzerland

FIG 43.8 ABSINTHE, Edgar Degas, Musée d'Orsay, Paris

the street activity and gaslight allowed businesses to stay open until well after dark.

Brasseries

Some cafés served beer and these became known as *brasseries* (French for 'breweries'). Beer had not been a popular drink in Paris before 1848 as it had been associated with rural living, but as provincials flocked to Paris for work and as the number of foreign visitors who drank beer increased, especially those from the German Lowlands and Great Britain, the popularity of beer increased. Manet included beer in several of his café pictures, such as *In the Café* (fig 43.7).

An image of hopelessness

Degas also depicts the negative side of those who inhabited the Paris cafés. In one of the most devastating images of public life, his *Absinthe* (fig 43.8) shows a woman sitting with shoulders slumped and legs splayed out, eyes cast down and an expression of hopelessness on her face. Obviously, she is a regular in this café and takes no interest whatsoever in either her surrounding or her companion.

The drink in front of her is absinthe, because of its greenish colour and the nearby carafe of water, while the man's has been identified as a mazagran, cold black coffee and fizzy water in a glass. A mazagran was a common hangover remedy, and since absinthe was taken at any time of day, the scene is probably set in the

morning, which fits with the grey light coming through the lace-curtained windows reflected in the mirror behind the pair.

Absinthe had been a working-class drink at the beginning of the 19th century, but, like beer, in the Second Empire it had suddenly become popular. Absinthe was a favourite target of France's temperance movement and by placing it in front of a woman, Degas related it to concerns of the time regarding women's drinking.

Clever composition

Although the picture may appear to have been painted from life, it was in fact a carefully planned studio set-up featuring a well-known actress, Ellen Andrée, as well as the artist's friend, Marcellin Desboutin, as models. Degas's clever composition plays a large part in its impact and the curious construction of space creates a zigzag effect in which we, the viewers, are also involved. On the table in the foreground we see a match container and a newspaper on a baton, while a folded newspaper forms a bridge to the next table, drawing us into the scene. We soon realise that we are seated at the foreground table and are, in effect, staring straight at the

FIG 43.9 CORNER OF A CAFÉ-CONCERT, Édouard Manet, National Gallery, London

FIG 43.10 CAFÉ CONCERT AT LES AMBASSADEURS, Edgar Degas, Musée des Beaux-Arts, Lyon

couple, although psychologically we are remote from them.

Café-concerts

Manet and Degas painted several scenes featuring café-concerts, another form of popular entertainment. These cafés often had huge stages, rather like music halls, and outdoor café-concerts took place in covered pavilions.

Manet tended to focus on waitresses, such as the girl in *Corner of a Café-Concert* (fig 43.9) who he asked to pose for him, but Degas concentrated exclusively on female performers and produced about 40 pastels and prints on the theme.

Le Café-Concert des Ambassadeurs (fig 43.10) is set in the famous café of that name on the Avenue des Champs-Élysées. The globes of the gaslights that lit up the theatre in a time before electricity can be seen behind the figure. They also light up the performers on the stage. Set along as footlights, they create unusual shadows and flesh tones while the darkness outside as well as the indistinct figures of the audience serve to highlight the vibrant red of the dress.

FIG 43.11 LA LOGE, Auguste Renoir, Courtauld Institute of Art, London

FIG 43.12 AT THE THEATRE (LA PREMIÈRE SORTIE), Auguste Renoir, National Gallery, London

FIG 43.13 DANCER WITH A BOUQUET, Edgar Degas, Providence Museum of Art, Rhode Island School of Design, USA

View from the opera box

Several of the Impressionists painted spectators at the opera and Renoir's *La Loge* (*The Opera Box*) (fig 43.11) was in the first Impressionist show in 1874. The scene is taken from the viewpoint of the opposite box. With its richly painted surface and depiction of the fine garments worn by a female opera-goer, it is one of the masterpieces of Impressionism. The woman wears an extraordinarily beautiful striped dress and the delicate white lace around her bosom is touched with flowers and surmounted by a cascade of pearls. Renoir returned to the theme of the opera box two years later with *The First Outing* (fig 43.12), but this time the painting features a young woman (perhaps 16 or 17 years old) who is not so self-consciously on display. In contrast to the woman in *La Loge*, who is accompanied by a sophisticated gentleman, in *The First Outing* the young woman's innocence is suggested by a female companion.

Dancers

The view from an opera box gives its occupants a privileged view of the performance. Degas's paintings involving opera boxes tend to involve the viewer in the

picture. In *Dancer with a Bouquet* (fig 43.13), it is as if we are seated in the darkness, just behind the fan of the woman in the box. The fan exactly mirrors the dancer's

FIG 43.14 THE STAR (L'ÉTOILE), OR DANCER ON THE STAGE, Edgar Degas, Musée d'Orsay, Paris

FIG 43.15 DANCER IN HER DRESSING ROOM, Edgar Degas, private collection

dress, and the dancer's bouquet is seen just under the nose of the woman in the box.

Views from above

Similarly, in *L'Etoile* (fig 43.14) we are in a higher loge (one that is close to the emperor's private box) with an uninterrupted view of the dancer making her entrance salute. Waiting in the wings are the other dancers and among them we notice the dark shape of a man's legs. It was very fashionable to attend the ballet, and those who subscribed to the most expensive boxes were permitted behind the scenes to observe from the wings of the stage, even during performances. Typically, these were middle-aged men who sought favours from the young dancers, attended rehearsals and walked freely about the dancers' foyer, even visiting dressing rooms. Degas included these men with the dancers in many of his sketches or shows us the dancers through an open door, which, in effect, places us in the position of peeping through the keyhole (fig 43.15).

Pastel drawings

Female dancers became Degas's favourite theme and he produced a huge number of paintings and pastel drawings on paper of dancers over his career. Pastel suited him, especially when his eyesight deteriorated and he could achieve the effects he desired. Sometimes he dampened the surface of the paper and often stuck on pieces of paper at the end or sides. He spent a good deal of time observing the dancers' movements at the opera and then had the dancers pose in his studio, where he

FIG 43.16 THE REHEARSAL, Edgar Degas, Glasgow Burrell Collection, Glasgow

combined his sketches into groupings of rehearsal and performance scenes or dancers on stage, entering the stage, resting or waiting to perform.

Oil paintings

Degas also produced oil paintings in quite complicated compositions. *The Rehearsal* (fig 43.16), painted in 1874, is a superb example of his early work. Figures are crowded into the upper left and lower right and are separated by a large area of floor space. A spiral staircase (a model of which was found in his studio after his death) forms a striking rhythm on the left, and this is accentuated by the dancers' legs that appear above, below and at its side. The dancers, stretching along the wall against the light of the window, are contrasted with the dancer resting in the foreground with feet splayed out, her blue-green shawl setting off the reds and russets of the girl and her mother next to her as well as the teacher's red shirt.

Mothers and daughters

The depiction of the mother in the picture is an example of Degas's keen observations behind the scenes of the Opera. Mothers of the dancers were constantly present at rehearsals, in the corridors and in dressing rooms. The reason for the mother's presence was that apprentices began official ballet classes at age seven or eight and studied long hours, without pay, for several years. They then had to pass several important exams in stages, by which time they could earn more money than their fathers. The time a mother spent in managing her daughter's progress was therefore an investment. Many parents no doubt lived in the hope that their daughter might become one of the premier dancers by her late teens and earn a really good salary. (In the 1860s, nearly all the dancers came from working-class backgrounds, but in the 1880s class divisions began to break down and the glamour of the star dancer attracted more 'respectable girls' to the profession.)

Degas frequently depicted these mothers in his paintings. In *Monsieur Perrot's Dance Class* (fig 43.17), for example, there is a mother hugging her daughter in the rear of the room.

Portraits of friends

Monsieur Perrot's Dance Class is one of Degas's most famous ballet pictures. It was shown at the first Impressionist exhibition of 1874. Jules Perrot, a famous

FIG 43.17 THE DANCING CLASS, Edgar Degas, Musée d'Orsay, Paris

FIG 43.18 JULES PERROT, Edgar Degas, Philadelphia Museum of Art

male dancer in his youth, was retired for many years when Degas made several life studies and a very fine studio drawing of him (fig 43.18), which he used in several paintings. It is a charming study. A complex arrangement of dancers and mothers are placed in groups on three sides of the famous teacher. At the rear, dancers relax in different poses with their mothers, one of whom is seated, wrapped in a red shawl, while another stands with her arms around her daughter, as though consoling her. In the foreground, there are a couple of typical Degas touches. These include the dancer seated on the piano who scratches her back and almost hides another, who absent-mindedly twists her earring as she reads, while at their feet near the piano we see a watering can used to keep the floor boards moist and a little dog, who presumably came with one of the mothers.

Carriage at the Races

Degas hardly ever painted portraits for money. He primarily painted people he knew, placing them in a setting typical to them. One painting is of Paul Valpinçon, an old school friend, and his family at the races. In a composition more about a family outing than the races, Degas painted the family sitting in their carriage (fig 43.19). The entire focus is on the infant, Henri, who has just fallen asleep after nursing (his wet nurse's breast is still uncovered). His mother bends under the sheltering parasol to look at him, while above, Valpinçon, suitably elevated above them and dressed in the formal clothes of a wealthy Parisian, gazes downwards towards his son. The dog by his side seems to follow his gaze.

The Orchestra of the Opera

Another friend of Degas was Désiré Dihau, the bassoon player in the orchestra of the Paris Opera. When Degas was asked to paint him (fig 43.20), he gave the matter a

FIG 43.20 THE OPÉRA ORCHESTRA, Edgar Degas, Musée d'Orsay, Paris

great deal of thought. In *The Orchestra of the Opera*, he chose to depict the bassoonist during a performance, but he changed the position normally occupied by the musician from the side among the other players to centre front. Although the studies were done in the studio, Degas presents a convincingly real image of the musician's controlled breath and well-practised fingers.

The picture is cleverly composed. It is divided into three almost horizontal strips. Several members of the orchestra are packed into the pit that is separated from us in the audience by the wooden side. This was the first of Degas's work to feature the ballet dancers for which he became so famous. In contrast to the men in dark suits, only the dancers' legs and the ends of the pink and blue dresses can be seen on the brightly lit strip of the stage. The brightest area of the dance is immediately above Dihau, and the deep bend of a dancing leg perfectly imitates the angle at which he holds his bassoon. Next to him, the scroll of the double bass breaks the line of the stage, drawing the two scenes together.

Conclusion

Degas had an awkward and aloof manner. He was sharp tongued and cranky and never really identified with Impressionism, but his colleagues always fully recognised his unique talent. Like Manet, he admired the solid traditions of the Old Masters, but his complex and clever compositions were distinctly modern and featured life in Paris at the end of the 19th century.

Questions

1. How did Degas differ from other members of the Impressionist group?
2. Name some of the modern subjects favoured by Degas in his painting.
3. Name some of the typical composition devices used by Degas.

Colour picture study

1. Examine *Absinthe* (fig 43.8) by Edgar Degas and describe the scene portrayed by the artist.
2. Examine *The Rehearsal* (fig 43.16) and describe what is happening in the scene. Use the painting to make comparisons with other paintings of a similar theme.
3. Examine *The Orchestra of the Opera* (fig 43.20) by Edgar Degas and describe the artist's unusual approach in depicting a portrait of a friend.
4. Examine the following paintings by Impressionist artists and compare the approach of both to their subjects and composition.
   - Edgar Degas's *Racehorses in Front of the Stands* (fig 43.6) and Édouard Manet's *Racecourse at Longchamp* (fig 43.4).
   - Édouard Manet's *Corner of a Café-Concert* (fig 43.9) and Edgar Degas's *Le Café-Concert des Ambassadeurs* (fig 43.10).

CHAPTER 44

CLAUDE MONET IN LATER LIFE

Carrying on alone

Claude Monet had little or no contact with the Impressionist group in later life and took pride in the idea that he alone carried on the modern tradition of change begun by Manet. In the 1880s, he and Alice Hoschedé went to live at Giverny. Even though his reputation was well established, Monet remained extremely conscious of maintaining his status as leader of modern art in France.

Challenges to Monet's position

By now new theories about colour were emerging, as well as challenges to Impressionism itself. Paul Seurat and the Neo-Impressionist movement in particular challenged Monet and Impressionism. Even Pissarro agreed that Monet's work was merely evolving rather than radically changing direction. Although Monet totally rejected this criticism, he had his own doubts. In fact, for some time he had been dissatisfied with what he was doing.

Change of style

Monet had become convinced that he no longer derived any benefit from working with others, so in order to advance his career he began to travel extensively, confronting nature entirely on his own. When he went out to paint he travelled with several canvases (which were kept in a specially designed case) so that as the light changed he could put one away and take out another to work on. In this way he created a remarkable series of deeply personal, highly informed landscape paintings. Nature – or rather, the sensations he experienced in the face of nature – became the sole source of his art. He took his ideas as far as possible by focusing on single moments in time. His work changed quite dramatically as naturalistic colour disappeared from his palette. Using thick, bright colours, he created paintings that went beyond being mere impressions to become objects that captured the complex relationship between the scene itself and the artist's own reaction to colour.

Monet in the 1890s

By 1890 Monet was very successful both at home and internationally. When Durand-Ruel mounted an exhibition that included a series of Monet's works entitled *Meules*, or *Grainstacks* (fig 44.1, fig 44.2),

FIG 44.1 GRAINSTACKS AT THE END OF SUMMER, MORNING EFFECT, Claude Monet, Musée d'Orsay, Paris

however, a dramatic change in the way Monet's work was perceived took place.

Grainstacks series

Always searching for a way to paint the elusive moment (or the 'fugitive effect', as he put it), Monet painted a multi-canvas series of *meules* (huge stacks of wheat or oats – they are not haystacks), which stood in the fields just behind his home at Giverny. He had begun work with these monumental forms, which stood 5 to 7 metres tall, in the mid-1880s, but returned with a new idea that a group of pictures on one subject could be seen as one. This was a totally new concept in art. To achieve his goal, Monet worked on several canvases together, moving from one to the other as the light changed, observing his subject for short periods under varying light and weather conditions.

In all, Monet made 25 *Grainstack* paintings and exhibited 15 of these in May 1891. They were not all one size, but were similarly simple compositions consisting of one or two stacks in a field, silhouetted against a line of trees, houses and distant hills under the sky. The compositions are strongly geometric, with the fields, hills and sky all reduced to parallel bands that in most cases extend across the entire canvas.

Works of art

Monet worked on the series in the studio until he had achieved the look he wanted. He altered them to improve their composition and sometimes enhanced the light by adding colours such as pink, red or orange for evening or summer sunlight. He even moved the direction of shadows. All this made them works of art that go well beyond the level of mere description.

Life and feeling

Monet was deeply involved with the French countryside and despite his emphasis on colour and changes in atmosphere, the shape of the stack remains the focal point of the paintings. They have not lost their identity and are never overwhelmed by the atmosphere. Sometimes Monet even goes so far as to outline them in bold colour in order to draw attention to their shape. The result is that these inert objects seem to quiver with life in the morning light, swelter in the heat of the midday sun, huddle together in the fading light of winter or stand mournfully alone in the evening, like actors on a deserted stage.

The 'discredited object'

People were perplexed at first by the concept of a series as one unit, of 'viewing the whole through its parts', and found *Grainstacks* hard to understand. They also found it difficult to comprehend the concept of the 'discredited object', that is, that the object itself has become an abstract motif due to its repetition over and over in various states. When the canvases were exhibited at Durand-Ruel's gallery in Paris, however, the show was an enormous success.

Monet's subjects

Grainstacks reflects values that were dear to Monet himself and to his native French culture. Monet was extremely anxious to hold the position of the leading landscape artist in France, and because of this he chose distinctly French subjects.

Monet was no ardent patriot, but his affection for his country was very strong. He did not want all his paintings to be sold to overseas buyers. He wished that a good selection would remain in Paris because that was the only place where 'there was still a little taste'.

An image of rural France

Grainstacks, therefore, is not just a series of examples of interesting shapes and colours. It is about the existence of nurturing, commitment and community that Monet felt were part of the countryside. The paintings represent the farmer's main source of income as well as the town's most substantial product. Breathing an air of contentment, they create an image of rural France that is wholesome, productive, reassuring and continuous.

This struck a chord with late-19th-century society and contributed much to Monet's success in that last decade.

Poplars

Like *Grainstacks*, Monet's *Poplars* (a series of paintings done of trees on the River Epte) (fig 44.3, fig 44.4)

FIG 44.3 POPLARS, Claude Monet, Fitzwilliam Museum, University of Cambridge, UK

FIG 44.4 POPLARS ON THE BANKS OF THE EPTE, Claude Monet, National Gallery of Scotland, Edinburgh

addressed another well-known element of rural France that contributed to its economy, stability and beauty. Poplar trees were a crop cultivated for the market (coal and wood being the only sources of fuel for heat at the time). As it happened, that summer the owners of the trees had decided to sell them for harvesting. Rather than lose his precious subjects, however, Monet bought the trees himself.

In the 19th century, poplar trees had significant commercial value. In addition, they possessed great decorative beauty – evident in their slender trunks, bushy heads, litheness and rhythmic arrangement. Viewing the *Poplars* series, people would no doubt have fully appreciated the symbolic nature of the work.

Rouen Cathedral series

By the time the paintings in the *Poplars* series were exhibited in Durand-Ruel's gallery, Monet was already working on a new series based on views of Rouen Cathedral (figs 44.5–44.8) that would to take him several years to complete. When the paintings were shown in May 1895, they caused a great sensation. The exhibition was something of an event, as new work by Monet had not been seen in Paris since the *Poplars* paintings three years earlier, and even they had only been on view for 10 days.

FIG 44.5 ROUEN CATHEDRAL, BLUE HARMONY, MORNING SUNLIGHT, Claude Monet, Musée d'Orsay, Paris

FIG 44.6 ROUEN CATHEDRAL, AFTERNOON (THE PORTAL, FULL SUNLIGHT), Claude Monet, Private Collection

FIG 44.7 ROUEN CATHEDRAL FACADE AND TOUR D'ALBANE (MORNING EFFECT), Claude Monet, Museum of Fine Arts, Boston, Massachusetts, USA

FIG 44.8 ROUEN CATHEDRAL IN FULL SUNLIGHT: HARMONY IN BLUE AND GOLD, Claude Monet, Private Collection

A Gothic cathedral

The new series was a unique departure for Monet. Although he had painted buildings in the past, he had never worked with such concentration on architectural views or spent as long on a single motif. As with *Grainstacks* and *Poplars*, *Rouen Cathedral* struck a chord in the public mind. France in the early 1890s was experiencing a considerable religious revival, but the choice of a Gothic cathedral was also a very special subject that was, once again, distinctly French. The Gothic style, which had begun in France during the Middle Ages, was so admired that it was adopted by artists throughout the rest of Europe. Once again, Monet's paintings affirmed France's position as a leader of things cultural.

Changing light on the cathedral

The weather conditions and the complex nature of the subject gave Monet considerable difficulty. He rented a room opposite the main façade of the cathedral in order to ensure the best view of the sun's magic as it moved over the building. In early morning, the sun lights up the sky behind the cathedral, making a dark silhouette before rising gradually to cascade down onto the façade, working its way downwards until the early afternoon, when the whole structure appeared to glisten in full sunshine before shadows once again creep up the façade from the darkening square. Finally, only the upper reaches pick up the last rays of the setting sun. Monet's paintings recorded the effect of this light as it changed, dissolving the architecture and turning grey stone to golden while rendering shadows in deep purple and red. During the project, he wrote to his wife, Alice, in Giverny, saying, 'Every day I discover something I haven't seen before.'

The garden at Giverny

All his life Monet was interested in gardening and even in hard times he spent money on flowers and garden projects. Now that he was wealthy, the first thing Monet did when he bought the house in Giverny was to develop a beautiful garden at his estate and employ a team of outdoor workers to tend it (fig 44.9).

He constructed paths, built raised beds filled with flowers (that were co-ordinated to bloom continuously from early spring to late autumn) and erected trellises to support climbing roses.

The water garden

In 1893 Monet bought another piece of land on the other side of the road and railroad tracks and here he built his famous water lily garden (fig 44.10). The project took quite an amount of time and effort and for a while Monet had to deal with some residents of Giverny who thought his plans to divert the River Epte would lessen the river's flow and pollute the river. They found the idea of foreign plants equally suspicious, but he overcame the

FIG 44.9 Monet's garden at Giverny

FIG 44.10 Monet's water garden at Giverny

difficulties and within a year the magnificent garden, with its large pond filled with water lilies, crossed over by a Japanese-style wooden bridge and ringed around with flowers, trees and bushes, was complete.

Influenced by Hiroshige's prints

Monet's gardens became his principal preoccupation for the last 26 years of his life. He enlarged the pond several times. The gardens were designed to complement each other. The flower garden was bold and profuse in colour, whereas the water garden was silent and meditative, mysterious and exotic. The Japanese bridge, the bamboo, the ginkgo trees and the various Japanese fruit trees that dotted the banks of the pond created an Oriental effect. This relates in many ways to prints by Utagawa Hiroshige, one of the most prolific and gifted Japanese artists (fig 44.11) who had recently been exhibited in Paris and undoubtedly influenced Monet in his design.

Towards the end of his life, Hiroshige produced a set of woodblock prints entitled *One Hundred Famous Views of Edo* (a city today called Tokyo). In this immensely popular series, Hiroshige conveyed a vivid vision of nature and man through his depictions of daily life in Edo that included famous sites, annual festivals and seasonal spectaculars.

FIG 44.11 THE BRIDGE WITH WISTERIA, Utagawa Hiroshige, Galerie Janette Ostier, Paris

Japanese bridge series

The gardens were Monet's pride and joy. 'Everything I have earned has gone into these gardens,' he once told an interviewer. 'I do not deny that I am proud of them.' But it was many years before he began to use them as inspiration for his paintings. In 1899 he produced a series of 18 paintings of the Japanese bridge (fig 44.12) and the light-dappled surface of the pond. Twelve of these were exhibited at Durand-Ruel's gallery in December 1900. Most were simply named *Water-Lily Pond*.

The paintings marked a turning point for Monet because for some time before working on the series he had done no painting at all. This was because of the illness of his stepdaughter, Suzanne Hoschedé, whose death in 1899 devastated the family. Even though he remained close to his inconsolable wife, Monet sought comfort by painting in the water garden.

'The revelation of my pond'

The death of Suzanne ended an era and closed the century, but the sparkling water, flowery surface and shimmering greens of the *Japanese Bridge* series mark the moment Monet described many years later as 'the revelation of my pond'. In 1909 Monet exhibited a series of paintings at Durand-Ruel's gallery entitled *Water Lilies – A Series of Landscapes of Water* (fig 44.13). The show was a sensation.

FIG 44.13 NYMPHÉAS (WATERLILIES), Claude Monet, private collection

Water Lilies series

The paintings were the result of several years' work that were also times of great frustration for the artist. Monet was suffering dizzy spells and blurred vision, but after a trip to Venice with Alice, Monet returned to his water lilies, as he said, 'with new eyes'.

Monet made a new series of studies of light on the surface of water that marked his most radical departure from conventional painting. Painting only the water lily rafts without the bank to act as a horizon and observing his subject in the moody half-light of dawn, twilight and dusk, Monet found the harmonies he had long been working towards. He had moved into the abstract. (Monet's work was so far ahead of its time that it was 1978 before someone realised that one of his water lily paintings in the Musée Marmottan Monet in Paris was hanging upside down.)

The last great project

Six years were to pass before Monet returned to painting water lilies. These were the most difficult years of his life.

The year 1910 started badly when Giverny flooded after the River Seine broke its banks. The Japanese bridge was almost submerged and the water crept well up into the garden. Monet was distraught about his beautiful garden and then, just when the flood had finally abated, Alice was diagnosed with leukaemia. Despite treatment and after a short remission, she died in May 1911. Monet wrote to a friend, 'My adored companion is dead ... I am wiped out.'

He stopped painting for a while ('Age and grief have exhausted me,' he said), but there was more to come. Monet's son, Jean, was diagnosed with a brain illness that would eventually kill him. Cataracts were found on both Monet's eyes, but he refused to be operated on. 'The operation is nothing,' he wrote, 'but afterwards my sight will be totally changed, and this is crucial for me.'

His son, Jean, had married Blanche, Alice Hoschedé's daughter, but following Jean's death in 1913 Blanche moved back to the family home so that she and Monet could comfort each other. She proved to be a devoted and loyal companion who not only ran the house and cared for Monet, but, as a painter herself, had a genuine interest in his work.

Les Grandes Decorations

Several years previously Monet conceived an idea to decorate a circular dining room in a series of *grandes decorations* consisting of paintings of water and water plants on fixed canvas panels hung around the walls under a dado rail. In preparation for this project he painted several studies of the water garden and its plants, but after Suzanne Hoschedé's death they had been stored in the basement, hidden like the water lilies submerged in the winter mud of his pond.

Seventeen years later, when tidying his studio before Blanche's arrival, Monet came across the preparatory studies he had made of the water lilies. The prospect of renewing his enormous 'project of water and water plants on a very large surface' was very exciting to Monet, but he felt that at the age of 74 he was too old to undertake such a task on so vast a scale. Fortunately, Monet's friend and fellow garden enthusiast, the statesman Georges Clemenceau, realised how important it was for the artist to lose himself in work. He wrote to Monet advising him to 'stop procrastinating ... You can still do it, so do it.'

A new studio

In order to proceed with the huge project Monet had to build a new studio. He worked through the dark days of World War I, even when the local people left Giverny because the battlefront was less than 40 miles away. Worried about his younger son, Michel, who was involved in the war, Monet shut himself up with work 'in order not to think any more of the horrors being endlessly committed' and to shield himself from the reality of 'this terrible, frightful war'.

World War I

Monet was at times so disgusted by the war that he felt he could not paint, but he somehow compelled himself to keep working on his great canvas panels. They were painted from outdoor studies and completed in his new studio, which had a glass roof to let in as much natural light as possible. The canvases were stretched and fixed to a wheeled chassis, making them easy to move. The panels were conceived to represent sunrise, moving to dusk. The Japanese influence can be seen in the composition as well as in the vibrant colours. Like traditional Japanese screen painting, trunks of willows

Fɪɢ 44.14 LES NYMPHÉAS, by Monet, at the Musée de l'Orangerie, Paris

feature prominently on either side of the screen, leaving empty space and distance in the middle.

A visit to the studio

The art dealer René Gimpel left an account of a visit to Monet's studio when the work was in progress:

> We found ourselves before a strange artistic spectacle: a dozen canvases stood on the ground, in a circle, all next to each other, all approximately two metres in length and over a metre in height; a panorama made of water and water lilies, of light and sky. In this infinity, water and sky have no beginning or end. We seemed to be witnessing one of the first hours of the birth of the world. It is mysterious, poetic, deliciously unreal; the sensation is strange; it is uncomfortable and pleasurable to find oneself surrounded by water on all sides without it touching you.

Monet's last works

Monet's vision deteriorated in the years after the war. His use of violent colours in his later works shows this, but by 1923 he was living in such a fog that he had the cataracts removed from his eyes. As he had expected, his vision changed completely, but he was able to use tinted glasses to restore a good deal of his sense of colour.

Monet kept the panels of his great *Water Lilies* series with him for the remainder of his life, but when he died on 5 December 1926, he left them to the state with strict instructions as to how they should be displayed. In accordance with his wishes, the panels in the *Nymphéas* (the *Water Lilies* series) were displayed unvarnished and glued to the walls of oval rooms built specially for them and to Monet's specification in the Musée de l'Orangerie (Orangerie Museum) in Paris (fig 44.14).

Conclusion

In the 1960s a second storey was added over the rooms displaying Monet's work, which greatly interfered with the light on the paintings. Between 2001 and 2007, however, the Orangerie was completely renovated. The glass roof was restored and now the natural light that the artist had intended shines through so that viewers today can once again appreciate the *Nymphéas* as changes in weather, seasons and hours of the day constantly alter their mood.

Questions

1. What art movement challenged Impressionism in the late 19th century?
2. What was particularly French about Monet's subjects?
3. Why did he choose to paint in series?
4. What did he create at his home in Giverny?
5. What was his last great set of works?

Essay

1. Monet became dissatisfied with his work and set out to develop a new approach to painting. Describe how he did this and the results he achieved.
2. Monet was the leading landscape artist in France for many years. Outline the progress of his work in the 1890s and in the early 20th century.

Colour picture studies

1. Examine *Grainstacks at the end of Summer, Morning Effect* (fig 44.1) and *Grainstack at Sunset, Snow Effect* (fig 44.2) and suggest how the artist has created such a monumental image of the French countryside in such simple compositions.
2. Examine Monet's *Poplars on the Banks of the Epte* (fig 44.4) and describe the composition of trees and river in the work.
3. Examine the photograph of Monet's water garden at Giverny (fig 44.10) and Hiroshige's woodblock print *The bridge at Wisteria Kameido Tenjin Shrine* (fig 44.11) and suggest how Monet was inspired by Japanese prints like this in creating his water garden.
4. Look at the paintings of the *Nymphéas* (fig 44.14) on display in the Orangerie Museum in Paris and describe the mood created by Monet.

CHAPTER 45

NEO-IMPRESSIONISM

Just as Impressionist artists had finally become widely recognised and more or less accepted as leaders of French painting, their position was suddenly challenged. A young artist called Georges Seurat moved Impressionism in a new direction and approached colour theory in a completely different way. His method involved placing hundreds of small touches or dots of complementary colours together. This Pointillist technique aimed to capture the effect of colour and light in a 'scientific' way. It was a direct challenge to the basic principles of Impressionism and was immediately recognised as a new direction for modern painting.

Scientific Impressionism

At the last Impressionist exhibition of 1886, Seurat stunned the Parisian art world with a huge painting called *A Sunday Afternoon on the Island of La Grande Jatte* (fig 45.1). All the Impressionists had become somewhat dissatisfied by now. Claude Monet was more Impressionist in his devotion to colour and light. Renoir had changed course dramatically, but was always interested in new ideas. Pissarro became involved with Seurat and the new theories that informed his Scientific Impressionism. Much to everyone's dismay, Pissarro enthusiastically adopted it, calling Impressionism 'romantic' and Monet's brushwork 'rancid'. He abandoned the methods of his former colleagues in favour of the Pointillist technique. This placed him squarely in the opposing camp and, to make matters worse, he insisted that Seurat and his follower, Paul Signac, be included in the Impressionists' exhibition. This led to a good deal of quarrelling. When Monet, Renoir and Sisley refused to participate with the new

FIG 45.1 SUNDAY AFTERNOON ON THE ISLAND OF GRANDE JATTE, Georges Seurat, Art Institute of Chicago

artists in the expanded exhibit, Impressionism as a movement was effectively over.

Divisionism

Pissarro exhibited with the Scientific Impressionists whose Divisionism or Pointillism was now attracting the attention, ridicule and sarcasm of the press. One art critic, Félix Fénéon was, however, very impressed, and in his ground-breaking pamphlet, *Les Impressionnistes en 1886,* he set the stage for a battle between the Neo-Impressionists and advocates of the early ideas of Claude Monet. Fénéon was the first to use the term 'Neo-Impressionism', which he described as a 'conscious and scientific' approach to the problems of colour and light.

According to Fénéon:
- Seurat's Divisionist art relied on structure and science, not intuition and chance.
- It resonated with references to history and past art, not the immediate and the mundane.
- It laid claims to higher realms and principles, to museums and the eternal, not to bourgeois drawing rooms and fleeting moments in time.
- It was therefore superior to Impressionism and deserved to be recognised as the most innovative and up-to-date style of the day.

He said, 'Future generations will remember 1886, because the age of Monet and Impressionism had come to its logical end and the age of Neo-Impressionism began.'

To help the public whom he knew to be confused by the work, Fénéon explained the ideas behind the new techniques in the following way:

> If one looks at any uniformly shaded area in Seurat's *Grande Jatte*, one can find on every centimetre of it a swirling swarm of small dots which contains all the elements which comprise the colour desired. Take that patch of lawn in the shade; most of the dots reflect the local colours of the grass, others, orange-coloured and much scarcer, express the barely perceptible influence

FIG 45.2 BATHERS AT ASNIÈRES, Georges Seurat, National Gallery, London

of the sun; occasional purple dots establish the complementary colour of green; a cyanine blue, necessitated by an adjacent patch of lawn in full sunlight, becomes increasingly dense closer to the borderline, but beyond this line gradually loses its intensity. . . . Juxtaposed on the canvas but yet distinct, the colours reunite on the retina: hence we have before us not a mixture of pigment colours but a mixture of variously coloured rays of light.

Pointillism and Georges Seurat

Georges Seurat, the leader of the new school, also wrote a good deal about his new theories. He and the other Neo-Impressionists analysed the colour of objects closely and the reaction of one colour upon the other.

The artists took account of insights from science and instead of blending colours they placed pure colours side by side on the canvas. Using small dots or points of colour, which gave rise to the name Pointillism, the colours combined before the spectator's eyes in an optical illusion, but remained glowing and light.

Pointillism was a response to the staleness of the established approach to the use of colour, which was systematic and logical. The real importance of the Pointillist movement was the part it played in the freeing of colour and the serious attention it paid to composition, both in line and in colour.

In the end, however, the Pointillist technique was quite laborious and proved to be unsuitable for working out of doors. Pissarro soon lost interest in it.

Georges Seurat (1859–91)

Georges Seurat was remembered as a tall and handsome man who was always neatly and correctly dressed. Serious and intense, his most pronounced characteristic was his secretiveness.

After completing his studies at the École des Beaux-Arts, Seurat became deeply interested in scientific theories on colour and vision. He spent two years devoting himself to mastering the art of black-and-white drawing and only then embarked on his first major painting – a huge canvas that depicted people swimming and relaxing on the riverbank at the popular bathing place of Asnières (fig 45.2).

Bathers at Asnières was hung at the first exhibition of a new group called Les Artistes Indépendants (Society of Independent Artists) that took place in a small building

near the fashionable Tuileries Palace. The show was a financial disaster, but it enabled Seurat to befriend Paul Signac, a younger, largely self-taught painter. Signac was influenced by the Impressionists, but was open to Seurat's theoretical ideas.

Seurat's next painting was set once again set near Asnières, but this time it focused on La Grande Jatte, an island on the Seine. With total self-discipline, he devoted himself completely to the task and travelled to the spot every day, sketching all morning before returning to the studio, where he painted in the afternoons. The giant canvas took two years to complete and was the main attraction at the Impressionist show of 1886.

Seurat's colours were spectacularly bright and the natural colours of objects were often mingled with complementary colours, such as red with green and orange with blue, changing subtly to give the effect of reflected sunlight. The overall effect was more formal than Impressionism and gave the paintings a timeless and slightly mysterious quality. So while *A Sunday Afternoon on the Island of La Grande Jatte* portrays the relaxed Sunday enjoyment of fashionable Parisians strolling by the riverbank, it captures none of the atmosphere and is in effect something that La Grand Jatte never really was.

Paul Signac (1863–1935)

Paul Signac came from a well-to-do Parisian family and was strongly influenced by Impressionism. Energetic and sociable, he was a member of the Société des Artistes Indépendants when he was exposed to the new theories of Pointillism (or Divisionism). He became an enthusiastic supporter of the new approach and helped to organise exhibitions. He also wrote articles of art criticism. A keen sailor all his life, Signac brought this interest to his paintings, mainly seascapes painted near Le Havre, Marseilles, Collioure, Saint-Tropez and even Venice (fig 45.3).

He was of immense moral support to Seurat and his more extroverted personality and enthusiasm provided just the right balance in their friendship as both artists set about making their mark.

Conclusion

Unfortunately, Georges Seurat died at age 31. Although Signac became the leader of the Neo-Impressionists, Seurat's death brought the short-lived movement to an end.

FIG 45.3 THE GREEN SAIL, VENICE, Paul Signac, Musée d'Orsay, Paris

Questions

1. What was Scientific Impressionism?
2. Who was the main art critic to support the Neo-Impressionist ideas?
3. What names were given to the techniques involved in Neo-Impressionism?
4. How long did the Neo-Impressionist movement last?

Essay

1. Discuss the theories of colour and light developed by Georges Seurat and the Neo-Impressionist artists.
2. Compare Neo-Impressionism with Impressionism and note the similarities and differences between them.

Colour picture study

1. Examine *A Sunday Afternoon on the Island of La Grande Jatte* (fig 45.1) and *Bathers at Asnières* (fig 45.2) by Georges Seurat. Describe the atmosphere of the works and the sense of movement (if any) in the scenes.
2. Compare *The Green Sail, Venice* (fig 45.3) by Paul Signac to *Regatta at Argenteuil* by Claude Monet (see Chapter 41, fig 41.7). Contrast the Pointillist technique used by Signac with Monet's Impressionist technique.

CHAPTER 46

THE INDIVIDUAL ARTIST

Impressionism revolutionised the nature of European painting. Artists had established the freedom to paint what they saw and felt, not what tradition dictated. With the importance of individual vision now recognised, the period that followed was one of the most exciting in the history of modern painting.

New art movements

Within a year or so of the closing of the last Impressionist exhibition in 1886 a number of movements began to appear, each with its own ideas of what the nature and function of art should be. Along with titles such as Neo-Impressionism, Synthesism, Symbolism, Divisionism and others, a new generation of great artistic names emerged – Gauguin, van Gogh, Toulouse-Lautrec, Seurat, Signac, Vuillard, Bonnard, Matisse, Munch and Picasso. In fact, the whole programme of 20th-century art was emerging. All of it can be categorised under the name Post-Impressionism.

Three recluses

While the rivalries and debates continued within the various artistic groups in Paris, three painters whose pictures would have the most profound effects on later generations were producing work far away from that city:

- **Paul Gauguin** left France in 1891 for the South Sea Islands (the islands of the south Pacific Ocean), where he was to die in 1903.
- Dutch painter **Vincent van Gogh** had forsaken Paris to work in the south of France, in a small Provençal town called Arles.
- **Paul Cézanne**, the figure whose achievements would dominate the history of late-19th-century painting more than any other artist, was painting in his native Provence (a region in southern France), rarely visiting Paris or exhibiting his work there.

Paul Cézanne (1839–1906)

A decisive influence

Cézanne was to have the most widespread and decisive influence on subsequent generations. For example, Cubism – a 20th-century avant-garde art movement that revolutionised European painting and sculpture – would certainly not have happened without him.

Very little in Cézanne's life or artistic career went smoothly. His most fervent wish was to exhibit his paintings at the official Salon, but every year they were rejected. For most of his career, however, he refused to exhibit anywhere else for fear of spoiling his chances there. Rejection and harsh criticism made him cynical and suspicious, a quality that stayed with him even after he achieved success. To the end of his life Cézanne found it difficult to accept praise, and he was profoundly distrustful of the admiration of younger artists.

Background

Cézanne was born in Aix, the capital of Provence, in 1839. He was the only son of a wealthy banker. Cézanne had a happy childhood, but his father was a domineering and authoritarian figure who fully expected that his son would grow up to be a lawyer or a banker. However, after studying drawing at Aix's municipal art school, Cézanne chose to become an artist and moved to Paris to continue his training. Here he met Camille Pissarro and, through him, the artists Renoir, Manet, Monet and Degas, who became known as the Impressionists. He exhibited with them at the first Impressionist exhibition.

A social misfit

Even at this stage in his life, Cézanne stood out from the other painters in the group. His tall, thin appearance was very striking, but he was socially awkward and he had a heavy Provençal accent and a rude, blustering manner. Behind his rough manner, however, was a sensitive, proud and easily wounded young man. Shy and timid, he rarely joined in the loud discussions held by the other Impressionists at the Café Guerbois.

Strange, turbulent paintings

Cézanne's paintings at this time were also very different from those of his colleagues. Made with paint thickly applied with a palette knife, they are turbulent and passionate works. They have highly charged, poetic and imaginary subjects, often of a violently erotic nature, as though painting offered some sort of release for Cézanne's dark imaginings.

Cézanne made little effort to exhibit or sell these powerfully original and disturbing works, apart from his attempts to get them shown at the official Salon. He was still spending part of each year at his parental home in Aix and still living off a modest monthly allowance from his father.

Hortense

In 1869 Cézanne fell in love with a model, Hortense Fiquet. Unknown to his father, they lived together in his flat in Paris and she secretly gave birth to a son, Paul.

The arrangement remained hidden, even after the couple moved south at the outbreak of the Franco-Prussian War in 1870 to live in a little seaside village of Estaque, about 30 miles from Aix. Here Cézanne spent most of his time painting landscapes, but he realised that his densely painted, frenetic style could not capture the subtle effects of nature. He also recognised that he needed technical help, so he returned to Paris to seek out Pissarro.

A pupil of Pissarro

Cézanne lived for some time near Pissarro in the Auvers area near Paris, and under his friend's direction he abandoned the palette knife and took to using lighter, purer colours in smaller dabs. Above all, Cézanne ceased painting in the reckless, frenzied manner of his earlier work and instead began to work slowly and methodically. He adopted Pissarro's practice of always working outside in the open air and carefully attempted to absorb the effects of light and shade. Now his energies were aimed exclusively in one direction – that of the careful and meticulous study of nature.

The House of the Hanged Man

Cézanne may have been working in the Impressionist manner, but his painting from this period had little in common with the flowing landscapes of Monet or, indeed, those of Pissarro. His technique was to first paint an outline of the work and then to apply several coats of paint to emphasise its three-dimensional nature, giving the scene a more sculptural look. Cézanne's vision is also quite unique. In the *House of the Hanged Man* (fig 46.1) the landscape is devoid of human presence. The abandoned dwelling is isolated, the walls cracked and the two slender trees, the chimneys and the edges of the roof protrude slightly from the dense and granular

FIG 46.1 THE HOUSE OF THE HANGED MAN, AUVERS-SUR-OISE, Paul Cézanne, Musée d'Orsay, Paris

surface of the painting. This painting is a key work in Cézanne's career. It is considered the most important painting of his Impressionist period.

Financial stability

Cézanne was, however, no more successful with this new style of painting than previously, and in the next decade of his life he began to spend more time in Provence, staying with his mother and his sister, and less and less time in Paris. He eventually married Hortense in 1886, after his father found out about the relationship. That same year his father died, leaving Cézanne a considerable fortune.

Now that he was financially secure, Cézanne's increasing isolation from the avant-garde in Paris made it inevitable that he would develop a completely independent style of painting.

He had grown very critical of the Impressionists and felt their attempts to capture light in their paintings caused them to lose structure. He disapproved of Pissarro's ventures with Seurat into the Divisionist style, was unhappy with Monet's series paintings and described Renoir's landscapes as 'cottony'.

Provence

The intense light of southern France, which heightens contrasts and contours, was perfectly suited to Cézanne's striving for timelessness and permanence in art. Brushstroke by coloured brushstroke, he worked forms up out of the white ground, letting them emerge from colour rather than from line. The result was an interweaving of objects on the picture plane in which the paint fulfilled a function entirely different from that in Impressionist landscapes. Nor did the urban scenes that figured so strongly in Impressionism hold much appeal for Cézanne – they were too transient in character. The landscape of Provence, its aspect and relatively constant vegetation throughout the year, offered precisely the quality of permanence Cézanne sought (fig 46.2).

Beyond Impressionism

Cézanne went beyond the Impressionists in his use of individual brushstrokes to depict the fall of light onto objects to create, in his words, 'something more solid and durable, like the art of the museums'.

Searching for grandeur and serenity, he lost any hint of the fleeting moment and instead of greying or lightening the colours towards the background to suggest

Fig 46.2 THE LARGE PINE, Paul Cézanne, Museu de Arte, Sao Paulo, Brazil

atmospheric perspective, he maintained the intensity of the tonal value throughout the composition. This served to pull background and middle ground forward into the foreground plane, creating a visually unified surface. The landscape seemed caught in a state of suspended animation, which lent it a timeless appearance.

In this way, Cézanne translated zones of space into zones of colour. This permitted him to suggest depth without the traditional method of perspective. The result is a relatively shallow space in which the objects seem interlocked in a consistent, dense and intensely coloured structure.

The cylinder, the sphere and the cone

Writing to his young friend and fellow artist, Émile Bernard, Cézanne explained his approach to composition very clearly:

> Treat nature by means of the cylinder, the sphere and the cone, everything brought into proper perspective so that each side of an object or a plane is directed towards a central point. Lines parallel to the horizon give breadth and lines perpendicular to the horizon give depth. But

nature is more depth than surface, so there must be resonance in light, represented by red and yellow and enough blue to give the feel of air.

Reproducing nature

Cézanne said this about his efforts: 'I wanted to copy nature; I couldn't ... But I was pleased with myself when I discovered that sunlight, for example, couldn't be reproduced, that I had to represent it by something else, by colour.'

For Cézanne, the Impressionist methods could not express the basic reality or vitality of nature. He came to the conclusion that nature's reality would have to be translated into terms of what was real in painting. This was why he spoke of equivalents and parallels. In other words, he would have to represent nature with colour equivalents to create a solid and valid impression that parallels nature, rather than opt for a superficial, coincidental representation of an ever-changing surface.

Nature itself and a painting of nature are fundamentally different entities, so any attempt at a direct transcription was bound to fail. Translation was therefore essential. The painter would have to mediate between the demands of nature on the one hand and those of the picture – the painted surface – on the other.

Slow, careful studies

Cézanne's *Mont Sainte-Victoire* (fig 46.3) shows his meditated and deliberate approach. This painting represents an approach to painting that is the opposite of Monet's quick and fluent recording of the nuances of light and shade. Cézanne undertook this painting after a lengthy contemplation of the subject. There is no attempt at creating atmospheric perspective, nor is there any hint of atmosphere. The painting is instead an intellectual organisation of nature and its many variations. The viewpoint is taken from a height, leaving little or no foreground, and the road leading off in the distance towards the mountain takes on the shape of a branch while the slight tilt of the tree itself is balanced by the thrust of the viaduct.

Mont Sainte-Victoire

Mont Sainte-Victoire was one of Cézanne's favourite motifs and over the years he painted it from many viewpoints and under different weather conditions (fig 46.4). He was rarely satisfied with his efforts and signed very few of the paintings. It seems that the mountain fascinated him. He worked relentlessly to capture the monumentality of its great limestone rockface (fig 46.5).

FIG 46.4 MONTAGNE SAINTE-VICTOIRE AU-DESSUS DE LA ROUTE DU THOLONET, Paul Cézanne, Cleveland Museum of Art, OH, USA

FIG 46.5 MONT SAINTE-VICTOIRE, Paul Cézanne, Hermitage, St. Petersburg, Russia

Stillness and dignity

On his return from Paris, Cézanne and his wife lived for a short while at Gardanne, a small town dominated by an unusual arrangement of houses which rise like stepping stones up a low hill topped by a church with tall towers. His depictions of this town are characterised by distant vantage points, careful compositions and architecture simplified to its most basic forms (fig 46.6). (These pictures are among the works that anticipate Cubism most clearly.)

Cézanne sought an attitude of stillness and dignity in a landscape and still life as well as in portraits. When he painted the art dealer Ambroise Vollard (fig 46.7), Cézanne had him sit for over 100 sessions in absolute stillness. In the end Cézanne said that he was somewhat satisfied with the shirtfront. When Vollard asked Cézanne why he had not applied any paint to the spots on his knuckles, Cézanne's reply was that he was not sure what tone to use and if it were wrong he would have to start the whole painting over again.

FIG 46.6 GARDANNE, Paul Cézanne, The Barnes Foundation, Merion, Pennsylvania, USA

FIG 46.7 PORTRAIT OF AMBROISE VOLLARD, Paul Cézanne, Musée du Petit-Palais, France

FIG 46.8 MADAME CÉZANNE IN A RED ARMCHAIR, Paul Cézanne, Museum of Fine Arts, Boston, Massachusetts

Cézanne painted his wife several times (fig 46.8). There is no record as to whether she found these sessions tedious. (Hortense could not settle in Aix – she found it too rustic for her taste – and she soon moved back to Paris.) The family home, Jas de Bouffan (fig 46.9), that Cézanne had painted on numerous occasions was sold and he moved into a small apartment in Aix. He was becoming more and more reclusive and difficult.

Rotting fruit

Cézanne found still lifes easier to paint than people, so he painted fruit and the same objects over and over. Even fruit could not be relied on – Cézanne found it necessary to use wax fruit and paper flowers because the real things rotted long before he had finished the paintings. The most striking feature of his still lifes is the combination of various perspectives of a single image. Table edges interrupted by a draped cloth continue on the other side at a different height. Jugs and glasses are frequently depicted from straight frontal and elevated position at one time. Table tops are tilted upward towards the viewer (fig 46.10). This lack of concern for traditional perspective reflects Cézanne's ability to focus his concentration on each individual object. In this

disregard, the principles of visible reality appear in his still lifes, landscape and portraiture. He was preoccupied only with art itself and not with the depiction of the objects before him. (His ideas later became the key source of inspiration for Cubism, with its inclusion of multiple viewpoints and perspectives.)

FIG 46.9 JAS DE BOUFFAN, Paul Cézanne, Narodni Gallery, Prague, Czech Republic

FIG 46.10 APPLES AND ORANGES, still life, Paul Cézanne, Musée d'Orsay, Paris

Past traditions

Cézanne consciously emulated past traditions. For example, his pictures of card players (fig 46.11) are a deliberate reworking of a favourite subject of the three Le Nain brothers, 17th-century French artists whose pictures Cézanne studied at the museum in Aix. Even in some of his self-portraits Cézanne seems to picture himself as an Old Master. In his pictures of his bathers more than any other, Cézanne concentrates on associating his painting with the past. These works echo the ideal nudes in the idyllic landscape settings painted by Renaissance artists Giorgione and Titian and especially those by the 17th-century French artist Poussin.

FIG 46.11 THE CARD PLAYERS, Paul Cézanne, Musée d'Orsay, Paris

The bathers

Cézanne painted a series of bather pictures in the studio, rarely even working from a live model. He depicted this subject throughout his career. Most of the works are quite small, and some, which he painted in watercolour, are tiny, miniaturist, jewel-like versions of the theme. It was only towards the end of his life that he attempted to paint the subject on a monumental scale, as though the hundreds of other versions he had produced during the previous 30 or so years had been so many preparations for a final, massive and conclusive treatment. He painted three large bather pictures in the last 10 years of his life. The final, majestic composition – so large that a hole had to be knocked through the wall of Cézanne's studio to remove it – was left unfinished (fig 46.12).

Painting to the last

In October 1906, at age 67 and suffering from diabetes, Cézanne was caught in a storm while painting in the open air. He collapsed and was exposed to the rain for several hours before he was found and carried home in a labourer's cart. He died a week later, but at least one of his deepest wishes had been fulfilled – he had died painting.

Vincent van Gogh (1853–90)

Van Gogh's painting career was one of the shortest and most intense in the history of art. He died by his own hand at age 37, only four years after he discovered his style and eight years after he began painting.

Despair drove him to paint after a series of failures in his life. The son of a Dutch minister, van Gogh was deeply affected by the poverty he saw around him and set out to be a preacher. He gave away all his clothes and slept in an outhouse, eating almost nothing. He condemned the drawing that he had done all his life as a distraction from his real work. It was a severe blow to him when his licence to preach was withdrawn under the pretext that he was not a good speaker (it was also taken away for his overenthusiastic practice of Christianity).

Painting as a mission

Van Gogh turned to painting, and from then on art became his mission. He worked hard to master drawing and lithography. Peasants and the hardships of their lives were the subjects of his early painting (fig 46.13).

Van Gogh came to Paris in 1885 and for two years lived with his younger brother, Theo, in his flat in an area of

Paris called Montmartre. Theo supported his brother with monthly payments from his own meagre salary, something that was to continue throughout the remainder of Vincent's short life. Vincent also received emotional and psychological support from his brother.

Van Gogh entered an art school, the Atelier Cormon, but formal education was far too rigid for him and he left the school after a short stay. While in Paris van Gogh saw the final Impressionist show and was introduced to Henri Toulouse-Lautrec, Paul Signac, Camille Pissarro and Paul Gauguin, among others. He was thus able to acquaint himself with all the leading tendencies within the Parisian avant-garde. Pissarro taught him the methods and aims of both Impressionism and Divisionism.

Colour

Van Gogh's contact with the French avant-garde had an impact on his work, especially in his use of colour. He abandoned the dark, earthy hues and grey tones of his earlier work and adopted the bright, pure, spectral palette favoured by the Impressionists and Divisionists. Van Gogh was, however, far too individual for the discipline of Divisionism and transformed the technique to suit his own purposes, which were personal and expressive.

This can be seen in a self-portrait (fig 46.14) van Gogh painted in 1887 where he had adapted the Divisionist style and bypassed the idea of complementary colour in optical mixing. Instead, van Gogh created vivid and insistent textures as well as a kind of aura or halo around his own head. He was later to write to Theo: 'In a picture I want to say something as comforting as music is comforting. I

FIG 46.14 SELF PORTRAIT WITH FELT HAT, Vincent van Gogh, Van Gogh Museum, Amsterdam

want to paint men and women with that something of the eternal which the halo used to symbolise.'

Arles

Vincent came to find Parisian life a strain. Despite the presence of his new artist friends and acquaintances in the city, he wanted to live in the country and longed for the sunlight and dazzling colour of the south of France. So at the end of February 1888 he left Paris for the small Provençal town of Arles, where he rented a room in a house close to the station. The outside walls of the house were yellow, which delighted him because yellow was his favourite colour (fig 46.15). He arrived when the town was covered in snow and was entranced by the beauty of the landscape.

The yellow house

During these first few months in Arles, van Gogh worked with a new intensity and drive. His brushstrokes broadened, his drawing grew more confident and his colours became stronger and brighter. He spent nine months on his own. He wrote regularly to Theo, sharing his thoughts and outlining his struggles with his painting.

Vincent also confided in his brother about the loneliness he felt in the evenings as well as his sense of domesticity and the reassuringly familiar look of things. The yellow

house in Arles was probably the closest van Gogh got to having a home of his own, and his desire to keep that security is represented in his depiction of his favourite chair and his pipe (fig 46.16).

FIG 46.16 VINCENT'S CHAIR, Vincent van Gogh, National Gallery, London

412

FIG 46.17 SUNFLOWERS, Vincent van Gogh, National Gallery, London

Expressions of emotion

Van Gogh was not satisfied to just record what he saw. He wanted to express the emotion of his whole being with pure colour. He exaggerated what he considered important and dismissed that which he considered trivial or insignificant. He used the contrasting colours of red and green to express the frightful passions of human beings or complementary colours to suggest the passion of two lovers.

He worked all day in the open air and in all weather conditions. He weighted his easel into the ground against the mistral, a strong and cold wind that blows in the region. On one occasion he sat all night with a crown of candles stuck in the brim of his hat to illuminate his canvas as he painted the stars over the River Rhone.

Despite keeping busy with his painting, van Gogh missed the company of other artists. He dreamed of a colony of painters living in the south of France like the one that had been established some time before in Pont-Aven in Brittany.

Gauguin

In the autumn of 1888 Theo had inherited a small amount of money from an uncle and used it to give some financial support to artist Paul Gauguin. He encouraged Gauguin to leave the artist's colony in Pont-Aven and make the journey to Arles to join Vincent.

Gauguin arrived towards the end of October. Van Gogh, highly excited at the prospect of his friend's arrival, had painted a series of sunflowers (fig 46.17) to decorate his new guest's room. For van Gogh, the sunflower was an 'earthbound metaphor of the sun's energy' with religious associations. It expressed all his optimism. Gauguin liked and admired these paintings, and painted a portrait of Van Gogh at work on one of them (fig 46.18).

FIG 46.18 VAN GOGH PAINTING SUNFLOWERS, Paul Gauguin, Van Gogh Museum, Amsterdam

Van Gogh also painted a series of paintings of his room, hoping to impress Gauguin. *Van Gogh's Room* (fig 46.19) is painted in the simplest manner with pure colour and strongly outlined shapes. Van Gogh painted two of everything, in harmonies of yellows, browns and pale blue: two pictures on the wall, two pillows on the bed and two chairs to celebrate the arrival of a friend and the end of his months of solitude.

A disastrous time

Gauguin's time in Arles was notoriously disastrous. Two more incompatible people could hardly have been found. Despite his passion for portraiture, van Gogh never painted Gauguin and only painted his chair or 'his empty place' (fig 46.20). It may be that Gauguin would not sit for van Gogh, or even that van Gogh was afraid to ask. Whatever the case, *Gauguin's Chair* can certainly be seen as a criticism of Gauguin because van Gogh's naïve, demanding and sensitive nature clashed with Gauguin's self-protective, cynical and almost brutal personality. Very shortly, relations between the two became antagonistic. Gauguin was exasperated by van Gogh's untidiness and van Gogh suffered from nervous exhaustion as he made every effort to make his friend's journey south seem worthwhile. Van Gogh's lifestyle over the previous few months had also weakened him. He had been eating very irregularly, often surviving for long periods on just coffee and tobacco. Van Gogh's work had

been so intense he had begun to drink heavily at the end of the day in order to forget how exhausted he was. Some sort of catastrophic collapse or breakdown was inevitable.

FIG 46.20 GAUGUIN'S CHAIR, Vincent van Gogh, Van Gogh Museum, Amsterdam

FIG 46.21 SELF PORTRAIT WITH BANDAGED EAR AND PIPE, Vincent van Gogh, private collection

FIG 46.22 SELF PORTRAIT, Vincent van Gogh, Musée d'Orsay, Paris

On 23 December, a few days after van Gogh had finished a portrait of Gauguin's chair, the two friends argued. Gauguin left the house to walk to the town square and van Gogh followed him, but then returned to the house and cut off part of his left ear with a razor (fig 46.21). He wrapped it in paper and then went to the brothel he and Gauguin frequented and presented it to one of the women there.

Saint-Rémy

Gauguin left and van Gogh was taken to hospital. Theo remained with him over Christmas, but his neighbours in Arles were not happy for him to return to the yellow house. Fearing another breakdown, he signed himself into a mental asylum in Saint-Rémy, a town not far from Arles, in April 1899. He was to live there for over a year.

It is not hard to imagine van Gogh's state of mind when one looks at another image painted in September of that same year, shortly after another attack (fig 46.22). The despair shows in the eyes and particularly in their colour. Swirls of the ice blue/green and white in the background seem to illustrate the mental anguish that lies behind the stern and passive expression. The halo effect has been abandoned, and instead the background has been filled with swirling flows of the same cold tones

FIG 46.23 THE STARRY NIGHT, Vincent van Gogh, Museum of Modern Art, New York

as in the jacket and waistcoat. The red of the hair and beard stand out dramatically against these colours. Just above the centre a fearful knot in van Gogh's forehead between the eyes completes this terrifying self-portrait.

Painting the stars

Shortly after he arrived in Saint-Rémy van Gogh wrote to Theo of his terrible need for religion and how when he felt like this he would go out to paint the stars.

Starry Night (fig 46.23) is a depiction of the night sky. The bright yellow moon and stars are painted in thick,

FIG 46.24 THE CHURCH AT AUVERS-SUR-OISE, Vincent van Gogh, Musée d'Orsay, Paris

FIG 46.25 DR. PAUL GACHET, Vincent van Gogh, Musée d'Orsay, Paris

sweeping brushstrokes swirling across the heavens, convulsed in fiery energy against a rich ultramarine blue. Below all the activity a dark but flame-shaped cypress tree unites the churning sky and the quiet village that is huddled against the equally rich blue tones of the hills.

The village was partly invented, and the church spire evokes van Gogh's native land, the Netherlands.

Auvers

After nearly a year at Saint-Rémy van Gogh decided to return north, hoping his attacks were symptoms of a southern disease, as though blown in on the mistral. Rather than live in Paris, he decided, on Pissarro's advice, to live in Auvers, a town about an hour from the city, where he could be looked after by a Dr Gachet. Gachet was an old friend of the Impressionists and he had built up a large collection of Impressionist paintings. Pissarro and Cézanne had stayed with him in the 1870s.

Van Gogh moved to Auvers (fig 46.24) in May 1890 and saw Dr Gachet two or three times each week. The two men evidently got on well. Van Gogh was attracted by the

older man's innate melancholy and tried to capture it in a portrait (fig 46.25). For a time, everything seemed perfect and van Gogh was much calmer and had not had an attack since February. But then he began to have a foreboding of another attack, writing, 'The weather outside is beautiful yet for a very long time – I don't know ... why – I haven't left my room ... I need courage, which I often lack, because since my sickness a feeling of solitude seizes me in the fields in such a dreadful way that I hesitate to go out.'

Nearly a year later he wrote again to Theo, 'I have painted three more big canvases. Fields of wheat under troubled skies and I did not need to go out of my way to express sadness and extreme loneliness.'

Wheatfields

In *Wheatfield with Crows* (fig 46.26), the crowded forms and deep colours convey an impression of chaotic density. Yellow cornfields wave and swell under a cloud of crows, houses buckle in spite of their strong drawing lines, trees weave dramatically into intense whirling skies. The painting is full of vigour, but even the deep blue of late summer appears heavy and storm laden and the black birds like prophetic symbols of death. As art critic John Berger has pointed out in his influential book *Ways of Seeing* (1972), our reaction to van Gogh's work

Fig 46.26 WHEATFIELD WITH CROWS, Vincent van Gogh,
Van Gogh Museum, Amsterdam

is forever conditioned by the knowledge that on 27 July 1890, the artist shot himself while working at his easel. He died two days later, attended by his brother Theo and Dr Gachet.

Violent epilepsy

Van Gogh has nowadays been diagnosed as suffering from a particularly violent form of epilepsy, one that was accompanied by both visual and auditory hallucinations. The episodes sometimes lasted two weeks or even a month, but afterwards, although exhausted, van Gogh would be totally lucid. Tragically, this most admired of modern masters sold only one painting in his life.

Paul Gauguin (1848–1903)

At the age of 34, Paul Gauguin gave up his career as a stockbroker. He left his comfortable life to take on a life of poverty, bitterness and suffering as an artist. His only consolation, but also his frustration, was the knowledge that he had followed his destiny.

A childhood in Peru

Gauguin had spent some time in Peru as a young child, which may explain his interest in exotic places later in his life. His father died on the voyage out, but his mother spent five years there before returning to France. The young Gauguin served a short while in the navy until his guardian found him a job in a stockbroker's office in Paris, a job for which he showed a surprising ability despite his reserved and unsociable personality. He married a Danish governess and the couple had five children, but all the while he was haunted by his desire to paint.

A 'Sunday painter'

As an amateur, or 'Sunday painter', Gauguin came in contact with Corot and spent many weekends in the country painting. In 1877 he met with Pissarro and became involved with the Impressionists. This was to be a turning point in his life. For the next six years or so he spent his holidays working with Pissarro at Pontoise, not too far from Paris, and under his influence he turned to primary colours. Years later, Gauguin, who was not always generous to his fellow artists, admitted that Pissarro was a master from whom he had learned a great deal.

Exhibited with the Impressionists

Gauguin exhibited with the Impressionists at five of their shows, though the artists did not fully accept him. Monet and Renoir in particular disapproved of their shows being open to 'any dauber', but Degas seems to have admired Gauguin and even bought some of his work. Gauguin's membership in the group was tolerated because of his friendship with Pissarro and also, perhaps, because of his wealth. In the early 1880s he accumulated a collection of Impressionist paintings. He particularly admired the work of Degas and Cézanne,

FIG 46.27 BONJOUR, MONSIEUR GAUGUIN, Paul Gauguin, Narodni Galeri, Prague, Czech Republic

418

despite the latter's acute dislike of him. Gauguin's advanced taste was an indication of the future direction of his career as an artist, even if at that time there was no sign of it in his own work.

A career change

In 1883 Gauguin resigned his job on the stock exchange and took his family to live in his wife's home in Copenhagen. Her family disapproved of him and his wife had no sympathy for his desire to paint and she resented the loss of her comfortable, middle-class life. Gauguin returned to Paris without his family and his career in painting began to advance. He became more determined. Far from shaking his revolve, poverty and illness served only to harden it. All he was lacking was opportunity.

Pont-Aven

In 1886 Gauguin made his first visit to Pont-Aven in Brittany, where he gathered a considerable following

about him and was at last in the role of a master. Here, his eccentric dress, moodiness and self-centred personality were seen as signs of genius (fig 46.27). To him, Pont-Aven was an escape from Paris and civilisation. He felt rural life was making him young again.

A new theory

Gauguin worked out a new theory, known as Synthetism. Simplifying forms and eliminating details, he used thick contours and large flat areas of uniform colour. He more or less did away with shadows, made very little use of linear perspective and suggested depth in his pictures mainly by the use of colour and by blocking planes of colour.

Gauguin felt that it was important not to paint too closely from nature, but to draw it out, to dream about it and think more of the creation that resulted from it. Everything around Gauguin served as a source for his imagination (fig 46.28), from the sound of the peasant's clogs on the granite soil to the rough sculpture of the Calvaries, a type of monumental public crucifix commonly found in the Breton countryside.

FIG 46.28 LA BELLE ANGELE, Paul Gauguin, Musée d'Orsay, Paris

An artist colony

Following the disastrous period spent with van Gogh in Arles, Gauguin dismissed the idea of building an artist colony there. On his return to Paris, however, he began to have ideas about establishing a colony of painters in the tropics, far from any taint of European civilisation. Ever since a trip to the French island of Martinique, in the eastern Caribbean, in 1887, Gauguin had become more and more obsessed by the idea. He was even prepared to go on his own, even if no one else was willing to join him.

Eventually Gauguin settled on a plan to go to the southern Pacific island of Tahiti – but to achieve this goal he needed money. It took some time for him to secure the necessary funds and for a while he had to return to Pont-Aven. He worked hard at promoting his work and ensured the publication of an article in the Symbolist press that argued that his paintings *Vision after the Sermon* (fig 46.29) and *Yellow Christ* (fig 46.30) were absolutely original in style. In doing this Gauguin failed to acknowledge his artistic debt to Camille Pissarro and Émile Bernard, losing both friends in the process.

An auction of paintings

Gauguin held a large auction of his work in Paris in order to secure the money he needed to book passage to Tahiti. His newfound literary friends and others of the Symbolist circle organised a grand farewell banquet in his honour at the Café Voltaire, but Pissarro and Bernard were not invited.

Tahiti

Gauguin worked for two years in Tahiti. It was not quite the paradise he had expected and he eventually left the main port town, Papeete. He bought a wooden hut and settled between the sea and a mountain with his new

FIG 46.30 YELLOW CHRIST, Paul Gauguin, Albright Knox Art Gallery, Buffalo, New York, USA

wife, a local girl who was 13 years old. Gauguin had brought a large collection of photographs and prints with him and some of these were part of the inspiration for his first works on Tahiti.

Shortly after his arrival Gauguin painted *Tahitian Women on the Beach* (fig 46.31), but his first major work, *La Orana Maria* (*Hail Mary*) (fig 46.32), was painted in 1891. This was followed by *Manao Tupapau* (*The Spirit of the Dead Watching*) (fig 46.33), which was based on a real experience. One evening he found his wife, Tehura, stretched out on the bed in their hut, terrified of the dark, which Tahitians believed was populated by dead souls.

Return to Paris

By the end of 1892 Gauguin was reluctantly preparing to return to Paris. For all his efforts to live as a savage, he still needed money, and his friends in France had been slow to provide it. In December that year, Gauguin had run out of canvas and he had only 50 francs left. When a little cash finally arrived from Paris, he was able to buy his passage home. He arrived in Marseille on 30 August 1893, with only 4 francs in his pocket.

For all the dazzling originality of paintings such as *Manao Tupapau*, the trip to Tahiti had in many ways proved a failure. Gauguin had not found it possible to survive without money. He had been unable to sell his

paintings there and his friends at home had similarly failed to find buyers for those he had sent back prior to his return.

FIG 46.32 LA ORANA MARIA OR I GREET YOU MARY, Paul Gauguin, Metropolitan Museum of Art, New York

420

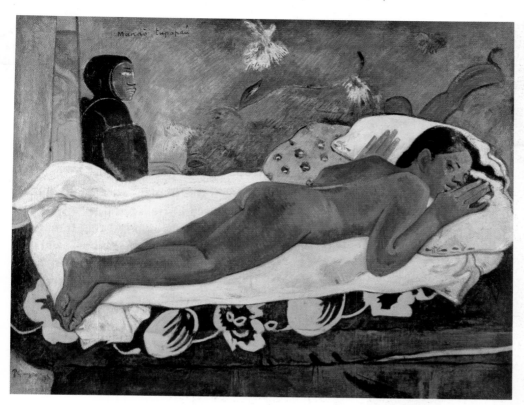

Self-promotion

During the two years Gauguin spent in France, he devoted himself tirelessly to self-promotion. He spent part of this time in Paris, living in a large studio that he painted bright yellow, and enjoying the company of some of the avant-garde artists and living with his 13-year-old Javanese mistress, Annah, and her pet monkey.

He found it difficult to sell his Tahitian work and he painted little during this period, spending his time writing an account of his life in Tahiti.

A return to Tahiti

Gauguin was determined to try Tahiti again, and in 1895 he returned to the South Seas. His work from this period in Tahiti is the finest he produced and has an exotic character that is not merely picturesque but expresses his deep feeling for life. Gauguin regarded the primitive life with nostalgia, but he was always aware that he could never be innocent enough to become part of this 'lost paradise'. This explains an element of the unsatisfied and melancholy in his work.

The women of Tahiti, with their gentle, classic beauty, fascinated Gauguin. He compared their behaviour and manner to that of the women of ancient Greece. He painted many works depicting Tahtian society, but two young women dressed in South Sea island manner represent Gauguin's dream of an idyllic society (fig 46.34).

They carry a basket of mango blossoms, the most typical flower of the tropics, like an offering of their innocence and purity of spirit.

FIG 46.34 TWO TAHITIAN WOMEN, Paul Gauguin

FIG 46.35 CONTES BARBARES, Paul Gauguin, Museum Folkwang, Essen, Germany

Money and health problems

Late in 1897, Gauguin suffered a series of heart attacks. He was also penniless and depended on his dealer in France, Ambroise Vollard, to send him a regular allowance. Buyers for his paintings proved unreliable, however, and the money never seemed to arrive. Gauguin was so deeply in debt that at one time he said he tried to poison himself. He constantly fell foul of the colonial authorities and he suffered a broken leg in a fight with French sailors, which left him with a bad foot to add to his troubles.

Cool, mysterious paintings

Gauguin's life in Tahiti was in many ways more difficult than the life he had lived in France and from which he sought to escape. Amazingly, none of this turbulence shows in his cool, timeless and mysterious paintings. The enigmatic and poetic images that emerged in his later works are softer, with paler colours than earlier, and the colours are handled so that one can almost smell the natural fragrances that waft deliciously in the imagination (fig 46.35).

When Gauguin began to work on a monumental canvas, he said it was to be a final testament to his endeavours and that he planned to commit suicide once it was finished. The huge picture, *Where Do We Come From? What Are We? Where Are We Going?* (fig 46.36), was finished by June 1898.

Its sheer size – it is more than 4 feet by 12 feet – and the strange title, which Gauguin wrote out in the top left-hand comer, indicate the ambitious nature of the work: it is as though in this single painting Gauguin wanted to embody one massive and comprehensive statement on his philosophy of life. He was hesitant, however, to clarify its precise meaning and he never provided an interpretation of it. He wrote to a friend in Paris that the dream was intangible and there was no allegory.

FIG 46.36 WHERE DO WE COME FROM? WHERE ARE WE? WERE ARE WE GOING?, Paul Gauguin, Museum of Fine Arts, Boston, Massachusetts, USA

A mystery

The painting presents a cycle from birth to old age – from the sleeping baby in the bottom right-hand corner to the aged lady on the left. Just to the right of centre, an Eve-like figure plucks a red apple from the branches above her (but a child to her left is already eating one). In the background, a large, wooden image of the Maori moon goddess Hina echoes Eve's pose with her raised arms. There is no Adam to complement this Eve and no angel to banish her from this shadowy, gloomy Eden.

There is no precise interpretation available of the painting and the narrative meaning of this massive work defies rational explanation. The viewer must, in the end, make up their own mind about it – which must have been very challenging indeed when it was first shown in Ambroise Vollard's gallery in Paris in 1898.

Death in prison

Ever restless in his search for utopia, Gauguin left Tahiti in 1891 and travelled to Hiva Oa, one the Marquesas Islands. Here he refused to pay taxes to the French colonial authorities and urged the natives to follow his example. This did not gain him friends in powerful positions and when he was charged with libel over an article he had published, criticising the governor, he was imprisoned. Already very ill, unable to walk and suffering from ulcerated sores on his legs, he died from a heart attack in prison in May 1903. News of his death only reached Paris in August.

Gauguin's legacy

Gauguin's words as well as his paintings were to influence 20th-century painting. He said he wished to 'bring painting back to its sources and to establish the right to dare everything'.

The Western artist's obsession with visual perception ended with Gauguin as his perception that 'everything takes place within my imagination. I close my eyes in order to see' became accepted. Cézanne, however, sharply criticised Gauguin's decorative, Oriental style. He said, 'It's all nonsense. He's not a painter. All he's ever done is make Chinese pictures.'

Towards Modernism

Post-Impressionist artists focused on the formal properties of colour, light brushstrokes and space as a means of personal expression. Dissatisfied with the merely visual, they investigated connections between painting, emotions and the intellect. Their achievements had the most profound influence on later artists.

Paul Cézanne

Paul Cézanne's artistic influence is pivotal to the generations of artists that followed. The lessons of his art are fundamental to an understanding of the development of modern painting and his accomplishments mark a turning point in the history of Western painting.

Les Demoiselles d'Avignon

Spanish artist Pablo Picasso's ideas about pictorial space were directly influenced by Cézanne's art and he referred to Cézanne as 'the father of us all'. The direct inspiration for Picasso's *Les Demoiselles d'Avignon* (*The Young Ladies of Avignon*) (fig 46.37), one of the most powerful paintings of the 20th century, was Cézanne's *Bathers* (fig 46.12), but during its long creation it changed and developed its own style. Picasso adapted the flat plains of Cézanne's work into angular forms as he distorted the faces and wrenched one feature out of line with another. The figures were also based on African masks, and in an attempt to portray several viewpoints at one time, Picasso moved the limbs about, making them appear almost dislocated.

Sexual frankness

The picture also broke new ground in its brutal sexual frankness. The women are prostitutes and even now the strange distorted angles of the five *demoiselles* ('young ladies') on show, with their eyes fixed firmly on the

Fig 46.37 LES DEMOISELLES D'AVIGNON, Pablo Picasso, Museum of Modern Art, New York © Succession Picasso/DACS, London 2011

viewer, is disturbing. The expressions are neither attractive nor inviting and the likely effect is one of discomfort or even anxiety. Picasso was at the time greatly in fear of contracting a venereal disease. That threat is felt everywhere in the painting, from the women's stony gazes to the melon in the foreground, which has all the appearances of a sharp weapon.

Towards Cubism

Les Demoiselles d'Avignon is widely considered to be the single most important picture in the early development of both cubism and modern art. Its flattening out of space and the breaking up of the shallow background also became some of the characteristic features of Cubism.

Cubism

Cubism was one of the most influential of all artistic movements in the early 20th century. It left a strong and lasting mark not only on the young artists working in Paris at the time but also on the very foundations of modern art as a whole.

The founders of the movement were Pablo Picasso, who left Spain in 1900, and Georges Braque, an artist who had started out with another group called Les Fauves but changed direction. Braque in particular admired Cézanne

intensely and started out painting in a similar style, but he gradually began to explore whether the solidity that so obsessed Cézanne could be pushed a little further.

Braque and Picasso

Braque and Picasso worked together, basing their efforts on a famous remark made by Cézanne in which he said that 'one must detect in nature the sphere, the cone and the cylinder'. They fragmented everyday objects in painting and brought them almost to the point where they no longer existed – in other words, abstraction.

They chose everyday objects like a bottle, a glass, a pipe, a newspaper, a guitar or a violin (fig 46.38), and sometimes the human figure (fig 46.39), but by painting 'as one thinks them, not as one sees them', they placed the thought process or 'conception' in artwork before imitation or the representation of reality. Therefore, the work of art itself became a reality or a 'pictorial fact'. As a consequence, painting became about itself and not about what it represented.

FIG 46.39 WOMAN WITH A GUITAR (MA JOLIE), Pablo Picasso, Museum of Modern Art, New York © Succession Picasso/DACS, London 2011

FIG 46.38 VIOLIN, Pablo Picasso, Pushkin Museum, Moscow © Succession Picasso/DACS, London 2011

Cubist stages

During the years 1907 to 1914, Cubism went through several stages. These were later categorised as **Analytical** up to 1912, then **Synthetic** and finally **Rococco**, at which time colour returned to what had been monochromatic paintings. During these years, Picasso and Braque were working so closely together that their work blended to make one body of work, the contribution of one almost undistinguishable from that of the other. The two artists were, however, completely different. Braque's progress was slow and deliberate, whereas Picasso was always in a hurry and advanced in fits and starts. Braque was seriously wounded in World War I, however, so Picasso continued on his own.

Closeness to nature

Cubism was not a rejection of reality. Far from ignoring nature, the artists were trying to gain a closer knowledge of it through new methods. Their theory held that we are always moving in the presence of reality and that as we move, the eye moves with us, shifting its range of vision. The eye therefore continuously reconstructs distances, surfaces and volumes.

The influence of Cubism was considerable and many were affected by it. Other artists contributed to the movement, but Picasso is the name associated with it more than any other.

Pablo Picasso (1881–1973)

Picasso first came to Paris in 1900 and throughout his lifetime worked constantly, searching for a way to express himself with complete freedom. His style changed continuously as he painted and sculpted and he experimented unceasingly right up to his death in 1973.

Styles

Picasso's first year in Paris, in which he painted sad-looking figures mainly in cold blues, is known as the Blue Period. This was followed by a Rose Period, when he painted harlequins, acrobats and itinerant circus folk.

Inspired by a visit to Italy, he shifted his emphasis next to large, Neo-Classical figures in sombre tones of grey, grey-blue and pink. Picasso did not abandon Cubism, however, and for several years he alternated between the two styles. In fact, the years between 1920 and 1924 have been called the Great Cubist Period. The *Three Musicians* is the title of two similar compositions he created during this period (fig 46.40).

FIG 46.40 THREE MUSICIANS, Pablo Picasso © Succession Picasso/DACS, London 2011

Spain

When Picasso returned to Spain in 1934, his enthusiasm for things Spanish returned, but he watched the oncoming tide of the war with anguish. His work at the time was characterised by violence and emotion, and he produced several versions of *The Weeping Woman* (fig 46.41), crying over a Spain torn apart by civil war.

FIG 46.41 WOMAN CRYING WITH A HANDKERCHIEF, Pablo Picasso, Museo Nacional Centro de Arte Reina Sofia © Succession Picasso/DACS, London 2011

FIG 46.42 GUERNICA, Pablo Picasso, Museo Nacional Centro de Arte Reina Sofia, Madrid, Spain
© Succession Picasso/DACS, London 2011

Guernica

The Spanish Civil War moved him from his preoccupation with his own artistic and personal problems. In response to the fate of the little Basque town of Guernica, razed to the ground by German bomber planes, Picasso created one of the greatest paintings (fig 46.42) in Western art history. Its universal and timeless theme represents man's inhumanity to his fellow man and is the most powerful denunciation of the brutality of war ever depicted in modern art.

The unique documentation of horror and despair features weeping women, a dead soldier, a horse in agony and the fragmented form of a bull. The perpetrators of this grotesquely violent act are never seen but their presence is everywhere.

An image in black and white

London and Paris newspapers carried eyewitness accounts of the bombing, which killed men, women and children on market day, and graphic photographs of its charred aftermath. Picasso worked out several versions of the painting, but from the beginning he seems to have felt that only black, white and grey could express the sadness of the event. The press had always been important to Picasso, and this huge painting echoes the screaming headlines of a newspaper reassembled in a collage.

At the centre of the painting is an electric light, which has taken the place of the sun, and the expressive figure of a wounded and screaming horse is countered by the brute force of the bull. Five figures express the horror, grief, anger and despair of the event. A woman kneels and a fallen warrior, lying between the horse's hooves, has a broken sword and a flower growing from his clenched fist. A woman in a burning house throws her arms to the sky, while another stretches from a window to light the scene, but discovers only a spectacle of death and destruction. A mother cries out in a deep howl of anguish for the dead child in her arms. The figures lament not only the tragedy of the town but cry out in fear for all of humanity.

Reaction at the World Fair

Picasso painted this work in just over a month for the Spanish pavilion at the 1937 World Fair in Paris. With its combination of Surrealist and Cubist imagery, it was just right for the mood of the time. The response from the civilised world was immediate. It touched the conscience of the public and was received with praise and unreserved enthusiasm.

After *Guernica* Picasso became a world-famous figure. Picasso refused to allow the work to be returned to Spain (which by then had been taken over by the fascists) and so it went to the Museum of Modern Art in New York City. It remained there until 1981, when, in accordance with the terms of Picasso's will, it was returned to Spain after democracy had returned to the country.

Modern art

Picasso created thousands of paintings, prints, sculptures and ceramics during the 75 years of his working life. No other artist is more associated with the term 'modern art' and he has influenced and dominated the art of the 20th century.

Vincent van Gogh and Paul Gauguin

Vincent van Gogh is perhaps the best-known artist in the world today. His life has inspired several popular films, but his paintings have also played a highly inspirational role in the history of modern art. His work, as well as that of Paul Gauguin, served as the inspiration for a short-lived and loose grouping of early-20th-century artists known as Les Fauves (the 'wild beasts').

Les Fauves

As an art movement, Fauvism had no strong philosophy or theory. Instead, its adherents believed that colour, with its sense of well-being, gaiety and energy, was the dominant force. Henri Matisse was the leader of the

group, which included André Derain and Maurice de Vlaminck, who was deeply impressed by van Gogh's painting – he himself used particularly bright colours, especially red. André Derain also used bright colour, but he was more influenced by Gauguin in his use of pure colour outlining and in sectioning the colours into separate compartments.

Colour harmonies

Like van Gogh and Gauguin, the Fauve artists did not limit themselves to simply using bright colour. They also discarded previous rules of painting by using strongly coloured shadow (reds or purples) and deliberately sought out unusual colour harmonies. Rejecting the traditional method of light and shade in favour of shapes constructed only with line and colour, they chose to see painting as first and foremost a flat surface to be covered with colours assembled in a certain order.

Henri Matisse

Henri Matisse, Vlaminck and others exhibited their work for the first time in Paris in the 1905 Salon d'Automne (Autumn Salon), an art show set up to counter the conservative Paris Salon. An art critic likened their work

Fig 46.43 Henri Matisse, *Femme au chapeau* (*Woman with a Hat*), 1905
oil on canvas; 31¾ in. × 23½ in. (80.65 cm × 59.69 cm);
San Francisco Museum of Modern Art, Bequest of Elise S. Haas;
© Succession H. Matisse/DACS, 2011

Fig 46.44 Henri Matisse, *The Green Line* (Portrait of Madame Matisse), 1905
oil on canvas; 40.50 cm x 32.5 cm (15.9 in. x 12.8 in.);
Stalens Museum for Kunst, Copenhagen;
© Succession H. Matisse/DACS, 2011

to *fauves*, or wild beasts, because of the strong colours. Matisse never liked this name, however. He realised that the random application of bright colours was not the essential point.

Shocked reaction

The south of France had been a source of great inspiration to Matisse and so he went to Collioure to work with André Derain. Here the artists developed the strong and vibrant tones that so shocked the viewers at the Autumn Salon. People were disturbed by the strange hues used in the paintings featuring the human figure. Matisse's paintings of his wife in *Woman with a Hat* (fig 46.43) and *The Green Line* (fig 46.44) caused a particular furore. He was quite taken aback at first by the hostility of the reaction, but came to accept that any publicity was welcome.

A long career

Matisse went on to have long and extremely successful career. His style changed several times and he inevitably came under the influence of Cubism for a short time, but he always retained his love of pattern and colour.

Conclusion

Along with Pablo Picasso, Henri Matisse dominated European painting in the first half of the 20th century. Like Picasso, Matisse used a wide range of media and techniques, but his willingness to explore the possibilities of pure line, colour and abstraction mark out his work as a bridge between van Gogh and Gauguin and the development of Expressionism.

Questions

1. Which three painters in the early 20th century had a profound effect on later generations of artists?
2. Which Impressionist artist was most inspiring and influential on Paul Cézanne, Vincent van Gogh and Paul Gaugin?
3. What movement did the work of Paul Cézanne inspire?
4. What did Pablo Picasso say about Cézanne?
5. How did Paul Cézanne interrelate with his contemporaries in Paris?
6. What did Cézanne search for above all else in his painting?
7. What famous phrase did Cézanne use in his advice to a friend regarding his approach to composition?
8. Why could Cézanne not 'copy nature'?
9. What was Vincent van Gogh's first career choice?
10. Describe the change in the work of van Gogh after he came to Paris.
11. Describe van Gogh's use of paint and brushstrokes.
12. Where did van Gogh live in Arles?
13. Describe the period spent in Arles after van Gogh's friend, Paul Gauguin, came to stay.
14. How did van Gogh influence modern art?
15. What did the other Impressionists think of Gauguin?
16. Where did Gauguin found an artist's colony?
17. How did Gauguin get enough money together to travel to Tahiti?
18. How did Gauguin manage financially while in Tahiti?
19. How did Gauguin's work change during his years in Tahiti?
20. What were the main characteristics of *Les Fauves* as an artistic movement?

Essay

1. Cézanne, Gauguin and van Gogh, often referred to as Post-Impressionists, were important influences on the art of the 20th century. Discuss the contribution of these artists to the development of modern art, referring to at least one painting by each artist. Illustrate your answer.

Coloured picture study

1. *Mont Sainte-Victoire* (fig 46.3) shows Cézanne's meditated and deliberate approach. Describe the evidence for this by examining the work and discuss the composition and Cézanne's use of colour to suggest perspective. Why do you think the artist was so obsessed by this mountain?
2. Examine *Still Life with Apples and Oranges* by Cézanne (fig 46.10) and comment on the arrangement of the objects as well as the artist's use of colour and brushstrokes to create volume. Discuss his use of various perspectives in the painting and his reasons for disregarding the principles of visual reality.
3. Examine *Starry Night* (fig 46.23) and *Wheatfield with Crows* (fig 46.26) and suggest how van Gogh created atmosphere in these paintings. Compare them to another quite different painting by the artist and give the reasons why you find it interesting.
4. Examine van Gogh's final self-portrait (fig 46.22) and describe why it illustrates his possible mental state. Compare this to an earlier or another portrait by the artist.
5. *Manao Tupapau* (fig 46.33) was painted by Gauguin based on a real experience. In your opinion, does the painting convey the atmosphere of the event? How does the work compare to other paintings of women in Tahiti?
6. Gauguin never clarified the meaning of his huge last work, *Where Do We Come From? What Are We? Where Are We Going?* (fig 46.36). Examine the work and describe the composition, colour and arrangement of figures in the work. What interpretation would you (as viewer) put on this work?
7. Examine the paintings *Woman with a Hat* (fig 46.43) and *The Green Line* (fig 46.44) by Henri Matisse and discuss his use of colour harmonies.

For permission to reproduce photographs, the author and publisher gratefully acknowledge the following:

© Advertising Archive: 62BR, 64BL; © Airvod: 66TL; © akg-images: 98B, 197, 202, 205R, 207BL, 207CR, 209R, 210T, 211B, 212BL, 227, 228TL, 272B, 340, 354, 382L, 395B, 411T, 414B, 195TC, 182, 228TR, 270T; © Alamy: 11, 18BL, 29TL, 30BR, 37BL, 37BR, 38BL, 38TR, 38BR, 38BL, 39TR, 44TL, 44BL, 45TL, 45TR, 48BL, 48TR, 57BL, 59T, 59BL, 59CR, 59BR, 60L, 60B, 61TR, 61CR, 61BR, 62TL, 62TR, 62BL, 63CR, 63BR, 64TL, 64TR, 65TL, 65TR, 66BL, 67TR, 67BR, 71TR, 71CR, 72TL, 102TL, 137L, 138R, 141L, 141R, 173T, 173B, 174, 175T, 181B, 183BL, 183BR, 185TL, 185TC, 184, 185TR, 190L, 195TL, 198T, 200CL, 200R, 201B, 206TL, 206BL, 207TL, 210B, 211T, 213L, 213R, 214T, 214B, 221T, 221B, 223TL, 223TL, 224L, 224R, 225R, 226L, 228B, 229T, 231T, 231B, 232TL, 232B, 233T, 233B, 234, 236, 238B, 239B, 239T, 240L, 240R, 242, 253BR, 263, 288TR; © Alan Counihan and John Coveney: 52T; © Art Archive: 371T, 420BR; © Armagh Public library/St Patrick's Church of Ireland Cathedral: 101B; © The Board of Trinity College Dublin: 164TL, © Bridgeman: 1TC, 1TR, 1TL, 2, 6, 14T, 14B, 15T, 15BL, 15BR, 17B, 18T, 23T, 57BR, 108BL, 119L, 119R, 120L, 120R, 121L, 121R, 122L, 122R, 146, 147L, 147R, 148, 149L, 149R, 151TL, 151TR, 151BL, 151BR, 152L, 152R, 168, 201T, 206TR, 212TL, 212TR, 226R, 235, 244, 245TL, 245BR, 245BR, 246L, 246R, 247L, 247R, 248, 249, 251L, 251R, 252TL, 252BL, 252TR, 252BR, 253TL, 253TR, 258T, 258L, 258R, 259L, 259R, 260L, 260R, 261, 262L, 262R, 264T, 264B, 265L, 265R, 266L, 266R, 267, 269T, 269B, 271, 272TL, 272TR, 273, 274T, 275, 276T, 276B, 277T, 277B, 278, 279, 280T, 280B, 281, 282, 282, 283, 284T, 284B, 287, 289, 293T, 293B, 294, 295T, 295B, 296L, 296R, 297L, 297R, 298, 301L, 301R, 302, 303B, 304TL, 304TR, 304B, 305, 306, 307L, 307R, 308, 309T, 309B, 310L, 310R, 311T, 311B, 315, 316TL, 316TR, 316BR, 317TL, 317B, 317TR, 318T, 318B, 319L, 319R, 323T, 323B, 324L, 324R, 325, 326, 327, 328T, 328B, 329L, 329T, 330L, 332, 333L, 333R, 334, 335, 338, 339, 341T, 341B, 343, 344, 345, 346, 347, 348, 349, 351, 352T, 352B, 353, 355T, 355B, 356, 357, 358, 359, 360, 361, 363, 364T, 364B, 365, 366T, 366B, 367, 368, 369, 370T, 370B, 371B, 372T, 372B, 373TL, 373BR, 374, 375, 379, 380, 381BL, 381BR, 382R, 383TL, 383TR, 383B, 384TL, 384B, 385T, 385B, 386L, 386R, 387T, 387B, 389, 390, 391L, 391R, 392TL, 392TR, 392BL, 392BR, 394B, 395T, 397, 399, 400, 402, 404, 405, 406, 407TL, 407TR, 407B, 408TL, 408TR, 409T, 409B, 410, 411B, 412T, 412B, 413T, 413B, 414T, 414TR, 415TL, 415B, 416L, 416R, 417, 418TL, 418BR, 419TL, 419BR, 420TL, 421TL, 422T, 422B, 423, 424L, 424R, 425B, 426, 504B; © British Library: 164TR; © Cleveland Museum of Art: 63TR; © Collins Agency: 27B; © Corbis: 30BL, 36TR, 37T, 38TL, 58T, 60T, 63TC, 75B, 157, 187T, 209L, 232TR, 238T, 241T, 241B, 303T, 381TL, 384TR; © Cork County Council: 34CL, 34BL, 34TL, 35TL, 35BL, 35CR, 45BR, 47TL, 47TR, 47BR; © Cork Museum: 93B; © Crawford Art Gallery, Cork and Dara McGrath 16B

Crawford Art Gallery, Cork and Dara McGrath: 17T; © Creative Commons/Mirsasha: 220B; © Dara McGrath: 27T; © David Lyons: 107; © Denis O'Connor: 33BL; © Department of Environment, Heritage and Local Government: 83TL, 85, 86TL, 87, 89B, 90T, 100L, 100R, 108TR, 108BR, 109BL, 111, 116R, 117T, 129, 130, 134, 135T, 135B, 137TR, 137BR, 139, 140L, 140R, 142L, 142TR, 142B, 143L, 144, 158T, 159B, 160L, 160R, 162L, 162R, 163, 171T, 171B, 172, 188, 189T, 189B; © Dyson: 64BR; © Elizabeth O'Donoghue: 29BL, 29TR; © Ennis Tidy Towns and Mike Mulcaire: 54T, 54B; © Garrett Weldon: 191T; © Getty: 12T, 16T, 58B, 59CL, 63TL, 70R, 86BR, 109TL, 156, 180L, 195B, 195TR, 196, 198B, 200BL, 205L, 218, 220T, 222T, 257, 274B, 286, 288BL, 300, 313, 425T; © Henry Dreyfuss: 61L; © Hugh Lane Gallery: 12B, 13TL, 13TR; © Hugh Lane Gallery and Patrick Graham: 3; © Imagefile: 91B, 256; © Irish Heritage Trust: 20, 21T, 22; © Irish Times: 13BR; © Jacques Bosser: 50TL; © Kat O'Brien: 49, © Ken Williams: 93TL; © Kevin O'Dwyer: 53TL, 53TR, 53BR; © Kobal: 72BL, 73TL, 73TR, 74TL, 75T, 76, 77TR, 78TL, 78BL, 78CR, 80; © Laois County Council: 33BR; © Louise Walsh: 26BL, 26T, 26BR; © Mary Evans: 381TR, 421BR; © Maurice Harron/Clare Dunne: 31BL, 31TR; © Mayo County Council: 51, 52B; © Michael Warren: 50TR; © Museum of Fine Arts, Boston: 127R; © National Gallery of Ireland: 330R, 270B, 4, 9T, 9B, 10, 23B, 187B; © National Library of Ireland: 29BR, 30T, 36TL; © National Museum of Ireland: 83TR, 83TC, 86BL, 90B, 91T, 93TR, 94BL, 94BR, 94TR, 95TL, 95TR, 96TL, 96TR, 96BR, 96BL, 97L, 97TR, 99, 101T, 102BL, 102TR, 103L, 103R, 104, 114, 123, 124T, 124B, 125L, 125R, 126L, 126R, 127L, 128, 153T, 153B, 154TL, 154TR, 154CR, 154BR, 155, 164BR, 165TL, 165BL, 165TR, 166L, 166R, 167; © Northern Ireland Environment Agency – Built Heritage section: 143R; © OXO: 66CR; © Photocall! Ireland: 18BR; © Photolibrary: 19, 34TR, 169, 177B, 179T, 179B, 181T, 191BL, 191BR; © Louis le Brocquy and National Gallery of Ireland: 8, © Provision: 46TL, 46TR; © Rachel Joynt: 32BL, 32TR, 32BR; © Rex Features: 67TL, 69T, 69B, 70L, 71TL, 72CR, 72BR, 74CR, 77TL, 79; © Royal Irish Academy: 112, 113L, 113R; © Rowan Gillespie: 41TL, 41TR; © Rowan Gillespie/Liam Blake: 40TL, 40BL, 40TR, 40BR, 41BL, 42TL, 42BL, 42TR, 43TR, 43BR; © Rowan Gillespie/Roger Kohn: 43TL; © Russborough House: 175B; © Sacred Destinations Images: 215R; © San Francisco Museum of Modern Art: 427L, © Seán Scully: 24; © Statens Museum for Kunst: 427R; © TopFoto: 190R; © Wikimedia: 215L, 225L, 170L, 170R.

The authors and publisher have made every effort to trace all copyright holders, but if any has been inadvertently overlooked we would be pleased to make the necessary arrangement at the first opportunity.